MW00637227

ONCE UPON
A TIME

ONCE UPON A TIME

The Captivating Life of
Carolyn Bessette-Kennedy

ELIZABETH BELLER

GALLERY BOOKS

New York   London   Toronto   Sydney   New Delhi

Gallery Books
An Imprint of Simon & Schuster, LLC
1230 Avenue of the Americas
New York, NY 10020

First Gallery Books hardcover edition May 2024

GALLERY BOOKS and colophon are registered trademarks of Simon & Schuster, LLC

Simon & Schuster: Celebrating 100 Years of Publishing in 2024

For information about special discounts for bulk purchases, please contact Simon & Schuster Special Sales at 1-866-506-1949 or business@simonandschuster.com.

The Simon & Schuster Speakers Bureau can bring authors to your live event. For more information or to book an event, contact the Simon & Schuster Speakers Bureau at 1-866-248-3049 or visit our website at www.simonspeakers.com.

Interior design by Jaime Putorti

Manufactured in the United States of America

10 9 8 7 6 5 4 3 2 1

Library of Congress Cataloging-in-Publication Data

Names: Beller, Elizabeth, author.
Title: Once upon a time : the captivating life of Carolyn Bessette-Kennedy / Elizabeth Beller.
Other titles: Captivating life of Carolyn Bessette-Kennedy
Description: First Gallery Books hardcover edition | New York : Gallery Books 2024. | Includes bibliographical references and index.
Identifiers: LCCN 2023050828 | ISBN 9781982178963 | ISBN 9781982178987 (ebook)
Subjects: LCSH: Kennedy, Carolyn Bessette, 1966–1999. | Kennedy, John F., Jr., 1960–1999—Marriage. | Press agents—United States—Biography. | Calvin Klein, Inc. | Aircraft accidents—Massachusetts—Martha's Vineyard.
Classification: LCC CT275.K458523 A3 2024 | DDC 659.2/974692092 [B]—dc23/eng/20231227
LC record available at https://lccn.loc.gov/2023050828

ISBN 978-1-9821-7896-3
ISBN 978-1-9821-7898-7 (ebook)

For Tom, Evangeline, and Alexander,
with love
and
For Carolyn and everyone who loved her,
with love

She loved to laugh. Many of her friends feel sad that she is being remembered primarily as a style icon. Carolyn should also be remembered for her warmth, for her kindness and generosity, for her wit, for her compassion and, most of all, for her great sense of fun.

—Colleen Curtis, *Daily News*, July 25, 1999

I remembered a story written by Henry James. It was the story of a young girl . . . who was as brave as she was beautiful, who was pure of heart and as unafraid to love. His description of Isabel mirrored that of Carolyn and I wondered out loud how it was possible for him to have known her when he wrote that story over a century ago. But, I suppose, it was because he was writing about his dream of a pure and brave American girl, one who comes along maybe once every hundred years, if we are lucky.

—Carole Radziwill in her eulogy for Carolyn Bessette-Kennedy at Grace Church in Greenwich, Connecticut, July 24, 1999

CONTENTS

AUTHOR'S NOTE

I n the summer of 1999, my interest in John F. Kennedy Jr. and Carolyn Bessette-Kennedy, the golden couple of 1990s New York, was merely casually curious. I then worked at Sotheby's and saw tabloids in delis on auction days, when lunch was a rushed grab bag between sessions. My colleagues and I stared at pictures of the glorious-looking couple; dazzling nights at galas and sun-drenched days on the Atlantic seemed worlds away from an art-house version of a chaotic Wall Street trading floor. But on July 17, when I checked the Saturday-morning headlines, my breath caught as I learned that John, Carolyn, and her sister Lauren had disappeared in a plane crash off of Martha's Vineyard. *No way*, I thought. *Not them!* And then: *But it'd be just like a Kennedy to get into a jam and find his way out.*

President Bill Clinton quickly involved the Coast Guard in the search, and we remained hopeful . . . that is, until Lauren's black garment bag, bearing her business card, which a friend had just recently placed in its plastic insert, washed up on the shore of Philbin Beach at the western tip of Martha's Vineyard: "Morgan Stanley Dean Witter, Lauren G. Bessette, Vice President" could still be made out despite being doused in water and sand. By the evening of Sunday, July 18, Coast Guard rear admiral Richard Larrabee explained they had shifted their focus from rescue to recovery. We all knew what this meant: John, Carolyn, and Lauren were gone. The August 2,

1999, cover of the *New Yorker* showed the Statue of Liberty shrouded in a black mourning veil. There was no mistaking it: The nation had lost royalty, but New York had lost more than that.

It was as though the brightness of our generation had dimmed. It had to do with age in general—they were our peers, *my* peers—but it also had to do with the fact that they seemed to be building up to something extraordinary. Carolyn's reluctance to speak to the press and John's deflection of rumors that he was running for office felt like they were saving their voices for the right time, the right causes, the right place. And now we would never hear them.

In 2019, two decades after the tragic deaths, I again found myself reading about the couple, and this time I focused specifically on the contours of Carolyn's story. My reaction was to defend her against the rumors—that she was difficult, manipulative, and icy—which began to feel like a repetition of misogynistic imagery that was both speculative and slanderous. Tabloids reiterated the charge that her vanity had been the cause of the fated plane's late takeoff, that she had made the pedicurist change her nail polish three times to exactly match a lavender swatch she had. Even flattery of her style was quickly warped into the narrative that Carolyn was a shallow, clothes-obsessed shrew. It seemed clear to me that she was not given due process in the court of public opinion.

There was an interesting disconnect between the pictures, which, though archival, seemed fresh and of the time I was living, and the articles, which seemed somehow from another era, which they were—the end of the century, the millennium, the last days of the fax machine, the world before 9/11 and, crucially, the full force of the internet. But there was something else that seemed odd: a compulsion to be dismissive of and even disparaging toward Carolyn that appeared to be the flip side to the obsessive attention she attracted. In theory, the relationship she was interested in was with her boyfriend, and then husband. But the other interesting relationship, reading these clips, was between the camera and its subject, the tabloids and their adversary. That her husband handled this attention with such an easy, graceful style threw Carolyn's attitude into stark relief. *What's the matter with her?* seemed to be the underlying question. What stood out was the implication that anyone who had a boyfriend like that—rich, handsome, famous, and, by all accounts, quite charming and nice—ought to have no complaints at all.

As my reading evolved from articles to books, especially the memoirs by Carole Radziwill and RoseMarie Terenzio, two intimate witnesses to John's and Carolyn's lives and characters, I began to realize that the people who actually knew her described a very different woman from the one portrayed in the tabloids. How could Carolyn, who accompanied the Radziwills to frequent hospital stays, really be an "ice queen"? How was it possible that a woman who went out of her way to comfort her friends during loss or grief, or to tend to a young teen in distress on the street, also be a coked-up bitch who screamed at John for no reason? There seemed to be a need to deprive her of nuance and humanity, as though she were required to play a villain role in a larger cultural narrative.

My interest deepened further, to the point where the decision to write about Carolyn Bessette-Kennedy was not so much a choice as a compulsion.

THE BACKLASH AGAINST FEMINISM in the 1990s is the historical and cultural context in which I now perceive Carolyn's story. Women who spoke up about workplace inequality or domestic abuse were dismissed as histrionic troublemakers. The new twenty-four-hour tabloid media—which skewered Anita Hill, reduced Marcia Clark to a "lawyerette," and blamed Monica Lewinsky for her affair with President Clinton—leveled unprecedented vitriol at Carolyn. It was all too easy to cast this unknown figure, who had no public profile until she met John, as a wild banshee, a vapid fashionista, or an undeserving harpy.

When reexamining her short life from a distance of twenty years, I found lessons about a dysfunctional culture and how women struggle to build a life within a patriarchal society. The nineties' media morphed into a newly minted sensation factory in which the burden of leading a public existence went from tolerable to excruciating for both Carolyn and John. While one part of the culture was basking in a champagne supernova of pared-down chic, another British music invasion, and languid cool, the tabloids began a feeding frenzy that forgot the objects of their fascination were human beings.

It wasn't just the tabloids and cable TV. Many of the books about the Kennedy clan written in the aftermath of the crash denigrated Carolyn as not good enough for America's prince. Any detail that could reflect negatively on her was scrounged up. John's childhood friend Billy Noonan's biography of

John, *Forever Young*, went so far as to say that Carolyn used Anthony Radzi-will's illness as her "cause célèbre" and a way to separate John from his friends.

In the renderings of John and Carolyn, most marital problems are laid at her feet. In this case, it wasn't Eden that was ruined, but Camelot. Carolyn, in these accounts, was crazy. She was cold, violent, emasculating, and a gold-digger. Both of them are being deprived of their humanity in different ways by this take. He is deprived of his complexity, and she is deprived of being more than the sum of her physical parts.

Sasha Chermayeff, who was close to both Carolyn and John, now sees Carolyn's anger at being hounded in a different light than she did at the time. "She had healthy anger that she couldn't express. Outrage . . . it's healthy! That kind of expression wasn't considered what someone married to JFK Jr. should be doing," said Sasha. "It wasn't considered feminine, and the judg-ment for what was a human reaction was fierce. Part of her anger was the constant misunderstanding of that. Everyone saying, 'Get your shit together' furthered her sense of isolation. She was feisty, and I loved the fact that some-one with cojones stepped into the picture.

"Yes, she was a caretaker, and John really loved that about her," Sasha con-tinued. "But she also stood up to him when he was wrong, and that was great. He had had it with the yes-people. But as for the press attention, John had been dealing with it since he could remember. He didn't know what it was like to walk into it. I like to think they could have made it. They were both compassion-based people."

We've seen people living in a celebrity fishbowl crumble again and again over the last twenty-five years, unable to sustain their equilibrium. I hope that amid the current intensified chaos—wars, post-pandemic social unrest and disaffection, and a cultural reckoning with systemic injustice—there is something afoot that, perhaps counterintuitively, makes a reexamination of Carolyn's life seem timely. I hope that witnessing her story will become a small part of the movement, already growing as the next generations come into power, in which we demand more personal responsibility and ethical consciousness than was required in the environment in which we were raised. Maybe even an evolution of the human spirit, where we not only recognize and empathize with one another but, to quote Robert F. Kennedy, we "make gentle the life of this world."

Perhaps what was most remarkable about Carolyn was that she was a super empath, which on the flip side makes one supersensitive. It's painful to think that someone who was able to care for friends the way Carolyn did, to read their emotions because she was so in tune with what everyone felt, was on the receiving end of so much jealousy that manifested in blind denigration. Case in point: A wedding boutique that peddled dresses similar to Carolyn's wedding dress displayed a cardboard cutout of John kissing what would have been Carolyn's hand upon leaving the church. Yet there was no Carolyn, or even a hand. He kissed the scarf dangling from a headless mannequin under a sign that read, "It could have been you." The wish to erase her is stark and unsettling.

It's a tragedy that Carolyn never had the chance to tell her own story—her thoughts, her feelings, her humor, her memories, and her truths were not something she got to share in her own voice. A lot of John's friends thought that if he knew he was going to die so young, he would have wanted his legacy preserved in writing. The same could be said for Carolyn. It stands to reason that a woman who focused heavily on helping those in need would wish to continue doing so, and there is much to learn from Carolyn's story.

Yet this book is written in an era that is much gentler on women like Carolyn Bessette-Kennedy. I think the growing (and reemerging) fascination with her shows that so many of us can relate to her, the kid who came out of the blue hoping to make not just an acceptable life for herself, but an *extraordinary* one. Many women identify with Carolyn; they are drawn to her vivacity, effortlessness, beauty, and style. In the age of social media, we can now draw a direct line between its attendant ills—intense public scrutiny, accompanied by anonymity that encourages toxic hostility, and the constant fear of being shamed or outcast—and a sharp increase in mental health issues. It seems Carolyn felt wounded by similar kinds of aggressions. Back then it was easier to dismiss the cause and effect as a character flaw. Over the last twenty-plus years, we've also seen a sea change in society's attitude toward depression and its treatment. The schadenfreude over Carolyn's bottle of antidepressants found washed up on the shore of Martha's Vineyard just days after the crash now seems shameful and ghoulish.

I wanted to recount Carolyn's story in a way that situated her at the center of her own narrative. When she appears in the volumes of Kennedy literature, it is often as a sidebar without empathy, compassion, or desire to understand who she really was. It's time she got her due.

ONCE UPON
A TIME

CHAPTER ONE

LAST NIGHT

July 16, 1999

The navigational pattern for a night flight from Fairfield, New Jersey, to Martha's Vineyard is to follow the lights up the coast of New England. Looking down from the small plane, the passengers and pilot would see the glimmering necklace of beach towns in Connecticut and then Rhode Island. The glow of bustling I-95 is enough to go by until Point Judith, Rhode Island, at the southwestern tip of Narragansett Bay. There, the pilot—Carolyn's husband, John—at the controls of the six-seat Piper Saratoga airplane carrying his wife and her sister Lauren, has to make a decision. If he continues along the shoreline, they can drop Lauren off to visit friends on Martha's Vineyard by crossing the narrowest point of Buzzards Bay, with only eight miles between points of land. On that route, he will still be guided by the lights of the mainland. But that route means an extra ten minutes, and Carolyn and John are already late for his cousin Rory Kennedy's wedding weekend.

John loved Rory, who was eight years younger than he, the daughter of his revered uncle Robert F. Kennedy. Yet this was the latest in an endless parade of Kennedy family events at which John's attendance, and therefore Carolyn's, was requested. Expected, even. John was the brightest star of the family. He was the man on whom they depended to guide the next generation into greatness. Outwardly, John wore this burden lightly—so lightly that he could also be depended on to be late. It was one of his many charms, except when it wasn't. Perhaps the hurry that night, as the plane flew up the coast, was to stave off the inevitable chiding, however good-natured, about missing any of the celebrations swirling throughout the weekend.

And so, having considered the Buzzards Bay option, he chose the alternative, banking right at Point Judith and setting the plane on a direct course for the Vineyard. The Rhode Island shoreline fell away.

Thirty-four miles of open ocean separated the plane from its destination. Thirty-four miles in a six-seat Piper Saratoga without someone instrument rated, or cleared to fly in clouds, rain, and fog in the pilot's seat. Thirty-three miles without lights.

Earlier that evening in New York, John had given his sister-in-law Lauren a ride to the airport in his white Hyundai convertible. They had both run late at work. He'd gone to the gym briefly before returning to his office at *George* magazine at 1633 Broadway in Midtown. She walked the three blocks from her office at the headquarters of Morgan Stanley, where she had been named vice president the year before, to John's office, and they left by 6:30 p.m. with the top down, battling gridlocked, rush-hour traffic. John made his regular stop at the West Essex Sunoco and bought a banana, a bottle of water, and six AA batteries. It wasn't until after 8:00 p.m. that John pulled up to the Essex County Airport in New Jersey and dropped Lauren off at the terminal, still in her beige work dress, so she could freshen up before takeoff. He parked the car and checked that the plane had already been pulled out from the hangar—a confirmation he had made by 3:00 p.m. that day, helpful considering he was still hobbling on his left ankle, which he'd broken after crashing his Buckeye—described by its manufacturer as a "powered parachute"—six weeks earlier on Memorial Day weekend. The cast had been taken off the day before, but he still moved gingerly, not yet back to full strength. John was checking the plane when Carolyn pulled up in a town car minutes later, also having left the city at 6:30 p.m. She was dressed simply in black pants and a black button-down shirt—black being her uniform whenever nearby paparazzi were a possibility.

John had owned the Piper Saratoga for three months. It had a Lycoming TIO-540-AH1A 300-horsepower six-cylinder engine driving a Hartzell three-blade constant-speed prop and was painted bright red and white. As John inspected the plane, he was, unbeknownst to him, being observed by two young girls at the airport. Overcome with the excitement of a John F.

Kennedy Jr. sighting, the girls had left a note on his car before retreating to watch his every move on the tarmac from a distance. John, they later reported, had been fastidious, checking the doors and ensuring that the ignition and both magnetos, the engine-driven ignition sources, were switched off. He pulled out the pilot's operating handbook and read through the preflight checks. Finally, he opened the rear door and, in doing so, gave the onlookers a glimpse of the beautiful upholstery inside.

Carolyn met John by the plane, and hesitated. Carolyn had ridden pickup while John piloted many times. Despite her unease, it had always been fine. Better than fine, at times—it was a welcome respite to be up in the air together, away from the claustrophobia of the incessant recognition.

Lauren then came up, bag in hand, and hugged her sister. The two, who had always been tight, had become even closer over these recent months when Lauren returned to New York after four years at Morgan Stanley's Hong Kong branch and bought a loft on White Street in Tribeca, just a few blocks from John and Carolyn's apartment at 20 North Moore Street.

Lauren entered the small passenger door of the plane first. There were four passenger seats in a club seating arrangement: the two rear seats facing forward and the middle seats facing aft. This way, the guests John and Carolyn loved to host on board could converse face-to-face. Lauren sat on the left of the plane; Carolyn was slow to follow her sister inside and sat on the right. Unusually, they chose the aft-facing seats, perhaps so they could talk in semi-privacy using the Piper's headsets. Carolyn usually sat beside John if there was no instructor, or if there was, she would sit in the third row, facing toward John at the controls. The control panel on the Piper was elaborate, and John began the process of starting the plane and preparing for takeoff.

IT'S TEMPTING TO SAY that the rest is history. What happened during the next hour is a matter of public record. John F. Kennedy Jr., who as a child experienced the shockingly abrupt and profound loss of his father, one of the most sudden, violent deaths in the history of American presidents, would experience his own sudden, violent death. His father died in the arms of his wife; the son died alongside his wife and sister-in-law. His father's death in the bright Texas sun was seared into the public consciousness with twenty-six seconds of amateur film footage; his son's death was consigned to the blackness of night and sea. The father's body was flown in its coffin from Dallas to Andrews Air Force Base, his blood still on his widow's dress when they arrived; the son's body was not transferred to its final burial ground. There was no final burial ground. It was an erasure. A vanishing from the sky to the sea. Like a myth.

The images of father and son are woven into an enormous and detailed tapestry of the most obsessed-over family in American public life, a family intertwined with some of the major plot points in the nation's history. Carolyn and Lauren Bessette's stories are embroidered on the fringe of that great fabric, threaded narrowly enough to be unperceived.

The plane began moving on the tarmac. "Essex Ground, Saratoga Nine-Two-Five-Three November on the ramp ready to taxi with information Mike for a takeoff," said John.

"Saratoga Five-Three November, good evening," the control tower responded. "Taxi to runway two-two." Approximately eleven minutes later, the plane's ascent tripped the Traffic Alert and Collision Avoidance System for a commercial American Airlines flight landing at Westchester County Airport. Neither air traffic control nor the pilot of AA1484 could reach the Piper Saratoga's radio; the pilot of AA1484 stated, "I understand he's not in contact with you or anybody else."

At Point Judith, John banked right over the ocean. Normally, at this point in the trip, one could make out Martha's Vineyard off in the distance, but an uninterrupted void of blackness yawned outside the windows of the plane.

They were flying through a darkness akin to that of a sensory-deprivation chamber, surface and sky indistinguishable. Only when John began to make multiple turns, climbing then descending, turning and descending again, might the sisters have noticed that it had been twenty minutes since they had seen the nebulous mainland lights, glimmering yet opaque as they receded in the distance.

CHAPTER TWO

WESTCHESTER

1966–1977

C arolyn, with her older twin sisters, Lisa and Lauren, had set the kitchen table with a bright multicolored tablecloth, perfect for the cake— lemon, Carolyn's favorite. Surrounding the table were boxes upon boxes that Ann, the girls' mother, was still sealing as she found the candles and located the ice cream. The room was bedecked with birthday decorations in the garish primary colors of the late seventies, in marked contrast to Ann's elegant furnishings. She had refined taste, eschewing the muddy brown and avocado green then overtaking homes across the United States. As soon as the celebration was over, she would start packing again.

It was January 7, 1977, Carolyn's eleventh birthday. Ann was worried about a move in the middle of the school year. She had been a single mother for a lot of their childhood. Her three girls had enormous reserves of strength, humor, and care—but still. The twins loved to dote on Carolyn and her friends, and with their help the cheer of birthday festivities might help distract her youngest from the fact that this was also a goodbye party.

Carolyn's whole class had been invited because Ann was the type who knew that the chaos incurred by hosting twenty children on a sugar rush was preferable to hurting the feelings of a child who might otherwise not have been invited. This was one of the lessons she taught her daughters: Never forget about those who are left aside.

Only as the guests departed did it sink in for fellow eleven-year-old Jane Youdelman that this was more than the end of a party. Eleven is an age where you can still ignore the inevitable outcome of certain actions— a house full of boxes means it will soon be vacated—until the moment is thrust upon you. After Carolyn had blown out the candles, the cake had been eaten, and the sun had begun to set, Jane stomped and cried around the perimeter of the Bessette home that was perched on a corner hilltop in White Plains, New York. The day, the year had ended, and her best friend was moving away. Was Carolyn as upset by the move as Jane? Was she excited about living in Greenwich, full stop, or did she feel slight apprehension mixed with joy at the lark of a new adventure? Carolyn, a child who usually bounced with exuberance, held a placid smile on her face amid the shouts of birthday and bon voyage wishes, her emotions concealed behind calm composure.

Jane and Carolyn shared a sense of freedom and joy in their young lives. Over the six years they had been friends, they'd run wild and free around their small White Plains neighborhood. Carolyn always made Jane feel welcome at her home and stood by her in the school hallway to stave off barbs coming from Jane's older sister, who wasn't as kind as Lauren or Lisa. Jane found herself writing in her third-grade diary, more than once, "I wish Carolyn was my sister." The sentiment was widespread among friends; Carolyn was sensitive and highly attuned to her peers.

Yuma Euell, who noticed Carolyn's kind nature early in their days at school, was also at the party. "I wasn't in Carolyn's class that year," recalled Euell. "But she went out of her way to invite me. She made sure you knew she was your friend.

"She was beautiful and strong, emanating a kind of light around her, but at the same time delicate," Euell said. "Mrs. Bessette was a substitute teacher at Richard J. Bailey School and friends with my mom. She had called my mother to say Carolyn wanted to ensure I was there because they were leaving the next day. My mom briefly sobbed when Mrs. Bessette told her the news. She always said that Carolyn and Mrs. Bessette were wonderful people." That the move surprised a few of their friends perhaps had to do with Ann having just sold her half of the house to her ex-husband.

⁓

INITIALLY, THE FAMILY LIVED in an apartment at 16 Fieldstone Drive in Hartsdale in Westchester County, New York. Then, on July 1, 1969, when Carolyn was three and a half, they bought the modest three-bedroom house at 12 Old Knollwood Road in White Plains, a ten-minute drive from Rex Ridge.

Neither Hartsdale nor White Plains was a bastion of affluence. In 1960, Hartsdale was a small, unincorporated area located within the township of Greenburgh, which had a population of around 76,000. Hartsdale covered about eight square miles when Ann and her daughters lived there. Historically, Greenburgh was predominantly Black. Many laborers had moved there during WWI, and, after WWII, middle-class Black families and large Jewish and Italian populations settled in the area. Though white middle-class households had become the majority in Hartsdale by the time Carolyn was of school age, the Greenburgh township was still fairly diverse, particularly in comparison to the rest of surrounding Westchester County.

In 1968, when Carolyn was two, Hartsdale witnessed an extremely contentious school-district merger, including the Bessette sisters' future school, Juniper Hill. The *New York Times* reported that some Hartsdale parents opposed on the grounds that it would compromise their children's education by mixing them with "slower children," apparently motivated by racial bias. Yet others lobbied on its behalf, wrote letters, and went to Albany and "pounded on the Commissioner's door." In August of 1968, the Hartsdale and Greenburgh school districts were merged and desegregated, resulting in a student body that was 75 percent white and 25 percent Black.

After the Bessettes moved to White Plains, Carolyn and her sisters remained at Juniper Hill School, indicating that Ann supported the merger and wanted a diverse environment for her girls. Ann sometimes taught as a substitute teacher at the school and was therefore a colleague of Carolyn's third-grade teacher, Mary Lou Darkenwald. Mrs. Darkenwald remembered Carolyn as "a very bright, confident, attractive child. She was outgoing but in a quiet way. Juniper School now had a diverse, integrated student population. Carolyn fit in nicely. She wasn't at all prissy."

Carolyn's criteria for friendship were kindness and humor. You had to be able to laugh, and even better if you could make her laugh. Yuma loved Carolyn's bubbling, infectious laugh so much that she was willing to risk getting in trouble to hear it. "I was sitting next to her, our desks side by side. I remember wanting to make her laugh all the time because it was so fun, so nice to hear that distinct laugh," she said. "So I did an impression of another kid who had complained that the classroom floor was dirty. Carolyn's giggle bubbled up and out into a belly laugh. I'd do whatever I could to hear that."

Carolyn and her classmate Jodi Savitch adored Mrs. Darkenwald, who conducted her classroom with a light touch, quieting the children with the French phrase *"Fermez la bouche!"* The kids thought this was very funny, but they obeyed. Carolyn and her friends braided each other's hair while Mrs. Darkenwald read to them from *The Lion, the Witch and the Wardrobe* by C. S. Lewis

"Every day did feel like it meant more," recalled Jodi. "The whole world was a wondrous surprise then. Carolyn was alive to it all, basking in words, transporting her mind through books and newfound equations, hopping on rocks, scrambling up hills, and exploring harbors. Behind Carolyn's house was a stream, and she had these many wonderful rubber animals that were a mainstay of our play—she loved animals. We made up our own magical kingdom and took turns naming our flock. I lived just up the street, and we would play like this for days. We were underwater explorers; we were horse trainers; we were on a jungle safari."

In fifth grade, just before moving to Greenwich, Carolyn met Howard Brodsky in her class at Richard J. Bailey School in White Plains, where she had gone after finishing third grade at Juniper. "She was so kind," Howard remembered. "My mom had died the year before, and not all the kids were considerate. Some were worse than inconsiderate and said things like, 'Ewww, you don't have a mom?' Kids will be kids, I suppose. But not Carolyn. When she heard that, she took me aside and put her arm around me. 'Don't listen to them. Just ignore them. They don't know what they're talking about.'" Howard developed a crush. "I lived further away and would walk the forty-five minutes to her house every chance I had, just to see if she would come out."

"What struck me most about Carolyn," remembered Jane Youdelman, "was that she was always full of hope. It's an undervalued characteristic. But she moved through the world brimming with a countenance that exuded 'What fun thing will I get to do or see today?' It made everything around her that much more enchanting. And it wasn't just because she was a child. It was a trait she held on to for a very long time."

The Bessette home was always the place to be, with Ann happy to have other children over. "It was a lovely house, and Carolyn always lit up a room,"

Jodi said. "She was so very sweet. Always. I remember her sisters smiling at us and helping us with snacks. Carolyn would make the most unusual flavor creations and insist I try them, too. One day we had cheese and crackers, and she held one aloft, adding a sprinkling of McCormick's lemon and pepper seasoning on top, one of her stranger concoctions. Or at least I thought it was strange until I tried it. It was too good."

Like Jane and Yuma, Jodi was devastated that her friends—not just Carolyn, but also Lauren and Lisa—and their warm, welcoming mom were moving away. And like Jane and Yuma, she does not remember ever meeting Mr. Bessette.

"Carolyn's mother came in for regular teacher-parent conferences," recalled Mrs. Darkenwald. "Her greatest concern was that Carolyn wouldn't be adversely affected by the divorce, that she didn't experience issues or problems because of it."

Mrs. Darkenwald allayed Ann's concerns about Carolyn. "She was the kind of child you wanted in your class," she explained. "Once you provided her with a framework for a particular subject—reading, writing, or math— she took off on her own. Carolyn was never a problem child. She was well-behaved, polite, and well-brought-up. She was active and had a number of girlfriends in class."

As continued to be the norm, her father was an outlying presence. "I don't know what role Mr. Bessette played in Carolyn's upbringing," Darkenwald said. "He evidently paid maintenance and child support for his three daughters. I think he saw them from time to time."

THE OFT-TOUTED MEDIA ASSUMPTION that Carolyn was a product of WASP privilege is laughable in light of the facts of her upbringing—Carolyn was raised in a predominantly Italian American household. Her maternal grandfather, Carl Calopero Messina, was born December 6, 1907, in Castellammare del Golfo, in the province of Trapani in Sicily. He emigrated to the United States in 1917, and by 1930 lived in Brooklyn with his younger brother, Giovanni, and his mother, Anna, while his father, Gioachino, stayed behind in Sicily. Tall with blue eyes, Carl married Jennie Venturalla, a beauty full of mirth and mischief, and the couple made their home near his mother on Bay 40th Street in Brooklyn. Jennie's father, Dominick, had emigrated from Italy at the turn of the century, so while she sounded American, Carl's Italian accent was strong.

Their daughter, Ann Marie Messina, was born on August 5, 1939, and her younger brother, Jack, arrived four years later. Carl was a screen printing and textiles foreman at Blum Screen Print Works, where he earned a salary of $1,600 per year while Jennie raised the children. In the mid-fifties, the Messinas moved to Ossining, another mecca of Italian immigrants in the postwar years. Carl and Jennie found employment at Printex, designer Vera Neumann's silkscreen-printing business housed in an 1810 Georgian mansion with views of the Hudson River. Carl was again a foreman, while Jennie was a sample maker for Vera's iconic scarves, which she began making with parachute silk after linen became scarce during WWII. Neumann's scarves— featured in a 2010 Smithsonian Museum retrospective—were as bold and bright as Lilly Pulitzer's, but with a New England, seasonal palette. While Vera may have been the designer, the Messinas were the artisans, their work a point of pride in the family.

To be an Italian American during the early 1900s was to be subject to appalling bigotry. A wave of nativist hostility engulfed the country during the Great Depression. Pseudoscientific racist theories claimed that "Mediterranean" types were criminal, even subhuman. From the twenties until the late sixties, Congress curtailed Italian immigration (along with restrictions on a broader range of nationalities) on racial grounds. Some prejudice subsided once immigration slowed, but tensions rose again during WWII. While the internment of Japanese Americans is well known, the US government also relocated ten thousand Italian Americans away from coastal zones to military camps throughout the United States and restricted the movements of six hundred thousand more. If Carl were to speak of Italy, where his father still lived, he could be tried for treason.

The epithets "dago" and "wop" were commonly used, even after Italian Americans had proved their loyalty to the US by their presence in the WWII armed forces. Carl signed his draft card in 1940, a year after his daughter, Ann, was born.

By 1983, the *New York Times* headlined an article with "Italian Americans Coming Into Their Own," but it had been a long and painful journey to social acceptance in white Anglo-Saxon America, and prejudice lingered. Carolyn grew up in a decade when, even more so than today, non-WASPs were considered socially subordinate—a far cry from the virulent racism that Blacks and others have long experienced in this country, yet a pertinent facet of the American sociocultural landscape.

Ann attended Ossining High School and participated in the Spanish Club throughout her years there. As a senior, in 1957, she was Classes Editor of the school yearbook, *Wizard*, and voted Best Looking by her classmates. Like Carolyn, her beauty was unconventional for her time, more Roman, with hints of Linda Evangelista and all the more riveting for it. Under the heading "Prophesies," where seniors made predictions for one another's future, Ann Marie was seen as "The Pepsodent girl with the million-dollar smile." All the seniors were pictured with their chosen pastime and ambition beneath their face. Ann Marie Messina's senior photo listed her pastime as "Playing 'hard to get,' " and her ambition as "Teacher." Carolyn would inherit all of these traits from her pretty, intelligent mother.

William Bessette, Ann's future husband, graduated from Crosby High School in Waterbury, Connecticut, two years earlier, in 1955. His yearbook photo shows a handsome young man whose smile suggests he knows it. Underneath the dashing photo is the caption, "Adept at all sports, Bill's A-1 swimming skill has made him a top-notch Red Cross Senior Life Saver. Next to swimming, basketball, and bowling, girls are foremost on his list of interests. An alumnus of Middlebury's Shepardson School, Bill will enter the University of Connecticut."

Ann enrolled at the University of Connecticut in fall 1957, and there met the good-looking junior William J. Bessette, who was majoring in civil engineering. William, older brother to Thomas, Dorothy, and Diane, was a member of the honor fraternity Chi Epsilon for civil engineering students and the American Society of Civil Engineers, which promoted professional contacts. William was also a member of the Newman Club, which was a Catholic student organization. And he is listed as Social Chairman, though of what we are left to guess, but his busy calendar anticipates his youngest daughter's gifts in the art of friendship.

True to her declaration in the Ossining High School yearbook, Ann was working toward becoming a teacher, determined and driven like her parents. She studied Elementary Education, becoming a member of Kappa Alpha Theta, and was again on the staff of the yearbook, *The Nutmeg*, where she helped write the Year in Review.

Carolyn's uncle Thomas Bessette recalled his older brother bringing their mother and him to meet Ann's parents, Jennie and Carl Messina, in Ossining: "I was quite young, but I was impressed by the fact that if you looked out their living room window, the prison was right there. Sing Sing in your backyard. Ann was beautiful; I loved her parents."

The *Nutmeg* of 1961, Ann's senior year, had a page covering the 1960 presidential race between JFK and Nixon, complete with photographs of each candidate. JFK's face—handsome, though with somewhat mournful eyes, and framed by his full head of hair—and Nixon's face, with its used-car-dealer smile, exist just a few pages away from Ann Messina's face. While flipping back and forth between the parents of Carolyn and John, one can't help but see the features the father passed down to his son and the mother passed down to her daughter.

Ann graduated with her bachelor of science in education in 1961. Though two years older, William, who worked throughout college, graduated in 1961 with a bachelor of science in civil engineering.

A year later they were engaged to be married. An announcement appeared in the August 30, 1962, issue of the *Reporter Dispatch* of White Plains. The headline read, "Miss Messina, Teacher, to Wed in Fall." Yet the article reported, "A Spring wedding is planned." In fact, their wedding took place the following summer, as that fall a tragedy occurred in the Bessette family.

William's father, Alfred Bessette, was a foreman for the Connecticut Light and Power Company. On October 11 of 1962, he was conducting a routine inspection of power lines in Middlebury, Connecticut, when he was electrocuted by 115,000 volts of electricity. He fell more than twelve feet from his ladder to the ground, sustaining burns on his face, neck, both arms, and lower body, and spent six weeks in the hospital "languishing in pain," as a family member put it. (While this private grief played out, President Kennedy, on October 22, alerted his citizens to the Cuban Missile Crisis, which sent a wave of shock and panic through the country.) Alfred died on November 9, 1962, at the age of fifty-eight, leaving his wife, Anna, a widow at fifty-three. William was twenty-six years old. His younger brother, Thomas, was sixteen.

Ann and William married on June 29, 1963. They were both two years out of college, during which time Ann worked as a school administrator and substitute teacher at Douglas G. Grafflin School in Chappaqua, New York.

William was working toward his New York State certification as a civil engineer.

Then, on November 5, 1964, Ann gave birth to twins Lauren and Lisa. Carolyn arrived just over a year later, in January 1966.

William experienced these major life events in the aftermath of his father's sudden death. Early parenthood is a time when you want your own parents to be there, if only to ask, "Am I doing this right?" But also, hopefully, to lend a hand—especially if you have twins.

At this time, Ann's mother, Jennie, became increasingly concerned about her daughter's marriage, and about her son-in-law in particular. Ann, she felt, had been left to care for three toddlers by herself even as she had to continue working. According to Roseann Flood, Jennie's colleague at Vera Neumann, "Ann and Jennie were very close. All Jennie spoke about was her worry for Ann because there were problems with William. Ann wasn't happy. Understandably."

As with college, William's engineering certification was prolonged. New York State requires four years of work in the field and one six-hour exam, which would have put William as earning his license in 1965. Carolyn would, years later, refer to this period as one in which her father "needed to continue his studies to be further certified." But she said, "Apparently it wasn't happening."

Acquiring the license took William until March of 1967, a year after Carolyn's birth. He went on to have a long career at Turner Construction International, where he worked on large public projects with a specialty in airports. William was a meticulous man who was, according to family members, "very, very anal-retentive," and his work took him to Las Vegas, Qatar, and Egypt. It often required long stays on-site, often for months at a time. On May 25, 1974, Ann filed for divorce from William in Westchester County Court, when Carolyn was eight years old.

ANN AND HER CHILDREN faced many difficult transitions over the course of their lives, but none so stark as becoming a single-parent household. "Eventually," said Roseann Flood, "Ann moved with her three toddlers to Jennie and Carl's for a while, who helped her with the girls when Ann was at work." Perhaps this is why Carolyn began kindergarten earlier than most children, at four and a half years old, rather than at five.

The split put the family under stress within and without—at home, the children had to make do with one parent around for day-to-day activities, and in the outside world, despite semi-liberated seventies proclamations of single mothers as superwomen, they were sometimes eyed with suspicion for breaching the norm. It was not just the mothers who felt the judgment—their children did, too.

Ann and the children moved back to Old Knollwood Road after William vacated the house in favor of an apartment elsewhere in White Plains. Carolyn intermittently asked her mother why they divorced but could never wholly wrap her head around it. William's absences would form Carolyn's experience of her father after her parents' divorce. "When we went out, just the two of us, she would talk about being hurt that her father was not around," said her friend MJ Bettenhausen. "She still wondered about all the memories, as she was so young when it happened."

Despite having little memory of her father in the house, on rare occasions, traces of her feelings toward him surfaced. She once explained to a colleague who had asked her why she always ate so quickly. "I got in the habit as a little kid," Carolyn replied. "I couldn't stand the tension surrounding my father, and the sooner I finished dinner, the sooner I could get away."

Carolyn's emotional and psychological makeup was also significantly influenced by her maternal family and had much to do with her unwavering curiosity, drive, and insistence on authenticity—they had an aversion to pretense. A nimble strain of humor ran in the Messina family, as evidenced by Jennie's frequent ripostes. Once asked if she was afraid to live so close to Sing Sing prison, Jennie shot back, "Sweetheart, trust me, if someone breaks out of jail in Ossining, the last thing they're going to do is stay in Ossining!"

Jennie had demonstrated the value of community responsibility by example: She volunteered at Phelps Memorial Hospital Auxiliary. Ann herself was always active in charity work with the Boys & Girls Clubs of America and Kids in Crisis. She imparted this caring spirit to her daughters, who participated in the Camp Fire Girls, the first co-ed, nonreligious, and multicultural organization for girls in the US; its playgroup counterpart for younger ones, the Bluebirds; and the three sisters sang to the elderly in retirement homes.

Throughout Carolyn's childhood, Ann's steady presence was the defining feature. Teaching her girls to make their own way and cultivate a solid work ethic was of the utmost importance to Ann, who had been raised among strong women with confidence, self-respect, and ambition as inherited traits. A friend of Carolyn's remembered Ann's sense of humor: "She laughed as much as Carolyn but suffered no fools."

Fortunately for the Bessette girls and their mother, a new father figure was about to come onto the scene. According to a friend, when Carolyn needed treatment for scoliosis at nine years old, Ann brought her to the acclaimed orthopedic surgeon Dr. Richard G. Freeman. Dr. Freeman was a recent widower; his wife, Marion, had died in 1975. He had three daughters of his own, Kathy, Diana, and Lori, and according to friends was an open-hearted and nurturing parent.

Dr. Freeman was calm and funny—a distinct change from intense William. Ann and Richard fell in love and were married in 1977. A few months later, "at my last conference with Carolyn's mother," recalled Darkenwald, "she informed me that they were resettling in Greenwich."

By January 27, 1977, when William bought Ann's share of the Knollwood Road house, Ann was no longer Ann Bessette; she was Ann Freeman. In Greenwich, the Bessette women joined the large Freeman household on Lake Avenue, a street of rolling lawns and stately homes. Although Ann's situation improved after marrying and moving to Greenwich (among other things, Freeman would turn out to be a loving stepfather), she never forgot where she came from—and nor did her youngest daughter. Carolyn's beginnings—in which her Italian American mother found herself single and raising her children alone after her husband's departure—would reverberate throughout her life.

CHAPTER THREE

GREENWICH TIME

1977–1983

Carolyn and Lauren clambered from the street up onto the bus. Lisa was not there yet, so the driver hesitated. The two sisters made their way along the aisle, smiling, screaming hellos to friends as only teenagers can, to sit in the back with the popular girls. The bus remained still. Why weren't they moving?

"Go ahead!" yelled Lauren.

"You don't need to wait for Lisa," Carolyn chimed in, the two of them laughing.

Sometimes the driver would wait anyway; sometimes he would not. It was only a ten-minute drive from the Freeman home at 722 Lake Avenue to Greenwich High School, but to walk took over an hour. If one of the girls missed the bus, Dr. Freeman or Ann would have to drive her.

Sometimes it was Carolyn who was late, sometimes it was Lauren, and sometimes it was Lisa (though usually not Lisa). Whoever it was, the other two sisters would urge the driver to go ahead. They thought it was hilarious.

Carolyn thought a lot of things were hilarious in her early teens. She was coming into her good looks, was giddy and excitable, and loved making friends. In the late seventies and early eighties, Greenwich was a safe enclave and a teen dream. High schoolers convened and shopped on Greenwich Avenue, at D.W. Rogers, a clothing store that helped bring your bags to your car; bought candy and greeting cards at Meads; and grabbed burgers and milkshakes at Neilsen's Ice Cream. Especially popular, though, was the beach at Tod's Point. The freedom to walk the avenue and meet with friends at the beach was exhilarating.

Despite the new stomping grounds, family was always close. Ann remained protective, and the sisters enjoyed the stability of a loving stepfather in a bright and spacious new home. Jennie and Carl Messina remained a large part of their lives, and together they attended their extended family's many baby showers and weddings. Carolyn expressed her love for her grandmother much in the same way Jennie would describe everything else—with a quip: "I have a little Italian grandmother with a hair growing out of a mole on her face."

Back then, Greenwich was not the ostentatiously wealthy place it is today. There were the old-school WASPs, but they kept their privilege understated. Shabby couches, beat-up station wagons, and worn-out Top-Siders were the order of the day. Many working-class Italians had recently come to the area to work as stonemasons. They were the artisans, and their craft is apparent in the stone walls that line the yards of the quietly expensive homes spread throughout the area.

The town was a peaceable mix of different families. Through the 1960s, Catholics were not admitted into many country clubs, which formed a large part of social life in Greenwich. One fellow Italian American Greenwich resident who lived there in the late sixties and early seventies remembered that "you feel that difference in that world of Connecticut country clubs. Catholics were not welcomed in Protestant clubs, so we joined Mamaroneck's predominantly Irish and Italian Winged Foot Golf Club. And we spent a lot of time at church, St. Mary's." By the time the Bessette sisters arrived, these old rules were just beginning to change and the town was opening up.

Ann Freeman's expertise was education, and she surely found the Greenwich public school system attractive. And though the need for her salary was less pressing, she continued teaching at Douglas G. Grafflin School in nearby Chappaqua. Mimi Stein was one of her fifth- and sixth-grade students in the late 1980s. "[Mrs. Freeman] was kind and open with us," Stein said. "She was in a second marriage, which wasn't super common at the time. She was around fifty, and when most other teachers were dyeing their hair, she was an elegant gray. She was the only teacher in front of whom I felt comfortable making mistakes.

"She had a deep level of understanding of what would work best for each student. She knew what it was like to be a kid, but she still had high standards and could work with her students in an individual way that is rare. Mrs. Freeman wasn't a hugger until you knew her. She was a warm demander."

Dr. Freeman's three daughters, Kathy, Diana, and Lori, were off to college and beginning independent young lives. Despite this, the six girls, Bessettes and Freemans, got along well—perhaps not living together on a daily basis precluded issues stepsiblings sometimes have. Most important, the Bessette sisters loved Dr. Freeman, and he loved them back, treating them as his own.

Ann and the girls settled in. She signed her daughters up for ballet at the Greenwich Ballet Workshop. The girls attended Central Middle School, which went through ninth grade. Lauren and Lisa then started their sophomore year at Greenwich High School, which at the time went from grades ten through twelve. Carolyn joined her sisters there for her sophomore year in the fall of 1980.

Classmate Peter Wilson attended Greenwich High School in the same era. "It was such a more free-spirited place as a teenager in the eighties," he observed. "The shops were still independently owned as opposed to the chains that now line Greenwich Avenue. Teenagers had big parties in their parents' homes when they went out of town. But the same teens throwing and attending the parties participated in Safe Rides, an organization that designated sober drivers to transport people from place to place.

"One night, I'd be a sober driver," said Wilson, "and the next, I caught a ride. It was great. It was more innocent and so much more fun. It was a time marked by trust, and we felt more freedom than kids do today. So we tended to live up to that trust."

Greenwich High was an enormous public school with over 2,200 students. Everyone convened at the student center, a vast open area that housed every clique. There were the usual ones: jocks, druggies, nerds, and a few special to Greenwich High, such as the tree people—the environmental enthusiasts. They all sat separately for the most part, but at the same time, they mostly got along. "Carolyn was in a smaller, different group," said classmate Sue Milby. "It wasn't jocks or stoners; it was just around four of them, Carolyn, one other girl, and two boys. They facetiously called themselves the 'Number Ones.'"

Lauren Holch, who rode the bus with the Bessettes, recalled: "All the sisters seemed gorgeous and popular and sat in the back of the bus with the popular kids, while I was shyer and sat in the front. It was hard not to notice them. Though Lisa seemed a bit less outgoing than Carolyn and Lauren."

By this point, Carolyn was taller than both her sisters, and as tall as most boys. While Lauren and Lisa, fraternal twins, had long, wavy brown hair and brown eyes, Carolyn's hair was lighter, even sun-kissed with blonde in the summer, and her eyes were bright blue. Still, they were often a tight trio, although they eventually found their way to different interests and friend groups. Other than ballet, Carolyn's main activity was work. She babysat and she took a job at Threads & Treads, the local sports shop that carried athletic wear with team insignias for the local high schools, on Greenwich's East Putnam Avenue.

Another friend of the Bessettes said, "It felt like the girls were in a bit of a pressure cooker, maybe like the family had a strict decree to be 'good girls,' to get all A's and do everything right. It felt to me that they were slightly stressed over what was expected of them."

While the Bessette sisters grew up comfortably, they were aware that their current lifestyle was made possible by their stepfather, an experience not unlike Jackie and Lee Bouvier's when their mother, Janet, married Hugh D. Auchincloss. Dr. Freeman attended Columbia University's Vagelos College of Physicians and Surgeons, completing his residency in surgery in 1959 and his residency in orthopedic surgery in 1964, both at Mount Sinai. He led a thriving practice in Westchester and was the chief of orthopedic surgery at White Plains Hospital.

At the Freemans' beautiful six-bedroom, five-bathroom home at 722 Lake Avenue, Carolyn's room was decorated in a French provincial style, a blend of Parisian polish with countryside rustic in various shades of white. She had neither a television nor a phone in her room—Carolyn was the type to talk all night if she had the chance, so Ann wisely kept the phones in family spaces. Lauren and Lisa both excelled academically. Carolyn got good grades but didn't put in the same effort as her sisters—her favorite subject was people. After Carolyn's first year at Greenwich High, Ann felt she was having "too much fun" and transferred her to St. Mary High School for her junior year.

"What this meant," said a classmate, "was that her grades were suffering. To be fair, Greenwich High, with the enormous student center that was so social it could feel like a nightclub in midday, required students to be very focused to keep up with a rigorous curriculum. Carolyn was magnetic, and people were drawn to her, vying for her attention. Add to this the fact that we were allowed to leave campus for at least one block during the day, and it was easy to fall behind."

In the fall of 1981, Carolyn began her junior year at St. Mary's, a mere four-minute drive along Clapboard Ridge Road from their Lake Avenue home. St. Mary's was smaller and less academically rigorous than Greenwich High, but also stricter. Ann T. Edwards, who taught English at the school, noticed that several students came to St. Mary's after having "too much fun" elsewhere. "It was a Catholic School, so a lot of protective parents sent their teenagers," Edwards recalled.

Irene Savage, a teacher at St. Mary's, remembered Carolyn as "vibrant and beautiful, but there seemed to be a bit of a drama. Perhaps it was just that she was new, because I don't remember it being a lasting issue."

While switching schools has inherent drama, this particular drama seemed to center on Carolyn having blossomed into a young woman of uncommon beauty. "Her looks attracted attention everywhere she went," said close friend and St. Mary's classmate Victoria Giorgi. "And she hated it. She would feel creeped out by the staring, and it often was creepy."

One friend first saw Carolyn as she made her way across the sand at Tod's Point to the concession stand. "That walk meant you were on parade, and you'd think, *I hope I look all right, I'm going to the concession stand*. Carolyn stood out, always had that charisma, that *it* factor," recalled the friend. "She was tall and thin—though not rail thin, as she later became—with eyes like a Siberian husky. But different looking, not Greenwich preppy pretty, not your usual 'pert nose, winged hair' beauty, and I mean that in the best way."

Ann kept a relatively tight rein on Carolyn as a defensive measure. "Carolyn's mom was welcoming to Carolyn's friends," recalled Giorgi. "She was truly warm and nice. But due to the excessive attention Carolyn's looks brought her, Ann was a little strict. So there were certain things Carolyn was not allowed to do. She was not allowed out late and had an earlier curfew than many of us. Ann needed to protect her. But of course, Carolyn snuck out once or twice."

Yet Carolyn was careful. "Many kids who lived in Greenwich came from very wealthy families, and the drug scene was intense. So while Carolyn might have been in the room while some partook, she didn't go near them," said Giorgi. "She was raised to steer clear of drugs or excessive drinking."

One weekend, Giorgi got permission to host a friend's sixteenth birthday party in the basement while her parents were in the house upstairs. "Everyone hung out together—St. Mary's and Greenwich High kids. So, as was always the case, it ended up being a massive party, and the house was trashed," she said. "When I headed to bed, my parents told me I'd go nowhere until I cleaned the house. There was a huge get-together the next day on the beach by Tod's Point, and I fell asleep resigned to missing it while I picked up cups and mopped beer off the floor. But Carolyn was sitting at the edge of my bed when I woke. 'Wake up! Come on, I'll help you clean, otherwise, you'll miss Tod's!' I couldn't believe she had come to help me. No one else had. But she did, and together we got the house clean. Carolyn was sweet that way, always thinking of others."

Other than house parties, Carolyn and friends would sometimes branch out for meals at local casual joints such as Casey's Tavern, Boxing Cat Grill, and Neilsen's. Mostly, though, the beach by Tod's Point was the place to be after school or on weekends. The boys played football while the girls would hang out or play volleyball. Everyone played Frisbee.

"We all got sodas and junk food from the concession stand, and by spring, it turned into proper beach days," Giorgi recalled. "Someone always blasted music from their car, usually classic rock. It was a sweet, innocent time."

Everyone also went to Tod's Point after prom. Many stayed the whole night.

"Carolyn was definitely never allowed to do that," Giorgi said. "She went to prom but did not stay out all night. She would've never tried."

"She wore a white slip dress to prom," said another student. "Carolyn was sophisticated and stunning even then." The other girls still wore poufed-up eighties constructions, so Carolyn, there with her boyfriend, Gene, stood out even further.

Carolyn had begun dating Eugene "Gene" Carlin, St. Mary's star football player, in her junior year. One student remembers Carlin as "a little conceited, a little bit of a player." (This rather ungentlemanly description tracks: When the press reached out to him in the 1990s, Carlin described his relationship with Carolyn as "hot and heavy. She's passionately sexy," and then added, "Use your imagination.")

But Carolyn could handle Carlin, who also described Carolyn as "someone who would make you jealous, and if you tried to do it back she'd ignore you. Then you go completely crazy."

The couple attended parties at mutual friend Rob Pedicano's house, which boasted the most sought-after luxury possible, at least for teens: a pool. Rob found Carolyn to be "incredibly kind" despite dating the big guy on campus. On Halloween of 1982, he hosted yet another party at his home. "Carolyn came dressed as a flapper. She was a knockout," he said. "And so nice. Later that same fall I was in a car accident, and it was Carolyn who came to visit me when I was stuck in the hospital for a week."

The picture of the pretty, compassionate, spirited high school girl that emerges from her friends and classmates of the time has another, darker corollary.

"Carolyn didn't see her biological father much. She never really spoke about him," said Giorgi.

Yet the Bessettes did see the girls for Christmas. "They split the day," said Thomas Bessette. "Ann had them in the morning, and in the afternoon we were all at my sister Dorothy's house in Woodbury [CT]. Dorothy always hosted; we called her The General. After a big dinner, presents. I still remember Bill sitting on the couch with two of his daughters nestled in his armpits."

"Additionally, despite her magnanimity, some girls were jealous, which didn't feel nice," said Giorgi. "Carolyn had no arrogance, but some girls were catty that she was so pretty and dated the cute football star."

Carlin was a year ahead of Carolyn, but he postponed going to college, so they continued dating throughout her senior year. "If I remember correctly," said one friend, "Ann was not crazy about Eugene."

When not with Gene, Carolyn spent time with friends. Unlike many of her peers, Carolyn didn't have a car, so she got rides from Giorgi and their mutual friend Carol Kleckner. "Carol's house was closer to mine, so she picked me up before Carolyn," said Vicki. "But Carolyn refused to sit in the back. Carol had a stick-shift Toyota, and Carolyn would squish in and sit between me and the shift. We'd laugh about it the entire ride, everyone jabbing elbows."

Lauren and Lisa would also pick Carolyn up or give her rides. "Her sisters were friendly to everyone, too. And they looked out for Carolyn," Giorgi said. "If we were at Tod's Point, they would come over to check on her, and bring her home if she hadn't already gotten a ride."

But really, Carolyn was doing just fine on her own at a different school. She seemed to be someone who always landed on her feet. Her fellow students found her to be full of joie de vivre. "I remember her as so sweet and also light-years ahead of the rest of us, emotionally and mentally," said one classmate.

"Carolyn was popular, but actively avoided becoming part of any clique. She was open to seeing anyone, [to making] any plan," Giorgi recalled. "She was a connector. She was close with Cathy Farrell, and the school always had them give prospective new students tours—because they were pretty, of course, but also because they were poised and personable in a way unusual for high school. I remember they were getting a little bit of local modeling work. Cathy's mother had made the connection for them."

But the modeling stint lasted only a short time. "Carolyn quickly found out she did not like the modeling work," explained Giorgi. "She didn't like the attention and wanted to move freely among her friends, under the radar." Dr. Deena Manion, another mutual friend, remembers the same, and sometimes it even extended to just having her picture taken by friends in casual circumstances. "Like everyone," said Manion, "I remember the first time I saw her. We were at Tod's Point on the beach, and she came over to say hello. I was thirteen to her fourteen and a half, and I was blown away by her beauty, thinking, *I want her fashion*. A jean pencil skirt, Tretorns with no socks, and a white oxford shirt. She was radiant. She was lively, with long hair that she threw around as she spoke. We saw one another over the years as our boyfriends were friends, and having her picture taken was never something she liked. It was true that pictures didn't do her justice. None captured how gorgeous she was, so maybe that was part of why. But even in casual moments with friends, if someone wanted to take her picture, she would often turn her head away from the camera."

Manion also made it clear that unlike a lot of teens in Greenwich, even ones they both spent time with: "Carolyn did not partake in drugs, even when we were out with people who were doing them. The times I spent with her, she didn't touch anything. She just didn't." But abstaining from drugs didn't mean she was particularly cautious or restrained.

"One evening, a group of us went into the city [New York City, an hour's drive or train ride from Greenwich]. We went to a private party, but it was held at a club. There were different rooms throughout the club, and one of them had a ball pit, like you would see at a children's indoor play center," said Manion. "We walked up to the room. She looked at me, raised her eyebrow as if to say, *I'll jump in if you will.* That was it. We spent the evening jumping around like kids in the ball pit, laughing hysterically."

Her playful side was evident to friends; to acquaintances it could appear to be a wild side. "After she switched schools, it seems like she chose a group of friends who were partiers, or at least appeared to be," said another friend. "They were loud, brash, and I remember being surprised. Her sisters were quite different. Lauren was very studious and goal-oriented. Lisa seemed more sensitive and bohemian, interested in art. Carolyn took a different tack, and although she was always nice to everyone, she hung with a tough crowd."

It's interesting to ponder the motivation behind the company she kept. Carolyn was not a heavy partier, but she spent a lot of time with those who were. Perhaps she felt the achievement-oriented path was linked to snobbery in a town where Catholics were unwelcome in clubs. She may have felt that while her French Canadian last name and blonde hair made her *look* WASPy, that was not who she really was, or at least who she had been while living in White Plains. She may have been self-conscious about the fact that the Freemans had had a whole life in Greenwich before she and her family even arrived. Finally, any difficulties in her relationship with her father weighed on her as well.

But none of these challenges were visible on the surface. "Carolyn was so poised, and she was mysterious even then," said Deena Manion. "If there was a party, we never knew if she was going to show up or not. If she did, she would often breeze in at the last minute, and usually didn't stay long. Even then, we knew she would do something spectacular with her life. We didn't know exactly what, but we knew." Carolyn had drive. She may not have known toward what, but already, in high school, she was manifesting the emotional intelligence that would be so fundamental to her professional life.

The caption to Carolyn's junior-year photo in the yearbook sums it up best: "Nice Eyes. Smile. Easy to talk to. Always screaming. Beautiful hair. *PRETTIEST."

It was in high school that Carolyn began to find her style. Catholic school girls often rolled up the waistband of their skirts to shorten them, but Carolyn did her own thing. The yearbook pictures show most girls in the uniform skirts, while Carolyn chose the less popular option: high-waisted, pleated pants.

"We had one of the nuns for homeroom," recalled Giorgi. "Her name was Sister Maureen, and she was so strict about shoes. But Carolyn really loved to wear her low-heeled pumps. Sister Maureen would admonish her, 'Those are not uniform shoes.'" Carolyn blew it off. "She already had a strong sense of what she liked to wear, and believe it or not, the shoes were Calvin Klein. She knew she'd get in trouble but would wear them anyway."

Carolyn kept a sense of humor about it all. Like most teenage girls, she hated gym class when you had to change clothes, or what was called "dress out."

"We had no gym facility, so we were constantly on the sidewalk battling rain and snow," said Giorgi. "To add insult to injury, a gym teacher named Ms. Miller was into disco, and she made us do aerobics to songs like 'The Hustle.' I can still see Carolyn rolling her eyes, barely doing the kicks. She looked at me imploringly, her expression pained, as if screaming, 'I can't believe this is happening. I can't believe this is happening.'"

Once at St. Mary's, classwork came easily to Carolyn. She got good grades but didn't have to put much time in. She did well without having to try very hard, according to classmate Trish Pulitano.

Sherry Mansing, a friend who was in English class with her, recalled Carolyn being sure of herself and contributing to class discussions: "She was down-to-earth and very smart."

A younger classmate, Claudia Slocum, retained vivid memories of Carolyn. "When I was a freshman and she was a big senior, she was incredibly sweet to me," Slocum said. "I remember when I burst into the girls' room one day just sobbing, probably over some lip gloss that my friends had made fun of or something. And she was there with her friends, and she came right over. She dried my eyes and tucked my hair behind my ears and talked me up. And after that, she always smiled and said hi to me in the halls. I was always so impressed by that because I was just a freshman and she was *it*."

CAROLYN WAS THRILLED TO get into Boston University. Her sisters had already left home by the fall of 1982, with Lisa heading to the University of Michigan and Lauren to Hobart and William Smith Colleges in Geneva, New York. Though she was already interested in fashion, Carolyn chose to major in education, just like her mother. Carolyn had a way with children—she liked them, and they liked her. Deena Manion remembered that Carolyn often spoke about wanting to be a preschool teacher: "Carolyn truly loved children and cooed at every child she saw. She always said she would make a career of working with kids."

The St. Mary's graduating class of 1983 conducted one of the requisite "Most Likely to" superlative polls. There was "First to Make a Million," "Wittiest," "Most Gullible," "Teachers' Pets," "Biggest Mooch," "Gets Dumped on the Most," and "Unluckiest." Carolyn, in a paraphrase of her mother's yearbook caption, was named "The Ultimate Beautiful Person." Valedictorian Deb Allis said Carolyn deserved the award because she "was beautiful inside and out. We kind of knew she was really in a different realm than the rest of us. Everybody in the entire class loved her."

Carolyn continued working the summer after graduation—for spending money, but also to supplement her tuition in Boston that fall. Though she had spent the last five-plus years in a prosperous suburb, she was not a spoiled young woman. Her job at Threads & Treads, which was described by a friend as "sort of a clubhouse" where teens would gather and hang out, was right up sociable Carolyn's alley. She could spend the summer making money, but was also in the company of her friends.

CHAPTER FOUR

BOSTON UNCOMMON

1983–1989

Carolyn and Dana Gallo pushed their single beds together in their dorm room, laughing and lounging as they ate Pepperidge Farm coconut layer cake straight from the box, sometimes barely defrosted. They lived on the thirteenth floor of Rich Hall, on Boston University's West Campus, and if anyone knocked on their door, the girls would shove the cake under the bed, which made them laugh harder. Once the interloper departed, they would pull the cake and their two forks back out. Many months and many cakes later—red velvet, chocolate, pineapple upside-down—the girls' friendship was firmly cemented.

"We laughed so much," Dana recalled. "Time with Carolyn was always, always entertaining. We would just hang out and have our own fun."

One of the heaviest things college freshmen carry with them on move-in day—among the clothes, music, books, posters—is continued romantic entanglements. They are certainly the most volatile. Gene Carlin, Carolyn's high school boyfriend, would drive up every weekend from Greenwich. He had not yet enrolled in college, even though he was a year older than Carolyn. For that first semester of Carolyn's freshman year, Dana recalled, "It was all about Eugene." Add the sweetness of reunion to the unfamiliar new landscape of Boston—indeed, of college altogether—and it's easy to imagine why, as per Dana, "Carolyn hardly left the dorm that first semester."

When she did leave, there were stares. Friends from that period of her life reiterate that college pictures didn't do Carolyn justice. "When I first met her, I thought, *Look at this tall, angelic, stunning girl; she's got to be difficult,*" said Dana. "But it was quickly clear she was the dearest person, so sweet and kind. There we were, a 4'11" dirty-blonde and 5'10" Carolyn, who knocked the breath out of people. And this is her in sneakers and a sweatshirt." (Carolyn, who often pointed out her own flaws—especially what she considered her big "Fred Flintstone" feet—dubbed herself and Dana "Mutt and Jeff.")

Dana explained that Carolyn was "very aware of how people were primed to judge her about her beauty. So she went out of her way to be kind and to make people comfortable."

Despite her inherently warm nature, Carolyn was still often met with judgment before people got to know her. Fellow BU classmate Jen Curran remembers seeing Carolyn for the first time. "I walked into our first class together, an art class, and was struck by her. I had never before, and haven't since, seen eyes as beautiful or expressive. I thought to myself, *This is a magical woman.* Nearly as soon as I met Carolyn, a few friends approached me, saying, 'She is going to skate by, charming the professor. She'll use her beauty to get more time with him.' I was in as much shock about girls that were supposedly her friends giving me this warning as I was at her beauty," said Curran. "It was more of a worry than complaint. They didn't really know her well at all, and it was a presumption—a presumption that was incorrect. She was extremely bright, with an elevated attention to detail."

An unwelcome aspect of beauty is the stereotype that it presumes a lack of intelligence—in this case, the dumb blonde. All this negative projection can be an assault on a young woman trying to step into adulthood. Luckily, Carolyn quickly forged friendships that allowed her to blossom even further.

The first night of the fall semester there was a fire drill, and all the students from the three giant West Campus dorms—Rich Hall, Sleeper Hall, and Claflin Hall—spilled out onto Nickerson Field, ordinarily home to BU's soccer, lacrosse, and football teams. It was like an emergency services social, a getting-to-know-you party. Another fellow freshman, Blaine Applegate, remembered how he, Carolyn, Dana, Marian Hughes, and Carrie O'Brien all met one another that night. From then on, they were usually together. Through the ups and downs of their time at BU, "we saw each other all the way through," said Applegate.

Applegate was having a tough time in his early days at college, and, as was her wont, Carolyn took him in. "I was grateful to have met Carolyn on our first week at school," he said. "I was damaged goods, but no one knew. The summer before I started college, my mom buried her father, my father left, and I had moved back to Bucks County. Befriending these people, especially Carolyn, softened the blow of being 350 miles away from home, a suburban guy in a city, and leaving Mom at that time. It turned out to be exactly where I should've been."

Boston University turned out to be exactly where Carolyn should be, too. The student body was enormous and varied, a dramatic contrast from St. Mary's. At BU, Carolyn's understanding of herself and the world was expanding, while she remained grounded in her roots. It was a balance she was able to maintain seemingly with ease. Fellow student Chris Hudson remembers Carolyn's affectionate "long, drawn-out tales of her . . . Brooklyn and Staten Island relatives. Concomitantly, she had this very regal, almost aristocratic quality to her. It was the combination of the two that made her so special." Her favorite cousin was a New York City cop who made extra money as a limo driver.

Carolyn, according to friends at the time, proceeded as if anything could and should happen, and part of her joy was living at full throttle. She concentrated intensely on making her friends feel valued. A hockey player she dated at BU mentioned that Carolyn "genuinely cared about the people around her and their day-to-day life experience." When a girl from her hall was hit by a car on the busy streets of Boston, Carolyn went with her to the hospital and insisted on staying until the girl's parents arrived. "Nurses had urged her to leave, as it was past visiting hours," the injured girl's roommate recalled. "But Carolyn wouldn't budge." When the parents got there, Carolyn consented to leave the hospital, but not before stealthily making her way from the emergency room to the maternity ward to peek in on the newborn babies.

"Even in college, you could tell she was smitten by kids," Colleen Curtis, who roomed with Carolyn in her senior year, would later write in the *Daily News*. "She worked as a student teacher, babysat for a coworker's child— though she did laughingly worry that people might think it was hers, some remnant of a wild past—and always peered into [baby] carriages."

Carolyn also participated in a tutoring program called Collaborations for Literacy, part of the School of Education's curriculum. It was designed to encourage parents to read to their children, and BU college students would go in and work with the kids at local public schools. Carolyn put much time and care into her position—an early display of her gift with children and a continuation of Ann's legacy.

"It was heartbreaking to see these children struggling at such a young age in under-resourced schools," recalled Carolyn's fellow education major Merrill Flood. The student-teaching work in those schools, she said, was "not for the fainthearted. I nearly cried when, within a week, some of the students started calling me 'mommy.' "

Carolyn was also a student assistant at a daycare facility in downtown Boston. She would come daily to work with the toddlers—feeding, reading, playing, and taking the kids outside. Carolyn was not only up for it all but seemed meant for it. One colleague recalled, "In the dead of winter, we had to take ten to twelve toddlers outside to the play yard in the back of the JFK Federal Building. Carolyn and I put on their snowsuits, which was a physically and mentally taxing job." She continued, "Carolyn came up with this system where we stood them in a row, and duct-taped their mittens onto the cuffs of their snowsuits so the mittens wouldn't come off, because if the mittens came off of one three-year-old, they'd get wet and start crying, then someone else would immediately start crying, and then it was a big shit show. We were young students, and we just thought, *Okay, we'll just put these kittens in a row and duct-tape their mittens. We can cut them off when we come inside.*"

Later, the media would imply that a lack of extracurriculars in school was the result of vacuousness or indolence on Carolyn's part. "She didn't play sports; she didn't join clubs. She studied being social," noted the *Los Angeles Times*. Indeed, she didn't have time for sports or clubs; unlike some of her BU peers, whose families provided them with unlimited expense accounts, Carolyn had to work. She needed the money. She babysat and worked as a host at several restaurants when she wasn't student teaching. Back home during the summers, she worked at the jewelry counter in Caldor, a discount department store that carried everything from clothes and electronics to gardening supplies.

Curtis wrote, "I can't think of anything less appealing than the months we worked as cocktail waitresses at a restaurant in Harvard Square, but the money was good, and four or five friends worked there together, which made the nights pass more quickly." What helped them get through was finding the humor in the situation: Carolyn "loved to laugh—hers was an unforgettable, contagious, belly laugh. She was always ready with a wisecrack."

TOWARD THE END OF Carolyn's freshman year, her relationship with Eugene became a little rocky. There had been some dramatic public scenes between the two, which hadn't surprised some friends. "Carolyn loved so much she was willing to fight for it," Gallo remarked. "And she was strong enough to fight for it. Strong enough about who she was. It wasn't about making a scene. Those fights were real love and passion." The truth was that even though Eugene would soon begin his freshman year at Northeastern University, a five-minute drive from BU, the couple was cooling down.

"With Eugene, it was mostly her being gorgeous and him being far away," said a friend. "She was not bitchy. She wanted to make sure they were dealing with the same truth."

By early in Carolyn's sophomore year, she and Gene were officially over even though he was now close by at Northeastern. It had been a long on-and-off summer, with the on due mostly to Carolyn going back to Greenwich between the spring and fall semesters. That year, Carolyn and her close friends Dana Gallo and Carrie O'Brien roomed together in the student housing at 1050 Commonwealth Avenue, a short walk from campus. Everyday wear for classes was often sweatpants and a T-shirt, yet when "going out," Carolyn dressed for the occasion, as was the practice among her classmates. It was often a black shift dress for Carolyn, and she stood out among many with permed hair that curled tightly at the ends while the roots remained straight. Through her teen and college years, Carolyn kept her hair natural— long with gentle waves.

The tabloids later tried to portray Carolyn as a wild banshee, but she was really just living the life—day and night—of an average college student. One friend from the School of Education worried that what she recalled would not paint Carolyn in the best light, but "not because it was anything bad. Carolyn loved to have fun; she loved to go out; she loved to dance like we all did."

The BU nightlife scene included many cliques: the studious nerds, the sports crew, the wealthy international students, and those dubbed the "black on black" crowd because it was the only color they wore and who congregated at the Paradise Rock Club, catching performances by U2, the Bangles, and Modern English. "But at home, we mostly listened to classic rock at the time, Crosby, Stills & Nash and James Taylor," Dana said.

A night out for Carolyn and her roommates might begin at the local watering hole Who's On First with two-for-one drinks on Wednesdays and lots of sorority girls, though Carolyn never joined a sorority. She was not a joiner, nor would the automatic networking have incentivized her—she liked having a wide circle of friends of her own choosing. The evening might end at T's Pub for last call. The girls knew the bouncers at their favorite places, and they would breeze right in. Dana recalled that heads turned when Carolyn entered; she was "tall [with] glistening hair. Every jaw dropped." One place Carolyn disliked was the Dugout, where the hockey groupies hung out—she wasn't a groupie, and didn't need to follow anyone around.

The BU Bookstore on Beacon Street was also a place to see and be seen. "Carolyn was always reading," Dana noted. "Jane Austen or a Brontë sister, and she kept what she was reading with her always—on her bedside table or in her bag to be taken out like a snack between classes."

Despite studying education, Carolyn's curiosity was piqued by fashion. Ann handled this enthusiasm with a light touch and understood that even though her daughter had to work for spending money, the spending wasn't always going to be practical.

"In truth, she spent a fair amount of money on clothes," wrote Curtis. "Carolyn loved them: She liked to hit Filene's Basement and the sales racks at upscale boutiques, hunting for bargains. When she found something she liked, nothing would stand in her way. If it didn't fit, clothes could be altered, and Carolyn even had a way of dealing with shoes that were too small. She'd buy them in the size that was available, then she'd 'lend' them to me—I was one shoe size smaller—and I'd wear them until they had stretched enough for her."

When Richard's daughter Kathy got engaged to Michael Ronan, one of the groom's many siblings threw her a bridal shower in the spring of 1985, which Ann and Carolyn attended. Ann arrived with Carolyn, as Lisa and Lauren were off at college. While this was first and foremost a family celebration, Carolyn and Ann knew that Michael's aunt, Roseann Flood, had a successful fashion career and was currently designing for Eileen Fisher. What they didn't know at the time was that Roseann had been a colleague of Jennie Messina—Carolyn's grandmother—for many years, the colleague who had witnessed Jennie's worry over Ann's first marriage.

The groom's mother, Ellen Ronan, whose maiden name was Flood, approached her sister-in-law Roseann with a tall young woman on her arm.

"Roseann, I want to introduce you to Carolyn, Ann's daughter," said Ellen.

"Hello, nice to meet you. Isn't this pretty?" Roseann announced, looking around the beautiful room. Carolyn politely agreed, and told Roseann it was nice to meet her as well.

"I know you work at Eileen Fisher," Carolyn continued, "and I hoped you might have suggestions on how I could start a career in fashion."

"I gave her a lot of encouragement," recalled Roseann, struck not only by how beautiful Carolyn was but also her affable sweetness and manners. "She had all the attributes of being a supermodel but wanted to work behind the scenes. She was slightly heavier than she became later, when she was under all that scrutiny. This was not a bad thing. She glowed. There was not even a hint of snobbery, of which she was later accused. She was thoughtful, kind, and very respectful."

Carolyn had a strong work ethic, always. She "knew her mom worked to put her through college and was very appreciative. Carolyn always wanted to have a job," Dana said. There may not have been an automatically refreshed bank account, but there was constant communication, connection, and emotional support from her mother.

"We loved when Ann came to visit," remembered Dana. "She was elegant and so funny, and Carolyn adored her mother." Whether seeing her mother, sisters, or grandmother, the occasion was marked by constant hugging and kisses. "When we went to visit Nana Messina, [Carolyn] never let her go. Towering Carolyn constantly stood by this short little Italian woman, her arms wrapped around Jennie, who would jokingly question the wisdom of things like students living on top of one another and eating in bed. 'But Nana!' Carolyn said in laughter. 'This is how we live.'"

The healthy relationship between her mother and stepfather was another essential marker in Carolyn's life. "Carolyn was so thankful her mom was being taken care of in the way she should," Dana said. Ann's remarriage created emotional security for the sisters. Carolyn's affection for her stepfather and stepsiblings made this stability not only more substantial but sweeter.

"She'd often call her mother for advice," Dana recalled. "It was a beautiful relationship. There was never yelling, but always an adoring 'Mommy!' And Carolyn usually took her advice."

Mother and daughter had a very loving, teasing banter. "I can see them in their kitchen in Greenwich now," Dana said. "Her mom was a schoolteacher, and very precise, and Carolyn tall, funny, sweet. She would stand by her mom, hugging her, teasing her, just pure love. And her mom laughing back at her while she was cooking in her sunlit kitchen with its wall of windows. Mrs. Freeman was kind, and so elegant. And she loved every second with her daughter."

AS CAROLYN BRANCHED OUT in her studies and work, she began to notice some of the men who noticed her. There were many of them, and not just fellow students. "Everyone was after her," Dana laughed. Sometimes, this attention was negative: "The attention she got from men bothered her," said Dana. "The guys who were overly attentive. Gawking. Even stalkers . . . Everyone wanted to be her friend because she was so pretty. She was gracious, and tried to be kind to those who were unrelenting. But she did get freaked out by a few people." For instance, a Boston photographer who had taken her picture for the "Girls of B.U." calendar "practically stalked her" afterward, said Dana. He was so persistent that Carolyn once ducked down in a car to hide from him as they passed him by. It was the beginning of the pattern of photographers being obsessed with Carolyn; for her, it was the beginning of life on high alert.

But her breakup from Carlin was a chance for Carolyn, whose dating had essentially been limited to the insular Greenwich scene, to learn more about what she wanted from relationships. Carolyn's relationship with John Cullen, the undoubted star center of BU's hockey team, began in the spring of 1985, their sophomore year. Cullen had been a phenomenon since his freshman season and would go on to play professionally in the NHL, but his college years began on an extremely difficult note—his mother had died of cancer the previous October.

Carolyn's friends all spoke of Cullen as a kind man who treated her well, and that their relationship was, in large part, a happy time, despite the groupies who followed his every move. Carolyn remained unfazed by the outsized attention to her boyfriend—she could readily hold her own, as long as the overwrought attention on her partner was not accompanied by hostility toward her for being his girlfriend. For Cullen, Carolyn's sensitive and generous nature was a boon in helping the still-shattered hockey player regain his confidence and enthusiasm for life after losing his mother.

In general, Carolyn maintained good relationships with the men in her life, both friends and lovers. Sure, she was accused of breaking hearts— one man swore she later broke Cullen's by carrying on with his hockey teammate—but Carolyn remained friendly with most of her former beaus, enjoying platonic relationships after breaking up. "A lot of people wanted to be around Carolyn, and she knew that not all the attention was beneficent. But most of the time," Dana said, "Carolyn used a very soft hand to carve out her boundaries."

When asked what he found irresistible about her, a BU ex-boyfriend laughed and said, "The reason she was so great with guys was that she was great with children."

"She was one of the best people on the planet," recalled BU hockey player and friend Chris Matchett. "She actively wanted other people around her to be happy."

However, at times, the scars of her parents' divorce, dormant for the years under the safety of her mother and stepfather's home, seemed to rise to the surface. One evening in Brighton, Carolyn "connected" with a hockey player whose girlfriend was her friend. It was a move at odds with her usually nurturing persona, but not necessarily with the fragility beneath that gentleness. "There were a few moments where it felt like she wanted to make sure her friends' boyfriends would be interested in her," noted a friend from that time.

Was it insecurity? "She flirted with a friend's boyfriend until he made some kind of move on her, and her friend was hurt," the friend continued. "Carolyn felt remorseful afterward, but it was wounding."

"It happened a few times," said another friend. "She would flirt until the guy made a move on her, making it obvious he would choose her over her friend, even if she didn't want to be with him." It was hurtful enough that the friend said, "I made a conscious decision not to be in touch with Carolyn after college."

Yet another friend was more generous, saying, "Yes, she sowed her oats.

But it wasn't vicious. There were a couple of guys she shouldn't have gone after." It was a behavior she outgrew, and after that she was especially careful in her relationships with men.

Carolyn sometimes juggled a couple of men at once, always leaving them before she could be left. A mantra she repeated with friends captures the nature of these relationships: *Date them, train them, dump them.* There was no shortage of men wanting to be with her, so while the declaration was glibly Carolyn-esque, it was also a defensive strategy.

It stands to reason that Carolyn would have difficulty trusting men after what happened between her mother and father. "The consistent presence of a nurturing father figure is tied to confidence, resilience, and emotional health, and can be a protective factor when the world feels overwhelming," notes Kimberly Wolf, a specialist in young women's mental health and the author of *Talk with Her: A Dad's Essential Guide to Raising Healthy, Confident, and Capable Daughters.* Perhaps, as a matter of self-preservation, Carolyn wanted an upper hand with men; it was better to be the conqueror than the conquered.

Did Carolyn's distance from her father affect the way she responded to male attention in college? According to Wolf, "When people experience loss or difficulties in any major area of their lives, they can make decisions that are out of line with their true selves. Grief can cloud your judgment."

Every child whose parents' marriage has fallen apart is prone to wondering, *Was it my fault?* According to one Bessette family member, "William was closest to Lauren, a go-getter. Lisa was a little more distant, she was shy by nature. But as for Carolyn and [her father] . . . we don't want to go there."

Whatever distance Carolyn may have had from her father obviously did not extend to her father's family, and specifically to the women in her father's family. Aunts Dorothy and Diane were constantly pulling the Bessette girls into their orbit, a warm, lively environment where Carolyn was clearly comfortable being playful. In a late 1980s Bessette Christmas photo, her sense of fun is on full display as she throws her leg over her cousin and grandmother as they pose on the couch with Carolyn's sisters. Another photo from the holidays shows the girls' young cousin Abbi pulling Carolyn's hair, whose mouth is open wide in surprise. Gatherings with these women occurred on a regular basis until the last months of Carolyn's life.

"Carolyn was a handful," the family member added, laughing.

What was it about Carolyn's dynamic with her father that may have made her relationship seem noticeably different from, for example, his relationship with Lauren? Did William, an engineer described as "anal-retentive" and "detail-oriented," see Lauren's academic excellence as a more valued trait than Carolyn's more sociable persona? Was he less comfortable around the more lively child?

Another close friend remembers Carolyn talking about the fact that there were issues with her father's share of the tuition. Thomas Bessette said there was a "disagreement and eventually a butting of heads between Ann and Bill about where the girls should continue their education. Both wanted them to go and get degrees. The discussion was about at what college."

Dana does not recall Carolyn's father ever coming to Boston, but Dana met him when Carolyn asked for her company visiting him in White Plains. Dana remembers that he was tall, tan, and very good-looking, with straight, light hair. Carolyn rarely spoke of her father, and those conversations were generally prompted by the issues with his tuition payments.

"It was not the greatest relationship, not easy," Dana says. "William was a civil engineer, out of the country a lot, travels presumably related to work. He never remarried, and lived in an apartment in White Plains, a step down. We visited him twice. She didn't really talk about him, but she did feel he didn't treat her mother well. And Carolyn was fiercely protective of her mother."

HOWEVER MUCH FUN CAROLYN had—with boys, at the bars, even with schoolwork itself—she was not one to take even a single step back from her friendships. Dana lost her mother to cancer their sophomore year, and Carolyn "never left my side," Dana said. "Never let go of me. It was amazing then and even more so thinking back on it now that a college student could be so nurturing during the death of my mother—[she was] incredibly caring." Dana often went home on weekends after her mother's death to nearby Medford, Massachusetts, where her father lived, and Carolyn frequently accompanied her.

In their junior year, Dana suffered another devastating loss, this time the death of her father. Again, Carolyn was there for her night and day.

Carolyn went with Dana to her father's wake, both keeping vigil and remaining lighthearted, a bright spot in very dark days. At one point, Mr.

Gallo's godmother walked in, looked at Carolyn (who had relieved Dana from the task of greeting visitors), and said, "And who are *you*?" Throughout the day, over and over, the elderly woman said the same thing to everyone she met. "So for years after," Dana said, "whenever we met someone and Carolyn wanted to make me laugh, she would say, 'And who are *you*?' in that same imperious tone. It sent me into hysterics every time."

The back-to-back deaths of her parents were blows that nearly felled Dana, and she credits Carolyn with helping her navigate her emotions at the time. "I'm not sure I would be where I am today had she not held me up when I needed a true friend. She was selfless when I was a mess. She did it without any expectation of reciprocation. In the years following my mother's and then father's deaths, she would sit next to me and rub my head, hold my hand. A loving touch was always there."

Carolyn's den was inclusive; in addition to her friends, the girls ended up taking in a husky named Silver that had belonged to Dana's father. Carolyn and Dana shared a room, and Silver slept with them. Unfortunately, as much as they adored the dog, it became clear that undergraduates living in Boston could not give Silver an ideal life. Their schedules were erratic at best, and the apartment had no air-conditioning, a very uncomfortable situation for a husky. Carolyn sobbed when they brought Silver to the airport, lightly sedating her before her flight to the farm in Utah where she would make her new home.

In their senior year, the girls moved again, this time next door to 1056 Commonwealth Avenue, a slightly nicer building considered off-campus housing. Throughout, Carolyn worried about Dana. On Dana's birthday, near the end of senior year, Carolyn tried again. She showed up with a basket, on top of which was a red bow. Inside was an adorable black kitten, also sporting a red bow.

"You got me a cat, Carolyn," Dana told her. "You know I don't like cats."

"Just give it a chance." Carolyn held the kitten up close to them both, making squeaking noises. "But she's so cute! Just look at that little face," she said. "How can you resist?"

Dana did not resist, and she fell in love. Carolyn also insisted that they name the kitten Madeline, after the heroic orphan in Ludwig Bemelmans's childhood classic.

"Carolyn wanted me always to have a companion," Dana said. "She was so conscious of my situation, that I didn't have parents. She was able to home in on people and make sure they felt attended to."

During senior year, Blaine Applegate—who'd remained part of Carolyn's friend group throughout college—injured his shoulder while playing football. His surgery was scheduled for January, and he would need to stay in the hospital for a few days. "With Carolyn as the ringleader, five girls came with me to the hospital, bringing all kinds of stuff," he said. "Food, blankets. It was a huge effort for them to gather all of it and come by taxi to the other side of Boston." The hospital wasn't in a particularly safe part of the city, "but the girls stayed until they got kicked out. The nurses told them that, 'For your safety, considering where we are in town, you'd better go now.'" Day after day, Carolyn and her crew returned to cheer on Applegate's recovery.

It was also in her senior year that Carolyn transitioned from waiting tables to being a public relations liaison for That's Entertainment, a night-club consortium owned by Patrick Lyons. She promoted two nightclubs on the other side of Fenway Park, 9 Lansdowne and the Metro, by arranging corporate parties for the clubs, chaperoning reporters to the events, and charming them into some good publicity—a piece of cake. If indeed Carolyn studied "being social," then let it be said she was a quick study.

The summer after senior year, Carolyn and Applegate found themselves both extending the undergraduate four-year plan into a fifth year—with the long hours she was working in PR, Carolyn needed extra time to make up the credits she missed. She moved again, this time to 1030 Commonwealth, where she and Applegate had apartments on the same floor. The building had a rooftop, where Carolyn loved to sunbathe. Applegate worked at Who's On First, so they kept similar hours: occupied until late at night, with free afternoons.

Applegate lived directly across the hall from the roof access. "Carolyn couldn't push the heavy lid off to get the door open," he remembered, "so she'd pound on my door and ask me to open it. I would climb up to get the lid off. She'd go up and sunbathe, and I'd have to put the lid back on after she left." Sometimes, he would join her. Summer was winding down, and they talked often, squinting at the sky. At times, the conversation got serious.

"Carolyn asked me if I was going to marry my girlfriend, Katie, which was complicated because I had another year of football eligibility, which meant graduate school for me. But Katie wanted me to graduate with her, and I didn't think I was ready for that."

"And you and Cully?" Applegate asked Carolyn, referring to John Cullen, whom she was still dating.

"Noooo," she replied. "I can't see it. I tell you what: In five years, after we're out of here and we've got nothing going on, let's find each other and see what happens."

They fist-bumped on it. Applegate thought of that pact for many years.

Carolyn's PR job for Lyons eventually became full-time. There, she refined her sense of who, what, and where was hip and current. Her coworker Joe Varange remembers her as "a good schmoozer and networker.

"She was always at ease," he continued. "She possessed a good mind for business, though business per se didn't turn her on. She was secure and strong, exceedingly sure of herself. She didn't take shit from anyone. In other words, it wasn't possible to intimidate her. She always stood up for herself. If she felt she was being spoken to in a disrespectful manner, she'd say, 'Excuse me, please don't talk to me like that.' "

One day, Carolyn was getting a ride to work with her friend Denise when Denise's car, an old beater, wouldn't start. Denise asked Carolyn to go knock on a nearby friend's door for help. Alessandro Benetton, heir to the Benetton fashion label, opened the door to see "two watery eyes framed by blonde locks that escaped a wool cap," Benetton later wrote in his 2022 memoir, *La Traiettoria*. "Every nuance of her charm captures me at first glance: certain gestures, the way her lips smile." Carolyn and Alessandro pushed the car while Denise hit the gas. As the car started, Denise called to Carolyn to hurry and get back in before it stalled again, but "she shakes [*sic*] her head amused, and before walking away, she greets [*sic*] me with a kiss on the cheek." However, Alessandro had just accepted a position in the London global finance sector of Goldman Sachs. Like Applegate, he would not forget Carolyn. "In her perfume," he wrote, "I want to read a promise of the future."

At the end of the fall semester of 1988, Carolyn had a degree in hand from the Boston University School of Education. That she'd graduated with the same major as her mother must have delighted Ann, who, given the success of her other daughters, already had much to be proud of. Lauren had not only graduated with a degree in economics from Hobart and William Smith Colleges but was also a member of the prestigious Omicron Delta Epsilon honor society. Carolyn marveled at how Lauren had learned Mandarin, a skill that would help her fly up the ranks at Morgan Stanley, where she was hired right after graduation. Lisa, the quietest of the three, had majored in art and was now pursuing her Ph.D. in art history at the University of Michigan. The girls were spreading their wings.

AFTER GRADUATING, CAROLYN MOVED on her own into a brownstone off Newbury Street, where she lived for a little over a year. Recalled Colleen Curtis in the *Daily News*, "My memories are of us sitting on the couch, watching *General Hospital* at three o'clock eating candy bars."

Though she was good at her job, Carolyn began to ponder her next move. Jonathan Soroff, a reporter for the *Improper Bostonian* who met Carolyn while he was covering the nightclub scenes she helped create in her role doing PR for Lyons, remembers her as a consummate professional and as much fun as you can be while maintaining that level of competence. "She had to be out at night, or in the late afternoon, showing prospective clients the spaces, hoping they would book it for a party or work event," Soroff said. "Like any client-services job, you can't pick and choose your clients. Some were rude and difficult, and plenty of them hit on her. She was overqualified for the job and was not the party girl some later claimed. I never saw her drink more than one glass of wine. She went nowhere near drugs.

"Ostentatiousness of any sort embarrassed her," he continued, "and she cringed when our transport to an event was a limo. We'd howl with laughter on the way about the gruesome 'champagne wishes and caviar dreams' of whoever hired these enormous, fuel-guzzling monstrosities."

"She would've rather been elsewhere," Dana said. "It was an awful job . . . That's why she switched to fashion."

As for the field of education, when some years later Carolyn was interviewed by *Women's Wear Daily* magazine for a 1992 feature on up-and-coming New Yorkers, she explained why she chose fashion over teaching. "At the time, I felt a little underdeveloped myself to be completely responsible for 25 other people's children," she said. "And to a large extent, I felt it wouldn't be provocative enough for me."

Around her December graduation, Carolyn was getting out of a cab to shop at the Chestnut Hill mall, half an hour away from campus. The store managers of the Calvin Klein boutique in Bloomingdale's happened to be out on the street, spotted her, and did a double take. She looked a lot like Elaine Irwin, who was a popular model for the brand at the time. They ran after her. Carolyn's resemblance to Irwin—tall, willowy, and blonde with a patrician profile—got her hired for a sales position on the spot.

Indeed, despite earning her degree in education, Carolyn's curiosity was still drifting toward fashion. Ann was supportive of Carolyn's branching out—she supported the choices of all her girls, as long as they worked hard.

It was in these last months in Boston when Carolyn ran into Alessandro Benetton again. He was sitting in a diner when she blew in, grabbing a large coffee before heading to work at the Calvin Klein boutique. Benetton described himself as "mesmerized," and ran outside to catch up with her. He asked her out for the same evening.

"Why not?" Carolyn replied.

She wanted to go ice-skating, and Alessandro readily agreed. He was a novice on skates, however, and spent the evening "paying the price for my bravado, hanging on Carolyn's arm in search of balance," Benetton later wrote. After a first kiss on the wall of the skating rink, they dated for a few months.

They had elegant dinners at the Waldorf Astoria in New York City and went hiking through the woods in New England. Carolyn and Alessandro even went to Boston Bruins games, where Carolyn's humor was on excellent display.

"Hockey fan to the core, Carolyn—here she is spewing unrepeatable insults, obscene turns of phrase capable of making anyone pale," Benetton wrote. "The following weekend walking hand in hand with me . . . before suddenly bursting out with words that sound like poetry, verses that rustle . . . like autumn leaves."

Benetton told *Vanity Fair Italia*, "Carolyn is half of my happiness during my Harvard years . . . and I think I can say it without betraying her memory, I'm half of hers." He goes on to say, "Why didn't it work? . . . I felt a stimulating affinity and yet we never managed to look further than a weekend."

Perhaps it *was* Carolyn looking much further than a weekend—she was looking into her future.

"And the goal was always to go to New York," Dana Gallo added. "In what capacity, she didn't know."

As it happened, New York City came to her. Susan Sokol, then president of the Calvin Klein women's collection, needed someone for VIP sales, and the New England regional executive quickly put Carolyn's name forward, saying, "I have the right person for you."

"Carolyn was perfect for her job at Calvin Klein," said Jonathan Soroff. "She oozed charisma and looked great. She could have been a highly success-ful model, but modeling didn't interest her."

Within weeks, Carolyn was brought to New York to interview directly with Calvin Klein. According to MJ Bettenhausen, Calvin's executive assis-tant at the time who became a close friend of Carolyn's, the designer was back fresh from rehab and determined to lead a healthy life, but still a little foggy. When Carolyn exited his office, she seemed worried.

"How did it go?" Bettenhausen asked her.

"I don't know, which is weird. I just can't tell, so I'm thinking perhaps I bombed," Carolyn said.

After Carolyn left the office, Calvin called in Bettenhausen.

"We've already cast her numerous times, and will again, so why am I meeting with Elaine Irwin?"

Bettenhausen soon called Carolyn back in to meet with the senior vice president, Paul Wilmot, who hired her on the spot.

Job in hand, in the early summer of 1989, Carolyn and another Bos-ton University classmate moved to a tenth-floor apartment at 166 Second Avenue, just a few blocks away from the East Village's legendary St. Marks Place and Tompkins Square Park. Calvin Klein corporate headquarters was a twenty-minute or so subway commute away, at 205 West 39th Street, the edge of the Garment District, and the epicenter of the New York fashion world of the "Naughty Nineties."

Carolyn's "What fun thing will I get to do or see today?" from third grade turned into "What fun thing will I do with my life in this city of endless possibility?" The answer would keep the city itself rapt for the next decade.

CHAPTER FIVE

CHAMPAGNE SUPERNOVAS

Spring 1989–Spring 1992

C arolyn represents a time that no longer exists," observed Michelle Kessler, Carolyn's colleague at Calvin Klein. There was a sense of liberty and possibility in the worlds of fashion and art in New York in the early 1990s, and that joy encompassed nearly every facet of Carolyn's life. These were, unbeknownst to the people living through it, the last years of analog, where certain kinds of improvisation and serendipity could be taken as a matter of course. Young people often journey west, or perhaps even to the Far East, to find themselves, but they come to New York to invent themselves. Who should I be? Who are my people? Where is my home? These were the questions animating Carolyn in the first months after her arrival in New York.

While Carolyn already had a clear idea of who she was on the inside, once in New York, she tried on a variety of exteriors. She dropped the sweatpants and sweatshirts of her college days. At times, when she was not at work, she dressed like a Bloomsbury bohemian in flowing dresses accessorized with Chuck Taylors. Other times it was jeans and a white button-down shirt. Carolyn's hair, always long and thick, was highlighted but had undertones that matched her darker, thicker eyebrows, resembling, in those first years in New York, more the Romanesque Monica Vitti than her later incarnation as a Grace Kelly diamond-ice blonde.

The way Carolyn looked was obviously a boon for a job in fashion, but her charm was an equal part of her appeal. According to friends and colleagues, she was completely at ease speaking with anyone.

"The Personals department on [the] eleventh floor was for 'personal orders,' where VIPs like socialites and actors, such as Bianca Jagger, Sarah Jessica Parker, Susan Sarandon, and Fran Lebowitz, were invited to come in within the days after one of the shows to place orders, anything from the runway," explained Kessler.

Another colleague explained, "Post-show, retail stores like Neiman Marcus and Saks were also placing orders at the same time, so everything would go into production at once. This was before the first Calvin retail store opened. When Carolyn did not have this parade of VIPs coming in, it was about following up with VIP clients and nurturing new relationships."

To succeed in Personals you couldn't be intimidated by celebrity. Carolyn was not, partly because unlike many others, she noticed which celebrities had substance and which did not. Anyone of substance was of interest to her.

She especially admired women whose lives and careers revolved around philanthropy and journalism. Clients like Blaine Trump, Annette Bening, Diane Sawyer, Patricia Buckley, and Sharon Stone needed to look sophisticated and modern, but they were not women whose lives revolved around fashion. "Carolyn was not 'expensive,' " said Kessler, "but she had a talent for handling expensive people."

Carolyn and her assistant, Rachel Bold, were both tall and blonde, so they jokingly called each other "Muffy," a playful dig at their many coworkers who came from blue-chip stock. The joke, however, alluded to a conundrum of New York Carolyn had not completely figured out. She had been able to sidestep whatever tensions of class and exclusion she may have encountered with the Greenwich elite, but New York City presented an entirely new social ladder, one that was especially conspicuous in the world of fashion, where many young women attained entry-level jobs because their parents were important clients. In the 1990s, people still checked the *Social Register*, and inclusion in the "upper echelons" just wasn't going to happen if your name wasn't in that book. Happily, there were places in New York for the young women, like Carolyn and Rachel, who were hired because they were bright, beautiful, and willing to work hard.

At one point, they even dated brothers. Sometimes they would scream at each other about what a client should wear, but the tirades always ended with the affectionate wink of their co-opted sobriquet. It also spoke volumes about Carolyn that in a world where assistants were often expected to cower, she encouraged Bold to not only voice her opinions, but fight for them. Their bond helped the two manage the moments when the office drama approached a summit. ("Calvin just came in on her broom," Carolyn would say during particularly chaotic days, raising her right eyebrow, a sure sign that mayhem was to follow.)

At the time, Calvin Klein gave his employees clothing allowances. The young, green girls didn't make sizable salaries, so this "gift" meant a lot—they would want to make it count. That spring, Sue Sartor, a design assistant who now has her own line of dresses, was relocated during construction along with her boss, Monica Roberts, near Carolyn's office. Sue remembers, "We were trying things on, all in these beautiful fabrics with earthy names like anthracite or nutria. I was self-conscious because I felt that I didn't have the same shape as a lot of the girls, who were usually model-tall and thin. We were putting on form-fitting silk kimono blouses, or three-button jackets, and she could see I felt shy and unsure. Carolyn walked close up to me and softly said, 'You have a beautiful body, and you should always be proud of it.'"

This is not something a lot of women in fashion were apt to say to one of their own who did not fit the tall, lean proportions of a model. Another employee remembered Carolyn once touching the hair of another colleague, remarking, "You look so beautiful today. I saw you getting out of the cab for work, and you just looked happy."

Carolyn valued her female friendships, and Calvin Klein was a workplace of many women; the feeling of sisterhood was predominant. Especially after growing up surrounded by Ann, Jennie, and two impressive sisters, Carolyn was perfectly suited for the office's amalgamation of female wisdom, empowerment, and verve.

In keeping with Calvin's habit of looking to his employees as sources of ideas and inspiration, Calvin asked that every employee take a Polaroid picture of what they had on every day and send them up to his office. For Carolyn, whose style had remained decidedly more bohemian in the very early nineties, this could vary wildly. Polaroids from the time show Carolyn in a black or white T-shirt, sometimes with a black pencil skirt and high-heeled black wedges, or with black leggings, no socks, and penny loafers. Another had her in a black shift dress over a white T-shirt, her eyes so intense and her hair so long and wild that she looked almost otherworldly. In a group shot, all the girls have on black, but Carolyn stands out with a black cap placed jauntily atop her head.

One former supervisor said, "Sometimes she would be wearing a fisherman's sweater, track pants, and sneakers, her hair wild. No makeup. Carolyn had an incredible eye and instinct, which is why she moved so quickly from sales to PR and then to shows. She was very creative, not a prima donna and not overly groomed."

Carolyn possessed an inimitably original, wildly engrossing brand of magnetism that held those around her spellbound. It's an energy that affects every facet of one's being. Mentally, emotionally, and intellectually, it's as if she brought just a little more with her to the planet. The "just a little more" had certainly been evident to her peers as a child, teenager, and university student. Now it was apparent to everyone on Seventh Avenue.

Carolyn's colleagues began imitating her clothes and manner. Assistant designer Jessica Wade remembered that "every woman who worked there was following [Carolyn's] style in one way or another. I remember thinking a lot about wearing no mascara" because Carolyn didn't. They had contests to see who could show up with the dirtiest head of hair. Once she wore a long midi Calvin skirt with Chucks on her feet and only a fitted black leather jacket as a shirt. Soon, Chucks, midi skirts, and jackets as shirts made appearances all over the office. If Carolyn ran out to the drugstore, she would bring back a lipstick or a vial of Abdul Kareem Egyptian Musk Oil, which she would buy from street vendors and share with the other girls.

"Here, try this. This shade will look beautiful on you."

"Try this oil. Doesn't it smell like clean, first love?"

This was Carolyn's signature scent. One can't help but wonder, in a fragrance version of Charles Foster Kane's Rosebud, if her father had brought this musk oil back from his work in Egypt.

But her influence went far beyond 39th Street. It was in her second year that she grew close to Zack Carr, who had been Calvin's right-hand man since 1970. "Whatever one thinks about what we stand for in terms of being non-traditional, modern, clean—that was Zack," Calvin has said. Over the course of their friendship, Carolyn became a muse and inspiration for Carr, and his pencil-drawn sketches in countless Hermès notepads began to feature her silhouette. Looking at the images, one understands exactly what Carr saw in her. Her long and slender form, with just the right amount of stylish disinterest, is animated by movement and energy. His sketches always look like a breeze has just blown through.

"Carolyn's first day, everyone at Calvin Klein was talking about her," said Zack's brother George Carr. "When Zack came home, his description to me was, 'She's different. She's special. Her body temperature is just higher.'

"I remember the first time I met her, she was already seated with Gordon Henderson outside Tartine, wearing a sleeveless black cashmere turtleneck and a midi black-and-white tweed pencil skirt, all Calvin. The only way to describe it," George recalled of approaching the corner of West 11th and West 4th Streets, "is that I suddenly saw this creature. And she was all in her hair. Laughing, with expansive arm gestures, and lush hair that seemed to have a life of its own."

Carolyn's influence on Zack (who died of a rare cancer in 2000) was profound. He often wondered, "How would Carolyn put this together?" Carr was the designer who convinced Calvin to "let Carolyn make him hip," said Carr's brother George.

Carolyn enjoyed an independence and sense of purpose in the early Calvin days that would stand in stark juxtaposition to the constrained orbit she would later occupy. She relished her East Village life, telling *Women's Wear Daily* in 1992 that she had "to step over drunks and crack dealers to get to my apartment. Everybody at Calvin thought I was crazy, but I couldn't imagine coming to New York and living anywhere else. Even with all the weirdness, I felt comfortable and had fun."

"In her apartment on Second Avenue, she had one chair, three champagne glasses, and mountains of clothes," Michelle Kessler said. It was a place to shower and change before the next round of excitement, and maybe sleep, of which she tried to do very little. Carolyn served as a tour guide to many of the coolest places downtown, corralling her colleagues to join the excitement at Buddha-Bar and MK.

Eric Goode, who owned MK, said, "She'd come in a lot, but she wasn't wild and crazy or anything. I really liked her." There was also Tunnel, Cognac, Nell's, Limelight, Palladium, Stereo . . . endless possibilities; Carolyn knew the particulars of each. Picture a taxi careening downtown, night air whoosh-ing through the open window as the radio blares Black Box's "Everybody Everybody."

Some of the clubs were havens for heavy drug culture, but that wasn't Carolyn's scene. She smoked Marlboro cigarettes, but no friends recall her being incapacitated. Not even from too many glasses of wine or dirty-vodka martinis, one of her standbys. What buoyed Carolyn was conversation, danc-ing, shrieks of laughter, and, above all, company. For all her confidence, "she did not like to be alone," one colleague pointed out.

"I was at dinner with a friend," remembered MJ Bettenhausen, "and we thought, let's call Carolyn. This was in the ancient pre–cell phone days when one would use a pay phone, which every restaurant had. She was there before we got back to the table, her hair wet from the shower, flying everywhere. She was so animated and lively in conversation that she was unfazed when a chunk of her hair grazed the candle and singed. Even though it sizzled and smoked, she shook it out and kept talking."

Carolyn became a New Yorker in a way particular to those for whom it was a dream they worked to make real. Stormy Stokes, who worked with Caro-lyn early in her tenure at Calvin Klein, said, "Carolyn would be up for anything NYC offered, in our early twenties—late nights at Rex, Bowery Bar, anywhere. The next day, we'd go for long brunches at Jerry's or Fanelli's in SoHo and then spend an entire afternoon wandering through downtown antique stores searching for the perfect gift for a friend. She found one—a five-pound Old English Bible—and hauled it home to the East Village. In the few years we worked and spent time together, we were young and had so much energy . . . four hours later, we would meet up at Noho Star and start all over again."

While she was decidedly a downtown girl, Carolyn did head up to the Upper East Side from time to time, to see love interest Scott Winters. They met in 1990 when he worked as a bartender at the Surf Club. Scott, an aspir-ing actor, was bartending to support himself. One of his first big breaks would be the role of the pompous Harvard student who loses the girl to Matt Damon in *Good Will Hunting*, but that was still years away. Eventually, he would lose Carolyn, too. She was out and about in the city and didn't seem interested in getting serious with a bartender, whom she uncharacteristically dismissed to a friend as "not enough to marry."

She then dated Scott's lookalike Stephen Dorff, who had been a child actor and was at the time playing Bobby Dean in a TV version of *The Outsiders*. Carolyn also dated banker Liam Dalton, who had, coincidentally, been hired a few years earlier by Jackie Onassis's friend Mike Nichols to consult on his film *Working Girl*. Like the others, he was seen by Carolyn as fun but without long-term potential.

More intense was a frustrating affair with Will Regan, owner of Rex nightclub. Regan and Carolyn had seen each other outside the club, and the fascination had been immediate. "It was a crazy chemical attraction, so powerful," Regan said.

"Carolyn adored Will," said MJ Bettenhausen. "He used to pull up to her building on his motorcycle and call out her name to her to come down. No phone call ahead of time. She was enthralled."

"She was crazy about this guy," a mutual friend confirmed. "One evening, I was heading over to Rex with some other friends, and Carolyn couldn't make it. She quietly said she needed to speak to me. Almost bashfully, she asked, 'Would you please not go?' She was concerned that Will would be interested in one of the friends with whom I was going. She was not being catty or mean; she just felt threatened. So while she presented very confidently to the world, she could be insecure. I saw a girl who had her heart broken at a very early age and wanted to protect it."

Carolyn's "not enough to marry" verdict begs the question: Not enough what? Whether from lack of interest in marriage or lack of interest in the men themselves, she kept most of her alliances casual. She was a vibrant young woman in her mid-twenties building her career in New York City. Mr. Right could come later. Call it sowing her oats, call it playing the field, but one shouldn't assume just because of her gender that she'd already be on the hunt for long-term love.

This fact was later used against her, as it was against many women who enjoyed the increased liberty that came with earning their own income, the legalization of birth control, and the loosening of conservative religious strictures. And Carolyn's dating existed within a haunted context: Her father leaving her beloved mother was reason enough to be extremely careful about commitment beyond the casual.

"You could kind of tell what had happened between her mother and father really bothered her. Carolyn would boast about how she had never been dumped," said one friend. "A little odder, too: She wore her mother's wedding band from her father on a chain around her neck. She told me, 'I felt like I could wear it only after I dipped it in holy water.'"

In her twenties, Carolyn was perhaps more invested in the crucial life-work of finding her community rather than her life partner. If you are lucky, you work with—or adjacent to—people who share similar interests, for whom friendship overrides competition. In the world of fashion, everything is extra—extra drama with dramatic personalities. You need a lot of luck in friendship. And, as with all luck, some of it is bestowed by fate, and some of it is self-made.

BY THE END OF 1991, Calvin had decided to promote Carolyn. "Calvin loved her," Paul Wilmot said. "After a while, he moved her into public relations." Carolyn was thrilled with the eventual change. "She had been lobbying to move to PR for some time," said a colleague. "It was where all the fun was."

At the start of 1992, Jules Watson became Carolyn's best friend and roommate. Eight months older than Carolyn, Jules was an agent at Click Models whom Carolyn had met when casting runway shows for Calvin. Like Carolyn, she was funny and larger-than-life, with an open personality and outsized sense of fun. They even looked alike, with long blonde hair and bright blue eyes. From the start, they were joined at the hip. But while Carolyn matched Jules's adventurous spirit, many of their friends would later note that Carolyn had more self-control. Jules was, according to one mutual acquaintance, "a louder, wilder version of Carolyn."

One friend spoke of an evening when they were out for drinks: "Jules loved to be loud and enjoyed the attention she got from it. There was a table of men sitting near us, and Jules was shouting at the top of her lungs and cursing like a sailor—every word in there was *cunt, shit, fuck, motherfucker,* and then she began to describe a hookup in graphic details—the guys moved tables." Carolyn found Jules great fun and loved that she could match or surpass her energy level. Yet while Jules didn't tone things down even when given a cue such as a group moving tables, Carolyn reined it in when required—she knew how to read a room.

In early 1992, after turning down several modeling offers, Carolyn agreed to a couple of photo shoots. Ann Mashburn of *Glamour* magazine convinced

Carolyn to pose in a small feature with three other women, including Sarah Laird, who also worked at *Glamour*. The shoot was built around the theme of "Me and My White Shirt." Mashburn explained, "I spoke with Carolyn almost every day, as did my assistant, Molly McMahon. And we saw her every couple of weeks, either when we went to the showroom and she showed us the line for a shoot, or when she brought samples over. To us, she was Carolyn at Calvin Klein like Tory Burch was Tory at Ralph Lauren."

McMahon recalled Carolyn being particularly kind when *Glamour* needed Calvin Klein samples for a shoot: "*Glamour* was not that high on the totem pole, and sometimes it was hard to get samples from other designers. Clothes would be reserved for *Vogue* or *Harper's Bazaar*, and the people working for other designers weren't always that nice about saying so. Carolyn was nicer than a lot of people in the industry. She'd say, 'Listen, *Vogue* has it reserved this afternoon, so just get it back in three hours.' She was supportive and knew we were all working hard."

Glamour readers loved the stories about "real women," such as the White Shirt feature, which highlighted more accessible styles than the high fashion found in *Vogue*. It meant the stories Mashburn created required more inventiveness, and she often called the designers' offices to get items for a shoot.

"I also needed the everyday girl, but a very pretty everyday girl, someone who worked in the industry or someone your cousin knew," said Mashburn. "I needed someone right away. 'Will you come to [the] studio for two hours?' I asked Carolyn and she said, 'Sure.' She was so at ease in her skin. She didn't wear a lot of makeup and was not self-conscious about the way she held herself. She was someone who made you feel great about yourself and was even super inquisitive about my son I'd just had, cooing over the pictures."

Glamour explained the shirt as "wrapped and tied for a feminine stamp that doesn't cater to frilly stereotypes," which echoed Carolyn's later style. In the accompanying text, Carolyn is quoted as saying, "I'm not comfortable in anything ornate. I like clean and understated looks [with] very classic colors—black, navy, gray, and white. If I want to add some impact, I'll do it with texture."

For the shoot, Carolyn wore a pair of jeans and a short-sleeved Calvin Klein Sport for Men white shirt tied at the waist as she sat on her knees with her feet tucked under her bum for support.

Xanthipi Joannides, a stylist on the shoot, said, "Although she did not like the cowboy boots I asked her to wear—in her quiet manner she told me that the boots were not something she would ever wear—she wore them anyway without much of a fuss. Most other women would make a fuss and say *absolutely not* but Carolyn was gracious and wore them. I do remember also how beautiful and stylish she was—there was a simple chicness about her. Carolyn's style did not scream for attention."

Soon thereafter, Jade Hobson, the creative director at *Mirabella* magazine—launched by Grace Mirabella in 1989 after her seventeen years as editor in chief of *Vogue*—asked Carolyn if she'd appear in the magazine. Jade was taken by Carolyn's energy and spirit. And even though Carolyn was neither a professional model nor a debutante who hung out with models, the fashion world was buzzing with her name.

It took some convincing before Carolyn agreed to do the shoot. As a young professional in the fashion business, she already understood the trade-offs between fame and freedom. "It's so much better to be able to model, but not model," she always said to her friends. If anything, given her experience of ducking down into cars to avoid the "Girls of BU" calendar photographer and having an early curfew because of the attention her beauty garnered, she felt the excessive focus on her looks to be a liability. Anyway, her looks were the luck of heredity, not something she labored over. Carolyn wanted to do something more with her life, and she could feel that she had that potential. She wanted, as a friend put it, "to be important." And to Carolyn's credit, she perceived that the smothering vanity of those caught in the swirl of the public's imagination was at odds with what she wanted to achieve in life. Carolyn wanted to keep herself free.

But Grace and Jade had an idea for their shoot that fit well with Carolyn's style and aesthetic. The feature was to be called "Friday Dressing," and the conceit was that six "regular" girls, all employed by designers, were found in their casual Friday clothes, between leaving the office and rushing off to a glorious weekend holiday. On the page opposite Carolyn was Sara Sereno, the young fashion agent who represented Carolyn's good friend, former Calvin Klein designer Gordon Henderson. Other design houses included were J.Crew, Isaac Mizrahi, Comme des Garçons, Crisca, Zang Toi, DKNY, Ralph Lauren, and Chanel, whose public relations manager Anne Fahey wore . . . a white cotton blouse tied at the waist.

"[*Mirabella*] wanted to often use real people instead of models, and when we did use models, we should choose one that didn't scream 'model,'" Jade later told the *New York Times*. And while Carolyn may have been against modeling per se, there was also that side of her that loved having fun. She wouldn't be dressed outrageously or undressed. She saw the part she was playing not as a catwalk but an impish cameo. (The next spread in the magazine featured supermodel Christy Turlington, where she is shown in a Kenar white silk charmeuse blouse . . . tied at the waist.)

The plan was to have Carolyn pose in Grand Central Station, wearing Calvin's poet shirt in washed-silk georgette and capri leggings. On the day of the shoot, Michelle Kessler, an assistant on the *Mirabella* shoot, met Carolyn in a location van outside the station. "Carolyn shows up and I thought— what kind of 'regular' girl is that? She was more than beautiful," Michelle said. "In fashion, we are surrounded by striking girls but Carolyn stood out as not just a beauty for the ages, but also smart, elegant, and self-possessed, especially for someone so young. Otherworldly."

As soon as she stepped onto the van, Michelle said, Carolyn was all questions: "We were in the van and Carolyn raises that one eyebrow and begins the inquisition." The questions were peppered with compliments, starting with asking Michelle in her best breathy Lauren Bacall voice, "Baby, what are you doing in this job? You're too good to be steaming clothes. You need to come work at Calvin, he will love you. Come bring your résumé tomorrow, and you'll meet with our head of our PR, Paul Wilmot."

Michelle showed up the next day, and within a week, after a meeting with Paul and then with Calvin himself, was hired. "My career trajectory was redirected by her uncanny intuition and insight. It was magic."

Michelle was far from alone in benefitting from Carolyn's support. Carolyn was a mentor to other women at a time when empowerment among women was less widespread. Some women, who had taken on more duties and responsibility than the men around them just to get a seat at the table, were not inclined to find more chairs.

But in the offices at Calvin, as one of the women who worked alongside Carolyn put it, "equality ruled," and many of the women at Calvin Klein either became fast friends, were amiable, or at the very least were not out to cut one another's throat.

That is not to say Carolyn never felt competition. Once, when she was still in Personals, a position she had been angling to rise above for some time, she was benched when a certain socialite came to shop. This client was friendly with the parents of one of her colleagues, someone who had already made her way past sales and was now in a coveted PR position. Despite Carolyn's poise, intelligence, and utter calm in the face of every type of luminary, this VIP requested the colleague—a new friend Carolyn had made amid the great leveler of hectic workdays—to help style her purchases. It was a harsh lesson: We only climb so far unless hands from upon high reach down to pull us up. All Carolyn could muster at the time was, "How do you *know* her?"

Carolyn became friends with Calvin's daughter, Marci, and his wife, Kelly. Some corporate environments would discourage developing friendships with the boss's family, but CK Enterprises implicitly encouraged closeness among colleagues, if just by virtue of long hours and the fashion world's inevitable blending of the professional and personal. MJ Bettenhausen, Rachel Bold, Michelle Kessler, and her assistant Jen Dermer were others in Carolyn's core circle, as was Monicka HanssenTéele, who had taken over in VIP sales. Monicka and Carolyn were often seen huddling in the elevator, rushing out to the theater or a foreign film, Carolyn's beret-clad head accentuating her constant motion. Often Carolyn, Rachel, Michelle, and Jen would grab dinner after work at Lucky Strike, in SoHo.

Carolyn was a touchy-feely kind of friend. If you rode in a cab with her, she would make sure her feet touched yours. If you were in close conversation, she was not content to simply listen to you: She would touch you, maybe cup your face, stare into your eyes, and say things she knew would make you feel good. "I saw you and Dan walking down the street this morning," she once said to a coworker, apropos of nothing, "and I could just tell by the way he looked at you that he is so very in love with you."

Some of their twelve-hour days were punctuated with incessant laughter, the tears-running-down-your-eyes kind. "We once found a mouse, nearly dead from poison," recalls MJ Bettenhausen, who would soon move over to Ralph Lauren. "Carolyn was always an animal lover; she had already had her beloved Ruby, a black cat known to scratch, but didn't take sides between species. We got a Tupperware container and gave it water and cheese, of course." Carolyn named the mouse Ralph, not just in honor of her departing friend but because, like her friend's new employer, he was little.

"She took people in and elevated them," said Heather Ashton, who worked at Calvin Klein as a receptionist in wholesale. "And hysterically took the piss out of them at the same time."

"It was simple things," recalled Michelle. "She'd call me Mesheee. She'd raise that eyebrow and ask, 'Is Calvin still here?' Meaning, Shall we bolt for the day?"

Sometimes the eyebrow was half humor and half threat. Noonan, in his book *Forever Young: My Friendship with John F. Kennedy, Jr.*, recalled that once, while she was about to dig into a slice of pizza, Carolyn heard a colleague berating Narciso Rodriguez, a new young designer for the women's collection, from behind one of the screens during a fitting. Carolyn stepped into the area of the scuffle. She looked at the pizza in her hand. She looked at the face of Narciso's attacker. She looked back at the pizza. Then, raising that right eyebrow, looked back at the attacker. Did this person want to stop berating her dear friend, or did she want this piece of piping-hot, dripping cheese pizza on her face? The colleague fled the scene and thereafter treated Narciso with due respect.

The photographer Bruce Weber recalls meeting Carolyn during her early years in New York. "She was so natural, such a beauty, but wild, like a jumping horse," he said. "She was also a fantastic mimic and could have us all hunched in stitches. She would imitate Zack [Carr], lovingly, perfectly capturing his excitement. 'Oh, we've got a design meeting, it's going to be excellent!' And then she'd do Calvin, re-creating his, 'Well, hold on, I don't know. Try it on. Try it on.'"

Even though Carolyn seemed to beguile everyone who crossed her path, she did not want fame but rather to be behind the scenes—successful, to be sure, and in a profession of importance, but simple. For all her sophistication, Carolyn once told MJ Bettenhausen that her ideal man was "a rugged guy with a pickup truck, preferably vintage, with a dog in the back." Carolyn was building a work family who knew and loved their colleague, a girl who wanted to have fun, and who figured love would find her soon enough.

CHAPTER SIX

ANN'S GIRL, JACKIE'S BOY

Spring 1992–Fall 1992

I n spring 1992, Calvin Klein was just getting back into menswear. None
other than John F. Kennedy Jr.—*People* magazine's Sexiest Man Alive of
1988—had an appointment for a fitting in the VIP room. At the time, the
thirty-two-year-old graduate of Phillips Academy Andover, Brown University, and NYU School of Law was working in the district attorney's office. He
would be an important client—notably, a walking, talking, biking-around-
the-streets-of-New-York-City advertisement for the menswear line.

So even though Carolyn usually only showed the women's line, Calvin—
along with Kelly and MJ Bettenhausen—decided it should be she, the most
effervescent person on the salesfloor, who would show John the selection of
clothing. Unsurprisingly, John came out of the meeting smitten, with a few
men's suits and Carolyn's phone number. He called within days.

"John invited her to join his group at a gala dinner; he was a board member and had purchased an entire table," recalled Bettenhausen. "Sitting next
to him was another woman that Carolyn either mistook as his date, or actually was his date." It was unclear, and Carolyn wasn't pleased. When John
invited her to the after-party at a local club, she coldly said, "I can't. I'm meeting people," and abruptly left.

Of course, she and Bettenhausen discussed this in detail later. Carolyn
had a list of whys and what-ifs: "Why would he invite me if he already had

a date? Should I have gone? I was pretty rude; I feel bad. He hasn't called. What do I do? Who does that, invite one woman when he has another date?"

Bettenhausen said, "I advised her to write him a thank-you note for inviting her to the event and explain she would've loved to have gone to the after-party, but that she had plans. She wrote the note, but he didn't call right away."

They met again on May 18 at the Don't Bungle the Jungle II fundraiser, on Pier 25, just off North Moore Street in Tribeca. It was another work night out for Carolyn, but also a new adventure. In the early years, when her job was mainly sales, Carolyn wasn't always invited to the parties. As Kelly got to know and befriend Carolyn, she included her in more events for which the company sponsored a table. Dozens of designers, Calvin among them, donated dresses to be bid on during a fashion show, with the proceeds going to help save the Amazon rainforests. Calvin and Kelly had a table with a prime view. Looking out, they could see Spike Lee, Bret Easton Ellis, and Richard Gere, among others.

The guests sat "eating intentionally cold smoked salmon and unintentionally cold chicken, and bidding on delightfully idiosyncratic 'jungle costumes' designed by the right sort of designers," reported the *New York Times* in an article titled "Don't Bungle the Benefit." The complaint, besides cold chicken, was that the event raised around $350,000 less than Don't Bungle the Jungle (I) in 1989, "when you could charge $500 a seat just to be within spitting distance of Julian Schnabel." The show was organized by art world notables such as Alba Clemente, Nessia Pope, and Schnabel's then-wife, Jacqueline Schnabel, with artists Ross Bleckner and Eric Fischl on the invitation committee.

As Claudia Schiffer came down the runway in a snakeskin dress, emcee Fran Lebowitz declared it "a simple dress for a simple girl." Just then, Kelly noticed Carolyn at the bar, in rapt conversation with John. Kelly was thrilled. John and Carolyn stayed there for over an hour, never looking away from each other. Lightning had struck.

Was the benefit meeting a chance encounter? Paul Wilmot later said that "John asked Kelly to introduce him to [Carolyn]," but maybe he meant reintroduce. John brought his close friend from Andover, Sasha Chermayeff, to the party, even though a huge fundraiser wasn't their usual sort of hangout. Sasha supported the idea that the encounter was intentional: "Eventually I spotted Carolyn. Just by looking at her I realized he has brought me here to see her, to tacitly approve . . . There was something about the way she moved, the tilt of her head. Carolyn was captivating. Without John even looking her way, my eyes went to her, and I knew." While John did not introduce them that evening, Sasha said she "knew it was only a matter of time."

Like Carolyn, John was magnetic. He hailed from the closest thing America had to a royal family, but he was also known to be kind and gracious. His chiseled features and warm brown eyes had made him a national heartthrob. He was the next great hope for the United States political dynasty of Camelot, and a man that women would approach even as he walked down the street holding the hand of another woman. Add to that, he was thirty-two to Carolyn's twenty-six years, but still, she wasn't unduly intimidated.

Her confidence in the face of such fame was exceptional. In nineties New York City, the interest in JFK Jr. was unsurpassed by any celebrity at the time, and very few even now. Watching him grow up, become a man of good spirit, and stumble in his career, all while making use of every amenity the city had to offer, was a sport and a pastime. Sightings were recorded everywhere: the subway, Central Park with friends and a Frisbee, swerving in and out of traffic on an ever-changing array of bicycles he forgot to lock up and were subsequently stolen, or even rollerblading against traffic, shirtless, while holding a box of pizza above his head and looking like Apollo on wheels.

After the benefit, John and Carolyn continued to see each other into the summer, in a haze of sultry dinners, dancing, and walks in Washington Square Park and Central Park. John even brought Carolyn to Sea Song, the Sagaponack, Long Island, home he rented with his cousin and best friend, Anthony Radziwill.

They dined at One Ocean Road, an airy restaurant with high-powered clientele located in a landmark building on the intersection of Route 27 and Ocean Road, with seascape photographs of nearby Straight Beach on the wall. After dinner they went to Murf's Backstreet Tavern, a low-key bar in Sag Harbor. Unlike so many Hamptons hot spots, Murf's is not a place to see and be seen. Like the dream Carolyn relayed to MJ Bettenhausen of finding a guy with a red pickup truck and a dog in the cab, Murf's was laid-back. The clientele was there for the local vibe, the craft beer, the ring game, and the dartboard that often fell apart when actually hit with a dart, which was "half the fun," according to a regular.

Sea Song is where she first met Carole DiFalco, then Radziwill's girl-friend (they got engaged on Mother's Day just two years later), a producer for ABC News's *Peter Jennings Reporting*. Carole and Anthony met when they were both assigned to cover the Menendez murder trial in LA in 1990, when brothers Lyle and Erik Menendez were tried for shooting their parents.

Carole wrote beautifully about that weekend in her 2005 memoir *What Remains*, describing the moment when Carolyn "walked across the living room and put a hand on my shoulder. She seemed to know me. Her eyes were as big as quarters and blue like a swimming pool and she spoke softly, almost whispering. She dismissed the barriers, the walls of politeness, the invisible personal space we protect. There was no awkward embrace with her, no hesitation. She hugged you tight, as if she might never see you again. That first day, I noticed light and movement and her hands." And then: "They broke up the next weekend, and I didn't see her for two years."

The breakup was messy, especially considering the brevity of the relationship. The week after their summer idyll at Sea Song, Carolyn met John for dinner at El Teddy's. The Tribeca mainstay was an unusual-looking place—a squat, two-story building wedged between two larger ones, with a replica of the Statue of Liberty's crown atop its roof.

Carolyn and John sat in a banquette, where, before they ordered a thing, John presented Carolyn with a letter. The author who sent it to him, a friend of his, came from the milieu of boarding schools, Ivy League universities, and "old money" families of New York, though he didn't divulge these facts until much later. The letter claimed Carolyn was a user, a partier, that she was out for fame and fortune. And in a grand flourish of the "slut versus the stud" double standard, the epistolary spy added that Carolyn "dated guys around town." John casually tossed the piece of paper at her, stood, and walked out the door.

Carolyn stared in shock at John as he departed and then at the correspondence that sat before her on the white linen tablecloth. She read the letter, folded it, and put it in her purse. Then she got up and left. She would carry it with her, in many ways, for a very long time.

At work the next day, her colleagues noticed she was not her usual vivacious self. She'd hardly told anyone that she had just spent two months falling for the "Sexiest Man Alive" nor that it had now blown up in her face. She was relieved she had kept mum about their relationship, but she did confide in one colleague.

For a girl who already had ambivalent feelings about men, the confrontation at El Teddy's was harrowing. It wasn't just the loss of a man she had begun to love. It was also the humiliation of the when, where, why, and how of the loss. Her pride at never having been broken up with was majorly wounded. She had made it to her mid-twenties without ever being on the receiving end of the kind of rejection—and accompanying pain—that she had seen her mother go through when she split with her father.

Eventually, she did open up. "Carolyn was upset, but not despondent. She knew that John was crazy about her, as she was for him," said a friend who wishes to remain anonymous. "It was Carolyn. She was resilient . . . and she also knew, deep down, that this would not be the end. John was a prize, and Carolyn had her eye on the ball."

But there was something shaming, wounding, about that letter, all the more so for having been delivered on an evening she thought would be another blissful date. John had taken the letter at face value, and it was ridiculous to her that there was no discussion, no words of explanation wanted or waited for, either from him or from her. She was rattled. "He just threw it in front of me," Carolyn said, "and got up and left."

Worst of all were the impossible-to-answer questions: Who and why? Carolyn would have already felt slightly at sea dating a man who'd had the world at his feet since birth. Was it easy to accuse her of being on the make because she wasn't born into a family off the *Mayflower*, or one listed in the *Social Register*? She'd grown up in a comfortable environment in affluent Greenwich, but just as her father's leaving the home lurked beneath the foundation of her identity, her time in Connecticut was in the home of her stepfather, itself a reminder that she was not fully of the place. She hadn't gone to an exclusive prep school nor an Ivy League college as John and most of his friends had. She also knew the rules were inevitably different when it came to dating a Kennedy—especially *this* Kennedy, a public man whose name and history conveyed money, power, and dynasty. But the main thing she liked about John, she told her friend, "was that he had always carried about him an 'I don't give a fuck about money and status' attitude. He cares about people for their minds and hearts. He is *intentionally* down-to-earth." Then she added, "And now this?"

It's not that she was oblivious to the distinction and potential that went with the man she was dating. "Of course these qualities in John appealed to Carolyn, although the money and fame did not matter," said a friend. "But she did want to have an important life, and she felt she could build one with John." For John's part, it would be impossible to never be swayed by society's leaden hand, even when he wanted to rise above it.

So, who wrote the letter? Given Carolyn's outsider status in John's world, it would make sense that it was one of John's friends. But there were many suspects, such was the sense of both possessiveness and protectiveness that John engendered in his family, his friends, and—it's not much of a stretch to say—the entire nation. He was, at the time of this encounter, just four years past being *People's* Sexiest Man Alive. He would later acknowledge that it changed his identity as a public figure, or rather made him one as an adult, no longer a subject of ardent, insider conversation, but a national celebrity. Having stayed fairly under the radar until the age of twenty-eight, he was no longer able to walk down the street, take a cab, eat in a restaurant, pop into a deli, or make use of his beloved Central Park without being recognized or approached. Chermayeff, his friend from Andover, told Kennedy biographer Steve Gillon (a professor and historian whom John befriended at Brown) that she sympathized with John's predicament, saying, "He used to make fun of it and complain to us, like, 'You guys get to meet new people, you get to make new, really close friends. I can't!'" He couldn't really go out in the world that way. It was too overwhelming. It was too much. John was too much for everybody. Everyone was just so blown away by him, that side of him. He was kind of stuck with the people he'd known for a very, very long time." Perhaps Carolyn, who seemed to have captured his attention in a unique way, threatened someone trying to keep it. Carolyn would not forgive this trespass. It took a few years, but she would find out who wrote this letter, and later freeze them out.

Jackie's longtime friend and John's longtime mentor George Plimpton told Kennedy biographer C. David Heymann, author of *American Legacy: The Story of John and Caroline Kennedy*, that Jackie was incredibly disturbed by the *People* coverage and that they spoke extensively about it at a dinner party she hosted soon after. By "'making John out to be a Hollywood hunk,' she said, 'the magazine has hurt his reputation. Nobody will take him seriously after this.'" What surprised Plimpton was that she referenced a future in politics at all for her son. "Jackie was jabbering away about how potentially damaging the article could be should John ever want to pursue a political career. I think it marked the first time I'd ever heard her mention such a possibility. Suddenly, the front door opens, and in walked John Jr. wearing a backpack. Jackie stopped talking. John said to her, 'Are you discussing me again?' Jackie giggled. John stayed for no more than ten minutes. After he went, Jackie picked up where she'd left off."

John picked up where he had left off, too. He had known the actress Daryl Hannah since the early eighties when their families met while both were vacationing in St. Martin. Daryl's stepfather was billionaire businessman and film producer Jerrold Wexler, who donated heavily to both the Democratic National Committee and the campaign of John's uncle, Senator Edward M. Kennedy of Massachusetts. They were an upper-class Chicago family who wintered in Palm Beach and belonged to its Everglades Club, where John's grandfather Joe Kennedy had served on the president's committee and board of governors. The Wexlers were also old money, having made their fortune in radio in the 1920s, and the Kennedys could possibly seem nouveau riche by comparison. When John's aunt Lee Radziwill married film director and producer Herbert Ross, Wexler called Ted, at Daryl's behest, and asked him to encourage John to spend time at the wedding with Daryl. In other words, she had been prescreened.

According to Billy Way, John's close friend from Andover and Brown, John had a lengthy phone call with Daryl either shortly before or not long after the contentious night at El Teddy's, and they decided to reconcile their tumultuous, on-and-off four-year liaison. (Among the many moments of drama had been the time Daryl called from the West Coast to break up with John the night before he took—and failed—the New York bar exam.)

Try as she might, Carolyn could not avoid John after the humiliating night with the letter. John was everywhere—magazine covers, late-night TV shows, and on the streets of New York. He and his sister, Caroline, appeared in a 1992 interview with Jay Schadler of ABC's *Primetime Live* to promote the Profile in Courage Award, named for their father's Pulitzer Prize–winning book and granted annually to politicians who challenge the status quo. Oliver Stone's movie *JFK* had been recently released, and Schadler, rather tastelessly, asked John if he planned to watch it.

"No," replied John, "because that's not entertainment to me."

Schadler continued, "You've heard the stories about your father," referring to JFK's numerous infidelities. "Do you think that had that been dealt with by the press, do you think it would have tarnished the image we have of him?"

Knowing how severely hurtful his father's cheating had been to his mother, John deftly replied, "I think the real question is whether or not, given the tenor of the times, my father would have gone into politics at this point."

It was not a hypothetical question for John. According to *The Men We Became*, the memoir by John's college roommate Rob Littell, after the July DNC, Bill Clinton had offered John an unspecified cabinet position. John had refused. It was not just that he was far from ready to take on the weight and responsibility that a position of such rank entailed; he was also all too aware of the scrutiny he'd be under given his heritage and pedigree.

Carolyn had already gotten the idea that spending time with John meant some loss of privacy. During their brief time together, they had already been hounded, their partnership noted in the press, even if her name was still unknown. As soon as a Kennedy ventured out, it seemed they were surrounded by informants. It turned out their time in Long Island had not been missed by the *Daily News*: "Kennedy sightings: John F. Kennedy Jr. had dinner two nights in a row with the same young woman at a restaurant called One Ocean Road in Bridgehampton. The second night, JFK Jr. asked the waiter where they could go where they wouldn't be bothered. The waiter sent them to Murf's Backstreet Tavern in Sag Harbor, which is described as a 'real drinking man's bar where a hunk like John-John might not even be recognized.'"

It's entirely possible that once the initial sting of the scene at El Teddy's wore off, Carolyn concluded that she had dodged a bullet. The summer of 1992 continued with the media noting John's every move—at the post-honeymoon reception at the family's Hyannis Port compound for his uncle Ted's wedding to Victoria Reggie, in the TWA terminal at JFK Airport with Daryl ("neither kissing nor fighting, which is how they are usually identified in public places," according to the *Washington Post*), and in the August issue of *M* magazine, which hit the stands July 23 with John's picture captioned "JFK as the once and future president."

Carolyn had been right. While the details of exactly how they moved past the El Teddy's letter as a couple are unclear, within a week of the scene at the restaurant, John tried to call Carolyn. And call. And call and call and call. He tried her at home, with no luck. He tried at Calvin Klein. "She's not in today" or "She's with a client, can I take a message?" was all he got. Even when he sent flowers, she didn't respond. The first bunch was an enormous, beautiful arrangement of blue hydrangeas.

"I'm not interested in seeing a guy who has a girlfriend," Carolyn told Michelle Kessler. Apparently, John had explained in one of his voicemails that he had spoken to Daryl, who wanted to reconcile, and that he felt he should give it a chance. MJ Bettenhausen told Carolyn, who was smarting, "He'll be back, but let him go figure it out."

The calls kept coming. Carolyn's friend and colleague Kim Vernon, who was then vice president of Global Advertising at CK, said that "John really chased her . . . This went on for some time."

DATING LIFE ASIDE, CAROLYN was busy building her career that summer of 1992. Her promotion to the PR department finally went through in July. By the time Michelle Kessler arrived that same month, Carolyn had become director of PR for the Calvin Klein Collection—which included the astonishingly fluid silhouette slip dresses that retailed between $300 and $900—and Michelle took over as director of PR for the CK line, the younger contemporary collection, along with Calvin Klein Jeans and Calvin Klein Underwear. For Carolyn, PR meant she was the liaison between the women's collection and the magazines, finding exactly what a magazine editor would need for a feature, whether it was a white column gown for a supermodel like Kirsty Hume, posing as a bored aristocrat leaning against a planter in an English garden for Arthur Elgort in *Vogue*, or capris and a sweater for a "regular girl" shoot for *Glamour* or *Mirabella*. Besides the day-to-day work of a press person, the PR girls at Calvin Klein were not only muses for Calvin and Zack, but walking advertisements for the brand, the original influencers.

Over time, Carolyn's responsibilities included creative production of the catwalks: the music (matching the songs to the looks), styling the models' hair, makeup, and the sequence in which the models walked. She and her assistant Rachel Bold moved from the eleventh- to the fifth-floor PR office, which shared square footage with the design department and the reception area. Their desks were one long counter that ran along a wall they all faced, the differentiation being what was on the wall in front of each. So Jen Dermer faced the wall, Michelle faced a mirror, and Rachel and Carolyn faced a window. Space was tight, and the PR area was thus named "the pen."

"It was an extraordinary time to be there," Michelle said. "The four of us sat together in the tight PR pen. . . . Carolyn was a big reader; there was always something literary on her desk, be it Charlotte Brontë or intellectual tomes on Henry James. I was incredibly organized; Carolyn was a tornado. She had so many sweaters piled on the back of her chair by the end of the winter, I would ask her, 'Do you have any clothes left at home?' Her eyebrow would shoot up, and she placed another sweater on top. I called it 'Mount Cashmere.'"

A couple of months earlier, Paul Wilmot, who had been with Calvin Klein since 1985, gave notice that he was leaving to join *Vogue* as director of public relations, where he remained for five years before starting his own communications firm. He stayed on at Calvin Klein during the transition, but before the arrival of his replacement, Carolyn answered directly to Calvin, which speaks to how much Calvin had begun to rely on her opinion. She was in her element during this interval, confident and decisive. For a twenty-six-year-old woman, she was remarkably poised. More than ever, she was an extra set of eyes for Calvin. "Carolyn was often popping into Calvin's office from PR, coming in to campaign for her opinion, or she would walk into his office and say, 'You have to see this person,'" remembered Michelle.

Eventually, a new supervisor was brought in to officially fill Paul's shoes. She and Carolyn did not mesh. Carolyn had, after all, been functioning as a direct liaison with Calvin. "I felt undermined at many turns," the former supervisor said. "She once said to me, 'We think that you think that we don't like you,'" placing this person squarely on the outside of the pen.

They forged on in an uneasy truce, with Carolyn concentrating on the work and stepping aside to let the new supervisor rule the roost.

"Everything [Carolyn] did was considered, and she had an air of *I know what's coming and no one else does*; it was exciting to watch," Michelle said.

She summed up: "She was like a good witch, and I wondered, what was she going to do with all of that power?"

A who's who of future fashion stars occupied the design department. "Narciso was there, John Varvatos was there, and Matt Nye was soon to arrive," Kessler said.

"I can't quantify how much PR affected sales," Kessler explained. "The magazines were how we did it. PR had to justify its existence and what we cost the company. We would clip out every mention of Calvin in every magazine.

"Later in that summer of '92," she continued, "someone says, 'There is a little girl here to see you.' She was an adorable creature. It was Kate Moss."

Kate could not have arrived too soon. Calvin had been in Hazelden for a Valium addiction, and a combination of wanting to have his hand on everything while said hand wasn't particularly steady had put his company in a vulnerable position.

"Calvin knew it was the young people who were going to get him out of this mess," said Madonna Badger, the company's advertising chief.

Three inches shorter than the reigning supermodels, clad in a pair of CK jeans with messy hair and no makeup, Moss walked with unself-conscious grace right past the herd of models, including Cindy Crawford, and into her meeting with Calvin. There, Kate simply sat on the floor. Calvin, in a move unlike any he had ever made, got down next to her.

When he emerged, he declared, "I love her, I love her."

But then he got cold feet. Calvin consulted with a couple of stylists, including his former employee Paul Cavaco. They worried she might not get much work, especially because she was so tiny.

Carolyn and Madonna Badger fought for Moss. Carolyn saw that Kate was exactly what fashion needed after years of the glamazons. And, like her mother taught her to be when she was sure of her position, she was unrelenting.

Later, Calvin would tell *Women's Wear Daily* that he knew right away. "A lot of women were getting implants and doing things to their buttocks," Klein said. "It was out of control. I just found something so distasteful about all that. I wanted someone who is natural, always thin. I was looking for the complete opposite of the glamor type." But while he might have known right away, without Carolyn's fierce advocacy, it's unlikely Moss would ever have entered the Calvin Klein universe.

"He changed everything on a dime one week before fall of 1992, for [the] spring '93 show," Kessler explained. Calvin had already been redefining the Calvin Klein universe. He hired "no-makeup" makeup artist Dick Page, who specialized in the dewy face, and went hyper-minimal. "This was Calvin making a statement," Kessler continued, "and it changed the entire fashion industry."

This was good news because something had to change. Back in 1990, the company had sustained a $4.3 million loss. The flagship Collection line was out of many young women's financial reach, and they again lost $14.2 million on the Puritan/Calvin Klein Sport division. In February 1992, the *Los Angeles Times* came out with an article titled "Can Calvin Klein Escape?" Explaining in past tense that "He Built an Empire on Raunch and Elegance," the article predicted that a more austere moment was ahead, and that the designer had both business and press problems. Calvin didn't comment.

He was about to reemerge on top with the Kate Moss and Marky Mark (otherwise known as Mark Wahlberg) underwear campaign. Harkening back to the famous "Nothing comes between me and my Calvins" tagline of the Brooke Shields era, the new campaign Klein launched further pushed boundaries with Mark eyeing Moss and saying, "Now that could definitely come between me and my Calvins."

The campaign revived Calvin, the company's fortunes, and made Kate a household name. Her career skyrocketed as her natural, puckish, seductive, delicate, and also androgynous look became the epitome of nineties beauty. "For me," Calvin said at the time, "Kate's body represented closing the door on the excessiveness of the eighties."

Despite her recent stints for *Mirabella* and *Glamour*, Carolyn consistently declined invitations to pose in front of the camera, of which there were many: *Vogue, Harper's Bazaar, Cosmopolitan.* That she turned them down was, and remained, part of her conviction that too much public attention could lead to nothing good. However, her desire to hide from the camera made her all the more tantalizing to those in the fashion world who'd seen her.

SOON AFTER SHE STARTED as the receptionist on the wholesale floor in late 1992, Heather Ashton got her first glimpse of Carolyn: Sitting on the counter of the office kitchen, she was eating pizza and giggling like a little girl. Carolyn was naked, except for a G-string. A posse of models such as Kate Moss and Bridget Hall, there for fittings for the forthcoming CK show, were milling about, so Carolyn tried on some clothes as well. Then she decided to have a bite mid-change. No surprise that Heather at first thought Carolyn was another model: At five feet, ten inches tall, Carolyn was the same height as Christy Turlington, Naomi Campbell, and Helena Christensen. It made sense to Heather that she was one of the lithe, gorgeous girls there for either a fitting or an audition to grace the billboard sailing over Times Square, or the pages of a magazine, draped in one of Calvin's delicate silk skirts.

A few days later, Heather was sitting at her desk, bored, when Carolyn walked in. In a bit of professional symmetry, Carolyn at first thought Heather, gorgeous in her own right, might be a model. The approaching stranger was dressed like the bohemian version of the brand's current emphasis on long, sleek silhouettes with a flowing floor-length black skirt, Chuck Taylors, and a snug white T-shirt. She promptly sat on the edge of Heather's desk, one hand on the table to prop up her frame as she leaned close to her subject and the other to grab Heather's hand, then her hair.

"What are you, then?" Carolyn asked. "Where are you from? Why are you at this desk? Why are you doing this?" Her questions came rapid-fire.

"You cannot imagine what it felt like to have Carolyn put her shine on me," Heather recalled. "Carolyn had *major* energy. She talked incessantly and was scary attractive. I don't know what I did to win her attention but I felt both lucky and a little terrified. I wanted to live up to it."

Heather explained that she had answered a *New York Times* want ad for a receptionist, got the job, and here she was. The plan was for Heather to learn the ropes and then roll into sales. She was tall and pretty, with beachy, unkempt hair. She told Carolyn that she had arrived in New York City two weeks earlier from Gainesville, Florida. A heat-seeking missile for a soul in need, Carolyn took Heather under her wing.

"She was the opposite of a corporate mean girl, stabbing her way up the workforce. She had a huge and generous heart," Michelle said. "I dated a guy Carolyn dubbed 'David the asshole' because he would play games and disappear for days. At a particularly low moment, I walked into work upset about the latest debacle but intent on keeping a professional face, but Carolyn knew something was wrong. I didn't want to talk about it at the office, but sometime after mid-night that night she called me and said, 'I know you're awake and lying in bed upset, but it's okay, you're too good for him'"—"him" being the man who had just broken Michelle's heart, or, given that the girls were in their mid-twenties, bruised her heart. She was used to Carolyn's caring, but what surprised Michelle now was that she hadn't spoken much, if at all, about her recent lovesickness, and somehow Carolyn not only could read her friend but be one hundred percent correct in that Michelle was indeed awake and stewing. "She saved me from mak-ing the phone call that one cringes about years later."

IN THE FALL OF 1992, Carolyn began a casual romance with model Michael Bergin. A former hotel doorman at the Paramount, Bergin would later, in a tell-all book, *The Other Man*, claim he was sexually involved with Carolyn from the fall of '92 until her death. There's no doubt Carolyn befriended Bergin, and, true to form, helped him with his career.

Michelle said that Carolyn booked a lot of her models, including Michael Bergin, through her friend Jules Watson, who was at Click Models. Carolyn and Michael had an on-off relationship, much more off than on. His later account of it is considered questionable by many of Carolyn's friends. "Bergin was not Carolyn's type," said a friend. He was just "one of the 'underwear guys' as far any romance goes. Though she was nice to him, he was not a serious boyfriend."

"I remember one day Carolyn was having words with Michael Bergin as he was leaving CK Industries," Heather Ashton said. "It was not that she was upset or interested in Michael, but more that she had a point that she needed to make to him, and apparently it wasn't sinking in. Every time the elevator door started to close Carolyn stuck her arm in to stop it; it would open back up and she continued lecturing Michael. There were other people in the elevator standing there, helpless, as Carolyn finished the heated discussion. I was doubled over with laughter."

John F. Kennedy Jr., meanwhile, had been spotted about town with Daryl Hannah that fall: at the movies, in Chicago, kissing in Central Park—all documented in the press. Put down the newspapers and magazines, and you could still come across a television clip of John and Daryl making out on a stoop near her Upper West Side apartment. That their reconciliation may have been catalyzed by Daryl's nasty split with her live-in boyfriend, Jackson Browne (John went to Los Angeles to pick her up and brought her back to New York), surely made Carolyn glad to be far from the perpetual JFK Jr. media mayhem and immersed in the Calvin Klein universe that provided its own high-octane originality, dear friends, and a platform from which she could flourish.

CHAPTER SEVEN

MUCH ADO

∽

Spring 1993–Spring 1994

Carolyn had been reporting to the supervisor she didn't respect for nearly a year when Lynn Tesoro was hired as the replacement. Tesoro had previously headed PR for the men's collection for four years, and her move to Carolyn's department was a renaissance for the label—and for Carolyn. The two self-made women quickly formed a mutual admiration society. Like Carolyn, Tesoro had gone to Catholic school, was of Italian descent, and had boundless energy.

Michelle said that Lynn "allowed people to be their best, and didn't put them in a box, which is hard to maneuver in corporate structures. Lynn saw exactly how everyone fit into the department—she was the absolute best person to work with and for, and an incredible mentor for us all."

While life in the office got more fun with Lynn's arrival, Carolyn was still having plenty of fun after-hours, too. "Carolyn was friends with lots of guys, and I mean platonically," said one former colleague. "She considered them worthy of true friendship and was able to develop nuanced relationships without the question of sex hanging over the room."

Carolyn was very close already to Zack Carr, Narciso Rodriguez, and Gordon Henderson. She began to include Michael Bergin in her platonic circle, as he had confessed to loneliness in the city after the romance ended. In keeping with her ability to remain on good terms with her former paramours, she brought him to clubs and hip restaurants, and made a mission of introducing him to many of her friends. Michael and Gordon became close and often went clubbing with Jules and Carolyn.

Among the adventures was Jen Dermer's wedding on Fishers Island that summer. "We had the best time," remembered Michelle Kessler. "Six of us went up—I went with my boyfriend Andy, Rachel brought her now husband, Franco, and Carolyn brought Michael as a friend. . . . We missed one New London ferry, then got the next and arrived just in time.

"When the priest finished the service—he had an unusually long drawl with the words 'foreverrrrr and everrrrr'—Carolyn and I just looked at each other and repeated slowly, 'Foreverrrrr and everrrrr,' holy shit," Michelle said. "Her eyebrow went up, and that was all it took for us to burst out into howls of laughter. Thankfully we were in the back of the church."

In June 1993, Carolyn pulled off a professional coup. Calvin was the honoree at the AIDS Project Los Angeles fundraiser at the Hollywood Bowl, and Carolyn produced a show that blew the house down. It was preceded by a seven-minute film of CK advertising over the years, including the infamous 1980 Brooke Shields ad—the shock of the past a prelude to the shock that came next: 350 models flocking out at the same time and then stomping down the long white runway extending into the audience of over 4,000 guests, while the song "Spiritual High" by Moodswings and Chrissie Hynde blasted over the speakers. Clad in heavy black boots, some topless, they showed the entire underwear collection. The music was booming, Hynde's voice singing about independence and freedom, culminating with the Reverend Martin Luther King Jr. repeating, "Let freedom ring." Kate Moss emerged, and Marky Mark dropped his jeans and grabbed his privates. According to one onlooker, the audience, having paid either $50 to sit in the bleachers or $25,000 for a box, "rose, cheering and screaming."

"How it all comes off is in God's hands," Calvin told the *Los Angeles Times* before the show. It had been in Carolyn's hands.

"At one point there was the concern the stage would not hold the weight of that many models at one time," Michelle remembered. But all was buoyant. "It was so exciting, it was unbelievable. And Carolyn had done the whole thing—the models, the music, all of it."

⁓

THAT SAME JUNE, JOHN was doing his own sort of modeling. Along with Elaine R. Jones of the NAACP Legal Defense Fund, he was featured in a *Vogue* profile called "Prize Partnership." At Jackie's suggestion, he had reached out to writer and *Vogue* editor William Norwich about doing a piece on the Kennedy Profile in Courage Award. The *Vogue* profile was a conscious effort on John's part to turn his image from "The Hunk Flunks"—he notoriously failed the New York bar exam twice, jeopardizing his position in the DA's office, before finally passing on his third attempt—toward a serious role of public service and civil discourse. It was, incredibly, the first time he had agreed to pose for a glossy magazine.

John had already flirted with the idea of journalism. His first big byline came the year before, in the summer of 1992, when he had published an article about a kayaking trip to the Baltic for the *New York Times*; in it, he channeled his gracious charm despite the harrowing journey he describes.

By the summer of 1993, the press speculated John was moving with Daryl to Washington, DC. She had put her apartment on West 69th Street up for sale, though by July, the *Daily News* ran a detailed account of a fight between Daryl and John at the restaurant Indochine, witnesses watching "the two scream at each other while madly pointing fingers in each other's faces." It's possible the fight had come from increasing tension ever since Daryl's visit to Martha's Vineyard over that Memorial Day weekend, which had culminated with a party at Red Gate Farm, Jackie Kennedy's thirty-four-acre oceanfront estate, after which "they left the place a shambles." In *The Day John Died*, Kennedy biographer Christopher Andersen wrote that Marta Sgubin, John's former nanny, who was still working for Jackie, scolded John in a way perhaps Jackie was unlikely to do, saying, "You should have more respect for your mother's house." John gave his word to do so in the future.

By the end of July, the *Star-Gazette* reported that John and Daryl were engaged. That was not true, but truth is often irrelevant for the tabloids.

Richard Wiese, another friend of John's from Brown, told Kennedy biographer Heymann, "It was a tough but interesting relationship. They were both a little spoiled. They were both used to getting their way. Daryl once commented to me that all of John's friends felt sorry for his having to put up with a Hollywood actress. 'But you know,' she said, 'he's no day at the beach.'"

In *The Men We Became*, Rob Littell put their issues down to the idea that good relationships have a gardener and a flower: One likes to nurture, and the other likes to be tended to. "The problem was that Daryl and John were both clearly, and admittedly, flowers," he wrote.

Thus began the merry-go-round of dating that John carried on for nearly a year—between Daryl, Carolyn, and old flame Julie Baker, too. Baker was a model who looked remarkably similar to Jackie. She and John had met at an Andrew Dice Clay stand-up comedy show in 1989. They dated for about a year, and after that she and John would occasionally reunite over lunch, or she would be his "date" between girlfriends.

Somehow, John convinced Carolyn to try again. And she gave it a shot. Granted, she knew she wasn't his only option. When she came across a pair of Julie's duck boots in John's apartment, despite them being a size too small, she made a point of wearing them. But Carolyn was guarded about the revival with John, treading carefully, perhaps as a matter of self-protection. Whether she was looking to protect her heart or her reputation, it was hard to say.

One night, Michelle Kessler noticed Carolyn getting ready to leave the office looking a bit more polished than her usual "relaxed perfection" style. It was after-hours, they had worked late, and the two were talking about guys.

"She was clearly getting ready to go out for a more formal evening, taking care with the tiny bit of makeup she wore. Carolyn didn't need much; if anything, she looked best without it. But I was curious, so I asked her what she was up to:

"'Car, you look dressed up. Are you going on a date?'

"'Oh . . . yeah,' Carolyn replied nonchalantly.

"'With who?' I asked.

"Carolyn—eyebrow raised—answered deadpan, 'A lawyer.'

"'Cool. What firm does he work for?'

"'Oh, he works at the DA's office.'"

That's all it took.

"I knew immediately," said Michelle. "'Carolyn, are you going out with JFK Jr.?!'

"She didn't say a word. Nothing. Just the eyebrow high and a smile on her face. It was just like her to keep it under wraps. She swore me to secrecy and I never told a soul, until the world found out."

When the world found out, Jen Dermer remembers being on phone duty when Carolyn and Michelle were at lunch.

"A guy called asking for Carolyn; I said she was out and asked if I could take a message. He sounded rather laid-back, and I couldn't tell if he said his name was Sean or John. So when Carolyn came back I told her a guy named Sean had called.

" 'I don't know anyone named Sean. Are you sure?' Carolyn asked me.

" 'It was hard to tell. Maybe John,' I said.

" 'Jen, this is important.' Carolyn laughed. 'Was it Sean or John?'

"We figured out that it was John, but that didn't mean when he called she jumped," Dermer said.

Carolyn's high school friend Deena Manion recalled an evening in October when a few friends were at Carolyn's apartment getting ready to go to dinner for Deena's birthday. "She was redoing her floors, and there were only two chairs and her bed," Manion recalled. Carolyn was pulling big black platform shoes out of her closet to give to Deena, who wore a similar size, when the phone rang. Carolyn let it go to the answering machine; when the caller left a message, it came out over the speaker and everyone in the room could hear.

"We were all a little gobsmacked. JFK Jr.'s unmistakable voice was on the machine, leaving a message saying, 'Hey, Car, it's John—where are you? I've been trying to get in touch with you. Call me when you can.'

"We couldn't believe it. As soon as he said 'John,' we said, 'Aren't you going to pick up?' She just shook her head, nonchalant. We said, 'Aren't you going to call him back?'

" 'He can wait,' Carolyn replied. And she didn't bring it up again the rest of the evening. There was no way Carolyn was going to put herself at the beck and call of anyone, much less a man who hadn't fully committed."

Despite his juggling act, John considered himself a serial monogamist. So when he and Carolyn were "on," he was "off" with Daryl. But Carolyn became increasingly irked that he wouldn't introduce her to his mother.

She had, after all, introduced him to *her* mother. "I took him to meet my mom," Carolyn told a friend. "John is sweet, charming, and his manners are perfect. But I could tell . . . she was not having it. She just gave me the eye the whole night. When we spoke the next day, she said, 'Carolyn, he's sweet, but that entire scene is just too much drama.' " The wisdom of moms.

"John told Carolyn he wasn't introducing her to Jackie because she liked Daryl, and that's what Carolyn thought was the case," a close friend remarked.

One night, during a dinner at Keens Steakhouse, John rushed Carolyn out a side door when he spied Jackie across the room with her companion Maurice Tempelsman, her stepbrother Hugh D. "Yusha" Auchincloss, and niece Alexandra Rutherfurd, according to Kennedy biographer J. Randy Taraborrelli. How the couple recovered from such a show of no-confidence is remarkable, but it would always gnaw at Carolyn, and when they fought, even years after Jackie had died, this issue would come up. How must it have felt to the girl from White Plains with Italian and working-class roots to be yanked out of a restaurant in order to keep her existence a secret from Jackie? Regardless, it didn't work, as Jackie later asked a friend about her son pulling the stunning blonde outside, "Does he think I'm blind?" Was John's reaction indicative of the fact he believed Jackie preferred the blonde actress who had moneyed connections?

But, in time, it became more evident that was not the case. Jackie's feelings about Daryl had never been overwhelmingly positive, and, as time went on, they got worse. Littell wrote that when Daryl was among the visitors at Martha's Vineyard, Jackie often "made herself scarce." Perhaps, rather, John worried that once he introduced Carolyn to Jackie there would be no going back to Daryl.

"Carolyn broke up with him a couple of times for not introducing her to his mother—it really bothered her," a close friend said. "Carolyn was very bohemian, a downtown girl, which John loved, and he himself would walk around barefoot and smoke pot. Not to excess, but he could be bohemian, too. But it's possible John was worried how that would go over with Jackie."

Carolyn began having doubts about her place in the world, as this was a serious setback. So much so that she reverted to a former bad habit she employed as a safety measure when she was feeling less than secure. She had a friend and colleague at the time who had a private school background and an old-money family name. One Friday, during this tumultuous back-and-forth with John, Carolyn noticed her friend leaving the office early with a suitcase.

"Hey," said Carolyn. "Are you taking off for the weekend?"

"Yes, I'm headed out of town now. I'm going to visit my dad."

"Oh. Well, have a good time."

When the colleague arrived at her father's place, something made her call her New York apartment, where she lived with her boyfriend. He picked up and said, "The strangest thing just happened. Carolyn called here and asked for you. When I told her you were visiting your father, she said I had to come out with her this weekend, that I couldn't just sit around alone." He ended up going to meet Carolyn with a few other friends. After the weekend he explained to his girlfriend that Carolyn had spent the evening flirting heavily with him, adding, "I don't think Carolyn has your best interests at heart, hon." Was the fact that the friend in question was the apple of her own father's eye, which Carolyn was not, part of why Carolyn made the mental leap to betray someone she cared for? Afterward, the friend did not cut Carolyn out completely, but there was a noticeable froideur.

Carolyn would never make another mistake like that again, and she was pained that she and her colleague were no longer close. What could have made a woman for whom empathy was a sixth sense behave so out of character? Was this low moment a reversion to fears about the advantages of having a strong family, and one with social standing at that? Was it just for a false rush of self-esteem? Or was it the fact that her friend had the adoration of her father, not unlike Jackie (who was worshiped by her father, Black Jack Bouvier), and Carolyn felt further pushed out of the inner circle?

IT WAS CLEAR THAT when Jackie had an opinion about John's paramours, she wouldn't hesitate to take a stand—the same could be said for her daughter, John's sister, Caroline. Early that autumn, when Jackie and Caroline found out that John was planning on bringing Daryl to Block Island for Ted Kennedy Jr.'s October wedding, the women canceled at the last minute. For Jackie—a stickler for manners and decorum—to have made such a sudden move, and one in which she was letting down the Kennedy side of the family, was about as strong a message as John could get. Video footage of John and Daryl's entrance to the wedding is a study in frustration, with John trudging so quickly past the photographers camped outside St. Andrew Roman Catholic Church that Daryl had to trot to keep up the pace.

William D. Cohan, John's friend from Andover and author of *Four Friends*, a memoir about his Andover classmates who died young, wrote that John's friend Charlie King had lunch with John in early November. Charlie told Cohan that John had looked dismayed. Charlie asked what was going on and John lamented, "I got into a fight with Daryl, and I'm living in the basement of a friend's house, and my mother doesn't really like Daryl all that much. It's the thirtieth anniversary of my father's death so I'm not really watching television. It's a difficult time. This Daryl thing has me thrown for a loop."

Richard Wiese—who had known Carolyn previously, separate from John—noted that John always asked about Carolyn when they got together. He observed: "Carolyn had a great sense of humor, while a lot of other women often tried to portray a 'fantasy' persona. She was challenging enough for him; a lot of women would've caved in a lot faster. John actually liked it when you teased him, he liked someone busting his chops. She could call him on things no one else would."

John had also been spotted with Julie Baker again, pictured in the *Evening Standard*, between dates with Daryl and Carolyn.

And yet Carolyn was still in the mix with John that fall, too. They were seen together watching the twenty-fourth running of the NYC Marathon on Sunday, November 14. Within days, a picture of the two of them sitting on the curb, surrounded by other spectators, was splashed all over the country. Carolyn was leaning her elbow on her knee, looking a little disinterested, while John seemed to be concentrating on the race. "So," went the caption in *Newsday*, "tall, blond, and skinny Daryl Hannah was replaced by slightly shorter, slightly less blond and certainly more voluptuous Lady X. At least, for the New York City Marathon."

The implication in this jeer that the relationship wasn't going to last was on the mark. Soon enough, John disappeared, again.

After Thanksgiving, Carolyn received a letter from her mother, sent to her office. Perhaps Ann mailed it there because the press had figured out where Carolyn lived on Second Avenue and had begun to chase her down. Ann included an article all about how John flew to Los Angeles to attend the December 1 premiere of Daryl's latest film and was staying at Daryl's Santa Monica house. In the article, when asked if she had been snubbed by Jackie, Daryl refuted with a simple "No." Finally, in parentheses: "(There were recent stories that JFK Jr.'s new romance was Carolyne Bessette, who works for Calvin Klein.)" To be relegated to a parenthetical would not have been flattering or reassuring, nor having an erroneous "e" added to the end of your first name, even if it was printed in bold.

Ann's note said, "Carolyn, please move on with your life." She also drew a frowning face, said a colleague.

When John got back from California, he called Carolyn, but she had gone dark. She'd instructed Jen Dermer, "Tell him I'm not here." He kept calling, with no success.

Other changes were afoot in Carolyn's life, and maybe a fresh start—without John—was part of the inspiration. She decided it was time to move out of her East Village apartment and offered to sublet it to her colleague Heather.

"I was living with a roommate who was driving me out of my mind," Heather recalled. "She was an actress and too dramatic for me." When Carolyn heard her complaining about the situation, she offered her place, as she was moving to Greenwich Village. "It's 166 Second Avenue," Carolyn told her. "Pretend you're me to the doorman. I'm done."

Heather did not know why Carolyn singled her out, but she was grateful. The move to Carolyn's apartment changed her life. Suddenly, she had her own place and a job where she felt welcomed, even if all she was doing for the moment was answering phones and typing memos.

Carolyn also tried to help Heather professionally. She knew that Heather was capable of much more than being a receptionist on the eleventh floor outside of Calvin's office. Carolyn wanted Heather to come to the fifth floor with her, Michelle, Jen, and Rachel. "There is a girl downstairs crying every day," Carolyn said. "You're going to take her place." Carolyn was aware that a fair amount of girls who had jobs in fashion PR came from a certain background: "The PR floor is the superstar floor; you have to be able to handle it," Carolyn told Heather. "There's a lot of girls there from Ivies and Smith, Wellesley. We are a little scrappier, and we can do the job. We can look like those girls but we are not those girls." In the end, Heather didn't get the promotion, but Carolyn had made her feel like a valuable colleague.

Carolyn found a ground-floor apartment in 112 Waverly Place, a beautiful building just off Washington Square Park. The lively tumult of the park—bustling with drug dealers, busking musicians, and chess players slapping their timers, day and night—was a short walk from her new place, but not close enough to be overwhelming.

Narciso Rodriguez lived in the building, as did Johnny Depp, who had a ground-floor, back-garden apartment, and Kate Moss could often be seen traipsing through the garden when she came to visit her boyfriend. Sara Ruffin, creative director of *Domino* magazine, lived on the second floor with her boyfriend, the actor and director Fisher Stevens, who, as it happens, had gone to college with John.

In addition to getting to know her new neighbors, Carolyn continued to hang out with the Calvin Klein designers Zack, Narciso, and Gordon, and spent even more time with Kelly Klein. Michelle Kessler had gotten a new job at Prada, so she migrated out of the CK offices that fall.

Carolyn also had her sister Lauren nearby; she was back at Morgan Stanley's New York City headquarters after earning an MBA from Wharton. A mutual friend remembers a dinner at Omen, a Japanese restaurant on Thompson Street in SoHo, that was a mecca for artists, designers, and gallerists. She found Carolyn and Lauren to be excellent companions, and always surprising. "Brilliant Lauren, of course, ordered in Japanese, so I had no idea what I'd be eating," the friend recalled. "It ended up being a delicious meal. We began one of those games, 'If you had to lose all but one of your five senses, which would you keep?' I, of course, said my sight, figuring at least Carolyn would agree with me since we both worked in a field where the visual is predominant. But both Carolyn and Lauren said, 'No, no, I could not live without a sense of taste!' They were both foodies. I was surprised."

Less enjoyable was the incessant ring of Carolyn's phones, both at home and at the office. "John called all the time, but Carolyn was resolute. What we came up with," says Carolyn's friend, "was an outgoing message on her answering machine for an imaginary boyfriend." Anyone who called would get a recording of Carolyn saying, "Hey, hon, I'll be back by seven o'clock, can't wait to see you!" The idea was that John would hear it and assume she'd moved on. John did hear it—and he called even more. "Eventually," says the friend, "Carolyn changed her number."

Yet some of her friends thought it was an audacious move—a numerical "hard to get"—and that Carolyn still carried hope that she and John would somehow work out in the end. Maybe Carolyn understood that when she made things official with John, there would be no turning back, and so she stalled. Or perhaps she simply didn't want to get burned again.

Carolyn's office hours were long and hard—she would often forget to eat lunch, though when she did remember, her favorite foods were mashed potatoes and scooped-out bagels loaded with tomatoes. But after work, she went out with her cadre of friends, sometimes grabbing dim sum at Jing Fong on Elizabeth Street, sometimes catching a movie. They often hit the dance clubs and were out until 2:00 a.m. Homebody nights in, watching a movie and going to bed early, were not her thing; Carolyn always wanted to be with other people.

One especially memorable evening was December 7, 1993, when she and a crew from CK attended the Metropolitan Museum of Art's Costume Institute Benefit. The December event was more relaxed than its current incarnation as the Met Gala on the first Monday in May. The party was honoring the late legendary *Vogue* editor and Costume Institute special consultant Diana Vreeland, with the exhibition "Diana Vreeland: Immoderate Style." It was the perfect chance for Carolyn and her colleagues, including Matt Nye, Wayne Scot Lukas, and Jessica Weinstein, to show Calvin's wares and their own impeccable style, all in Vreeland's signature red and black. Carolyn wore a dress from Calvin's 1993 spring collection, looking just as enticing as supermodel Christy Turlington, who had worn it on the runway. The dress was long, silky, black, sleeveless, and simultaneously sexy and elegant.

Bergin wrote that it was during this stretch that he and Carolyn renewed their romance. His modeling career had hit its peak when he was chosen to be the new Calvin Klein underwear model. Carolyn called him after the shoot, telling him he did a great job.

Bergin claimed that when his agents told him he would be going to Milan in January to model in the winter shows there, Carolyn invited him to her family home in Greenwich for Christmas Eve dinner. He had met Ann a couple of times, and now he met Richard, Lauren, and Lisa.

"They made me feel as if I was part of it, and I got the impression that they were rooting for us as a couple," Michael wrote. Whatever they thought of him, Ann made sure Michael slept in the guest room.

IN JANUARY 1994, BOTH Jackie and Anthony Radziwill were diagnosed with cancer. Anthony, having found a small bump on his abdomen, was first told it was a hematoma. When the surgeons removed it, however, they realized it was a fibrosarcoma. Jackie had been on holiday, sailing in the Caribbean with Maurice Tempelsman, her companion since the mid-eighties, when she became ill, coughing, with swollen glands and abdominal pain. The doctors biopsied her lymph nodes and discovered she had non-Hodgkin's lymphoma.

John was no stranger to losing loved ones, but these two, his mother and first cousin, were his helm and ballast. He spent much of his time walking in Central Park with Jackie, and, as Rob Littell later wrote, "The only thing John enjoyed during those sad months was his mother's company. Among the most important things she told him then was not to be afraid of his name. This had a profound effect on John."

Jackie had remained optimistic that she would recover. Gillon wrote in his biography of John, *America's Reluctant Prince*, that she told John not to worry, saying of her disease, "This is the good kind. We can beat this."

That winter was the first time John spoke about Carolyn to John Perry Barlow, a friend whom he had met when Jackie sent him, aged seventeen, to Barlow's Wyoming ranch, Bar Cross, in the summer of 1978, after he had poured wallpaper paste down the mail chute at 1040 Fifth Avenue. She had hoped this would teach her son some life skills, self-sufficiency, and maturity. Barlow, who had also been a lyricist for the Grateful Dead, was thirty-one, but still, he was more a friend than a father figure.

John told Barlow that he was not with Carolyn because of Daryl, but that "he couldn't get his mind off of her" and that she was "having a heavy effect on him." Kennedy biographer Andersen wrote that when Barlow asked who Carolyn was, John replied, "Well, she's not really anybody. She's some functionary of Calvin Klein's. She's an ordinary person."

Throughout his life, he had always enjoyed being in the world, in the city, without fanfare. Maybe Carolyn promised a life without the drama, or at least life on a smaller stage. As a sort of king-in-waiting, John had long been expected to marry within an imperial court, and Daryl, being a movie star with a billionaire stepfather, fit the formula much more than an "ordinary person" who spent much of her childhood in White Plains.

IT WAS DURING THIS period that John realized he didn't want to be a lawyer after all. He quit his job at the DA's office in July 1993 and formed a business partnership, Random Ventures, with his friend Michael Berman, a publicist he'd met nine years earlier when they were both at the New York

City Office of Business Development. Gillon wrote that one of Random Ventures' first schemes was to mass-produce affordable kayak kits that people could assemble themselves. The kayak kits never took float, but their next idea did: They began hatching a plan for a magazine that would cover the cross-section of politics and popular culture.

By 1994, John and Michael were at serious work on a business plan, finding an editorial voice and, of course, raising money. John took an office in Berman's public relations company, PR/NY, and the two of them raised $3 million to seed the venture. It was a start, but not enough. Enter Hachette Filipacchi, the French publisher of *Elle* and *Paris Match*, which kicked in $20 million. RoseMarie Terenzio, John's assistant at *George* from its inception in February 1994 until his death, eventually earning the title chief of staff, wrote in her memoir, *Fairy Tale Interrupted*, that "it was as if he and his slightly demented rescue dog, Sam, worked at PR/NY, only none of the staff, except for Michael, knew what he was doing there." Eventually, Michael dissolved PR/NY to concentrate full-time with John on launching the magazine they christened *George*, after founding father George Washington.

President John F. Kennedy had wanted to be a journalist, but after the death of his older brother, Joe Jr., in WWII, he assumed the mantle of the Kennedy family's political ambitions. Early in his career, he wrote the Pulitzer Prize–winning *Profiles in Courage*, a book that was published at a time in America's political history when it was possible to discuss world events without everything filtered through an exclusively partisan lens. The magazine *George* was the print version of much of John Jr.'s theories, hopes, and conflicts about politics, as well as his ambivalence about celebrity culture and his residence within it. *George* may also have sought to extend some of the themes of positivity and patriotism without partisan rancor.

Beyond building *George* from the ground up, John also spent a lot of the next month with his mother, walking around the Central Park Reservoir (which was later named after her) and talking over her life, and their lives together. Yet when Jackie collapsed and was hospitalized on May 15, John was not there, having been summoned to Los Angeles by Daryl, who wanted him to bring the ashes of her recently deceased dog from New York and then attend the pet's funeral. When he arrived, Daryl became upset because John had placed the ashes in a simple box rather than something more elaborate.

"He was livid," said Gillon, who often gave John editorial advice for

George. "But John resisted making any waves, and once he'd done his Daryl dog duty, he simply rushed back to be with his mother."

Four days later, on May 19, Jackie died, with John and Caroline at her bedside. John somehow found the strength to walk out to the press gathered under the canopy of his mother's building and announce her death. He told them his mother had died "surrounded by her friends and her family and her books and the people and the things that she loved. She did it her own way and on her own terms, and we all feel lucky for that, and now she's in God's hands. Thank you, and I hope now we can have these next couple of days in relative peace."

The funeral was held at the Church of St. Ignatius Loyola on Park Avenue at East 84th Street on May 23. Even before then, New York City had gone into mourning. Over eight hundred people had camped out on Fifth Avenue and outside Jackie's apartment. John had peered at the crowd in quiet amazement.

John's childhood friend Billy Noonan wrote that as John waved at the crowd from Jackie's fifteenth-floor balcony, he said, "Can you believe this? They've been here for days."

The bond tying John and Daryl had been thinned to almost nothing, and now the threads had frayed to the last hold. According to a guest, "Daryl made small talk at Jackie's funeral about how she met Jackson Browne."

And "even after [Jackie] died," Gillon later told *InStyle* magazine, "Daryl had another dog that was sick and John was up in Martha's Vineyard or Hyannis Port, and Daryl's on the phone talking about her dog all the time and John is there in the kitchen with Sasha Chermayeff, and he says, 'Can you believe this. I just lost my mom and all she wants to talk about is her sick dog.'"

Jackie's death created an enormous chasm in John's life—physically, mentally, emotionally, and spiritually. She had been his world, supportive and loving at every turn, and very sure and forceful in her opinions of what was right and wrong for him. Marta Sgubin, John's childhood nanny (who, like Carolyn's grandfather, was also an immigrant from Italy), said that "when he suffered the most is after Madam died. It was a big, big void in his life." Over the next weeks, it simply felt right to have Carolyn there. She was supportive of John and his magazine, and full of love for him but willing to turn a cold shoulder if he didn't do what was right for himself, for her, and for their relationship. The echoes were strong.

And soon this "ordinary person," as he described her to John Perry Barlow, would become someone extraordinary for John.

But that he had never introduced Carolyn to his mother was an omission John now knew was a mistake. Billy Way told Cohan that "John regretted that he never introduced her to his mother. Carolyn, like Jackie, was Catholic and the product of divorced parents. They both had a smart, minimalist look and sexiness. Carolyn wasn't exactly the girl next door, but she also wasn't a spoiled, preening film star or a fashion model. She seemed very New York, the quintessential Downtown Girl."

John told Way, "I can't believe I let her go the first time around." He wasn't going to make that mistake again.

CHAPTER EIGHT

WORKING GIRL

Summer 1994–Fall 1994

Despite Carolyn's steadfastness after John's mother's death, their relationship was still touch and go. He was officially with Daryl when Jackie's life was coming to a close, but his commitment seemed fragile. With the stress and sadness over the loss of his mother, he was at loose ends.

"John was mixing and matching all these women at the same time," Billy Way said. "I suspect it had something to do with the anxiety he felt over his mother's suffering."

And while Carolyn was no doubt happy to be a sounding board—a particular talent of hers—she would never be a doormat. Carolyn made this very clear. Once, John was an hour late for a dinner date; he arrived in his usual blithe spirits, explaining he had decided to pop by the gym. Carolyn's answer to this was to throw her glass of wine in his face and leave. Certainly a wake-up call.

In early summer, Calvin Klein hosted a party at Odeon where Carolyn and John's relationship status perhaps went from "on the down-low" to "on the up-and-up." Carolyn was in professional mode at the event when John approached the entrance. The Odeon maître d' Bruce Hanks said, "I told John, 'Sorry, there's a private party,' and John, always polite, says, 'No problem,' and begins to leave. Suddenly Carolyn came running toward me saying,

'Who was that?' I told her it was JFK Jr. and she said, 'Send him back in.' So I did, and then Carolyn and John sat together in deep discussion all night. They were an item ever since."

Hanks mistakenly thought that was the moment they first met, though it may have been the moment they became an official couple. Why John didn't say, "I'm here to see Carolyn, who works with Calvin," or why Carolyn feigned unfamiliarity can only be guessed at. Maybe they were still guessing themselves.

The fact was, Carolyn needed stability. She knew this about herself. "She needed to know that she was a priority for John," said MJ Bettenhausen.

As the summer went on, John began to give Carolyn fewer reasons to doubt him. The two became nearly inseparable, traveling together, spotted at restaurants, and messing about in boats in Martha's Vineyard. Yet John still played it lightly when they were with others.

It was their mid-August trip to Martha's Vineyard where the thong seen around the world made its debut. A series of photos announced that Carolyn was now John's bona fide steady. She stands like a figurehead on the bow of a small motorboat, John a few feet behind and below her at the wheel as they tool through Menemsha Basin, where Jackie had kept her boats since buying Red Gate Farm in 1979. They would not have expected a telephoto lens trained on Carolyn's derriere when passing the spare, rustic harbor that, in local parlance, was "up island"—the most remote, sparsely populated part of the Vineyard, known for its high elevation and dramatic oceanside cliffs. Then again, emblazoned on the side of the boat is MS 109 PT to honor his father's command of the PT-109 cruiser in WWII. *A Current Affair*, a prime-time TV version of supermarket tabloids, found the thong newsworthy enough for an entire feature.

That same summer, they joined Kelly and Calvin Klein in East Hampton, basking in the seclusion of their ten-thousand-plus-square-foot house on Georgica Pond. In the nineties the Hamptons were still half potato fields spread among the mansions, and the couple kept under the radar. At the time, the Kleins were renovating the house but had a spectacular poolside lounge area that Kelly had designed in the late eighties. Her 1992 photography book, *Pools*, came about when she was researching designs to build it, but couldn't find any architectural books on the subject. Now there was interior work to be

done, and Carolyn was there to offer advice and tend to Kelly in general, as she
and Calvin were having an ebb in their marital flow. John had known Calvin
and Kelly for a few years, and Kelly and Carolyn had grown close.

For all the private, heady romance, they kept their cards close to their
chests in public. Carolyn could not have been pleased to have her picture in a
bikini on public view—she wanted to keep a low profile for as long as possible.
John had told Carolyn when he went back to Daryl the last time, as he had told
his girlfriend of five years whom he met at Brown, Christina Haag, when they
took breaks, that he was faithful to his girlfriends, once official. Once he was
sure, he was in—Carolyn and John spent that summer becoming sure.

BY THE TIME LABOR Day arrived, John was ready: After two years on and
off (mostly off except the last three months), he would now introduce Carolyn to his extended family. They went together to the Kennedy compound
in Hyannis Port. Dinner was at his aunt Ethel Kennedy's house, where selec-
tive rules of decorum were observed—John advised Carolyn to call Ethel
"Mrs. Kennedy."

She felt somewhat insecure about meeting them, especially as John had
never introduced her to Jackie. Her friend MJ Bettenhausen said she was
anxious and tried to dress and act as she thought a Kennedy should, or at
least a guest of the Kennedys should.

Carolyn and John arrived in Hyannis Port on September 3 and had a
day full of activity—swimming, walking, and kayaking—before Carolyn
even laid eyes on Aunt Ethel, as told by J. Randy Taraborrelli. The compound comprised three Kennedy residences across six acres on Nantucket
Sound, with the Shriver house a short walk away. Joe Kennedy Sr. bought
the largest of the three in 1929, called the Big House, which Uncle Ted had
taken over in 1982. JFK bought a nearby house on Irving Avenue in 1956,
close to his father's place. It served as headquarters for his 1950 presidential
campaign and was thereafter called the President's House, which siblings
John and Caroline now jointly owned. Initially, Ted owned the RFK house,
which presided on a great lawn between the President's House and the Big
House, but he sold it to Bobby and Ethel in 1961. The RFKs had access
to the beach, and, much to John's chagrin, he had to cross Ethel's yard to
go for a swim or kayak. But he was respectful to his aunt, and he brought

Carolyn on time to find many cousins and their spouses already present and dressed for dinner. It was not a shorts-and-flip-flops affair but suits-and-cocktail-attire. Carolyn, for the most part, had nailed the dress code: She wore a white silk skirt and a mauve blouse, with a new, bubblegum-pink scarf wrapped around her neck. The conversation was garrulous and drinks were plenty as they awaited the arrival of their hostess.

Ethel made an entrance in white linen pants, a blue blouse, and a string of pearls. Everyone stood up, and Carolyn scrambled to rise as well, just a second behind, quickly catching on to the ritual. After Ethel took her seat, they lowered themselves back in their seats. Ethel regaled them with a story of the chef botching a soufflé for dessert, leaving him so distressed that they shared a few glasses of Grand Marnier to ease his mind.

"He had to carry me out of the kitchen." Ethel laughed.

The next morning, Carolyn woke to find John absent from their room. He had gone off sailing with his cousins. In Ethel's kitchen, Carolyn saw a chalk-board with two breakfast shift sign-ups—one at 6:30 a.m. and one at 7:30 a.m. "Ethel then told Carolyn that she was supposed to sign up for one of the two shifts the night before," Ethel's assistant Leah Mason recounted to Taraborrelli. "The poor dear had missed both shifts. Carolyn then looked at the sign-up sheet and saw John's name on the 7:30 roster; he'd signed up but neglected to do so for her. You could see that she was sort of crushed. I told her he probably figured she would sleep in. It was always better to not be on the list at all than to be on it and then not show up at the reserved time. 'He sort of loses his mind when he's here, doesn't he?' she asked me. I said yes, that was true."

The big event of the holiday weekend was Ted's clambake. There were two tents and, on an enormous mound of sand, a rowboat filled with sea-weed and covered with a tarp. Vast amounts of food would come up from the baking pit—lobsters, soft-shell clams, potatoes, and corn slathered in butter—and be placed on the rowboat, which would serve as the buffet.

At the end of the weekend, Carolyn felt that she had just bungled an audition—and wasn't sure she'd be getting a callback. Photographer Stewart Price told Taraborrelli that when he suggested the next visit would be better, Carolyn responded, "Oh, there won't be a next time." She didn't usually have a hard time winning people over, but Ethel was a hard nut to crack. Dinner conversation had been challenging—talk of politics, world events—and even though Carolyn was able to keep up, she felt like she was somehow lacking.

John, on the other hand, with his ineffable ability to wrest the positive from an ambiguous situation and happily move on, considered the weekend an unmitigated success. Carolyn had handled herself—at least outwardly—with poise and good humor. But that isn't to say that she carried no insecurities into the evening, or into the whole weekend, for that matter. A close friend mentioned that when Carolyn felt insecure or unsure of herself in situations where she felt judged, she would put up a bit of a facade. Perhaps she did so that weekend, thus giving Ethel reason to doubt her authenticity.

Maybe it was a matter of being a girl among boys. Arnold Schwarzenegger, once a newcomer, could tumble along with the Kennedy nephews, cousins, brothers, and uncles—playing flag football, going fishing, and "dragging," in which a gang of them would jump into the ocean, grab a rope tied to a swiftly moving sailboat, and hold on for dear life—as one of the guys. Carolyn had her humor and composure, and her bubblegum-pink scarf.

THAT FALL, CAROLYN AND John continued spending most of their free time together. On weekends, he brought her to Central Park for touch football games with friends like Rob Littell and Richard Wiese. Wiese, who had known Carolyn from downtown hangouts like Au Bar and MK before she and John became official, recalled that one of the things that stood out about Carolyn was her ability to treat John like any other man on the street.

"Carolyn showed up and chirped right back at all those guys bantering while they knocked one another around, including John," Wiese said. "Nothing got by her, and she enjoyed the repartee as much as anyone. She would stay on the sidelines with John's German shepherd Sam, and later their high-strung Canaan dog, Friday, calling plays, and teasing everyone mercilessly, laughing. John loved it."

But behind closed doors, friends knew that Carolyn and John were developing a real kind of intimacy, beyond the playful banter and antics with friends and family. They would spend long, loving evenings confiding profound moments from their lives, and, especially, the subsequent emotional challenges. Carolyn still felt ambivalent about her parents' divorce; like John, she had been raised Roman Catholic. Though she was sporadically in touch with her father, she also felt left behind. Stewart Price once noted that Carolyn had confessed to him, "I have these weird daddy issues."

For his part, John told her about having ADD and dyslexia, and how Jackie had moved him from Saint David's to Collegiate, both all-boys private schools in Manhattan. Overcoming these obstacles required learning specific tools and behaviors. (These were helpful, though not so much they could overcome the ordeal of taking the bar exam sitting in the glass-walled Javits Center while in the crosshairs of photographers just outside.) Jackie felt that Collegiate was better equipped to teach her son how to manage his learning challenges as well as some emotional ones. According to Christopher Andersen, there were kids who had taunted him, saying, "Your father's dead, your father's dead!" Suffice to say, John was traumatized by the assassination of his father, whom he could scarcely remember, but was grateful to his mother for her focus on her two children while coping with her own PTSD. He regretted the moments he felt he had let her down, such as failing the bar—his shame exacerbated by the attendant "The Hunk Flunks" headlines.

Rob Littell recalled how John kept up a good face for the press but was privately devastated. He took a bottle of Macallan up to a motel in Lake George, New York, and "slowly drank a bottle of Scotch over the course of the weekend, alone and listening to self-help tapes."

John desperately wanted to live up to Jackie's hopes—and everyone's expectations, including the extended Kennedy family's as well as the public's. Gillon documented that Jackie had written him a note just before her death, saying, "I understand the pressure you'll forever have to endure as a Kennedy, even though we brought you into this world as an innocent. You, especially, have a place in history." Historian Doug Wead said that Jackie "knew in her heart that, someday, the stars are going to line up, and he's going to be president."

John's predicament as inheritor of the myth of Camelot tugged at Carolyn's heartstrings. They shared a similar language—that of people who had grown up without fathers, be it from an emotionally absent one, or, in the worst case, a physical loss such as John faced. This could have been one of the many forces that pulled them toward each other—additionally, they had both been raised by loving, devoted mothers.

Carolyn was emotionally strong and caring enough to feel to John like a balm in the aftermath of losing his mother. Like Jackie, she could guide him in nearly every facet of his life. While still holding down a demanding position at Calvin Klein, Carolyn consulted with John on the creation of

George magazine. This not only required business acumen and developing an editorial voice, but also the never-ending task of filtering those who wanted proximity to John for their own gain from those who had his best interests at heart. Carolyn's good instincts about people were indispensable to John. She was looking after him, a real partner in more ways than one.

People changed their behavior when John was around. Some would suddenly jockey for position, or simply lose their cool and turn into a sort of panting sycophant. Carolyn went from surprise to annoyance to indignation at how people would throw themselves at John every time they walked into a room. The problem wasn't that people were paying attention to him, it was that they demanded attention *from* him. Carolyn wasn't just annoyed; it embarrassed her on behalf of the very people behaving so cravenly. She had never engaged in such self-demeaning behavior, and she was shocked and not a little concerned at the lengths people would go just to get his attention.

Jack Merrill, a friend of John's dating back to 1987, noted that "people lost IQ points the minute he walked into a room. They spoke louder, gestured wildly, and stared, of course." This was not a normal life.

Yet Carolyn was not a normal girl. At this juncture—before she, too, became a figure upon whom people projected all kinds of hopes and dreams, not to mention disappointment and anger—she had every reason to believe she could handle these extraordinary circumstances.

Merrill remembered, "Once, we went to a birthday party in a huge SoHo loft, and as we stepped off the elevator right into this huge space, the room got darker the deeper it went, which made it feel like we were walking into klieg lights. As we moved into the space and could actually see people, the crowd looked super sophisticated, but still a ripple went through the room, and it was like the floor tilted up, and everyone started sliding toward us. 'Uh-oh . . .' Carolyn said. 'Here it comes: the freak show.' You could see Carolyn visibly deflate. 'Oh no,' she said. 'Even these people are freaks.' *Freaks* was her term for those who lost themselves in the face of celebrity of any kind. It unnerved her. 'Let's go,' she said. 'Nothing interesting here.'"

That September, when John gave a speech on behalf of his uncle Ted Kennedy at the Codman Square Health Center in Boston, the clinic's capital campaign director, Arlene Fortunato, became cognizant of John's predicament.

"I felt a little ashamed," said Fortunato. "Nobody seemed to care about who he really is. He was like a prop, and it seems like such an awful life for him."

All the people hovering around John who wanted something, who sought the proximity to his celebrity and family legend, gave John an understanding of how Carolyn was different. She was in the relationship for *him*.

Some variation of "she was seeking neither power nor fame" has been echoed by all of Carolyn's friends and colleagues. Intentionally or not, she had passed a trial by fire. Not once since she and John first met in 1992 had she gone to the press or spoken about him with anyone but the closest confidantes. She was not vying to be "seen out" with him. In fact, when he began calling her after the scene at El Teddy's with the letter, he wasn't sure that Carolyn would go out with him again at all for some time. When she finally agreed, she did not change who she was.

And she wasn't just being paranoid. Despite a whole summer spent falling in love, there were still things that gave Carolyn pause, like John's habit of taking off at a moment's notice.

"Everything would be going along swimmingly," said one of Carolyn's colleagues from Calvin Klein. "And then suddenly, [John] would disappear. It was very hard for her."

John had been a world traveler his entire life, drawn to high-octane, physically thrilling adventures. He could be off heli-skiing, scuba diving, or climbing a mountain at a day's or even a moment's notice. "Carolyn had to accept John going off the grid often," the colleague said.

Even John's close friends sometimes wondered about his need for daring physical feats. "It's a thrill-seeking thing these guys need just to be able to survive," Sasha Chermayeff told William D. Cohan. "There's no way I can explain to you why a man needed to go and be, like, dropped off alone in the Arctic to kayak."

Though John and Carolyn had traveled together—and he had brought her to Hyannis Port to meet Ethel and the clan—he did not bring her to all of the weddings he attended that summer of 1994, including that of his first cousin and best friend, Anthony Radziwill, to Carole DiFalco in East Hampton. *People* magazine reported: "Stag was also Kennedy's preference last fall [*sic*] at three weddings—of his friend and *George* business partner, marketing executive Michael Berman, in Manhattan; of his cousin Tony Radziwill, a television producer for ABC, in Manhattan [*sic*]; and of his Washington attorney pal Daniel Melrod on Martha's Vineyard."

Two out of three claims were correct. Carolyn went with John to

Michael Berman's wedding, where she was seen looking merry next to their close friend Jack Merrill. The *Daily News* reported that "the race for JFK Jr.'s attention is officially on and Caroline Bissell [*sic*] seems to have opened up a slight lead over Julie Baker. John-John escorted Caroline [*sic*] to the big wedding reception of his buddy and magazine partner—Michael Berman—at the Boathouse Friday night."

The next day they went to the Manhattan Animal Care Center in East Harlem to look at dogs. The sole human occupant of the large kennel area, filled with dogs in cages, was Libra Max, daughter of artist Peter Max, who was also looking for a dog to adopt. She turned to see John dressed for a day in the park, while Carolyn was clearly in her dress from the evening before.

"The shelter was completely empty of potential adopters, which was sad," Max recalled. "There were long rows of dogs behind bars vying for attention or crying. Carolyn and John walked slowly by each dog, stopping and giving each one a little acknowledgment, and I was struck by that—their compassion." They didn't adopt that day, but wanted to give a dog in need a home.

Of the two weddings Carolyn was not invited to, the lack of invitation to Anthony and Carole's wedding may have stung the most. Carolyn knew how close John was with Anthony, who was one year older than him. They had been through a lot together. Anthony was there when John saluted his father's coffin, and they had also shared glorious summers together—on Skorpios (John's stepfather Aristotle Onassis's Greek island), the Italian resort town of Ravello, and Martha's Vineyard—laughing and clowning with each other alongside their impeccable mothers, Jackie and her sister Lee. The cousins were each other's safe space. Was the lack of invitation an indication of John's lack of dedication to her?

Add to this that Carolyn was still haunted by the anonymous letter of two years prior—less by the letter itself than John's reaction to it, how he had taken it to heart. His first instinct was to make her answer for it. Their relationship was new, and John was trained to be wary of newcomers' intentions given the decades-long visibility of his family. The irony would be that John would come to rely on Carolyn running interference with just the sort of people as the one who wrote that letter.

This sense of unease in Carolyn quickened when a photograph was taken in October of John on the street with the ex-girlfriend whom he had dated off and on, though mostly off, from 1985 to 1993, Julie Baker. Appearing in the

Globe and the *National Enquirer*, Julie and John were giving each other a kiss. From the angle it's hard to tell if the kiss was on the lips or if it had been a platonic peck on the cheek. Carolyn kept her cool, but "seeing photos like this was unnerving," her friend MJ Bettenhausen said. Not only was she not one hundred percent sure where the relationship was going, the added caveat was that the press already had her on their radar. If the press knew she had been seen with John, then they would know if she stopped being seen with John, and a public breakup would not have been comfortable for a young woman who had been careful, said her colleague, to "have never been dumped."

It was becoming clear that dating John was going to impact Carolyn's life in bigger ways—both in terms of public optics and her private, everyday existence. Her beautiful, bohemian 112 Waverly Place address had been discovered by the paparazzi that summer, and their constant camping out in front made it impossible for Carolyn to continue living there. Even the *Boston Globe* chimed in, making sure to mention that she was a Boston University alumna before squawking on, "She recently had to move out of her New York apartment because the press had staked it out and so far, her new location has been kept a pretty good secret." This was the second move in as many years, and it wouldn't be her last.

Happily, Carolyn had a soft landing. She moved in with close friend and former Calvin Klein designer Gordon Henderson in a second-floor apartment he rented in a brownstone on the corner of West 11th and West 4th Streets in the heart of the West Village, owned by a motherly figure named Marlaine Selip who had a teenage daughter, Erin.

"She was a force the moment I met her," Erin, now Erin Lippmann, said. "There was a strong, big, bright light around her." Marlaine would invite everyone in the building to her first-floor apartment for Sunday dinners. "Our building was full of people who worked in fashion," Erin continued. "Carolyn was one of my favorites. She was an older sister, mentor, and friend. It was a turbulent time in my life; I was acting out, and she was very kind at a difficult time, when I was maybe not so open."

Regarding Erin, not only did Carolyn use her innate ability to read people and respond in ways that calmed and cheered them, but also she may have employed tools she had learned while earning her degree in education. It's not everyone who can focus on a troubled teen without making them back further away.

"I immediately warmed to Carolyn. I wasn't easy and she knew exactly how to talk to me . . . to break through those barriers," said Erin. "She was always kind to those she knew needed it. She gave me advice on what to wear and encouraged me to keep it simple: 'Put your wet hair in a bun, put on some lip gloss, and go!'"

Erin adored both John and Carolyn, and in watching them together, "I could see that she and John were madly in love."

"You know how you always hear about meeting a girl and knowing instantly that she's the one, and you think, nah . . . that kind of instant connection doesn't happen in real life," John said that summer to Gustavo Paredes, the house manager for what was now the Hyannis Port home that John shared with his sister, Caroline, but which everyone still called the President's House. "Well, that happened to me."

CAROLYN SURROUNDED HERSELF WITH close friends, but John had an outsized life full of friends from New York, Andover, and Brown, not to mention the enormous array of Kennedy cousins and associates, including Jackie's multitude of friends. It was such a large group that he instinctively compartmentalized; there was no other way to handle it. With some, such as Anthony Radziwill and Billy Noonan, whom he had known since boyhood, time together was marked by a carefree banter; with Sasha Chermayeff, he had fun but also serious emotional and psychological discussions; with Gary Ginsberg and Steve Gillon, both friends from Brown, he shared an affinity for political theory and discourse; and with Rob Littell and Dan Samson, he had an all-out, wildly infectious appetite for adventure.

A month or so after bringing her to meet the touch football crew in Central Park, John began to introduce Carolyn to more of his close friends, such as Brown friend and rugby teammate Kenan Siegel and his girlfriend Betsy Reisinger, Dan Samson, and finally, properly, to Sasha Chermayeff at a mellow home dinner, after having her "check Carolyn out" two-plus years earlier at Don't Bungle the Jungle II. All of them loved her immediately, and Littell was particularly taken not just with her beauty, but her entire persona. "It was obvious that she was as bright a star as John," he wrote. "And it wasn't just because of her fierce, compelling beauty. It was because she seemed to look right into your soul, and then wink."

Carolyn introduced John to Narciso, Gordon, Jules, and MJ Bettenhausen. Bettenhausen, it turned out, had known John for a few years from various events in the city. So she had a unique perspective when she first saw them together. "What was most noticeable about them was how much they laughed together. It was striking," she noted. "Carolyn had always been full of joie de vivre, but depending on the company, John could sometimes be more introverted. Carolyn brought out his joy."

"[Carolyn] and John made few public appearances," said Billy Way, "because any function they attended automatically assumed the proportions of a major event. When they did appear in public, John took it upon himself to protect her."

They joined a book club started by filmmaker Michael Mailer, a son of Norman Mailer, in part because they could evade the media in a private setting, but mostly because it was a bright, fun group of friends. When it was John's turn to host at his loft, he chose *Neuromancer*, a science fiction novel by William Gibson. Mutual friend Karen Duffy missed that meeting, but later heard that the dinner was an endless feast that "went on forever. And ever," she wrote in *Glamour*. Everyone was so exhausted by the time they finally finished eating that the book talk never happened. The friends joked later that John had probably never read the novel and came up with the hours-long dining experience to "weasel out of leading the discussion."

John brought Carolyn to the Odeon to meet Jack Merrill, who, in addition to being a fellow boxing fan, was a founder of the Naked Angels theater group. Merrill said, "John told me he met someone and he wanted me to meet her. She was late. When she finally showed up, she made me laugh, which made her laugh and made John mad, which made us laugh more. She was smart and fast and funny. A real New York City Girl. And we both found ourselves in the position of 'deflectors.'"

Carolyn and Jack immediately appreciated each other as people who were in John's life for authentic friendship, but also ones who would help John keep the would-be groupies at bay. But while for Jack this deflecting was a once-in-a-while gig, for Carolyn it became a full-time necessity because, as Jack put it, "John always had people coming at him, and it's hard to explain, but she and I knew when to pull in the wagons close, in a way that wasn't rude, and he could feel at least a little safer. I think most of his best friends knew instinctively how to do that."

Carolyn managed to stay centered amid the obsessional chaos in which she found herself thanks to her coterie of good friends and her dedication to her job at Calvin Klein.

"I remember Carolyn's work ethic," Merrill said. "She was 100 percent on top of things. She would wake up at 6:00 a.m. to do paperwork before heading to the office."

Carolyn, at this juncture, had worked at Calvin Klein for five years, starting as a salesgirl in a store in Boston, moving to New York to work as a bespoke salesperson for VIPs, and then onward and upward to public relations. Now, at age twenty-eight, she was a publicist and a producer at one of the most prominent fashion labels in the world. Her confidence in her abilities had grown along with her accomplishments. She was able to navigate the warp-speed-paced fashion industry that catered to frequently outlandish celebrity demands, and, perhaps most importantly, she understood her talent with fellow human beings. It was at this time that she confided to Reisinger exactly what it was. "I know this sounds odd," Carolyn told her, "but I can always feel what everyone is feeling. Before I talk to them, I can tell."

With such faith in her instincts about people, and with such savvy and success in her career and other relationships—it's no wonder that Carolyn thought she could handle dating John F. Kennedy Jr.

CHAPTER NINE

MEET THE FAMILY

Fall 1994–Fall 1995

By November, John deemed it time for Carolyn to meet his sister. Caroline Kennedy's thirty-seventh birthday was on November 27, two days after John's thirty-fourth birthday. The two of them were uniquely close, having been through unthinkable loss together. Caroline kept John steady and on course as best she could, and he, in turn, provided levity and a sense of merriment. Yet since Caroline had married Ed Schlossberg in July of 1986, things had changed.

"It was as if once Caroline married Ed, he built a wall around her," said a close friend. "Possibly, it was what she needed at the time, having been through so much in her young life. But it shut some of us out."

John was not shut out, but by most accounts, he was not a fan of Ed's. And Ed, according to Bobby Kennedy Jr., was not a fan of Carolyn's. Schlossberg had a Ph.D. from Columbia and a nebulous job description that involved architecture and design. In 1994, John and Ed got into a fight regarding a film about President Kennedy's contributions to the arts that Ed was trying to make for the John F. Kennedy Center for the Performing Arts in Washington, DC. "John, hearing of Ed's efforts thirdhand, was angry," Rob Littell wrote. "It was all he could talk about one racquetball session." He felt Ed should have consulted him first. John made a call to the Kennedy Center and the project was scratched. It might have been one of the first times John stood up to Ed in any way, and Ed may have suspected Carolyn's presence behind John's newfound backbone.

"We all have certain roles in our families that we are assigned from childhood," Carole Radziwill would later observe about this conflict. "And most families, despite how one grows and changes over time, are comfortable keeping everyone in their roles. When you go back to visit, you find yourself in those same roles, even if you've perhaps outgrown them. I think John, now an adult starting his own magazine, had changed. And Carolyn helped him realize that he had grown into someone wiser, more professional, and more nuanced as a person than what everyone in his family was used to."

Carole, fresh from her honeymoon with Anthony (to Australia and New Zealand), was unequivocally thrilled to see Carolyn at Caroline's Park Avenue apartment for her birthday party. "This is her official coming out," she wrote in *What Remains*. While Carole remained quiet and watchful among the crowd, Carolyn was decidedly not. "She walks into this guarded room radiant and stubbornly original," Carole wrote. "Impulsively affectionate." Caroline was less impulsive, and, after hugging John, "hesitates for a brief moment before greeting his date, *So nice to meet you*. Her friends smile politely and then shift their focus to John."

Carole and Carolyn, however, jumped right back into friendship, glad to finally get to know each other after their auspicious start two years earlier at Sea Song. They would likely have been friends during the two-year hiatus, but Carolyn held back. "I think John kept in touch with her," Carole said, "but Carolyn was very careful to keep a low profile and didn't want to get involved with his family during the time he was still dating Daryl. She was wise."

Yet now their friendship was off and running. The women, who both came from Italian middle-class families, had an easy camaraderie, and became fast confidantes. "Neither of us came from a tony private school background. We didn't go to Brearley or Chapin, nor an Ivy League university," Carole said. "We had also both, oddly, worked at Caldor's Department Store. We joked that while John and Anthony water-skied off Onassis's yacht *Christina O*, as it traversed the waters around his island, Skorpios, Carolyn and I were wearing our blue smocks at the jewelry counter."

And then there was the fact Carolyn was also just a very good, attentive friend. "She had such energy and was so authentic," Carole continued. "She was one of those people who adds energy to a room. Carolyn was a lot of fun, but she could also quickly go deep."

Anthony, after a successful surgery in February, had just weeks before the birthday soiree received the bad news that his cancer was back. In fact, they had just returned from surgery at the National Cancer Institute, a branch of the National Institutes of Health (NIH) in Washington, DC, after finding another lump in Anthony's leg on their honeymoon that August. Carole recalls the diagnosis: another fibrosarcoma, but now high-grade and metastatic. Yet Anthony was only thirty-five at the time, and remained optimistic, as the doctor said surgery was the best option and Anthony's last one had been successful, with clear margins. Carole later wrote, "No chemotherapy. This is all Anthony hears. I hear something slightly different: Chemo doesn't work. But I file that away."

Regarding Caroline, despite the commonly held belief that it was dislike at first sight, one friend maintains that Carolyn and Caroline got along right away: "Caroline saw how much John and Carolyn laughed together. She was happy for them both."

Carolyn and Caroline were seen lunching together quite a few times around town and one acquaintance who saw them observed, "The two women seemed to really enjoy each other, and the conversation flowed, peppered with laughter here and there."

WHEN THE HOLIDAYS CAME around, it seemed that Carolyn and John didn't spend them together. Two days before Christmas Eve, John was ticketed in Madison Square Park for walking his dog without a leash. On January 16, 1995, *People* magazine published an issue on an untethered John, headlined, "JFK JR. ON HIS OWN," going on in the subtitle to cite his breakup with Daryl Hannah and call him "a dreamboat adrift." *People* was a Kennedy-friendly magazine: They gave him accolades for founding Reaching Up, "a nonprofit organization whose goal is to better train and bring recognition to New York State hospital orderlies, home attendants and nursing aides," and for serving on the boards of both the Institute of Politics at the John F. Kennedy School of Government at Harvard University and the JFK Library Foundation. They acknowledged the "massive weight of expectation and interest," yet cast doubts on the wisdom of starting a political/cultural magazine.

The *People* article mentioned Carolyn in passing—but not without citing John's exes in the same sentence. "Yes, there are occasional spottings of lovey-dovey reunions with ex-girlfriend Julie Baker, a model, and with Hannah look-alike Carolyn Bessette, director of public relations for Calvin Klein. But on a typical night out recently, he showed up at the trendy Film Center Cafe with three women. 'They were all just friends,' says the owner."

But Carolyn's presence in John's life had developed much further than this glimpse suggested, and in the following months, she would become integral to the founding of what would be John's lifework: *George* magazine.

A couple of months into the year, everything solidified. Carolyn began to accompany John to official events, including the Naked Angels theater company's semiannual Valentine fundraiser, for which John was the co-chair. He arrived solo on his bike, but inside "rendezvoused with a cool blonde in a clingy black dress." By the end of the night "they had snuck off to the darkened bar where Bessette coquettishly climbed onto her suitor's lap."

They were snapped at a March dinner inside the National Arts Club. A neighbor of John's in Tribeca recalled, "I looked across the room to see John, who was impossible to miss," he said. "But equally striking was the blonde woman next to him. Not unusual for John to have a beautiful woman on his arm. I made some wise remark to my wife such as, 'Oh, here's John with another one. I wonder how long this will last.' My wife looked over at them and immediately said, 'Oh, no. This one is different. Trust me, she will stay.' I think it was about a remarkable grace in the way she held herself, and her interest in the people around her, not just John."

People began to know Carolyn when they saw her. She became one of the celestial, bold-faced entities who traipse around Manhattan unencumbered, free-range. For a while, Carolyn was able to go unnoticed, but that wouldn't last long.

Initially, the attention Carolyn received focused on her burgeoning relationship with John. But when the press dug a little further, they discovered that she had also been involved with Michael Bergin, whose naked torso was, at that very moment, looming over Times Square in a Calvin Klein underwear ad shot by Bruce Weber.

"Don't be so quick to envy Carolyn Bessette," wrote George Rush and Joanna Molloy in their eponymous *Daily News* column on March 2, 1995. "Yesterday we told you how the fetching Calvin Klein exec has had her hands full dating John Kennedy Jr. and hunky model/actor Michael Bergin. Her friends say she wasn't at all amused to see her love life splashed across the *Daily News*—particularly since she no longer goes out with Bergin."

"I sympathized with her," said Rush, looking back on that time, "even while being part of the plague that afflicted her. Our first meeting was at Elaine's. She was smiling, pleasant, seated next to Paul Wilmot. You could tell she wasn't offended by the coverage."

Rush and Molloy's item speculated, "She also suspects Bergin, who's up for a part as Jeanne Moreau's love object in the movie *La Proprietaire*, engineered the story to hype his career."

Despite the *People* piece and the occasional sighting or blip in a newspaper or magazine, these were the halcyon days before the paparazzi stalked Carolyn, when ubiquitous cell phone cameras and Twitter were an Orwellian nightmare still of the future. Thus, the spring and summer of 1995 was a time when the world allowed Carolyn and John their time alone, so necessary to help them find their footing with each other and in the world. It was as if they had their honeymoon before their wedding, instead of after.

Which is not to say there was no press. John was spotted April 7 backstage at the Calvin Klein fall 1995 show. A reporter from the *Sun Sentinel* wrote about John as though he were a rare white leopard spotted on safari: "If you blinked, you missed him. John Kennedy hid backstage at Calvin Klein until the lights dimmed, then took his seat out front. Just before the finale, the would-be magazine publisher (a poli-sci rag tentatively titled *George*) quickly returns to the paparazzi-free backstage area and to his latest squeeze, Carolyn Bessette, a Calvin Klein marketing executive."

The press wrote as if John were still a young child, and thus gave themselves carte blanche to assume a guardianship of sorts. Yet "the latest squeeze" was more than that. And the press began to figure it out. Carolyn's hideaway safehouse on the corner of West 11th and West 4th had been discovered. Erin Lippmann, née Selip, remembered that after Carolyn got together with John, "photographers would jump out at her once they figured out she had lived here. They would shout names at her, screaming out horrible things to get her to look upset. And she was a young girl."

That spring, Carolyn and John made two moves indicative of their commitment. First, they bought a black-and-white Canaan dog from breeder Donna Dodson, who owned Pleasant Hill Farms in Kingston, Illinois. David

Golden, a Canaan breeder in Virginia, explained that Dodson told him, "They clearly researched Canaans, because as John said, they were 'intelligent and independent.'" Golden said Dodson laughed when recalling that "Carolyn was the one that really wanted a dog. I had several phone calls with them, including one when Carolyn kept me on the phone forever, discussing the necessity of training *both* the dog and the people."

After getting to know the couple, Dodson selected a puppy named Friday for them out of a litter born in May. Dodson would ship "Pleasant Hill Friday" (his AKC registration) to them when he was nine weeks old. John and Carolyn were so taken with Friday that they commissioned Herb Ritts to do a photo shoot of the dog. One of the photos was used for a mock *George* magazine cover, which they framed and sent to Dodson.

It was around the time of Friday's arrival that Carolyn moved into John's Tribeca loft on North Moore Street. Situated between Varick and Hudson Streets, it was right next to a neighborhood bar called Walker's. The building held seventeen apartments and was a prewar co-op, but the entrance was a nondescript gray, with two steel steps leading to a small metal platform and double doors resembling something you might find at a high school gym. No awning. No doorman. No security. It had been an industrial space, and still looked like it—Carolyn and Carole jokingly called it "Home Depot" and "the Warehouse." Their loft on the top of nine floors was a bright, skylit open space of 2,700 square feet with polished hardwood floors and fourteen-foot-high ceilings. It was an open floor plan, which gave the apartment an expansive feeling of space.

Tribeca, still a relatively quiet and deserted neighborhood, also somewhat resembled a warehouse. Yet it was growing rapidly, with Robert De Niro positioning his film company, Tribeca Productions, in office space on the corner of Greenwich and Franklin Streets, just above Miramax Films, the company that was taking over the indie film industry and bringing it to the mainstream. The Tribeca Grill was quickly becoming a neighborhood fixture. Carolyn was happy for the anonymity Tribeca initially offered, but that didn't last nearly long enough. She told friends she missed the Callery pear trees that canopied the intersection of her former home on West 11th and West 4th Streets, one of the most charming spots of the city.

The attention only magnified. That May, Carolyn's presence outside Jackie Kennedy Onassis's apartment, after a memorial for the first lady, was a provocation to the press. Her attendance at the memorial, an extremely private affair, was a sign that she was more than an interloper. The chase was on.

ON THE FOURTH OF July weekend, John and Carolyn were in Martha's Vineyard. John asked Carolyn to come out fishing with him in the morning. Fishing was not her favorite thing—Carolyn liked to stay cuddled up in bed with her cat, Ruby. But she was game to get out on the water, something one had to get used to when spending time with John.

Once John's boat left the shallows, he turned to Carolyn and said, according to Terenzio, "Fishing is so much better with a partner." Then he put a platinum band of diamonds and sapphires on her finger. It was a replica of what Jackie called her swimming ring—pared down and elegant, perfect for swimming. It was also perfect for Carolyn and her understated elegance. John had decided that it was Carolyn or no one. She understood the pressure he was under, the predicament of all the scrutiny intermingled with tragedy. But she also knew she would have her own impossible situation once she married him. Carolyn told him, "I'll think about it."

Carolyn told very few people of John's proposal. She invited Carole Radziwill to North Moore Street and showed her the ring but asked her not to share the news. Carolyn was becoming more aware of the swirl of ambition and judgment that surrounded John and knew it would be a heavy burden. Rob Littell later wrote, "[Carolyn] resisted his proposal for an entire year."

"They loved each other, and it was a given that they would spend their lives together," said Carole. "But she was in no hurry to make an engagement announcement."

In *Fairy Tale Interrupted*, RoseMarie Terenzio quoted Carolyn as saying, "I've been a nervous wreck ever since I got off that boat. We had people up that weekend, and I had to pretend like nothing happened. I just don't want anyone to know yet."

"I could hear the jitters stemming from her excitement," Terenzio recalled, "and also from her nervousness over how people would react when they found out."

Carolyn's concern was warranted. The proposal stayed secret for all of two months. On Friday, September 1, the *New York Post*, citing an "anonymous friend," printed news of the engagement. A friend who also mentioned that Carolyn was taking her "sweet time" to think about it.

Adding insult to injury, it was one week before the official launch of *George*. Michael Berman was apoplectic. This would be one of many disagreements the partners would have over not just the magazine, but Carolyn.

Terenzio wrote that Michael shouted, "This is going to take thunder away from *George* . . . How did she let this get out?" He may have meant RoseMarie, as she was John's gatekeeper, but the implication that Carolyn had let it get out was impossible to escape.

"Who cares?" John replied, raising his voice as well. "This is my life. I'm going to do what I've always done—ignore it and move on."

The sting of Michael Berman's accusations was the suggestion that Carolyn would do anything to undermine the launch of *George*. It had been John's passion, and Carolyn had been supporting and working alongside him these many months despite having her own full-time job. As John developed the business, Carolyn advised him on everything from cover designs to layouts to editorial content. As her BU roommate Colleen Curtis wrote, Carolyn "was more involved in her husband's magazine than anyone really knew."

Carolyn got along especially well with *George*'s creative director, Matt Berman (no relation to Michael)—they were fellow creatives. One day, when they were still putting the first issue together, Carolyn was chatting and eating pizza in Matt's office when John walked in and asked her what she thought of the magazine. "[John] was trying to be cool," Berman wrote in his memoir, *JFK Jr., George, and Me*, "but I heard trepidation in his voice. Her mouth full of pizza, Carolyn assured him, 'John, it's exactly what it should be.' To this day, I'm awed at how emphatically the twenty-eight-year-old Carolyn was able to put things in perspective."

Carolyn and Curtis went to lunch before the launch of *George*, and she recalled that Carolyn was "bursting with enthusiasm for the project, trying to make me guess who was on the first cover. Her hint was that 'this person embodied pop culture at this moment.'" Curtis guessed incorrectly a dozen times, prompting an eye roll from Carolyn, who finally disclosed that Cindy Crawford dressed as first president George Washington would grace the inaugural cover.

Carole, who watched John and Carolyn bring the magazine to life, said that "she absolutely counseled him the entire way through. He relied on her professionalism and savvy. Carolyn went with him to business meetings, fundraising endeavors, everything."

While she still had her own career, Carolyn's wisdom of what was au courant was invaluable to the magazine. She had made understanding the worlds of fashion, business, and culture a priority. Someone once suggested they approach Galen Weston as an investor, but John was not sure who he was. Carolyn jumped in and gave him the rundown, *Women's Wear Daily* later reported. "With the speed and accuracy of a top presidential aide, she filled him in on the Canadian billionaire's holdings, his wife's elected office, and gave a thumbnail sketch of the couple's social world."

"She was fluent in the vernacular of style and design," *George* editor Richard Bradley (formerly Richard Blow) wrote in his book *American Son.* "Carolyn could spend hours with Matt Berman talking about the trendiest models and photographers—she seems to know them all. If you walked into Matt's office while she was there, you never wanted to leave; she was a more vivid creature than any of the models in *George's* many advertisements."

In fact, the advertisements were key to *George's* creation and sustainability. Everyone knew it, and getting ads for the magazine was the top priority to get the entire enterprise up and running. With Carolyn's insider knowledge and connections to all the fashion and design firms, she was an enormous asset—sometimes unknowingly.

For instance, one evening John and Carolyn were having drinks at Bubby's in Tribeca with Betsy Reisinger and Kenan Siegel. "All of a sudden, a couple who owned an international design label walk up to us and thank Carolyn profusely for having helped their teenage son recently," Reisinger said. "Carolyn responded quietly, 'Oh you're so welcome, he's a lovely boy.'" Reisinger added that Carolyn didn't elaborate, but when she went to the bathroom, John explained, "Apparently a few weeks ago, Carolyn was walking home by herself after dinner with a friend when she sees this boy, huddled over and crying, clearly in deep distress. So Carolyn being Carolyn, she made a beeline for him."

"And?!" asked Reisinger.

She recalled that John answered, "So, she kneels down to speak to him, getting on his level. She could tell he was pretty anguished. She stayed with him for a long time. And she made sure he was heading home. The next day I get a call at the office. Turns out it was the son of these designers, and after talking to Carolyn, the kid had been able to lighten the load he had been carrying. The next day, he got out of bed willing to give the world another go. I don't know exactly what she said to him, but apparently it was pretty uplifting." And then they took out a full-page ad in *George*. Said John, "Carolyn got us our single most important ad sale to date."

John was incredibly grateful. Securing ad sales was taking up a lot of his time. Earlier that year, he had agreed to speak at the Adcraft Club of Detroit, a two-thousand-plus association of advertisers, in the hope of engaging interest from the car companies in Detroit. The executives went berserk in the presence of the president's son—but leveraging his family name was something John had reservations about; he wanted to succeed on his own terms. But there was no way for John to separate from his legacy. That *was* his authentic self.

"It was bizarre. I can't think of anyone else in this country who could have drawn the range of interest that he did," one publisher told the *Los Angeles Times* after John spoke for the third time at the Adcraft Club. "Everyone wanted to see the guy. Everyone. I've seen GM and Ford keep the likes of Ted Turner and Si Newhouse waiting. But the people there were waiting on [Kennedy] like he was visiting royalty."

This objectification was exactly what John had spent his life looking to escape. It's no wonder that he dreamed of piloting his own plane, a dream he would put on hold at the behest of Jackie and Caroline, then Carolyn, for another two years. Apart from the thrill of careening through the blue sky unencumbered, it was a way to travel without having to spend time in commercial airports, where he felt trapped. If at first Carolyn felt his desire to fly was unwise, she soon understood why escape was enticing. John's friend John Perry Barlow told Cohan that she said, "He's all alone up there. He couldn't be happier."

Unfortunately, Carolyn, too, was beginning to understand the strain of being under a microscope with the press and the public. Everywhere she went, cameras were there, photographers coming ever closer. "She suddenly found herself surrounded by camera crews," said Paul Wilmot. "It was her first exposure to this sort of thing, and it became a real problem. When she met with fashion editors of various newspapers and magazines to discuss Calvin Klein, they only wanted to know about John. When he began appearing at the shows to support Carolyn, the press went crazy. There was this terrible frenzy. They began hanging out in front of the offices. At night Carolyn had to take a circuitous route out of the building to avoid the press. She once asked me, 'When will all this press business end?' I told her, 'It'll end when you and John get married.' That turned out to be a bit of very bad advice—if anything, it got worse."

When it became clear that she would not be a cooperative subject, photos capturing her in an expression of avoidance, annoyance, or abject fear became the highest prize—or at least the highest-paid pictures. How much of this could Carolyn have anticipated when she finally said yes to that sapphire-and-diamond ring?

On Thursday, September 7, the official launch of *George* magazine was announced at a colossal press conference at Federal Hall in downtown Manhattan. Almost three hundred reporters were in a frenzy to catch every moment, but especially John's speech. The crowd hushed when he began; he joked about not seeing this many reporters in a room since he had last flunked the New York bar exam and seemed completely at ease speaking to such a large group. The most widely reported part of his speech, other than "Ladies and gentlemen, meet *George*," was his humorous forestalling of questions on his private life before they could be asked by providing a litany of preemptive answers: "Yes. No. Honestly, we're just good friends. It's just a possibility. Somewhere down the road, maybe. Never in New Jersey."

It had already been declared the most successful magazine launch in history, with 175 pages of advertising in its first issue. For fear of distracting attention from the magazine, Carolyn, despite having worked closely with John and other staffers for months, was not in attendance. After the tense atmosphere created when the news of their engagement threatened to overshadow the magazine launch, Carolyn was more careful to keep herself behind the curtain. Plus, she was still with Calvin Klein, and it was the middle of New York Fashion Week—Calvin's CK show for spring was the following Monday, so she would have been busy at 205 West 39th Street. (And perhaps she was reluctant to leave their still-young puppy, who frequently accompanied her to work. Friday was sweet, but needed minding—he could always be counted on for comic relief. Noona Smith-Peterson, who, as senior vice president of international public relations, ran Calvin's Milan office, often came to the New York office. "Once [Carolyn's] dog pooped under my desk in the office in New York," Noona said. "That made everyone's day, and we all had a huge laugh.")

In her absence, some reporters mistook Carole Radziwill for Carolyn and rushed her. "I was there with Anthony and Maurice Tempelsman," Carole said. "Carolyn chose to skip it. She often avoided events where she knew there would be a lot of press. They weren't yet married so there was considerably less pressure to show up, so she didn't.

"I told a reporter that Carolyn 'wouldn't be caught dead here,' referring to the press spectacle that she knew would ensue if she showed up," she continued. "The next morning John and RoseMarie Terenzio, who handled the PR at *George*, were considering how to handle press questions about her absence, and then that article came out and they laughed, saying something to the effect of, 'I guess Carole took care of that.'"

With the first issue of *George*, John stepped into public life in a way he had not before, and it was just in time for the gloves to come off between the gawkees and the gawkers. The press acknowledged as much, with the *Daily News* crowing about their new tactics: "Spurred by tabloid TV shows and willing to pay big money, a new breed of paparazzi is hunting celebrity prey with a new weapon—the video camera—hoping to provoke the rich and famous into looking small and mean on tape. 'If he yells, it sells,' is the new modus operandi."

CAROLYN AND JOHN, DISCONCERTED by the media crush, made a plan to go to Honduras for Thanksgiving with a large group of friends, including Michael Mailer and his girlfriend Pam Thur, Barbara Vaughn, John Lambros, Peter Alson, and Kevin and Helen Ward. It was on the week of John's birthday and also the thirty-second anniversary of his father's assassination. He liked to avoid the press during that week if he could help it.

Peter Alson remembered, "One measure of that trip was when we had to take a bus through the countryside to a small plane before flying to the island. The bus stopped in the middle of nowhere so we could get sodas and food, and suddenly, all the Hondurans show up to see John. He handled it gracefully; he was used to it. John shook hands and said hello. Carolyn stood off to one side bemused. No one said a word about it back on the bus. It was a matter of course."

Alson really began to understand how different John and Carolyn were—and yet, how these differences complemented one another. "John had a well-plated armor. He was diffident, at a bit of a remove, and one can see from the pictures he was often sitting off to the side by himself," Alson said. "Carolyn, on the other hand, when she turned her focus on you, you felt like you were the only person in the world. She had an intoxicating quality.

"During the trip they had a couple of fights. You could tell there was a tension there. Then they would make up and be like new. It felt like they had a very private, intense connection."

Alson added: "They were both gorgeous . . . When [John] went diving, he would come up, and his hair would be perfect."

Yet on one particular dive, Carolyn went down deeper than she was supposed to, and then came up way too fast. This can cause the bends, decompression sickness when a quick change of pressure causes bubbles of nitrogen to dissolve into the blood and tissues, and it can often be fatal. Even though she was okay—she didn't actually get the bends—it felt like a close enough call that Carolyn was scared and upset when she got to the surface. Alson remembered, "John was even more upset with her for not being more careful with herself, even though he was fearless himself. It was ironic."

As the weekend went on, Thur found that Carolyn was drawn to her. Thur had just started dating Michael Mailer and was also new to the crowd. Neither she nor Carolyn had the background of private schools or the personal or generational wealth shared by a lot of those present.

Thur's impression of Carolyn was that "she was completely original. She didn't care that everyone came down to dinner at six. She came down when she was ready, often barefaced, with wet hair and in a silver shift she had picked up in Chinatown for $10 just days before the trip. She was stunning.

"But not everyone was nice to her," Thur recalled. "Kevin and Helen felt like they had ownership of John. It bothered Carolyn the way they behaved without boundaries. An engaged couple should have a sort of private access to one another, but some people refused to respect it. John himself didn't adhere to normal expectations. He would not say, 'I can't.' For him it was inconceivable to let people down. And some people took advantage of that.

"Especially," said Thur, "concerning one of the female friends they all had in common. 'This woman is calling John at eleven p.m., on his private phone,' Carolyn said. 'They used to date, so this woman has his private number. John would pick up and chat with her.' And it bothered Carolyn—understandably.

"It's hard to build a life, a nuclear family, which is what he wanted, if everyone is clamoring after you and one finds it hard to say no," said Thur. "If Carolyn was going to be in this, she asked him not to choose between her and the world, but to shift ever so slightly."

Carolyn and John returned to the city refreshed after their week away. They had dinner, just the two of them, for John's birthday at the Tribeca Grill on December 2, with a more public celebration afterward at the Mudville9 bar. John asked for the lights to be turned down, "whereupon, he and Carolyn and about 100 friends proceeded to have a dance party that lasted till the wee hours," the *Daily News* reported. John didn't mention that he had celebrated his birthday there before with Daryl, but at this point that was fully in the past.

In mid-December, the couple headed to Arizona, where they stayed at the Phoenician in Scottsdale. Their trip to the luxury resort that sits on the base of Camelback Mountain was picked up by the *Daily News*—they reported that the hotel was "also known for John John and his lady Carolyn Bessette prancing about. Our pals spotted Kennedy buying golf clubs and baseball caps."

It seemed a pattern that Carolyn and John would repeat, time and again. When the tumult in New York became acute—with the press, with their relationship—they flew to a far-off destination to reset, unwind, and regain their balance. Most of the time, it worked.

CHAPTER TEN

SUNDAY IN THE PARK
WITH *GEORGE*

February 1996–March 1996

The early months of 1996 posed, perhaps, the most challenging for the young couple yet. They had been engaged for over six months, yet hadn't quite set a wedding date or begun planning in earnest. And they were about to feel the full force of the media storm that would test them—Carolyn especially—beyond anything they could have imagined.

On February 25, 1996, Carolyn and John were coming out of brunch at the Tribeca Grill when they began to argue. First, they argued in front of the restaurant, both making wild gestures and obviously screaming at each other. John's face was full of fury, and Carolyn gave it right back to him. They went home to get their dog, Friday, and, completely unaware their every move was being captured on camera by paparazzo Angie Coqueran, brought him to Washington Square Park, where they continued their quarrel.

John grabbed for her hand and pulled the engagement ring off her finger. They were both crying, pushing each other, and yelling at the top of their lungs. John stormed off, and Carolyn ran after him, not one to stand for being left in the lurch. When she reached him, she leapt on his back. He turned around, shoved her off, and then they yelled more, close up in each other's faces.

After a time, they stopped and sat on a bench for a few moments looking shellshocked. Eventually, they continued walking, but were at it again after a few blocks. Finally, John just sat down on the curb, buried his head in his arms, and cried. Carolyn was pacing back and forth, and then offered her hand, and John put the ring back on. Carolyn tried to take Friday's leash, and John screamed, "You've got my ring, you're not getting my dog, too!" Eventually, Carolyn and John wrapped their arms tightly around each other and walked home, Friday trotting along beside them.

Two days later, Carolyn accompanied John to the Municipal Art Society's gala, held at the 69th Regiment Armory on Lexington Avenue and East 26th Street. Carolyn wore a black Calvin Klein evening gown that Christy Turlington had recently modeled for the spring/summer collection. With its long sleeves and loose curvy fit, the rayon dress was the perfect combination of demure and sensuous—the best possible advertising for Calvin Klein. Journalist Richard Corkery of the *Daily News* surmised, "Seems like this must be the real thing for John-John." Going by her facial expression, Carolyn was not thrilled by the horde of photographers corralled at the entrance and inside, but neither was she terrified or aggravated. Her relationship with the press had not yet become dysfunctional.

Up until that winter, Carolyn's hair had been a light brunette with two lighter highlights framing her face, but now her hair was a bright, cornflower blonde with "buttery chunks" throughout. It was the exact color of Carolyn's third-grade locks, a feat that colorist Brad Johns once described as "hair color that looks natural, like a child's hair after a day at the beach."

Johns was the colorist at Clive Summers Salon on East 57th Street. He had gotten his start working at Oribe, the famed Fifth Avenue hair salon where the nineties supermodels went to get their hair blown out and up into impossibly glossy manes befitting their Amazonian frames. Johns's assistant Christopher Simonetti remembers Carolyn coming in wearing casual boot-cut jeans, black boots, and a black turtleneck. She was warm, very friendly, without pretense. "When you met her and spoke to her, you can easily understand how John fell in love," said Simonetti, who goes by Zane and now has a chair at Louise O'Connor Salon on East 61st Street. "Carolyn was one of those women who became more and more beautiful when you spoke to her and spent time with her. She asked us all about our lives and was genuinely interested in the answers; she invited Brad to dinner at their loft. She was a delight."

Carolyn let Johns go with his instinct and lighten her mane. "Do what you think is best," she had said. This was also the time when Carolyn lost weight, and plucked her eyebrows from a thicker, more Italian-looking brow to small wisps. A close friend at the time said that "consciously or not, she was beginning to transform into what she believed was expected of a 'Kennedy Wife,' leaving her bohemian scrappiness behind."

And so when Carolyn stepped into the gala on John's arm, she had metamorphosed from an earthy, wavy-haired Roman beauty to a platinum, ethereal, fair-skinned siren whose cheekbones had emerged diamond-sharp. Intentionally or not, she adopted Princess Diana's habit of looking down when walking past the press corral. She looked up only occasionally to smile at her date and other guests, who included the architect I. M. Pei and Caroline and Ed Schlossberg.

What Carolyn and John didn't know—couldn't have known—was that their spat on the downtown streets of Manhattan two days earlier had been captured by a telephoto lens across the street. With video. And it was about to be blasted around the world.

"Fights, Camera, Action" was the headline George Rush ran in the *Daily News* when he reported that a weekly television tabloid show called *Day & Date*, on CBS, had won the bidding war for the tape and would be broadcasting the entirety of the fight in living color over five days beginning on Monday, March 11. "Amid the prolonged tempest," Rush wrote, "the couple allowed manners to get the best of them. As they bickered on a park bench, the pair fell silent when a child stopped to pet their dog. Kennedy broke a brief smile as the dog, a black and white mutt, licked the child's face. But when the kid moved on, the argument resumed." It was also noted that contrary to reports of Kennedy roughing Carolyn up, it appears that Kennedy was "merely trying to pry her arms off of him when she jumped on his back." Both the tape and photos were initially bought by the *National Enquirer's* Steve Coz, who told *Newsweek* the bidding for the tape was "in the $100,000 range." They ran the photos in their own eleven-page spread.

Soon enough, more photos of the fight appeared. Each report was worse, more salacious, more vile than the last. "Hunk and lover's quarrel," proclaimed the *Daily Mail*, with a follow-up the next day noting the "loud, public donnybrook." The *San Francisco Examiner*, getting the park wrong, touted "JFK Jr., girlfriend scuffle in Central Park," and even the *Cincinnati Post* got in on the action with "JFK Jr. rips ring off in lovers' spat."

The accounts grew more creative by the day. The *Philadelphia Daily News* trumpeted, "JFK Jr. & squeeze had swinging time in park," and told how John and "his bony girlfriend" fought until "the lengthy scene ended with Kennedy sobbing on the curb and Bessette mumbling in his ear." The next line: "*That* is not the kind of low profile Jackie taught her kids to maintain."

Among the many things the press outlets got wrong was that the fight was about Carolyn's jealousy over John flirting with another woman. Some reports had the other woman as Sharon Stone, some claimed it was O. J. Simpson's girlfriend Paula Barbieri, and some didn't name anyone specifically but noted John's "roving eye."

Others more accurately reported that the original spark was Carolyn's anger that John was letting himself be exploited. This is corroborated by Steve Gillon, who noted that the fight was not about an imaginary "other woman," but caused by Carolyn's concern that John let others take advantage of him, most recently at a wedding they had just attended. The evening before the skirmish, they attended the wedding of Naked Angels' artistic director Toni Kotite, where, Gillon explained, they found "themselves seated next to [the style] editor of the *New York Times*. Carolyn surmised instantly that the bride wanted to get the *Times* to cover her wedding and was dangling John as incentive . . . she was furious at John for not making a statement by walking out."

Carolyn's friend Dana Gallo said that Carolyn was not one to back down when she thought she was right. "That fight we all saw in the park with John Kennedy Jr.? I saw it many times."

The Washington Square Park fight left Carolyn making her public debut in the role of a hysterical, unhinged woman. John was snarked at, too, but for him, this moment was but a blip on the long exposition that was his life as the son of a beloved president. David Spade sat under John's photo on *Saturday Night Live*'s "Spade in America," and lightly called him out: "Excuse me, I have to go rough up my girlfriend and pretend I run a magazine. Be right back." Was it merely in jest, or was it indicative of John's reputation for being less than civil with his girlfriends—to which there were seldom any consequences? After all, he had been seen screaming at Daryl Hannah in the street as well, and it hadn't changed the public notion that he was Prince Charming.

For Carolyn, this moment was a turning point—not the fight itself, but the video and its aftermath. To be the interloper into John's parade was always going to be dicey. In the court of public opinion, this was the first glimpse of the defendant. And yes, she became a defendant.

"I know John regretted it but, unfortunately, it was Carolyn who suffered the most in the court of public opinion," wrote Richard Bradley. "On the video, she definitely looked like the aggressor. It helped to set in stone an unflattering image of her as being dramatic and unhappy. We all knew John had a temper, but the public didn't. It looked like Carolyn had brought out the worst in America's Prince, that she was changing him, and a lot of people held that against her. In the end, I think Carolyn was more angry at herself that she'd let John get to her in public than she'd been at whatever they were arguing about."

When Carolyn got word that the fight had been photographed and taped, she was distraught. She had already felt judged by John's friends, family, and some of the staff at *George* who thought her job at Calvin Klein was vacuous compared to their politically charged journalistic endeavors, even if they were publishing articles like "If I Were President" by Madonna.

The whole saga caused Carolyn to have doubts about marrying John. She talked openly to friends about her reservations, about the prolonged engagement, and her delay in taking the next steps. But she also talked about how John ultimately won her over. "She knew it was a huge commitment, not just to John but to everything being married to JFK Jr. meant—which was legion," said MJ Bettenhausen. Carolyn told Bradley that John "was the only man she'd ever known who was so strong, so patient, so sure of what he wanted. She hadn't realized how much she needed that until John provided it."

For his part, John had told Bradley, as well as Littell, that Carolyn just needed a little time. Littell was one of John's closest friends, an ally who wanted nothing but the best for his college buddy John. In his memoir, Littell wrote that he and Carolyn "had an easy rapport . . . and liked each other by virtue of the fact that we both loved John. And we trusted each other right away to make him happy." He went on to say that "[Carolyn] was, basically, a complex and talented woman with a great sense of humor and sparkle to spare. I think she had no idea if she could handle being married to John."

John's desire to keep his personal and professional lives separate was dealt a severe setback when the "action-packed videotape" of his fight with Carolyn surfaced. Carolyn's introduction to the world at large was sullied by being captured, as if in amber, forever, at one of her worst moments.

Chris Oberbeck, one of John's closest friends from Brown, said, "The fight created a frenzy that John and Carolyn simply weren't ready for."

There was damage control necessary on behalf of *George*, an undercard to the headline fight. Michael Berman was incensed that John would behave like that in a public park when he was now the face of their joint business venture, and that John didn't warn him or anyone else at *George* that the fight was going to be publicized. Berman suggested an official appearance where the couple displayed the loving side of their relationship. But from Carolyn and John's perspective, why placate the press, especially as most other pictures *did* show their loving relationship? Public affection, such as holding hands or her sitting in his lap, was their usual modus operandi—the images from the Municipal Art Society's gala a case in point. Berman hoped that if they wouldn't pose for a photo op to head off the negative press, at least they would issue a quote to a previously complimentary press, thereby minimizing the incident. However, John and Carolyn refused.

Steve Gillon wrote that John said, "This is personal," and to that, Berman replied, yelling, "This is not just personal. This is the point where your personal life and professional life mesh in ways they don't for other people."

"Carolyn was embarrassed," said Bettenhausen, "but also a little defiant. She worried what the Kennedys would think, but she knew that couples fought and she was not the first girlfriend to have a fight with John in public." It seemed that he could get away with quite a bit, in the eyes of the press, and it was becoming clear very quickly that Carolyn would not be granted the same clemency.

As for Caroline, on March 5, she and Ed made the *Daily News* for their attendance at the premiere of the movie *The Birdcage*, Mike Nichols's update on *La Cage aux Folles*. When asked about John and Carolyn's recent fight in the park, she replied with a simple, "John's doing great." No mention of Carolyn.

John was summoned by his uncle Ted to discuss the matter. Senator John V. Tunney, of California, recounted to Taraborelli that Ted said that "He spoke to John about it to sort of parent him through it, but he told me he didn't get far because the kid was so shaken and embarrassed."

After the fight, it became increasingly difficult for Carolyn to even walk into the building where they had been living together for a year. The elevator was key-operated, and without a doorman, Carolyn worried she would find herself in a dangerous situation. Tribeca was still full of deserted warehouses in the 1990s, without much other foot traffic around, and so the fear that no one would be around to call off a swarm of photographers was not unfounded.

The emotional and mental toll of the media coverage is encapsulated in a paparazzi photo taken of John and Carolyn in a cab that same March. Carolyn is dressed in her new uniform of black, with her head bowed so low that it seems she's looking at something on the floor of the yellow taxi. But this was not the demure, lowered gaze of the gamine who made her debut at the Municipal Art Society's gala—this was avoidance by a woman pursued as prey, as her means of survival.

Contrary to so many young women's desire for fame and fortune—even back before the world had its ingenue influencers—Carolyn did not yearn for the spotlight.

Jack Merrill would agree. "She was interested in the world around her, not her looks or herself," he said. "And having that attention on her locked her in, which was anathema to her."

Some interpreted this as something larger haunting Carolyn— something the press had not yet dug up. Michael Berman, of all people, was the one to respond to one such rumor: an implausible defender of an even more implausible theory. In reaction to rumors from "inside sources at Calvin Klein" that Carolyn was pregnant, Berman was quoted in the *Daily News* on March 4 as saying, "It's absolutely untrue. It's ridiculous, absurd. She's not pregnant. I've spent the last three days with them and I would know."

That Berman felt a right to comment is odd, given that there had been no official statement about the fight in the park. Even more odd is the idea that Carolyn would have spent three days in a row with him.

Gossip columnist Liz Smith chimed in on March 18, saying, "Now take it from me or don't, but the rumors surrounding John F. Kennedy and his girlfriend, Carolyn Bessette of Calvin Klein, are totally media-manufactured. Carolyn is not pregnant, and the couple is not getting married, not anytime soon."

While Smith was spot-on that the pregnancy rumors seemed to be just rumors, she was perhaps wrong about plans for a wedding. Around this time, Carolyn began to carry around a large black three-ring binder, which was full of tabs and highlighted labels. She brought it to Hyannis Port, she carried it to Bubby's, and she was seen with it frequently tucked under her arm at the office of *George*. Billy Noonan described it in his memoir, *Forever Young*: "Contained in a three-ring binder, it was cataloged and tabbed like something she was coordinating, maybe a fashion show . . . or so I thought."

Carolyn was planning their wedding.

A COUPLE OF WEEKS after the fight, Carolyn officially left her job at Calvin Klein. *Day & Date* had just aired their video coverage of the fight over a five-day series. It had become increasingly impossible for her to walk into the office due to the stalking paparazzi's presence. With the chaos of the press tracking her every move, perhaps even taking attention away from the brand, it no longer made sense to stay on.

For someone who had worked since she was a teenager, this was an enormous decision. From retail jobs in high school to waitressing in college to the seven years she had spent at Calvin Klein, Carolyn had always been a working girl. It was how she had been raised. "What people don't realize is how central work was to Carolyn," her roommate Colleen Curtis explained. "She always worked. Always, always, always. Look at her sister, her mother. They were powerhouses."

"Carolyn always wanted to be part of something. She wanted to be with people," MJ Bettenhausen observed. Carolyn thrived on her connections to others, especially in a creative, collaborative environment. Losing that at this crucial juncture would be difficult.

It seemed that Carolyn was also beginning to envision how she could put her talents and gifts to work in other fields. It didn't have to be fashion, and it didn't have to be PR. Curtis wrote that Carolyn "recognized that the fashion industry could be one-dimensional," and that she "talked about translating the skills she learned in fashion PR into something more meaningful—such as fundraising for non-profit organizations." A Calvin Klein colleague said, "Although she worked in public relations—and did a great job—I don't think that's what she wanted to do in terms of a career."

Carole Radziwill reiterated this, noting that "Carolyn had for the most part outgrown her position at Calvin Klein. She was thinking about ways she could make a difference in the world. She thought about going back to school for psychology, making use of her innate talent at homing in on the heart of someone's troubles and uplifting them."

Christiane Amanpour, a Peabody Award–winning journalist, reflected, "The voracious and often vicious attention paid by the tabloids and the press to her at the time had the terrible secondary effect of chasing her away from the workforce. I am sorry a talented person like Carolyn was not afforded that space, just because she married a man who was a huge celebrity, my great friend John Kennedy."

"When people parse over her trajectory and say that she had no career, they forget that she was only in her twenties, a time where plenty of people these days are still struggling to find work at all," Carole said. "She was very young and had already done so much. With so much attention on her every move, she felt she had to navigate the next steps extremely carefully. Whatever she chose to do, she had to be very sure of it in a way that most people aren't pressured to do."

"Friends from the fashion world couldn't necessarily see her in the same way" after she was engaged to John, Carole said. "Their experience of her had been as a consummate professional, absolutely sure in her abilities and a warrior for her creative ideals. It's no wonder they didn't understand that this different, unusual blitz was an entirely different beast, and something from which she did, unfortunately, need defending."

"Calvin was very upset," a colleague remembered. "He felt left behind."

What do you do when you've just handed in your notice, your former boss is mad about it, and you're being chased everywhere by cameras? You go to Paris.

CHAPTER ELEVEN

SPREZZATURA

April 1996

Carolyn was no longer bound to a job in New York, and the experience of sudden freedom spurred the need for adventure. Carolyn and John's European tour—Paris, Milan, and Geneva—was the change of scenery that they needed that spring. Carolyn's sister Lisa was in Munich working on her dissertation for her Ph.D. in medieval art history, and she would meet them in Milan—an especially welcome part of the trip for Carolyn.

First, however, there was some *George* business to attend to. After an astonishing number of ads in the first two issues, each with 175 pages, it was inevitable that after the initial enthusiasm about the Kennedy name on a magazine, the excitement would reduce to a simmer. By issue number three they were down to one hundred pages of ads, so it was crucial to keep the buzz for the magazine strong. On March 25, Carolyn and John flew to DC, where *George* held a party at legendary hosts Peggy and Conrad Cafritz's art-filled home in the Foxhall area.

This semi-public soiree at the Cafritz home was exactly the sort of thing that Michael Berman had been advocating for after the video of the fight surfaced—a display of the couple's warmth, humanity, and political engagement. Peggy Cafritz was charmed by her guests of honor, noting to the *Washington Post* that Carolyn had "a broad frame of reference to her conversational skill" and "didn't seem like an ornament" for John, concluding, "I am a good observer, and they seemed solid. She had dimension."

John and Carolyn took advantage of a moment when the crowd was preoccupied by a speech to have a mini-adventure. "With a mischievous smile, John slid the window open and dropped to the patio a few feet below. Carolyn slipped off her heels and followed, grasping the windowsill as John held out his arms and eased her to the ground, then reached for her hand," Richard Bradley wrote in *American Son*. "They didn't return until the party was winding down, and when they did, smiles danced around their faces like little waves lapping at the edges of a pool."

Bradley later wrote he "wished that everyone could see them like this."

In all, the party was a success—for the magazine and for Carolyn and John, who seemed reinvigorated, in their element, and ready, once again, to take on the world. Just two weeks later, they left for an eleven-day holiday to Europe.

IF PARIS IS FOR lovers, it's especially for lovers fleeing an overexcited swarm of American press. Carolyn and John arrived on April 12, checking into the Ritz. Soon enough, the city worked its magic. Carolyn and John were seen outside the Ritz in the 1st arrondissement, John sitting on a wall and Carolyn beaming at him with adoration, holding his face in her hands. John is wearing an ensemble of athleisure, black sweatpants and a beanie on his head, a very American look. Carolyn, however, in her large black coat, hair swept up into an unstudied bun, a few strands escaping around her face, looked completely Parisian.

The photo brigade in France captured them at the Ritz and the Luxembourg Gardens. Both Carolyn and John look deliriously happy, awash in that flushed, reflective Parisian light. They went to the Louvre. Carolyn loved art—her friend Hamilton South, who was then chief marketing officer for Ralph Lauren and is now vice chairman of Standard Industries, recalled Carolyn as knowing every exhibition going on in town and wanting to see everything, while Carole said that "creative art was high on Carolyn's list of priorities." Often, after a long workday, "Carolyn jammed a beret on her head and off she went to attend a foreign film or gallery opening," recalled colleague Sue Sartor.

After three days in Paris, John and Carolyn traveled to Geneva, Switzerland, where they attended a Cartier Foundation dinner for the presentation of the newest iteration of the Cartier Tank watch, on April 15.

John donned his usual tux and Carolyn, who always understood the assignment, was in a two-tone black-and-tan jersey dress that encapsulated the evening's note of dark to light. Kate Moss had recently showcased the dress down the runway in the 1996 Calvin Klein collection, the last show Carolyn had produced for her former employer before she resigned.

From Geneva, it was off to Milan, where the young couple shopped and went to fashion shows. Prada was high on the list—both for attending the runway show and for shopping. Most important for Carolyn, she would be getting together with Lisa, who provided some much-needed familial support after the debacle they had left behind in New York.

Lisa traveled in from Munich, where she was studying at the Zentralinstitut für Kunstgeschichte on a two-year stipend from the Kress Foundation. Her dissertation, "The Visualization of the Contents of the Psalms in the Early Middle Ages," focused on three medieval psalters, books containing separately printed psalms: the Corbie Psalter, which was made in the ninth century and was the most illustrated psalter in the West; the Utrecht Psalter, thought to have been made at the monastery of Hautvillers in Reims; and the Stuttgart Psalter, believed to have been made at the monastery of Saint-Germain-des-Prés in Paris. She conducted her research at Munich's Bayerische Staatsbibliothek, the largest collection of books and pamphlets printed up to 1500, the earliest printing stage in Europe. Lisa was shyer and quieter than both Carolyn and Lauren, but she shared their intellectual curiosity and parlayed the same drive with which her sisters rose to the tops of their fields into her work as an art historian.

Carolyn and John had dinner with Krizia founder Mariuccia Mandelli and took in the city. While Carolyn, John, and Lisa were surrounded by centuries of masterpieces in Italy, back in New York a different kind of exhibition was underway.

THE ESTATE OF JACQUELINE Kennedy Onassis had been on display at Sotheby's headquarters on York Avenue since April 19. Interest in the items was so intense that the house announced a lottery method for a select number of viewers, choosing just 30,000 of the 105,000 people who had purchased a catalog to receive two tickets each to attend the exhibition in person. There were still lines formed around the corner by those without tickets hoping to get lucky anyway and make it through the doors to get an eyeful.

Unlike most exhibitions at Sotheby's, this was pure pandemonium—velvet ropes were required to clearly delineate the space between over five thousand items and the ticketed viewers, all eager to see a piece of Camelot up close.

The auction itself—with its swarm of bidders in the room and on the phone, while absentee papers waved like mad white flags—was more like an ancient agora with shoppers bartering for meat and produce. Each new price, announced with a satisfying smack of the gavel, sent a shock wave of nostalgia and consumerism as the Kennedy memorabilia turned upon the podium. Many saw the estimates and thought they might have a chance at winning the bid. They were soon disabused of this notion. Items that would not have sold in a rummage sale skyrocketed to thousands of dollars—such as a tape measure for over $5,000. The president's MacGregor woods golf clubs sold for $772,500, more than eight hundred times the $700–900 estimate. Arnold Schwarzenegger, then-husband of John's cousin Maria Shriver, was the buyer.

Jackie's simulated pearl necklace, estimated as worth $700, received an enormous bump from the moment captured on camera in 1962 when Jackie laughed as two-year-old John grabbed at them. The necklace sold for $211,500—more than ten times what it would have cost had it been real, and setting a record for faux pearls. Caroline's childhood rocking horse sold for $75,000, and John's high chair for $85,000. Even an ashtray went for $37,000, though it did bear Jackie's initials. Most of the items were not exceptional works of art or craftsmanship, nor were they even from the White House era. They were all Jackie. Not one item went unsold; the proceeds from the sale totaled $34,457,470.

AFTER MILAN, JOHN AND Carolyn headed north to Gianni Versace's estate on Lake Como to visit the designer and his sister Donatella. Donatella later said that "John seemed totally entranced by his partner. He had a completely open mind about Carolyn's fashion friends, who were different from his friends. He adored her personality, her outlook on life."

One of the evenings, they went to dinner at a friend of Versace's, where smoking was not permitted. "You couldn't smoke inside the house," Donatella said. "So Carolyn and I went upstairs and smoked on the balcony, and then we couldn't get back in. The door had locked behind us. John finally came by looking for us and let us in."

Donatella added, "I was a little envious of Carolyn—who wouldn't be?"

Next stop: Rome, where they stayed for two days at the Hassler. Designer Valentino Garavani threw a dinner party for them, but apparently the designer and his business partner, Giancarlo Giammetti, were unaware that John and Carolyn had gotten engaged—and so they had invited some of Rome's loveliest sirens. "[John] didn't care about the others," Valentino said. "He didn't so much as look at them. He told me he was in love."

Earlier that day, Associated Press Television News was awaiting the arrival of John, hoping to catch a glimpse of him on his way to see the Garavani art collection in the Accademia Valentino, which included da Vinci's Codex Leicester, a leather-bound, thirty-six-page notebook containing the Renaissance creator's scientific observations and theories on the properties of water, the placement of fossils, and the luminosity of the moon. As John approached the opulent Maison Valentino nestled into Piazza Mignanelli, a large square presided over by a towering nineteenth-century bronze statue of the Virgin Mary, the crowds were out to greet and gawk at him. Carolyn was wise to sit this one out, given the pestering John received.

When they asked him, "Mr. Kennedy, why are you here?" His reply was simple. "To visit this beautiful museum!"

When John had gone inside the building, the reporters began interviewing one another. When asked about the value of a John Kennedy Jr. photograph, an answer comes from Rino Barillari—one of several photographers who claim to be the inspiration for the term *paparazzo*, coined by Federico Fellini, which translates roughly into "pest"—"He's worth between 15 to 20 million lire" ($10,000 to $13,000 in US dollars). In perhaps the most honest description of the job of a paparazzo of all time, Barillari added, "The important thing is to invent, create, and ridicule!"

On April 21, there was a delightful conspectus of Carolyn and John's quick Roman holiday in the Italian daily paper *la Repubblica*:

A little bit of mom, a little bit of dad, a lot of himself. John Fitzgerald Kennedy junior opens his eyes wide on the genius of Leonardo told in the exhibition on the 'Hammer Code' at the Accademia Valentino and Rome opens his eyes wide to him, the sexiest man in America. Beautiful much more than the ordinary, very elegant in the gray-beige mohair signed by the designer who yesterday opened the doors of his art-space as well as his home, the 'delfino' of the 35th president of the United States returns to the capital twenty-five years after his visit with the charming and severe mother Jackie . . . John is used to feminine charm and has shown a (almost genetic) predilection for actresses. Already boyfriend of Daryl Hannah, a flirt with Madonna and another with Julia Roberts, today he is romantically linked to Carolyn Bessette (28-year-old pierre [*sic*] of Calvin Klein) who seems to have appeased the chromosomal passions of Kennedy hit-and-run.

Things felt lighthearted in Italy in a way they hadn't in New York. Carolyn had *sprezzatura*, defined as "certain nonchalance, so as to conceal all art and make whatever one does or says appear to be without effort and almost without any thought about it," in 1528 by Castiglione in *The Book of the Courtier*. One might guess she didn't mind being a footnote in the *la Repubblica* article—a slight mention being a relief after the onslaught of attention she had been given by the papers in her home country.

After just eleven days away, it was time to return to New York. And while Europe may have left Carolyn refreshed and revitalized after spending time with her sister, good friends, great art, and exceptional fashion, she was coming back to a life of unknowns—and a wedding to plan. As she and John boarded the flight back to New York, it was hard to say if Carolyn was happy to be going home.

CHAPTER TWELVE

BACK TO WORK

Spring 1996–Summer 1996

In a rare case of running away making a situation better, the press hoopla actually did lessen in the months following their European sojourn. Upon their return to New York, Carolyn was stepping back into a life without a career at Calvin Klein, but she certainly still had work to do.

"From my limited time with her many years ago but knowing her strong character, I believe that Carolyn understood that by agreeing to marry John, she was also taking on a role," said Michelle Kessler. "It was a job, but one that she was determined to do very well. She was refined, discreet, and correct."

Carolyn accompanied John to a memorial mass for Jackie on May 19, now two years after her death, which was held at St. Thomas More Church on the Upper East Side. She was becoming part of the family. She wore a striking black Calvin Klein pantsuit from the 1996 autumn/winter collection, with a plunging neckline, and carried a black Prada handbag. The clean, streamlined look was meant to attract no attention but was cutting-edge all the same. Her style and her look had changed since the days of long flowing skirts with Chucks and contests with colleagues to see who could go the longest without shampooing their hair, when she sometimes turned to a friend and said, "Is this too Stevie Nicks?" First, there was the blonder, more polished hairstyle, and her wardrobe began to take on a more subdued, simple flavor. Perhaps it was simply the changing tide in fashion, or Carolyn not wanting to give the press anything to write about, or her transformation into what she thought Mrs. John F. Kennedy Jr. should look like—a woman Jackie would have approved of.

Soon enough, looks such as this would be replicated by women all over the country. Already, her ability to seamlessly combine high and low, such as a Calvin Klein slip dress under an oversized fisherman's sweater, had been emulated by her colleagues and those who knew her personally. Now that she began to be pictured out on the town with John, Carolyn was becoming, like Jackie, a style icon in the making—whether she liked it or not.

Alexandra Kotur, a former *Vogue* editor who saw Carolyn and John at events throughout that spring, observed Carolyn's transition from a more bohemian style into refined minimalism: "We were coming out of grunge, no more waifish slip dresses or smeared mascara," said Kotur. "Once Carolyn came into the spotlight, she never made a mistake. Her own sense of style was innate. As Anna Wintour said, 'You either have it or you don't.'"

That summer, Carolyn and John lived a full life in downtown Manhattan, where they were for the most part left in peace, inhabiting the moody, underpopulated world of Tribeca, where the bustle of Manhattan felt far away, and moving through the greater downtown area when it had a distinctly different character than today's version.

"The uptown people had not come in," remarked Nancy Haas, a writer for the *New York Times*'s *T* magazine, who lived nearby. "It was emptier. There were no phones with cameras and a much greater sense of privacy. John and Carolyn were very present in the neighborhood, in Tribeca but also downtown more generally. It was a source of pride to have them out and about. People respected their privacy because they regarded them as part of the same world of downtown, the restaurants and bars. Il Cantinori was their favorite spot in the Village."

Carolyn was not big on cooking, to put it mildly, but she had reached out to none other than Martha Stewart for advice on cooking and decor. While Carolyn and John often hosted weekends in Hyannis Port and Martha's Vineyard, Jackie's personal assistants, Providencia Paredes or Efigenio Pinheiro, respectively, did the cooking. They had both been employed by Jackie for decades. Yet when in New York, "Carolyn preferred going to dinner parties rather than hosting them," said MJ Bettenhausen. "She loved to see friends, to socialize, and she would stay and chat all night. Eventually, John would pull her home."

Bettenhausen, who also resided in Tribeca, remembers how much fun she had going out with her: "There was a place near us we used to call 'the hidden barn.' It was attached to a longtime speakeasy that's now known as Smith and Mills. We sat outside and we always brought the dogs. John would be with us a lot, but sometimes he would be walking by as we were in fits of laughter and just shake his head, such as when we would shout, 'Act now,' and double over. It came from an evening after I had just had surgery; I had been in a horseback riding accident. Carolyn came over, and apparently a few nights before I partook in the unfortunate combination of heavy painkillers and the Home Shopping Network. Suddenly all these packages started arriving. Carolyn saw what was in them, and that was it. She got on the phone to call Jules Watson and said, 'You have to get over here now.' The two of them helped me open package after package of onion slicers, graters, and whatever else I impulse-bought. We were laughing so hard it was just silence, tears running down our faces. From then on, all it took was for one of us to repeat the network prodding, 'ACT NOW!' and then it was hysterics."

It was a time when Carolyn still felt free enough to do silly things, like when she and Bettenhausen found themselves at a punk bar, and "unbeknownst to us it was one of those places where everyone did that sort of ramrod, pogo dancing where they bashed into one another," said Bettenhausen. "We thought, all right, and jumped in. No one could move the next day."

It seemed that Carolyn's constant challenge was to find a way back to herself, the girl roaring with laughter. But at the same time, she still had a fragility about her. Rob Littell described it in *The Men We Became*, writing, "By then I'd come to know Carolyn well enough to believe that John had met his perfect match. . . . Carolyn had a quick wit and a seductive mix of manners, able to swear like a sailor and converse easily with heads of state. More than anything, though, Carolyn had an uncanny ability to read people. This could manifest itself as compassion or as wary surveillance, but she was never not paying attention."

Carole Radziwill had similarly observed, "It was obvious from the moment I met her that she was the one for John, and John knew she was the one for John. Only the two of them could have matched each other; they were enthralled. Carolyn was very confident, which he adored. She was very authentic and could be fierce! She was both contemplative and vivacious. It was instantaneous attraction for them."

John said much the same to Rob upon their return from Europe, when the two met to play racquetball at the Downtown Athletic Club. "She's the best chance I've got," John told him, divulging the upcoming nuptials, a secret to savor while they searched for the right location, far from the madding crowd.

FINDING A BEAUTIFUL, ROMANTIC location where Carolyn and John could keep the ceremony private would be a priority. They needed something off the radar, so obviously Hyannis Port wouldn't do. Steve Gillon described how, at the suggestion of RoseMarie, they flew to Nova Scotia. Upon their arrival, Carolyn called RoseMarie and said, "Honey, what the fuck are you doing to me? This is the most depressing place in the whole world. I'm not getting married here."

Eventually, they came upon magical Cumberland Island, Georgia. Or rather, John had come upon it years earlier with Christina Haag. But the perfection of the locale—remote, romantic, wild and yet peaceful—surpassed any expectations. Cumberland is a thin, seventeen-mile-long barrier island off Georgia's southeast coast, with a maritime forest and protected beaches. Horses roam freely around the island, and graze on lawns around the many island salt marshes. And the best part about it: The island was home to less than fifty human residents.

The downside was that pulling off a wedding on the island would require near-military-level logistics. Part of the island's appeal was that it was only accessible by helicopter, private boat, or ferry. In late June, Carolyn and John booked the entirety of the Greyfield Inn for Thursday, September 19, through Sunday, September 22. Privacy was aided by the inn's discreet owners, Gogo Ferguson, a sixth-generation Carnegie, and her husband, David Sayre. They arranged for caterers and a band, as well as the wedding license, all kept strictly hush-hush. The next three months were a study in clandestine party planning, with Carolyn arranging shipments of wine, silverware, and tents in small quantities so that they looked like regular orders for the inn and therefore would draw no undue attention.

The planning process was, in a roundabout way, an opportunity for Carolyn to connect with her late mother-in-law's legacy and traditions, as she found herself consulting with Jackie's friends. Denis Reggie, Ted Kennedy's brother-in-law, was enlisted as the official photographer. Bunny Mellon, who had helped Jackie design her exquisite White House Rose Garden, recommended Robert Isabell, who had done the flowers for both Jackie's funeral and Caroline's wedding, for the arrangements.

RoseMarie was happy to help; she also loved the subterfuge involved in a secret wedding. But the lines between John's assistant, PR manager, personal secretary, and friend could sometimes get blurred. She wrote that Carolyn spent time with her after work hours, and once went to her place after a tense moment with John, reasoning that RoseMarie "could certainly relate; the burden of being close to someone so famous meant you had to watch everything that came out of your mouth."

In fact, the intermingling of home life and work life for the couple was increasing. Carolyn was showing up more and more at the *George* offices. Matt Berman's office was her unofficial desk. Several *George* staffers were people John had known from Brown or were graduates of other Ivies, and often from the privileged backgrounds. Carolyn, decidedly not from that background and growing increasingly wary of those who were, preferred to spend time with RoseMarie and Matt. In his memoir, *JFK Jr., George, and Me*, Matt wrote that some of the "Waspy Ivy Leaguers, good students from upper-middle-class backgrounds . . . often dismissed me as John's *airheaded creative director* and pegged Rose as his *dumb secretary*." Carolyn was comfortable in Matt's office, where she would flip through magazines, smoke cigarettes, and give him and John advice and support. John would walk into Matt's office to seek her two cents when Carolyn was there.

Her familiarity with fashion houses and what they looked for in marketing was an enormous boon with *George*'s ad sales. Kim Vernon, her former colleague who organized Calvin Klein's advertising, met with John and *George* vice president Elinore Carmody at Carolyn's urging. "Carolyn asked me to do a lunch with John and Elinore," said Vernon, "which she half-attended. She didn't want to get in the way, and at the same time was very supportive of John and the magazine in general. It took a while to get the lunch on my calendar, but she was persistent. Carolyn had her own spirit, which was a bit unpredictable, and was part of her great sense of humor. She was surprisingly funny."

Elizabeth "Biz" Mitchell, a fellow Brown alum and former *George* senior editor who had recently been promoted to executive editor of the magazine, corroborated to Gillon that "[Carolyn] knew what those advertisers were looking for in the magazine. She had a lot to offer, and most of her suggestions were very helpful."

Just when things were beginning to feel normal, a series of challenging events, both personal and public, were once again upon them.

Toward the end of May, Anthony and Carole Radziwill were due back in DC for the third operation to remove tumors from Anthony's lungs. In *What Remains*, Carole wrote, "I am starting to fade, to feel heavy, and Carolyn reaches in right here to pick me up. 'Why don't I come with you this time,' she says. . . . She is not asking but telling me she will come. Everything changes when Carolyn comes to the NIH. I am in danger of losing my optimism, and she distracts Anthony and me both." In person, Carole spoke about how Carolyn always brought a picture of Friday and put it on the wall whenever Anthony was hospitalized. "It was endearing and brought some levity," she recalled. "There are so many stories to exemplify her kindness and wit."

Soon more official events arose, such as the Robin Hood foundation dinner in mid-June at the Hilton, where Carolyn climbed into John's lap, and some of the iconic photos of the besotted couple were snapped. In one they are beaming at each other and laughing. In another, she is still smiling and looking down, while John kisses her cheek. The *Daily News* noted that the happiness the couple displayed was "in stark contrast to their fight footage a couple months back."

As much as the press fed off their public feuds, they ginned up news about their joy, too.

"Talk is percolating that JFK Jr. is on the brink of announcing his engagement to Carolyn Bessette," proclaimed the *Philadelphia Inquirer*.

"The fashion-minded folks at *W* magazine see a wedding tux in John F. Kennedy Jr.'s more-or-less immediate future," said the *Los Angeles Times*.

"The wild speculation goes like this: Carolyn Bessette, 29, his longtime gal pal and co-star of that spat-in-the-park episode, has left her job flacking for Calvin Klein in New York, a career move supposedly designed to position the Boston University grad as suitable Kennedy marriage material. 'No more wild friends. No more male models. No more late nights,' the mag theorizes."

Carolyn began going AWOL if she wasn't entirely comfortable with an occasion. Even in her own home, she would simply recuse herself if she didn't like the company. "Once in a while, when John had someone over whom Carolyn didn't like or thought to be using him, she would say she had to run out for a moment to pick something up," MJ Bettenhausen said. "But really, she just couldn't take being around people with false agendas, and she would come over and hang out until she felt sure the person had left. We always had a good time together, but it meant she lost time with John and peace in her house."

The paradox of this time in her life was that it seemed, from the outside, that her world was getting larger, when from Carolyn's point of view the world seemed to be shrinking in ways that simply made her sad. She had always been a social creature, and the necessity of reining in her circles of acquaintance, out of distrust, dislike, or sheer exhaustion at the neediness and bad faith of the seekers, was not a welcome development. The early stages of her reclusiveness were the first occasion for speculations in the press that had no basis in fact, most notably that she was constantly doing drugs.

THEIR WORLD GOT A little smaller in a different way when they lost their friend Billy Way that summer. Carolyn and John were spending the Fourth of July weekend at Hyannis Port when they got word that Billy, after dining at Nello on the Upper East Side and crossing Madison Avenue, was struck and killed by a taxi. Way's parents lived in Bermuda, so John volunteered to go to the morgue to identify Billy's body. John was haunted by the experience.

Billy had suffered from drug addiction, and John, Rob Littell, and Bobby Kennedy Jr. had attempted to stage an intervention for him some years before, unsuccessfully. Bobby had gone through his own dark years with addiction, but John had always been careful. In the eighties and nineties, recreational drugs were often part of the atmosphere, and John would occasionally smoke pot. But he was always sure never to get out of control, and, as Littell wrote, "John's attitude toward drugs was more cautious, perhaps because getting caught would have been worse for him. He was too committed to being healthy and fit, too conscientious, maybe too afraid of the consequences."

Carolyn felt the same way, though with a different set of motivations. When she was in college, the consequences of getting caught were not nearly as outsized. But there was a similar sense of caution. As her Boston friend Jonathan Soroff, who was a reporter on the club scene at the same time Carolyn was doing PR for the clubs, remembered of their club days, "She would have a glass of wine, maybe two. Maybe smoke the tiniest bit of pot once in a blue moon. But that was the extent of it."

MJ Bettenhausen pointed out, "Carolyn would not like to be out of control. Yes, we had fun—I remember one concert we snuck tequila in by pouring it into Ziploc bags, which we then tucked in our boots, but more in the spirit of fun than getting wasted."

Hamilton South noted, "The one thing Carolyn never needed was an accelerator."

Yet, the Party Girl epithet began to define her in the media, partly because her distance gave them room to make things up. Mostly the conjecture was due to the whiff of a wedding that was in the air. No one, no matter who they were, what their family name was, what they did for a living, or how smart, beautiful, clever, or kind, was going to marry John F. Kennedy Jr., son of JFK and Jackie, the little three-year-old saluting his father's coffin now turned handsome grown-up magazine executive, without being subjected to incredible scrutiny.

For Way's funeral on July 16, his parents had asked that mourners attend not in customary black, but to wear bright colors to celebrate their son's life. Carolyn took the grieving parents' wishes to heart and wore a floral-print shirt dress from Chanel's Resort 1996 collection. Of course, there were pointed comments in the press that she had dressed inappropriately.

The constant drumbeat of wedding rumors continued through July into August. Papers as far-flung as the *Spokesman-Review* in Spokane, Washington, snarked, "Carolyn Bessette has left her job as a publicist at Calvin Klein and is preparing to become Mrs. John F. Kennedy Jr. But we still kinda doubt she's his first lady."

The *Miami Herald* chimed in with their thoughts on how she would stack up, saying, "No more late nights. . . . She's working hard to become the quintessential helpmate."

Closer to home was *W* magazine, which quoted a former Calvin Klein colleague who described Carolyn as "a cool blonde. . . . There's something sexy—even raunchy—about her. Any man would want that."

According to Claire Sisco King, associate professor of communication studies at Vanderbilt University, "What used to be a push-pull environment for news changed with the intensity behind the new twenty-four seven channels and the internet, and the need to churn out more content," she explained. "It had always been commonplace to be cruel to women in the media, but this exponentially increased in the nineties. For Carolyn, there was also the unspoken rule where John and his family had been through so much tragedy, that treating them (too) poorly was unacceptable. So you need heroes and villains, and unfortunately that meant scapegoating Carolyn."

Very telling is an interview John conducted with *National Enquirer* editor Iain Calder for *George*. John brought up a contretemps that had occurred when he was still at Brown, when the tabloid called to say they had pictures to prove John was gay. The press, and people like Anita Bryant, had begun a full-scale onslaught on the LGBTQ community. John laughed, unconcerned, and told them to take their best shot. They turned to Ted Kennedy and tried to blackmail him. Ted didn't give them a penny. John figured they had pictures of him at a "gay bar," which he went to with gay friends—and he didn't care if people knew that or what they thought of his sexual preferences. John's question to Calder was, Why didn't they run the pictures? Calder exclaimed, "We would never, ever have run the pictures!" When John wondered why not, Calder explained, "Because our readers consider you a beloved figure, they would have killed us for doing that. You're the little boy saluting his father."

John was aware of the stark differences between how he and Carolyn were treated by the media, and he tried to defuse the situation by asking them to go easier on her. But he also fell a little short of the mark in truly grasping how deeply it would alter *her* life, and subsequently her ability to enjoy it, using the old family adage favored by Lee and Jackie: "This is the rent we pay for this privileged life." However, Hamilton South pointed out, "It was difficult for John to see, and therefore understand, that the price was much higher for her as an individual than it was for him."

While John did his best to protect Carolyn, it was hard for him to articulate the easy, nuanced manner he had cultivated with the press over a lifetime. John's suggestion to "just relax" was at once good advice but also missed the point. As Carolyn told one friend, "You don't understand. When I walk up the street, they walk in front of me backward, knocking over old ladies and mothers with children. They don't care."

John had learned how to handle the press since his earliest years, watching his mother live a private life within a public sphere. Littell wrote: "He was one of the most famous people on earth and he rode the subway, played in the park, and hung out with his friends in full view of the world. No bodyguards, no Secret Service, no subterfuge. By refusing to be a recluse, he forced people to give him some space. And he returned the favor by being a generous and gracious public figure."

THE ABSOLUTE PANDEMONIUM, HOWEVER, came in mid-August when it was announced that a team from *George* would attend both the Democratic and Republican National Conventions. When John entered the Republican Convention floor in San Diego, people lost their minds.

"Almost instantly the space around him started to crackle with energy like the horizon before a thunderstorm," Richard Bradley wrote in *American Son*. "At first, John tried to be polite to everyone swarming around him, reaching for his hand, touching his shoulder, holding out programs for him to sign. But the mob kept growing; things were getting out of control. So he and Gary [Ginsberg] bolted, striking out for the safety of the outside building."

The Democratic National Convention, held in Chicago, featured Bill Clinton and Al Gore accepting their party's nomination and a speech by Ted Kennedy, but nothing matched John's ability to attract a crowd. Seeing him, they went absolutely wild. RoseMarie, who was waiting for John outside, wrote that she said, "John, this is crazy."

"This is exactly what we want," he assured her. "We're the biggest game in town."

CAROLYN ATTENDED NEITHER OF the convention parties. She was busy wedding planning—or rather, dress planning. Carolyn chose her old friend Narciso Rodriguez, who by then was with the design house of Cerruti, for the honor of designing her dress. They collaborated on this for many months. They were spotted together in Paris, where Carolyn had flown several times for three-hour couture fittings in order to ensure the sublime, pearl-colored silk crepe dress fit like a glove. The estimated cost was around $40,000; Narciso gave it to her as a gift.

In addition to being ecstatic with the work of art that Narciso was creating, she was thrilled with the diversion. The papers spotted her dining in Paris with Narciso during one of their trips and speculated that he was a new mystery man, and that Carolyn and John had split, claiming she turned up in "a sighting last week in Paris at a Chinese eatery on Rue de la Roche. Broke lo mein with a Frenchman, in his 30s, at the back table where they also shared a nuzzlement. JFK isn't talking." They were both amused by this gossip—Carolyn because it got the press off her trail, and Narciso because he was flattered that he could be considered her paramour.

The media's attitude that summer seemed to be that they were happy for a story about the wedding but would be equally happy for a story about a breakup. Bad news sold as well as good news—if not better. "Kennedy marriage watch: Opinions are split," the *Daily News* crowed.

Was harsh, polarizing commentary what the news now looked like? It didn't matter, as Professor King noted that "this was no longer responsible journalism reporting the news and responding to public interest. They had to fill that time, and if they had to, they would make things up." Such as claiming Lee Radziwill had said that Carolyn wasn't right for John—"Lee loved Carolyn," Hamilton South said. "She thought she was special . . . a rare combination of charm, humor, and great looks." But the false narrative that Lee was against her nephew's fiancée was fodder for tabloids, with the *Daily News* claiming that Lee had been telling friends that Carolyn *"wasn't right for him anyway."*

The razzing increasingly affected Carolyn. She often used what Carole Radziwill called her "Secret Agent voice" on the phone—a low-toned whisper—but when she called an old friend from Calvin Klein that August her voice was full of fear and trepidation. Carolyn, her friend said, was in distress: " 'Hey, how are you?' Carolyn whispered. She asked after my parent who had been not well, and told me about Anthony and how concerned she was for him, Carole, and John, given how sick he was. She explained it was a lot of pressure between the magazine, Anthony being ill, and the press attention. 'It's like I am a prey animal. They are everywhere. And anyway do I really want to be a wife at home? . . . Can I still go to Film Forum at three p.m. on the spur of the moment on a Tuesday? . . . Am I supposed to stay here cooking dinner every night? I don't cook! The last thing I'm going to do is cook every night! I'm not sure I can do this,' she said."

Becoming Mrs. John F. Kennedy Jr. would mean she couldn't just go to the Film Forum on a Tuesday—or anywhere ever, really—without being noticed. Was it dawning on her that the spotlight might only intensify? That would be the last time she called this friend.

CHAPTER THIRTEEN

THE WEDDING

September 1996

Carolyn's call to her old friend was a brief spell of cold feet. Carolyn and John's relationship "was really based on the idea that they were soul mates. That they'd found the counterpoint of each other," Rob Littell later said in the docuseries *Final 24*, "*JFK Jr.*" And as the summer of 1996 came to a close, these soul mates were headed to the altar. The wedding of Carolyn Bessette and John F. Kennedy Jr. was on.

Carolyn worked feverishly on the planning while keeping it all under wraps. Their vows would be said in a beautiful location that was not only far from the New York and DC power corridors but also a bit lost in time. Stepping foot on Cumberland Island, it was hard to tell what year, perhaps even decade, it was; there weren't even landlines in the rooms, only one main line in the office of the inn. The Cumberland Island National Seashore legislation had helped keep the number of visitors to the island at three hundred per day. There were only around forty guests, all arriving on either the Thursday or Friday before the Saturday ceremony.

Carolyn spent weeks discussing flowers with Bunny Mellon, which served as a lesson in landscape architecture, horticulture, decorating, and, saving the best for last, an intensive study in "How Jackie Would Do It." It mattered to Carolyn, who had never met Jackie, that the wedding would have met her late mother-in-law's approval. The hardest part was keeping the guest list down to the number of people who could be accommodated on the island. It was not an easy task, but it was crucial for the couple's ability to actually enjoy their own wedding weekend. Carolyn and John needed the intimacy of a small group that was close to both of them. Carolyn's list began with her family—her mother Ann, stepfather Richard, sisters Lauren and Lisa, and one of her stepsisters, Kathy Freeman, with her husband, Michael Ronan. Of her friends, she included Gordon Henderson, who designed John's tuxedo, and Jessica Weinstein, Jules Watson, and Narciso Rodriguez.

JOHN WENT INTO PROTECTIVE mode as the wedding day approached. He lost his usual cool in Hyannis Port on Labor Day weekend when a photographer crept up on Carolyn at the beach. Jonathan Soroff, her old friend from Boston, was on the beach that day as well, and he was just about to go say hello. "I was sitting with friends, and I look over and there is Carolyn on the beach, happily watching John kayak. Suddenly, this guy comes up in jeans and long sleeves carrying a heavy backpack. It was a paparazzo, and when he saw Carolyn solo he pounced. It was awful. She put a towel over her head. After a few minutes, John came bounding out of the water and he was livid."

John's anger made the news, caught on videotape as he rushed up yelling, "Don't come up to my girlfriend when she's on the beach alone and start taking fucking photographs!" John wrested the camera away. Later, being the gracious public figure that he was, John ended up apologizing. Yet a line, literally and figuratively, was drawn in the sand. Carolyn was going to be his wife, and he wanted the press, if they couldn't completely leave her alone, to at least treat her with dignity and respect. The couple told themselves that this would be the case soon enough—after the chase of the wedding was over, they could live happily ever after.

Carolyn and John were indeed happily planning all the details. John had kept their impending matrimony quiet at *George*, but no one was fooled. Carolyn and RoseMarie were copying invitations in the office after-hours because they couldn't trust a printer not to leak the story, and John was walking on air. "John seemed distracted after Labor Day 1996," Richard Bradley wrote in *American Son*. "It could mean only one thing: after about a year and

Carolyn as a toddler, circa 1969.
Courtesy of the Bessette family

Carolyn's third-grade class at Juniper Hill School in 1974. Carolyn is seated third from right. *Courtesy of Jane Elezi and Jodi Savitch*

Carolyn at the Bessette family Christmas celebration in Woodbury, Connecticut, circa 1977. *Courtesy of the Bessette family*

The wedding announcement for Carolyn's parents, Ann Messina and William Bessette. *Courtesy of the Bessette family*

Zeller Photo

MISS ANN M. MESSINA
Fiancee of William J. Bessette

Miss Ann Messina Becomes Engaged To W. J. Bessette

Mr. and Mrs. Carl Messina, Ossining, N. Y., announce the engagement of their daughter, Miss Ann Marie Messina, to William J. Bessette, son of Mr. and Mrs. Alfred Bessette, Middlebury. A spring wedding is planned.

Miss Messina was graduated from University of Connecticut and is on the faculty of Douglas G. Grafflin Elementary School, Chappaqua, N. Y.

Mr. Bessette was awarded a BS in civil engineering from UConn where he was a member of Chi Epsilon, honorary fraternity. He is assistant engineer in the Department of Buildings of White Plains, N Y.

The extended Bessette family in a photo from Christmas 1980. Carolyn, in the top row, second from left, was almost fifteen. *Courtesy of the Bessette family*

Carolyn (top left) and her sisters with their Bessette cousins, Christmas 1980. *Courtesy of the Bessette family*

Carolyn's senior year photo from the 1983 St. Mary's High School yearbook.

Carolyn's graduation portrait from St. Mary's High School in Greenwich, Connecticut. *Courtesy of the Bessette family*

Carolyn with her cousin Abbi Nori Nelson, their grandmother Anna Bessette, and her sisters, Lisa and Lauren, at their aunt Dorothy Bessette De Somma's house in Woodbury, Connecticut, circa 1985. *Courtesy of the Bessette family*

The Bessette sisters and cousin Abbi flank their grandmother Anna Bessette. *Courtesy of the Bessette family*

Carolyn and Lisa lounge together at their aunt Dorothy Bessette De Somma's house in Woodbury, Connecticut, circa 1982. *Courtesy of the Bessette family*

Lauren with William Bessette at her graduation from Hobart and William Smith Colleges, 1986. *Courtesy of the Bessette family*

LEFT: Carolyn posing for portraits for *Women's Wear Daily* on August 25, 1992, in New York City. *David Turner/WWD/Penske Media via Getty Images*
RIGHT: Carolyn and Deena Manion in New York City, 1992. *Courtesy of Deena Manion*

Carolyn and her Calvin Klein colleagues attending the City of Hope fundraiser hosted by Bloomingdale's on October 28, 1992, in New York City. *Eric Weiss/Penske Media via Getty Images*

FROM LEFT TO RIGHT: Jenny Landey, Carolyn, Marci Klein, and Suzy Drasnin, circa 1990. *Patrick McMullan via Getty Images*

Carolyn with on-and-off boyfriend Will Regan, owner of Rex nightclub, at Bloomingdale's in March 1993. Regan often arrived unannounced at Carolyn's apartment, and the two would ride off on his motorcycle. *Patrick McMullan via Getty Images*

Carolyn with Jack Merrill at the Central Park Boathouse for Michael Berman's wedding to Victoria Hagan in October 1994. *Courtesy of Jack Merrill*

Carolyn directs backstage action in April 1995 in preparation for the Calvin Klein fall 1995 ready-to-wear runway show in Bryant Park; John was spotted in the wings. *Kyle Ericksen via Getty Images*

John and Carolyn at the Municipal Art Society Gala at the 69th Regiment Armory in New York City on February 27, 1996, just two days after their big fight in Washington Square Park was secretly videotaped; two weeks later, the tape was sold and made public. *Richard Corkery/*NY Daily News *Archive via Getty Images*

Carolyn's notably blonder hair made its debut at this event. *Richard Corkery/*NY Daily News *Archive via Getty Images*

Carolyn and John beam at the Cartier presentation of the new Tank watch in Geneva, Switzerland, on April 15, 1996. Along with her engagement ring, the watch was one of the few pieces of jewelry that Carolyn regularly wore. Her dress is from the Calvin Klein spring 1996 ready-to-wear collection, the last show Carolyn produced before resigning. *Stéphane Cardinale/Sygma via Getty Images*

Carolyn and John embrace at the wedding of Betsy Reisinger and Kenan Siegel on March 21, 1998, in Miami. *Courtesy of Robert Curran*

John and Carolyn's extremely private wedding on September 21, 1996, on Cumberland Island, Georgia. *Courtesy of Denis Reggie*

John tenderly kisses Carolyn's hand after the couple was declared married. Designer Narciso Rodriguez got his big break after this image was highly publicized. *Courtesy of Denis Reggie*

John and Carolyn arrive at a May 29, 1997, reception in Boston in honor of the annual Profile in Courage Award on what would have been his father's eightieth birthday. *Brooks Kraft LLC/Sygma via Getty Images*

Carolyn and John on Madison Avenue entering *George* magazine's second-anniversary celebration at Asia de Cuba on November 5, 1997. *Ron Galella/ Ron Galella Collection via Getty Images*

John and Carolyn arrive at Milan's Teatro alla Scala in December 1997 to see Giuseppe Verdi's *Macbeth*. She is wearing her signature Bobbi Brown Sheer Lipstick in Ruby. *AP Photo/Luca Bruno*

FROM LEFT TO RIGHT: John's aunt Lee Radziwill, hotelier André Balazs, Carolyn, and close friend Hamilton South in deep conversation at the Supper Club on May 5, 1998, celebrating the Parsons Dance Company's premiere of composer Shelly Palmer's "Anthem." *Richard Corkery/*NY Daily News *Archive via Getty Images*

Carolyn, wearing a black Yohji Yamamoto gown with a wraparound back bustle and long silk gloves, smiles while John whispers in her ear at the October 1998 Municipal Art Society Gala at Grand Central Terminal to celebrate the building's renovation. *Richard Corkery/*NY Daily News *Archive via Getty Images*

John's cousin Maria Shriver and Carolyn share a laugh at the 9th Annual Fire and Ice Ball in Los Angeles, a fundraiser for the Revlon/UCLA Women's Cancer Research Program, in December 1998. Carolyn is wearing a Versace evening dress. In a rare moment of speaking to the press, Carolyn commented, "The whole evening was spectacular." *Jim Smeal/Ron Galella Collection via Getty Images*

John and Carolyn at the annual White House Correspondents' Dinner on May 1, 1999. She is wearing his dinner jacket over a Jean Paul Gaultier dress with a clamshell neckline. *Tyler Mallory/Liaison*

Carolyn at the Newman's Own *George* fundraiser at the U.S. Custom House in New York City on May 19, 1999, in a ruffled opera coat from Yohji Yamamoto's spring 1999 collection. *Ron Galella via Getty Images*

Carolyn smiles as she and John speak to reporters outside the May 1999 Newman's Own *George* fundraiser. *Ron Galella via Getty Images*

a half of dating, John and Carolyn were getting married. Everyone at *George*, I think, guessed John's secret."

Carolyn came in to see Brad Johns a few days before the wedding to get her hair colored. "She was still her lovely self, maybe a little quieter, slightly nervous," said Chris Simonetti. "So we were surprised when RoseMarie later called on Carolyn's behalf to apologize if she had been more 'particular' than usual. She had been wonderful, like she always was. That's Carolyn. She's thinking about our feelings just before her wedding."

How well Carolyn and John felt someone could keep a secret determined the timing of when they got the call to clear the weekend of September 21. Some, like Anthony and Carole, had been told several weeks earlier, since Anthony was John's best man. Christiane Amanpour, one of John's roommates in Providence (she attended the University of Rhode Island while he was at Brown), was also told weeks ahead so she could make arrangements to fly to the US from Sarajevo where she was covering the Bosnian War for CNN. Others—such as John's friends Ed Hill, Kevin Ruff, George Sherell, and Chris Harty, and his cousin William Kennedy Smith—were told the location and allowed to book their plane tickets to Jacksonville International Airport themselves. Sherell was tasked with picking Ed, Kevin, and William up from the airport. Narciso Rodriguez, Jessica Weinstein, Jules Watson, and Gordon Henderson arrived in Cumberland before even the bride and groom. RoseMarie had booked sham tickets to Ireland for the bride and groom that same weekend.

On Thursday, September 19, Carolyn and John chartered a private plane via Million Air from Teterboro to Jacksonville, Florida, the closest airport to St. Marys, Georgia, where they would catch the ferry to the island. Accompanying them were Billy, Kathleen, and baby TJ Noonan; and Rob and Frannie Littell. The two couples arrived at the airport before John and Carolyn without a clue where they were headed. Littell later wrote, "About twenty minutes later, John and Carolyn came flashing in, like creatures from a diamantine planet. . . . The soon-to-be bride and groom giggled the whole way down. We all had this tingly sense of 'Can you believe this is happening?'"

Gogo Ferguson had thoughtfully arranged for the Georgia clerk of court to sneak on the plane once it landed for the couple to secretly take their blood tests and fill out their marriage license application. "I had no idea who she was," said chief clerk of Camden County Probate Court Shirley Wise. "When I asked her what her surname was going to be, she said, 'It's going to be Bessette-Kennedy.' And my face just dropped." When Carolyn saw that the woman was just realizing who the license was for, she begged her to stay mum. "All I want is to get to the ceremony without the helicopters," Carolyn said.

Soon, the couple rejoined Billy and Rob and their families. "We climbed into an old fishing boat and motored across an otherwise silent bay to Cumberland Island," Littell wrote, "reaching the Greyfield Inn just in time for dinner with about a dozen early comers." Everyone was met at the dock by a security man, who handed them a card on which an Indian Head penny and a Buffalo nickel were affixed, which they were instructed to always have on their person. It was their pass, their way through the velvet rope. If security found anyone without it, they would be unceremoniously tossed off the island.

The Greyfield Inn, built in 1900, has the feel of both a family home and a grand hotel, with its wide veranda spanning the width of the house. The bar on the main floor is well-stocked, and guests can pour themselves drinks anytime they wish, with an honor system implied by the bar's name, Honest John. There are sailing trophies in the form of silver bowls, and the library houses numerous first editions and author-signed copies of hundreds of books, as well as bound editions of *Harper's Weekly*.

Carole and Anthony were staying in one of the cottages called the Chicken Coop. They had just gotten good news from Anthony's latest scan, lending an even happier note to the occasion. "There is a general exuberance on the island, and we are all proud to be conspirators," Carole wrote in *What Remains*. "They have pulled this off, and no one yet can believe it."

There were cocktails in the parlor before dinner, and it was a fairly large crowd; most of the guests were already there. Those arriving the following day included Christiane; Chris Harty; and Caroline, Ed, and their children, eleven-year-old Rose, nine-year-old Tatiana, and three-year-old Jack.

During dinner on the veranda, guests met and mingled. It went swimmingly, as people from the fashion world mixed with John's Andover friends, and Carolyn's Italian granny, Jennie Messina, met John's Boston Irish friend Billy Noonan, who described her as "a real pistol." The Greyfield Inn was "like a Clue game come alive," Noonan wrote, "with graceful rooms filled with unusual guests . . . Narciso introduced himself as 'the other man,' [Jules], an outrageous blonde who was speaking with an affected British accent—somehow she was funny instead of annoying—and Jessica, who was looking a little tired."

That evening, some guests turned in early, exhausted from a day of travel, while others stayed and kept at the champagne until late. The next morning, hangovers were worked off as guests swam in the ocean, walked along the white-sand beaches, marveled at the live oaks covered in moss, and listened to the nickering of wild horses.

Chef Jodee Sadowsky prepared smoked scallops for the Friday-evening rehearsal dinner, once again on the veranda by candlelight. Gordon decorated the five tables with delicate flower arrangements, surrounded by low candles so that guests could easily converse with one another across the table. Sasha Chermayeff was seated next to John, and at one point, he leaned over toward her and said, "That's where my mother would have sat." Was he thinking of his father, too? Was Carolyn thinking of hers, who was not invited to the celebration? At a different table, Carolyn sat next to Billy Noonan. She asked him, he wrote, "What do you think Mummy—Jackie—would think? Would she approve of this? Would she think it's okay?" Noonan "assured her that Mrs. Onassis—as I always called her—would've loved the setting, this wonderful leap they'd taken, to get married in this exotic place."

Throughout the evening, the guests hit the bar. Ted Kennedy and Noonan were perhaps a little better skilled at handling their alcohol than John Perry Barlow, who had a few drinks and made a crude remark about the good looks of the Bessette sisters. Noonan recounted how John took him aside and had a little talk, and somehow Barlow returned to the dinner, demonstrating his skills from his days as a lyricist for the Grateful Dead to give a lively speech. Ted Kennedy also spoke, reading a poem Caroline had written about her brother when they were young, and he delighted Carolyn by saying how much Jackie and Jack would have basked in this event.

Other speeches were more reserved, however, including, surprisingly, that of Carolyn's mother, Ann. As Littell recounted in his memoir: Ann "expressed reservations over the union, implying that it might not be in the best interest of her daughter." Carolyn, after all, had always been a private individual; marrying a public figure would be tantamount to being thrust under a microscope—every aspect of her personal life would be explored and exploited by the media. Littell described how the crowd, happy and enthusiastic about the union, moved on quickly from the moment, but that John was "visibly stung by his mother-in-law's remarks."

Littell wrote that "the emotional ripple was absorbed by the crowd, most of whom had no such worries, and after dinner we all piled out to the beach, where a bonfire blazed and a bar had been set up under a big tent in the dunes. Some people went to bed, others kept the party going. Although I've hardly seen them since, I felt related to Narciso and Gordon by the wee hours. The hardiest souls ended up talking in a small house, set to the side of the inn, that was serving as Carolyn's wedding suite that weekend. She, wise woman, had gone to sleep hours ago."

One guest got so drunk he fell asleep on the pasture and woke up to see the long craning necks of the horses grazing above him. But then it was back to the beach, with Frisbees and swimming and football, working the alcohol from their systems as the day went on. Lauren and Lisa came to the beach but kept about a football field's length from the crowd. Littell says several of the crowd went to say hello and came back "impressed" and "smitten."

Suddenly, there were a few planes overhead. Most were too entranced with the pristine sand and water to worry much; they even waved from the picnic. Later, word came out that a couple of intrepid reporters had been skulking around the island, but between the dense underbrush full of thistles, the heat, and a couple of wild boars, they were glad to be rescued and bounced by security.

Around 4:15 p.m., a convoy of old Chevy pickup trucks appeared at the inn to transport guests to the dusk ceremony. Chippendale chairs from the Carnegie dining room were placed on the flatbeds for the women to sit on; the men sat right on the flatbed. Honored guests—the bride's parents, grandmother, and Ted—rode in the trucks' cabs. They at first drove right on the beach, along the water, before turning off it onto an unpaved road through seven miles of Southern live oaks, magnolias, and wax myrtles.

John went to Anthony and Carole's "Chicken Coop" house to take a shower, and from there they relocated to a home closer to the chapel to get dressed. "Gogo told the owners there was a wedding and asked if the bride and groom could use their house to change," Carole Radziwill wrote. "Carolyn is already there when Anthony and John and I arrive. There is an elderly maid at the house and she almost faints when she sees John. He invites her to the wedding, and she comes and sits in the back pew."

The impromptu invite speaks to John's and Carolyn's general attitude toward life and toward themselves. The guest list was not a who's who of celebrities or even of the political landscape. It was people they loved—though whittling down the list was difficult, and the couple went to great lengths to extend their regrets to those whom they wished could share in their nuptials but they literally could not fit on the island. Kenan Siegel and Betsy Reisinger, who were and remained dear friends, got a phone call a week before the wedding from Carolyn and John expressing their love and explaining their predicament. "They called and explained the need for a small list," Reisinger said, "and they were concerned that we understood how much they loved us and that we would celebrate together soon. It wasn't necessary, we understood, but that's who they were. They went out of their way to make sure everyone felt included, even if they weren't physically present."

The couple gave a nod to both JFK's and RFK's dedication to civil rights by holding the ceremony at the First African Baptist Church. The one-room church was built in 1937, replacing the original log cabin from 1893; some of the founders had been born into slavery and emancipated after the Civil War. Carolyn and John had planned a Catholic service, and John said they had "turned Catholicism on its head" in order for Father Charles O'Byrne, the Jesuit priest who had conducted Jackie's funeral, to conduct the ceremony in a Baptist church.

The ceremony was scheduled to begin at 5:00 p.m. Guests milled about outside as both the bride and groom were late. John had misplaced his shirt, and Carolyn tried to put her dress on in the car on the way to the chapel. She forgot that she needed to put the dress on before attending to her hair and makeup, which meant redoing her hair and makeup after she had pulled the form-fitting work of art over her head. She wore her beach-streaked hair in a low, twisted bun at her neck, a long veil attached, with barely there makeup. She looked polished, but natural, reflecting the simplicity and unaffected spirit that infused the whole weekend.

Efigenio Pinheiro, Jackie's longtime butler and now Carolyn and John's on North Moore Street, drove back to the Greyfield to look for John's shirt, while everyone admired the flowers Effie had placed inside the eleven-pew chapel, the garland on the door, and even palms he'd planted outside after the flowers originally slated to adorn the chapel went missing in action. Bobby

Kennedy Jr. ran after armadillos while the sun began to go down. Some arranged the Chippendale chairs brought in the truck, others placed fans on the pews.

John finally arrived and was relieved that he was not later than Carolyn, laughing while he guessed who had hidden his clothes from him. Noonan? Radziwill? (Neither of them had.) Meanwhile, Jessica, Gordon, and Narciso hurriedly remade the bride. It was getting dark, and there was no electricity in the chapel. The windows had been painted over in white years ago, so no remains of the setting sun beamed in. Effie collected candles and placed them throughout the church, and a few people had flashlights.

Just before sunset Carolyn arrived at the door of the church, and was walked down the aisle by her stepfather, Dr. Freeman, as gospel singer David R. Davis sang "Amazing Grace."

As Noonan described it, "Carolyn was stunning and very stark—as if the few lights were just for her, with the rest of us in darkness and her betrothed's face leaning into her halo."

Billy Noonan captured the wedding on videotape (the basis for his documentary *JFK Jr. and Carolyn's Wedding: The Lost Tapes*). When John fumbles with the ring, Carolyn gently puts her hand on John's shoulder and laughs. "That moment right there," Noonan said. "The moment that she put her hand on his shoulder to reassure him that everything was okay, that was quite a loving subtlety. But that was her."

"Have I mentioned how beautiful she was?" Littell wrote. "I'll say it again—you couldn't look away from her . . . in her simple and flawless wedding gown, with her hair swept back and a smile on her face, we were all dazzled."

And then there was three-year-old Jack Schlossberg, who was used to seeing the bride in jeans or swimsuits at Hyannis Port. He asked, "Why is Carolyn dressed like that?"

Narciso maybe put it best: "I'll never see anything more beautiful than that."

On the footage Noonan eventually made public, Carolyn and John stood in front of a cross made of sticks and twine as they said their vows, presided over by Father O'Byrne. With Caroline standing as Carolyn's matron of honor and Anthony as John's best man, the crowd cheered upon the pronouncement that they were husband and wife. Everyone filed out to Davis singing "Will the Circle Be Unbroken."

As Carolyn and John stepped down from the church, the wedding picture of the century was taken. Denis Reggie captured Carolyn and John's happiness as the groom lifts his bride's hand to his lips, a gesture of unabashed adoration. Carolyn is clutching a bouquet of fresh lilies of the valley and smiling at him, perhaps even laughing.

Reggie later said, "It was an incredibly magical moment. I saw it as it was unfolding, almost in silhouette. It was virtually dark outside. John reached for the hand of Carolyn; she was caught off guard. I'm walking backwards in the light rain at dusk, and John does this amazing gesture, taking her hand and bringing it to his lips . . . It was lovely, the spontaneity of that gesture."

As Carolyn stood outside talking with the well-wishers, one of the wild horses came and nibbled on her bouquet. She sent the picture someone had captured of the moment to MJ Bettenhausen, who Carolyn knew loved horses, having ridden since she was a child.

The trucks took everyone back to the Greyfield Inn as a light rain began. The heat was broken with lightning high in the clouds, and the weather passed as quickly as it had swept in. Everyone sat with those whom they knew, as opposed to the rehearsal dinner. Rob and Frannie Littell dined with Billy and Kathleen Noonan, along with Timmy and Linda Shriver, as they listened to speeches, all of them gracious that night. Anthony spoke lovingly of John and Carolyn, saying everyone understood why John would marry her, and chided John for teasing, pranking, and generally torturing him his whole life, and then spoke of "his caring, his charm, and his very big heart of gold." Tatiana and Rose Schlossberg sang the "K-I-S-S-I-N-G" song, and Ted gave another heartfelt speech in which he recited a poem by Irish poet Daniel Kelleher that the Irish ambassador to the US had sent to John's parents when he was born:

We wish to the new child
A heart that can be beguiled
By a flower that the wind lifts as it passes.
If the storms break for him,
May the trees shake for him
Their blossoms down.

In the night that he is troubled,
May a friend wake for him,
So that his time be doubled,
And at the end of all loving and love,
May the Man above
Give him a crown.

Ted's meaningful words captured the sensibility of the night. Then the senator danced wildly to "YMCA" and "Macarena."

Carolyn and John cut the cake, frosted with vanilla buttercream and adorned with flowers, her hair now released from its bun and falling into her face in a tousled mass. She wore his jacket over her shoulders while they danced under a tent on the lawn to a DJ set heavy with Prince songs from *Dirty Mind* and *1999*, joined by most of the guests.

The next morning, there was some confusion during check-out—the newlyweds had covered the costs of their guests' rooms at the inn, but since the Radziwills were in the Chicken Coop, Carole and Anthony "were presented with a bill for our room and meals," Carole fondly remembered in *What Remains*. "John is horrified and tries to straighten it out at the last minute, but it gives Anthony wonderful ammunition. *'You made us pay to eat at your wedding, you cheap bastard!'* " Carole and Anthony saved the bill, and the card holding the Indian Head penny.

Carolyn and John ferried to the mainland as their friends scattered, flying back to their homes, enchanted to have been a part of this special weekend on a beautiful island. Those who had been there were all giddy that the bride and the groom had achieved their wish to marry privately, evading the media and invasive paparazzi.

However, Carolyn and John's hopes for a reprieve from further intrusions after their marriage were dashed. At the exact moment the couple had banked on the paparazzi losing interest, the unrelenting media onslaught would only escalate.

CHAPTER FOURTEEN

DAYS OF WINE AND ROSES

September 1996–November 1996

Carolyn and John arrived back on the St. Marys, Georgia, mainland on Sunday to meet Gogo's husband, David Sayre, himself a charter pilot, who flew them to Miami International in his Beech 18, a single-engine plane from the 1940s.

Sayre later told *People* that John came to the open field where the plane was parked and asked where the photographers were, saying that he was "ready to have some pictures taken at that point. He loved the plane, the whole scene. He wanted to have a record of it." John was awestruck by the machine, its once-shiny body now a duller gray, with a thick build and low-set wings. It sat on its own at the end of the airfield, beckoning them. ("If Marilyn Monroe had been an airplane," wrote David Freed in *Smithsonian Magazine*, "she would have been a Beechcraft Model 18.")

"This looks like something Amelia Earhart might have flown," John said, circling the machine.

"Let's hope we do better than she did," said Carolyn, less entranced.

By the time Carolyn and John landed in Miami, word was out about the wedding even though they had not yet made the announcement themselves as they had planned, with a press release to the AP. John's cousin Patrick Kennedy, Ted's twenty-nine-year-old son, a Democratic congressman from Rhode Island, had been campaigning in Steubenville, Ohio, for Democratic

Ohio state senator Robert Burch, who was running for a seat in the House of Representatives, when he inexplicably took it upon himself to announce to the Associated Press via local station WTOV: "Besides the hot news on the wires this morning, my cousin John did tie the knot yesterday."

Carolyn and John had been hoping to sneak off to their honeymoon before the press got wind of the wedding. But Patrick's speech let the cat out of the bag, and on Monday, September 21, the *Washington Post*'s Ann Gerhart announced the marriage with the headline "John F. Kennedy Jr., a Bachelor No More."

The newlyweds did manage to leave the country without hassle, flying from Miami to Istanbul. Using the alias "Mr. and Mrs. Hyannis," they checked into the Çıragan Palace Hotel, formerly the palace of Sultan Abdulaziz, thirty-second sultan of the Ottoman Empire, which Christiane Amanpour had recommended.

Carolyn and John basked in the flavors, sights, and sounds of the city, finally alone. They visited the Hagia Sophia mosque and drank Turkish coffee. John bought Carolyn a jewelry box as they strolled the thriving markets of the Grand Bazaar. It was heavenly for all of one day.

By that afternoon, they were spotted by a group of Midwestern tourists who bellowed their names from a tour bus, blowing their cover.

"John-John!!"

"Carolyn!"

"Hey, John!!"

The paparazzi found Carolyn and John on day two of their honeymoon. *Globe* paparazzo Russell Turiak explained that his paper had bribed a travel agent for the information that Carolyn and John were in Istanbul, staying at the Çıragan.

"I was on the next plane over," Turiak said. "When I arrived, I saw John by the pool, and Carolyn must have been in the room. I was there with two colleagues, another photographer and a writer. The writer was in charge of the story, so we went where he told us to go. As it happened, he was in the concierge's office at the hotel buying cigars, and there was John. My colleague overheard him asking for advice about where to go after leaving Istanbul, and the concierge gave him an itinerary. We now knew where to be and when."

That evening, the newlyweds enjoyed a quiet, romantic dinner by the sea, then went to see dancers of the Mevlevi Order, who practiced meditation started by the poet and mystic Rumi: They spun in continuous circles with arms open to the sky "to embrace all humanity with love," and were otherwise known as whirling dervishes.

The restaurant where they dined, Körfez, is housed in a *yali*, a waterfront mansion, nestled in a cove on the Asian Bosphorus, where the patio tables offer gorgeous views of the fortress of Rumeli. Manager Emil Gabron told C. David Heymann how he sent them a bottle of champagne and befriended the couple. "I told Carolyn that it's all right for a Turkish woman to go 'crazy' for two months during her life," said Gabron. "The month after her wedding, and the month after the birth of her first child."

"American women don't require special occasions to go crazy," Carolyn replied. "We're always considered nuts."

Gabron found them both witty and "very sweet." They exchanged contacts, and when Gabron brought his wife to New York later in the year, Carolyn and John invited them to their loft. "They confessed that before leaving Istanbul, they went to a tattoo artist who plastered their respective behinds with shamrocks."

Despite the symbols of luck, the rest of the honeymoon was marked by both the media and random American tourists chasing them wherever they went.

"Though we had their itinerary for Ephesus, I had no idea where they would be their one day in Istanbul. But I guessed correctly," said Turiak. "I walked over to the Blue Mosque, which takes up the entire block. I was going one way on the block, and Carolyn and John walked right by me to head in."

Turiak hadn't gotten the shot he wanted and was in a quandary about what to do next. "I couldn't go into the mosque and trail them; it's dark in there, and using a flash in a mosque was not going to happen. There were several entrances and exits, so I had no idea which way they'd come out. I was at a loss. So I stepped in after them, and I saw lines of shoes. I knew then that Carolyn and John had taken off their shoes and would be coming out the same way they went in to put them back on before leaving."

When Turiak saw them coming out of the mosque, it took a few moments for Carolyn's and John's eyes to adjust to the light. Turiak got his shots. And then he got luckier; or rather, Carolyn and John got unluckier. Turiak mulled over the main tourist spots, speculating on their next destination. They could have been anywhere in a city of fifteen million people with an enormous bazaar. Yet Turiak banked on the couple heading to places with historical significance, and he was right.

Carolyn and John headed to the ancient Basilica Cistern, one of the hundreds that lie beneath the city, this one under the Basilica Stoa.

"I stood on the corner and watched them walk in, again stuck as to how to find them on the way out. Suddenly, a young Turkish boy approached me and patted me on the shoulder.

"'Who are you waiting for?' he asked. I told him I was waiting for JFK Jr. He said, 'They don't come back out from here.' Then he pointed in the opposite direction, about a block away. 'I'll show you,' he said.

"So I stood outside the exit of the Basilica Cistern, and eventually, out they came. I got many beautiful shots of them. John, always aware of us and where we were, spotted me immediately. He was a kind and gracious guy, and what he did was good for my paper and good for them because it gave us what we needed, on deadline, no less, and bought them some peace.

"As they stepped out through the doors that framed them like the chapel doors at their wedding, he paused and took her hand, picked it up, and kissed it. It matched the photo from the wedding exactly," Turiak continued. "From there, he took a couple more steps and then looked at me questioningly. Then he shrugged. His face changed, and it was more of a 'C'mon. You're not going to get a better shot than that. Off you go.' So off I went back to the hotel. At least for the rest of that day."

But what had worked for John before was no longer sufficient. The economy of celebrity stalking had changed. Now that there was endless airtime and web pages to fill, the notion that the media would show a target any semblance of respect was outdated, especially when a female was involved. Had John been traveling solo or with one of his Brown compatriots, a few shots would have sufficed. But because Carolyn was a new, unvetted female in the Kennedy family with the double appeal of disliking having her photo taken but looking mesmerizing in them, the chase was on.

Turiak had their whole itinerary, and his chase led every other newshound to follow them on the middle leg of their honeymoon in Ephesus. He got another shot of the newlyweds shortly afterward in a cab, where Carolyn appears to be in tears after realizing they've been spotted yet again.

"They eventually stopped at a small roadside café, and I got a few beautiful shots of them having coffee and Turkish pastry at an outdoor table. Afterward, they got in the car, and we followed them," said Turiak. "But suddenly, their Mercedes came to a screeching halt. John got out and gave us a look we only got when he was furious, which was not often. He crossed his arms. He'd had enough. Then all of a sudden, he and Carolyn hopped into another waiting car, and they lost us. We tried to find them in Ephesus again the next few days, but we were off the trail. We'd gotten more than we needed."

Not everyone decided to call it quits, however. Carolyn and John hoped for privacy as they spent the rest of their trip cruising the Aegean on a privately chartered 123-foot double-masted schooner, the *Althea*, but that would prove impossible. While in the port of Marmaris, they decided to eat at a low-key rooftop terrace. Suddenly, the couple overheard a group of ten speaking English at a nearby table. "You won't believe who I just ran into at the bazaar. John-John! He was gorgeous," a woman announced.

"Did you see *her*?" one of them asked.

"She was with him, and let me tell you, that woman is no beauty queen," said the woman.

A gentleman piped up, saying, "I think she's cute!"

"Nah, Julie Nixon is better-looking than she is."

Carolyn stood and bolted out of the restaurant. The unfortunate incident was depicted in the *Daily News* within weeks.

The couple continued their honeymoon, with Carolyn smarting from the encounter. Henceforth they rarely left their chartered boat, other than to swim, as it cruised the Greek isles.

IT CAN'T BE SAID that John and Carolyn were unaware of the statement a wedding would make and what it would mean in terms of bringing Carolyn into the fold. Perhaps, in an effort to control that narrative—shift it from "royalty" to "power couple"—the October issue of *George* told a different story.

The first-anniversary issue of *George* hit the stands the day after their wedding, with a vintage photograph of Richard and Pat Nixon on the cover and headlined in pink: "Love & Politics: America's Most Interesting Power Couples." In his editor's letter of the magazine that month, John wrote, "It's true that political life can be a strain on marriage. The husband (usually) gets all the attention while the wife is expected not only to give up her career, but gaze adoringly during every photo opportunity. They have little privacy and even less time together. But in another respect, the crisis and isolation of a public life create a sense of shared burden that can bring a couple closer." So despite what, up to this point, had been John's burden to bear alone, Carolyn was now in it for the long haul.

Having left America and its power couples behind for the moment, Carolyn and John also finally managed to elude both the American travelers and photographers. After the three days in Istanbul, and the encounter with the rude tourist in Marmaris, the rest of the two-week honeymoon was, according to friends, heavenly.

WHEN THE NEWLYWEDS RETURNED to 20 North Moore Street on October 5, they were greeted by hordes of paparazzi. Exiting the car upon arrival at the airport, Carolyn was startled by the onslaught of cameras. Her hope to have become uninteresting to the papers upon marrying immediately evaporated, and she ran upstairs looking like a frightened deer, while John gathered their luggage.

MJ Bettenhausen explained: "Returning from the honeymoon to a relentless press, she felt like she had to pay attention to her looks in a way she wasn't that interested in doing on a daily basis . . . Carolyn was more like a tomboy, which you can see from the early photos of them in the park or stepping out for dinner. She wasn't into girly things or makeup. Carolyn loved to move about the city freely, making spur-of-the-moment plans, and now she felt she had to 'present' before walking out the door. She had thought that the interest in her would wane once they were a married couple. It was just one more way that what had been her free spirit was confined."

When they finally went back downstairs later that day, they did not step out into the crowd unawares. RoseMarie wrote that John had been on the phone with her while he and Carolyn looked out the window of the loft and saw the mob. "[Carolyn] pulled the phone away from John. 'I don't want to go down there,' she insisted. 'I'm not sure this is a good idea.'" Rose reassured her that she should trust John's instincts. "'They just want a shot of you two together, the newlyweds. And then they have it. I think it's a good idea. You don't have to say anything or even smile. Just stand there.'" The couple took great pains to get dressed and went downstairs. Carolyn made her first appearance as Mrs. Kennedy, but only after John pleaded for space. She waited in the vestibule while John stepped outside to face the press.

"Getting married is a big adjustment," John said gently, addressing the swarm of photographers standing on the sidewalk outside the building. "This is a big change for anyone, and for a private citizen even more so. I ask that you give Carolyn all the privacy and room you can."

John did not expect the moon; he knew they would always have an interest in him—and therefore his wife—and this fact would need to be reckoned with throughout their life, as evidenced by the qualifying phrase "you can." Carolyn understood the odds and simply hoped to live under less scrutiny than a prisoner in a supermax lockdown.

John went back into the building to retrieve his wife. Carolyn held tight to John's hand, nestling herself as closely under his shoulder as possible. John tucked her in and showed her the "give them a little and step away" waltz he had perfected over his lifetime.

So, on the first day after her honeymoon, Carolyn stepped out of her front door in a barrage of flashbulbs, and one of those snaps became nearly as well-known as the wedding photo. Carrying a black Prada tote bag, she wore a camel midi pencil skirt, a simple black sweater, and knee-high mahogany boots, also Prada. The look was the height of nineties minimalism—the outfit telegraphed, "If you must look, here I am, but only look briefly, please." It was a concession to the inevitability, even necessity, of being exposed and the need to do it on her own terms to whatever extent possible.

Once on the sidewalk, Carolyn peered at the throng of cameras with trepidation. Finally, when one of the reporters asked her if she was "enjoying married life," she smiled before heading toward John's '94 black Saab, with a surf and ski roof rack with the logo MAIN BEACH. It was hard to tell if the smile was because she was happy to be asked a polite question or because the scene was over.

"But the truce lasted the length of John's statement," wrote Steve Gillon in his biography of John. "As soon as John and Carolyn started walking toward their car, the cluster of photographers 'broke rank' as everyone scrambled to get the 'money shot'—the one picture that no one else could capture. The melee petrified Carolyn." Within seconds John put the pedal to the metal, and they sped off at full tilt.

For a few days after, the press favorably compared Carolyn with Jackie, with *Newsday* calling the wedding "a momentary revival of the Kennedy mystique." Some journalists claimed proprietary, even clairvoyant, knowledge of Jackie's opinion of Carolyn. The *Daily News* headlined "Connecticut beauty won Jackie's approval," which is a bold claim considering the two never met. Elisabeth Bumiller of the *New York Times* wrote that armchair Freudians have also noted the many similarities "between Ms. Bessette-Kennedy, as she has chosen to be called, and Mr. Kennedy's famous mother, the late Jacqueline Kennedy Onassis. Like Mrs. Onassis, Ms. Bessette-Kennedy is Roman Catholic and the product of divorced parents, with a French name if not heritage. Like Mrs. Onassis, Ms. Bessette-Kennedy is athletic, with an almost mysterious allure in public and, former colleagues say, a short temper in private."

John Perry Barlow told Kennedy biographer Christopher Andersen that "Carolyn became a 'thing' in the eyes of the public, and she was treated accordingly." Photographers were there to capture it when Carolyn fell on the front steps of 20 North Moore, dropping her groceries everywhere. *Women's Wear Daily* later reported that the paparazzi took pictures instead of assisting her.

"I realized that a lot of the photographers really didn't like me," Carolyn told the publication. "They wanted me to do something wrong so they could photograph it."

This cruelty extended to another incident days later, when the press took an opportunity to swarm Carolyn. Caroline and Ed were hosting a wedding party on October 10 for everyone Carolyn and John hadn't been able to fit on the whittled-down guest list for Cumberland Island. Caroline's Park Avenue apartment, near the corner of East 78th Street, was a ten-minute walk from where Jackie had lived on Fifth Avenue. John pedaled up to the building on his bicycle, gliding right past the photographers. He was too quick for them to catch anything other than a blur. This was not his first rodeo. Carolyn arrived a little later, on her own, to the crowd of hungry photographers. She stepped out of a taxi wearing a black Prada slip dress, and, unusually for her, a string of pearls around her neck. The photographers pounced.

Despite her vow to never speak to the press, Carolyn used her voice. "Please, I can't see," Carolyn said to the mob. She looked utterly miserable in the pictures, despite having retained a slight glow from the Turkish sun. The only photo of her smiling at the party was taken when she was holding Caroline's toddler son, Jack. The coda to the evening came with the discovery that someone whom they trusted enough to invite into Caroline's home made off with a stack of pictures from the wedding.

It's safe to say that since the tabloids did not splash the pictures across the nation, the family managed to stop the leak before it could go far.

CAROLYN PREPARED BOTH MENTALLY and physically for her first official outing with John as his wife. The Whitney Museum of American Art's benefit celebrating the thirtieth anniversary of its move to the Marcel Breuer building on Madison Avenue was an important evening to John—his mother, who had been a trustee of the museum from 1963 until her death, had attended the Breuer's opening party in 1966. Hosted by Prada, the event was attended by a wide range of glitterati, including Miuccia Prada, *Harper's Bazaar* editor in chief Liz Tilberis, *Vogue* editor in chief Anna Wintour, Evelyn and Leonard Lauder, and Flora Miller Biddle, the granddaughter of the museum's founder, Gertrude Vanderbilt Whitney.

Once again in black Prada—a clingy, midi-length dress under a suit coat—Carolyn wore her hair long and loose, and had very little makeup on. The couple was running late, so Carolyn trotted quickly into the museum. The gathered reporters booed Carolyn flying past the step-and-repeat post. A reporter asked Carolyn what she was wearing. She didn't answer.

A reporter then complained to John about Carolyn's silence, to which John "leaned over" and replied, "It's more dignified if you try to find out for yourself . . . Hint: It's on the back of the invitation."

"Okay, she was wearing Prada," wrote Rush and Molloy. "But what about the Big Question? 'Have you started a family?' the happy hunk was asked. Kennedy put both hands out defensively, his body language saying, 'Don't go there.'"

What might a slightly tight dress mean? The lack of a champagne glass in a photograph? A bad mood? Headlines such as "Papa John-John" and "JFK Jr. doesn't say no, doesn't say yes—& Carolyn's mum," blasted around the rags.

"'I had to ask,' the reporter said.

"'You had to ask,' [John] conceded."

It became clear, over time, that she was not pregnant. The harassment they received regarding the status of their family was undoubtedly a major factor in Carolyn's retreating further and further into her shell.

"This is ridiculous," she told a friend. "If I don't leave the house before eight a.m., they're waiting for me. *Every* morning. They chase me down the street." This was not the friendly hellos and banter John received as he hopped on his bicycle to head to work. Carolyn was physically afraid of the people who stalked her.

FEAR LED CAROLYN TO hide away, something completely at odds with her personality. MJ Bettenhausen explained, "Carolyn used to be out late at night because she wanted, *needed*, to be with people, not because she was out partying. To see her shut in, feeling like she couldn't do that anymore, was heartbreaking. She loved to spend hours chatting and truly focus on someone; she was smart and funny, and was always completely entertaining." Her world was shrinking even further.

RoseMarie tried to help, advising Carolyn to remain silent. "I always stressed to Carolyn that she shouldn't let the press, the paparazzi, or cameramen hear her voice," RoseMarie wrote in *Fairy Tale Interrupted*. "A person's voice is personal and intimate. If they never heard hers, I thought, they wouldn't get what they wanted." It was wise advice at the beginning. But as time wore on, Carolyn's silence allowed too many Greek choruses to shout their stories, true or not.

"We forget that Carolyn was only thirty when she got married," said Carole Radziwill. "She was a focused, intelligent and intuitive young woman who was still getting used to all the public attention. I don't think anyone, including her, could ever understand how much that kind of attention could destabilize one's life. Carolyn would have gone on to do great things. But we didn't know then that there just wouldn't be enough time."

Still, Carolyn didn't shirk the duties that came with being John F. Kennedy Jr.'s wife, and at the first-anniversary party for *George* magazine, held at Asia de Cuba, she worked the room. She was dressed in a long, black nondescript Yohji Yamamoto sheath, in her bid to make her image less newsworthy. She stood for two hours in polished-calf Manolo Blahniks, greeting guests and happily chatting them up. Attendees included Lee Radziwill, Conan O'Brien, and Ian Schrager.

Happily describing her dedication to the design and booming ad sales of her husband's magazine, Carolyn told William Norwich of the *New York Observer*, "I'm Georgie's girl."

Although the party was a smash hit, and John went on a press tour that included an appearance on Candice Bergen's television show *Murphy Brown*, it was no golden ticket for the magazine. Despite Carolyn's contributions, despite the party, the magazine was still up against declining newsstand and ad sales. It's common for a magazine to struggle to keep momentum once the novelty and shine have worn off, but neither John nor Carolyn was going to accept anything less than success—for their magazine or their marriage.

CHAPTER FIFTEEN

FRIENDS AND FOES

November 1996–January 1997

To escape the cameras, the couple traveled to Hyannis Port nearly every weekend in November and December, staying at the President's House. They were often joined by John's friend Billy Noonan and his family. According to Noonan, John told him, "My accountant told me that it made more sense to charter a plane and fly here every weekend than sell." Noonan recalled that John said that he wanted their children, when they had them, to partake of the house and the compound. "We would often drive down [from Boston] to meet them and have a party," Noonan wrote. "It went on like this for a while, and we were never closer as couples. John liked to make huge dinners, and we would get into huge arguments"—political arguments, as Noonan leaned right.

Besides creating a menu to each guest's liking, Carolyn organized the groups according to who she thought would most enjoy one another. Robbie Littell remembered that "she stressed over the guest list, once calling me in a half-serious panic to say, 'There's a lot of alpha dogs this weekend. Too much testosterone. I'm not sure it's going to work.'"

Friends from college, friends from work, friends from their travels, they kept and tended to them all. As Carolyn told Donatella Versace, "I'm never going to give up my friends, but at the same time, I will be the best wife for John."

Less seamless was the mix with John's family, particularly with his sister, Caroline. A large part of it was John's tension with his brother-in-law, Ed, but, moreover, "John's and Caroline's friends never crossed over," Sasha Chermayeff, who spent considerable time with John at Red Gate Farm on the Vineyard, told Steve Gillon. "We stayed separate. She didn't think much of his friends, and he didn't think much of her friends, but I always felt there was an old closeness between the two of them. They really loved each other."

And although it was never clear how close Carolyn and Caroline were or were not, it seemed that—if only for the sake of seeing her brother happy—Caroline appreciated Carolyn. As one friend noted, "It simply wasn't true that Caroline immediately disliked Carolyn, because she saw how much they laughed together."

Caroline had also given a thoughtful wedding gift to her new sister-in-law. From the outtakes of the exquisite material from the dress, tablecloths, and other pieces used during the wedding, Caroline had a talented costume designer create a pillow that was then embroidered with pearls and monogrammed CBK.

It stands to reason that Caroline and Ann Freeman were on good terms as well, as one of the Bessette-Freeman gifts to the couple was a white bedspread, also painstakingly embroidered with matching material and monogrammed with both Carolyn's and John's initials. With these elegant yet useful gifts, both sides of the family seemed to be expressing their happiness that the couple would be sharing their lives together, and the sisters-in-law a set of initials.

The sisters-in-law were filmed together on November 26, coming out of St. Thomas More Church on East 89th Street off Madison Avenue after attending a private memorial for JFK on the thirty-third anniversary of his death. It was finally an intimate moment for the family to have together, and one of the few times Carolyn publicly wore color, wrapped in a green plaid coat from Valentino's 1996 autumn/winter collection—the green perhaps to honor the Irish family history. Caroline and Carolyn popped into the back of a two-door car, tucking in expertly, carefully avoiding eye contact with the camera.

The wish for privacy was what they most had in common. Otherwise, their personalities were extreme opposites. Carolyn was demonstrative, sometimes boisterous, and very often found the humor in a situation. Caroline was quieter, more studious, and reserved.

It should be noted, however, that Carolyn met John's sister when she was grieving. Caroline had just lost her mother, and by the autumn of 1996, she likely knew that soon, she would also lose her cousin Anthony.

Problems arose, as they often do, around the holidays. As a Christmas present, Ed gave Carolyn a shelf of books—many of his favorites. It was a gift that Ed would love to receive himself. However, John was livid: "How dare you insult my wife by sending her this . . . this syllabus! As if she is unintelligent and needs to catch up on her reading!" This likely wasn't Ed's intention, but maybe things were too far gone between Ed and John for anything to be taken lightly, even a Christmas gift. (At least Ed hadn't included his own book, *Einstein and Beckett: A Record of an Imaginary Discussion with Albert Einstein and Samuel Beckett.*)

While John felt judged by Ed, he also made a habit of poking fun at Ed's career as an experimental design artist, which had not entirely come to its full fruition in the nineties. When someone asked John what it was that Ed did, John would laugh and say, "You tell me!" John felt that his brother-in-law was pretentious.

John and his sister remained close, regardless, but John's feeling that Ed and Caroline's friends thought him a dunce was a raw spot.

THAT FALL AND WINTER, John continued to run everything at *George* by Carolyn. She was already holiday shopping for the staff in November. "If John was on the phone, Carolyn would often wait in my office sitting with her legs draped over the side of a chair, her hair spilling over the other side," Richard Bradley wrote. "Carolyn made me a little afraid to move. In any event, keeping her entertained was always my priority. When John finished whatever he was working on, he would come in and stand behind his wife, gently stroking her hair or, more often, massaging her back. Teasing him, she would pretend not to notice and carry on talking to me, and eventually, he would throw up his hands in mock frustration and stomp out. Then Carolyn would smile and ease out of her chair and amble into her husband's office, sometimes closing the door behind her."

Matt Berman had been after Carolyn and John to pose for the cover in a mock-up of Grant Wood's classic painting, *American Gothic*. He asked seriously once or twice and then relentlessly in jest. "It would have been amazing: John wearing overalls and staring stone-faced into the camera, Carolyn in a Depression-era housecoat," he wrote in his memoir, *JFK Jr., George, and Me*. "She usually didn't smile in pictures anyway, and she wore her hair pulled back in almost the same style as the farmer's wife. However, as I got to know John and Carolyn better, I began to understand their sensitivity to the way they were perceived in the public eye, and I really appreciated their need for privacy."

Their need for privacy grew, as now it wasn't just the gossip columns offering their conjecture. The big guns of opinion journalism had begun to weigh in, starting with none other than the *New York Times*'s Maureen Dowd. Eschewing the usual rumination on what Jackie would have made of her daughter-in-law, Dowd clutched her pearls over what patriarch Joe Kennedy, who "introduced Hollywood illusion to American politics, spinning magic and mayhem from great teeth, great hair and great public relations," would have thought of his granddaughter-in-law. Noting that Joe Sr. liked Oleg Cassini "because he was refined," she wondered, "What would he have made of the Kennedy name being linked to a designer such as Calvin Klein, associated with unclad Marky Mark, kiddie porn and heroin chic?"

Ann Gerhart of the *Washington Post* jumped in, describing Carolyn as a "raging party girl." While acknowledging her degree in education from Boston University, she quickly slaps it down, writing, "How can you face 30 chattering second graders at 8 a.m. when you've been out all night at the Buddha Bar?" However, the *Washington Post* did publish "The List: 1997, What's out, what's in as 1997 dawns," which pronounced John as "out" and Carolyn "in." A small victory perhaps, but why did it have to be one or the other?

A more compassionate take is found in the words of George Plimpton, founder and editor of the *Paris Review*, who raised funding for his nonprofit literary magazine by asking friends for donations (something John would have despised doing but may have saved him some trouble). He invited John to the magazine's fall 1996 benefit. When John arrived, his presence changed the dynamic of the room; everyone stopped what they were doing and stared. "It was embarrassing," Plimpton told the *New York Times*. "I was just so sorry. I think it's going to be very difficult for them to fit in."

All the same, Plimpton was thrilled about their marriage. "It seemed like an idyllic union. They were both bright and beautiful," he said. "If Carolyn had the persona of a vaguely soulless mannequin, it was because she loathed the press. Privately she exuded the profound femininity of a Jackie Kennedy, with the same toughness and sense of humor. Although they weren't given to using baby talk," Plimpton continued, "I once heard her call him 'Mouse,' while he called her 'Catty Cat.' They were truly in love. They were soul mates."

Despite the incessant media intrusion and the tumult of *George* magazine, they were still newlyweds, and those who spent time with them remarked on the evident love and affection for each other. "They were a smitten couple," Hamilton South said. "They exuded happiness and laughed all the time. John loved Carolyn deeply. They were trying to build something away from the limelight."

Carolyn was further cheered by a visit from her nana, Jennie Messina, in December. Upon her arrival, Messina took one look at the loft and said, "So you married this famous man, and you're in every newspaper, and this is where you live?" Despite Carolyn's attempt to soften the space with throw pillows and her dozens of picture frames (though empty), the apartment was still, essentially, a bachelor pad. John had spent over $100,000 renovating the plumbing and electrical, adding architectural details and enormous glass windows facing north, east, and south, and a modern, open kitchen. He had put in a small library, and the walls were hung with tribal masks that he had collected on his travels throughout Asia and Africa. A brown velvet sofa and chairs from Jackie's library were set around the TV, and her painting station (one of her hobbies was painting in watercolors, and she once gave Stanislaw Radziwill a small portrait of him walking with Kennedy advisor Chuck Spalding) sat nearby in stylish balance with the modern decor.

Carolyn had bought an exquisite mahogany Edward Wormley midcentury modern dining table, signed DUNBAR BERNE INDIANA in applied brass to the underside. When the three twelve-inch leaves were inserted, the table reached a length of ten feet, fitting perfectly with the highboy laid with the initials JFK and the presidential seal. Yet, the apartment still felt like what it had originally been: a warehouse.

Carolyn appreciated John's efforts at domesticity. Once, he had purchased an enormous wooden construction that housed dozens of cubbyholes. Jack Merrill came over to visit, and Carolyn, smiling, said to him, "'John went out and bought this thing . . . it takes up the whole wall with these antiqued squares.'" said Merrill. "Carolyn didn't have the heart to tell

John that it was hideous and made me promise to praise the monstrosity when John arrived home. 'You have to be surprised, Jacky, and act like it's a great piece of furniture.' So of course, I asked something about it, and she lit up, saying to John: 'You see? He likes it, too!' I loved her for stuff like that."

Eventually, Carolyn purchased a sleek, modern Dunbar desk as well, and it was there that she read newspapers and piled her books throughout the day.

Carolyn and John's social life contracted into mostly outings with good friends in private places. When they did venture out, it was to low-key spots in their Tribeca neighborhood: Bubby's, the Odeon, Walker's, and for the occasion of Carolyn's nana's birthday on this December visit, they chose a traditional, hole-in-the-wall restaurant in Little Italy. *George* staffers had become like family to both Carolyn and John, and they invited Matt Berman along for the celebration.

Waiting inside were Carolyn, her best friend Jessica Weinstein, Rose-Marie Terenzio, and Carolyn's grandmother. "Nana was a tiny, frail version of Carolyn," Matt wrote. Like most who met Jennie Messina, the silkscreen artist for Vera Neumann known for her ripostes, Berman found her endearing. "Carolyn had spent the afternoon shopping at Barneys with Nana and told us that when she tried on a pair of high-heeled Prada pumps, Nana shouted across the shoe salon, 'Carolyn, take those off, you look like a prostitute!'"

For the holidays, Carolyn and John gave each *George* staffer thoughtfully personal gifts. Richard Bradley said he was "stunned at the beautiful engraved Mont Blanc fountain pen they had gotten" for him. Matt Berman wrote about the bounty, "a juicing machine to Jen, the vegetarian, a Dunhill lighter to the English editor who smoked like a chimney. Hermès scarves, Mont Blanc pens, and Knicks tickets were given to others. John handed me a large, gift-wrapped rectangle. When I unwrapped it, I found an original print of a 1950s stripper in gold body paint by the photographer Weegee. I was floored; I'd seen and admired this image in books and couldn't believe that John had actually bought it for me. I loved it. Later that evening Carolyn warned me, 'You better like that thing; we almost had to mortgage the house for it!' Rose later told me that Carolyn had told her, 'I want Matt Berman to open his present in front of the whole staff so they see that John takes him seriously.'" RoseMarie received "stacked boxes and garment bags on her desk, along with a check for $5,000."

John and Carolyn endeavored to create an atmosphere of camaraderie at *George*. Associate editor Hugo Lindgren, who was one of John's first hires, remembered John pulling long nights in the office with his staff. If he was going to ask them to work hard, he would as well.

Lindgren also remembers that while it was great fun to work at *George*, there was lots of jockeying for John's attention—so much so, that for each interview John conducted for the magazine, he would assign its editing to a different colleague each month to avoid anyone feeling left out.

"People do get a little crazy around someone like John," Lindgren told *Esquire*. "Michael and he, I think, had a really good friendship at some point, and then didn't, and I think that can be very disturbing to people. They sort of lose their special 'in,' and that's what really fucks people up."

Lindgren later added, "I think what happened with [Michael] Berman is that he used to feel like in their partnership, he was in control of John's image in some way and could direct him. When Carolyn came on the scene, he felt like he was losing control. And there are some people who, when it comes to a perceived loss of access to John, can become pretty distressed."

Michael felt like Carolyn was interfering, and Carolyn felt like Michael was someone who had attached himself to John for the wrong reasons. Carolyn's exasperation with Michael's office tactics occasionally resulted in a confrontation. Gillon wrote, "Once, she had a conversation with an executive at Condé Nast who complained that John had canceled lunch with him three times. When she asked John about it, he said he never had a lunch scheduled. She discovered that Michael had made the appointments, promising John's attendance, and then canceled."

John hated conflict and was, at times, happy to have Carolyn run interference. He especially avoided run-ins with those whom he saw as male authority figures. It was something John understood about himself, and he had been working on it. In the meantime, Carolyn took on the task; she even called Michael and shouted, "No one in the office wants to deal with you. You're bringing down the business, and you're bringing down John!"

One instance of sidestepping was how, usually, John and Michael had an implicit agreement to give modest gifts to the staff each holiday season, with a few bonus checks in the mix. Michael apparently had his assistant contact John about picking out the gifts for the year but did not get a response. When John and Carolyn gave staff the expensive, thoughtful gifts without his contribution, Michael felt slighted. John and Michael's working and personal relationships continued to decline steeply from there.

All this put Carolyn in a tricky spot. John wanted and appreciated the deflection Carolyn provided, but it provoked anger and envy in others. John sometimes wanted to back away from friendships, and it was easy to let Carolyn provide a barrier. He also backed away from the press in the hope of protecting his wife, but their response was to become infuriated and to home in on Carolyn even more. Every move she made, they looked for fault.

The press called her out that fall for subletting her East Village apartment "illegally." Of course, the legality depends on landlord approval. And while Carolyn's landlord never commented publicly, it is possible that he or she had only just realized that Heather Ashton, Carolyn's friend from Calvin Klein, not Carolyn, was living there once it was made public by the *New York Post*. Comedian Argus Hamilton came to Carolyn's defense in the *Los Angeles Times*, saying, "You can't blame her. Kennedys come and go, but a rent-controlled apartment in New York comes along only once in a lifetime."

Ashton explained: "The press found out I was Carolyn's friend who was staying in her place and then stalked me . . . I got a taste of what she had been dealing with, and it was terrifying. I was walking into the building, and hordes of cameramen jumped out at me, chasing me. I ran into a nearby coffee shop to hide. When I tried to leave, they chased me across the street."

Dealing with the onslaught every single day, Carolyn went into crisis. John, upon seeing his wife in pain, tried to do something about it. On Sunday, December 15, the couple was walking home arm in arm from brunch at Bubby's with Friday; Carolyn, who was carrying a copy of the *New York Times*, had wrapped a black scarf around her ears and over her head to stave off the biting cold. When they spotted Angie Coqueran, the paparazzo who had brought them so much trouble the previous February by taping the fight in the park, staking them out in a Chevy Blazer, John rushed over to the car and began shouting at Coqueran. In a moment of fury, he jumped on top of the hood of her car. He hopped down only to reach his arm in the driver's window to try to grab the keys, and Coqueran rolled her window up on his arm. Carolyn, standing beside him, began to cry and tried to pull John away while the entire debacle was filmed by yet another paparazzo, Marcel Thomas, across the street. Thomas said that "they ducked into a hallway, and he was holding her in his arms and [Carolyn] was crying." Carolyn and John managed to get the attention of a passing police car, who told the photographers to leave. They did, but only for a day or so.

Coqueran later told Christopher Andersen, "I didn't blame him one bit for getting angry. Before he got married, he was gentle as a bunny with us—even when he was pissed off. He had spent his whole life being hounded by the press and he knew how to handle it. But when your wife is upset and the paparazzi are making her cry, your first instinct is to protect her. I don't blame him at all for coming after me. In a way, I think it shows what a great guy he was. He tried to strangle me and I still love the guy—that's how great he was."

Coqueran went on to tell Andersen she did have some sympathy for Carolyn, noting she had gone from a casual tomboy to a femme fatale. "I think she was trying to live up to something when she would have been happier just staying the sort of fun-loving person that she was," Coqueran posited, either blissfully unaware or tap-dancing away from acknowledging that it was the behavior of people like her, and her specifically, that was the cause of so much of Carolyn's despair.

The tune is so familiar: An antagonist shows fondness and forgiveness toward John but gets frosty on the subject of Carolyn. Richard Bradley pointed out that "everyone knew that John was chivalrous, but they hadn't seen him react with anger at the press, at least not in their face. But attributing the change to Carolyn somehow ruining Prince Charming was simplistic at best, manipulative at worst."

Why was it so difficult to understand that John's anger wasn't because he suddenly hated the press but rather that they were hurting someone he loved? In this, he was a true partner. The tabloids refused to acknowledge the havoc they wreaked on the couple. Also, it was just more dramatic to blame her, and it sold more papers.

FOR NEW YEAR'S OF 1997, Carolyn joined John in Bozeman, Montana, where even the locals in a dive called Half Moon Saloon had a knee-jerk antipathy toward the new Mrs. Kennedy.

The mountain view at Big Sky Resort was framed by the large window of the bar, where skiers and snowboarders joined truckers and locals, whose taste did not run toward what one described as the "tight black sweater and very tight black flared pants" Carolyn wore—and especially not her "boots with four-inch heels." The exaggeration is obvious, as are the reactions from all of the females in an article that appeared in the *Irish Times*, written by journalist Anna Mundow.

Mundow was in to see her hairdresser, and all the talk was of *Star* magazine's headline "JFK Jr. and Bride Talking BUST UP as Secret Vacation Turns into a DISASTER." One stylist claimed she knew it would never last. A beautician chimed in, laughing at Carolyn's high heels. "She damned near broke her neck when she slipped on the ice in the parking lot."

"'Him I liked, her I couldn't stand,'" a female truck driver told the *Star*. ". . . I said to him, 'Hey, you need a haircut, Mister.' He laughed and said, 'What I need is a beer for me and my wife' . . . but his missus, she said, 'Really, John, is that necessary?'"

Enormous offense was taken at Carolyn's remark. Mundow went on to say, "When a woman who takes size six in clothes asks if any of that is 'really necessary,' trigger fingers start to itch."

It's an overblown response on many counts. Let's be clear that the town wasn't new to posh tourists—Big Sky Resort up the road is one of the most elite ski areas in the country. So, it's fair to say that the locals saw their share of tight clothing and high-heeled boots. But the particular disdain for *this* posh tourist is telling—whether the comments on Carolyn's weight, wardrobe, or demeanor were based in jealousy or just plain cattiness—it was the age-old tradition of women turning on women.

By January 1997, Carolyn could hardly do anything without intense scrutiny and its subsequent criticism. Ms. Mundow put her finger on why women were so critical of John's new wife when she explained, "[My stylist] has a vested interest, however imaginary, in John Jr.'s future." The irrational fantasy that they might one day be in John Kennedy's life perhaps explains the swift backlash against Camelot's newest princess.

The accusations against Carolyn's character went beyond her not being "good enough" for John. Even friends had employed trite archetypes to explain away why John chose Carolyn as his wife. One acquaintance told the *Guardian*, "She managed Kennedy really well . . . She was smart in terms of her approach. She knows how to disappear; she knew how to drive him nuts." And the tabloids erroneously reported that Carolyn was seeking to increase her prenup from $1 million to $6 million, should they be married less than three years, which got many tongues wagging about how she "landed" John.

"Unbelievably, it got worse. Less and less would she go out to dinner or anywhere public," MJ Bettenhausen said. "She took solace in Friday—we both adored animals. There was an empty parking lot near our apartments, and one day Carolyn said, 'Let's just make this our dog run.' Next thing I know, she is bringing down a few chairs, giggling. We walked into the lot, and she shut the gate. Carolyn sat with her back to the street, and we had hours of fun watching Friday and my dog play, chatting and cooing over our canines. It was so good for Friday, who was a nervous dog. Partly because of his breed but partly because his parents were often chased when they walked him. It was good for Carolyn, too. We spent a lot of time at 'our run,' and let the dogs go wild. The press never found us out, and we went several times a week."

Carolyn also found reprieve in their family homes. Despite the shaky beginning, she did enjoy Hyannis Port. It seemed a place where she felt welcomed. John's cousin Kerry Kennedy Cuomo told the *Washington Post* at the time that Carolyn was "a very bright, sweet, wonderful, creative woman whom John has fallen madly in love with. She has been to the Cape on several occasions, and we all love her. We especially love her because he does."

The *George* offices at 1633 Broadway also served as a haven—it was one of the few places outside her apartment where she felt safe, and she trusted most *George* employees because John had already vetted them. Carolyn felt at home there, treating so many of the staff as friends. Gillon wrote, "She delivered baby clothes to a pregnant senior editor. She joked and told stories. She would often invite editors for drinks after work and treat them to dinner. [Michael] Berman saw sinister motives behind her actions."

One editor who worked there at the time remarked, "It was like he got it into his head that Carolyn was this Yoko Ono character who was taking John away from him, which was absurd because he was not Paul McCartney. He wasn't even Ringo."

Other staffers agreed that Carolyn was not intentionally subverting Michael's authority. As Gillon wrote, "She was there to relax and find an outlet for her energy, two things she could rarely do anywhere else," and he quoted Biz Mitchell as saying, "She knew what those advertisers were looking for in a magazine . . . she had a lot to offer."

Carolyn, as ever, aligned with Matt Berman, the creative director. "As a result, a tug-of-war emerged, with Matt and Carolyn lobbying for more creative content and less dense stories, and Michael prodding the magazine in the opposite direction," wrote Gillon. "Carolyn seriously complicated Michael's already difficult relationship with John."

John's fight with Carolyn in the park had made headlines, but John's fights with Michael in the offices of *George* were no small thing—and over time they became more frequent and much louder. The staff could only sit in their offices and try to pretend it wasn't happening. One day, Richard said to Biz, "Mom and Dad are fighting again."

Biz replied, "Yes, but which one is which?"

"If a quarrel began in Berman's office, Michael might pursue John down the hallway," wrote Gillon. "One editor recalled Michael walking a few feet behind Kennedy, belittling him in a voice loud enough for bystanders to hear, 'Who's going to save you now that your mother's not here?' John would try to ignore him, but Michael persisted: 'You're nothing. You're a loser.'"

The more John and Michael's relationship devolved, the more Carolyn protected John. Once, she called Michael while he was on a business trip and shouted, "You should leave! John could be so much more successful if you weren't there!"

Carolyn told John that Michael was a "schemer"—"He's using you," she said.

Michael's quest for control over their magazine, and his desire that it should feature more serious political content and less popular culture, seemed to be conflated with his desire for control over John. It was a recipe for disaster.

IN EARLY JANUARY 1997, Carolyn and John invited Steve Florio, president and CEO of Condé Nast, to dinner at their loft. Florio had managed to expand the company, even though the decline of print magazines had already commenced in the face of online content. He was a heavily mustachioed man with a capacious personality, and part of his business success was due to his own sprezzatura. In a proposal for an autobiography, he wrote of himself, "I was, after all, Steve Florio. The Godfather, the Samurai, the leader, the warrior." (Though not, apparently, the author, as he abandoned the project.)

Still, he was at the time a larger-than-life figure, Si Newhouse's deputy overseeing the famous stable of glossies that set the terms for fashion and fashionable chatter, including the *New Yorker*, *Vanity Fair*, *Vogue*, *GQ*, and *Architectural Digest*. They all sat companionably on the floor while John and Carolyn showed him pictures of their wedding. Florio knew Carolyn from her days at Calvin Klein.

As Florio recounted to Heymann: "I always liked her. Their dog, Friday, camped in my lap and we sorted through the photographs. There was Uncle Teddy doing the Macarena. It looked like any Irish family wedding. Everybody was drinking, dancing, and looking happy. I saw that wonderful picture of John kissing Carolyn's hand. They were so beautiful. She was a riot. John adored her. Did they bicker from time to time? Well, hello. You're damn straight they bickered, just like I've been bickering with my wife for 32 years—we're still battling it out. I'd be finished without my wife. I know John felt the same way about [Carolyn]. I never met or knew a married couple that didn't argue now and again."

Knowing Florio loved boats, John showed him several pictures of the presidential yacht named after Rose Fitzgerald Kennedy's father, the *Honey Fitz*. "My God," said Florio. "Every once in a while, I have to remind myself that you're the son of an American president. My grandfather came to this country with five bucks in his pocket and a bag of carpentry tools."

"That's why you're here, my man," John replied. "That's why you're the CEO of a major company. Because your grandfather got on the boat and said, 'I'm going to find a better place.'"

It was never stated that the evening with Florio was anything other than a purely social occasion, but it stands to reason that John was cognizant at the time that the situation with Michael Berman, as well as the publisher, Hachette, would not hold. Perhaps he and Carolyn had their eye on a better home for *George*.

In the middle of January, the paparazzi captured Carolyn and John leaving their apartment for DC to attend Bill Clinton's inauguration. John came out and got into the car first, a cameraman's tape rolling on him the entire time. Carolyn emerged a minute or two later, carrying an enormous roll of cerulean-blue wrapping paper that she points directly in front of her, parting the sea of cameramen who jump in her path. She had perfected the technique of waiting a beat after John had settled in the car to give him time to realize he might have forgotten something—a wise modus operandi with a disorganized husband.

Once Carolyn was sure John didn't need to run back in for his wallet or keys, she trotted to the car. As if on cue, John reversed the car at full speed, whipping into a rear-facing three-point turn. It was a wild maneuver, but he executed it perfectly and they eluded the buzzing paparazzi, only to be flagged down by a nearby cop. John did not get a ticket, but they were told that the cameramen had a right to be there.

Throughout his life, John needed organizational help from the people, mostly women, in his life. As his life grew in complexity, the task became more Herculean. He tortured RoseMarie with this often and Carolyn with it even more often. RoseMarie might have to give no fewer than five reminders to stand up from his desk and leave the office to be on time for an appointment. He would often realize, when he got in a car to the airport with no time to spare, that he had forgotten his wallet, which meant calling Carolyn or RoseMarie to FedEx it to his first destination, as he was going to Europe directly afterward.

"[Carolyn] sighed in mock exasperation—moments like this with John were routine—and joked, 'Better you than me,'" RoseMarie wrote.

But to others, she might vent. "We can't get out the door without taking an hour to find his keys and wallet!" she yelped. "Sometimes he'll be a no-show somewhere, and I'll call the house to find him there, having totally forgotten."

As the press closed in on them, John became increasingly preoccupied with *George*, partly out of necessity and partly because he wanted to put his energy into something he could actually control. Unable to make the press insanity go away, nor the subsequent problems it was causing his wife, John began to turn his attention away from it to block it out. Carolyn felt she had to carry it on her own. The simple act of leaving the house was now an experience that was impossible to navigate without the lurking paparazzi and their clicking cameras. It was like a leaving-the-house tax. It had to be paid every day.

"The onslaught was brutal," recalled Jack Merrill. "The press constantly created drama out of thin air. John was used to it. Carolyn took it personally."

When John was there, the exchanges with the waiting photographers were more like friendly banter: "Hey, John, how are you doing?" He might even answer them, and even if he didn't, he was usually gentle with them. He knew the easiest way was just to give them a moment, a word, a glance, a smile. But that was what worked for him. From Carolyn, they wanted something different, and their approach reflected the nature of their wish. What they wanted from Carolyn was a fall, a mistake, a sour face. John had grown up knowing he was beloved everywhere. For Carolyn, life had been different, and while she had dozens of friends who adored her, there were also many who were jealous and malicious toward an unknown girl walking in and creating such thunder.

The incessant insults shouted by the paparazzi ("bitch," "whore") and insinuated by the tabloids ("vapid," "cold," "crazy," "manipulative," "moody")—were taking their toll on Carolyn. "One afternoon she was supposed to meet me uptown in my office; she called and was crying," Carole Radziwill wrote. "She had been out, and they had tailed her the whole time, and she couldn't bear to go out again. I went down to see her. Photographers were sitting in parked cars, some with engines running because it was cold, in twos and threes. They held cigarettes out the window. I could see them talking and laughing, on stakeout."

As run-ins with the press were becoming more frequent, John was beginning to lose his famous cool. On January 28, the couple was having brunch at Bodega, a neighborhood café in Tribeca, and had tied Friday's leash to a bench outside. They were eating happily, reading the Sunday paper, when suddenly they saw someone outside the window. It was a woman named Ruth, who had been stalking John for ages. She had gone so far as to show up in the *George* offices once, trying to use the Xerox machine in the hallway. Now she had the audacity to untie Friday and put him in her lap. Some paparazzi joined in on the fun and petted the dog as well. John tore out of the restaurant, grabbed Friday's leash, and went ballistic on them: "If you guys are going to be inhumane to my wife, you shouldn't pet my dog!"

JOHN'S NOTION THAT THE media would get their fill of Mr. and Mrs. Kennedy and then move on to other carnivals wasn't coming to pass. Would they have to move out of New York City in order to raise a family? Was the best way to get rid of the media's ravenous appetite for them to give a little here and there, which was hard for Carolyn, or completely hide away, which was impossible for John?

They could go nowhere without scrutiny. For example, in February when they missed a flight out of LaGuardia to West Palm Beach, *Daily News*'s Hot Copy seemed to have the scoop: "One of the beauties of being John Kennedy Jr. is that you can get star treatment at airports . . . Even the ones not bearing your family's name." Carolyn, John, and Friday had "waited by the First-Class check-in until they were told there was a Delta flight they could get on. This prompted the trio to hop into a cab for the Delta terminal. And here's where our worlds are a world apart. Even though John forgot his briefcase back at the TWA terminal, the Delta folks, more or less, held up their flight until the case was couriered over. If it were us—or you—they'd have left before our grandmother made it down the gate with her walker."

It was around this time that John became consumed with the notion of piloting his own plane again. Richard Bradley noticed that before an editorial meeting in early 1997, John was reading Hachette's aeronautical magazine: "While John waited for his staff to assemble, he leafed through a copy of *Flying*, another Hachette publication, gazing happily at the pictures of new planes," Bradley wrote. "He was talking about taking flying lessons. He always wanted to learn to fly. Plus, the ability to fly his own plane would allow him—and Carolyn—to bypass the exposure of airports and commercial flights."

Carolyn, however, continued to take the commercial flights, even as John began flying himself back and forth to Hyannis Port or Martha's Vineyard on an instructor's plane, even with the instructor on board.

John wanted to pilot his own plane, as well as his magazine. What decisions would Carolyn make herself, and what could she leave to John's navigational skills, in the plane and with their future?

CHAPTER SIXTEEN

HELP WANTED

February 1997–April 1997

Carolyn was once again caught in the crossfire when, at John's office, the pot was beginning to boil over. One afternoon that February, John and Michael Berman had their final blowout. John burst into Michael's office and shouted, "We are not doing any of this," making a move to grab the paperwork related to a possible TV deal on the horizon that could have potentially generated desperately needed revenue. "I'll be the editor, and you can be the publisher. That's the way it's going to be."

The two men tussled over the folder, and, in the process, John ripped Michael's shirt cuff. One Hachette alumnus recalled being told that at one point in the fight, John took a pair of scissors, raised them over Michael's head, and had to be held back by staffers. When Michael said that John would need to be the one to explain to the networks why they were backing out, John had an answer at the ready: "I took care of it; I told them that you were doing this behind my back."

Michael, once again, redirected his anger onto Carolyn.

"When you come in the office, you're unrecognizable!" Michael yelled. "You're exhausted. You're unfocused. Whatever your problems, keep them at home. Don't let them spill over into the office. That's all I ask. Get her the hell out of the office."

"That's not true! Don't say that about her," John warned. "She has legitimate friends in this office. You're jealous because they like Carolyn and no one likes you."

"Her behavior is deplorable!" Michael shrieked.

"She's the best thing that ever happened to me. Why would you try to ruin that? I can't tell her what to do." With that, John stormed out of Michael's office and into his own, locking the door.

Michael went maniacal and chased after John, screaming, "Open the fucking door! Open this door!"

He tried to pick the lock with a letter opener he had grabbed from a nearby desk, to no avail. On the way back to his office, he took John's datebook from RoseMarie's desk. When RoseMarie noticed it was missing, she looked everywhere, and ended up asking Michael point-blank if he took it. Although he denied doing so, a few minutes later he approached her desk.

"Here, you left this in my office."

Michael's taking of John's datebook is the perfect metaphor for what he felt he'd lost: control over John's time, and over John's life.

The press got wind of the skirmish and on March 14, the *Daily News*—under the headline "If he keeps this up, they'll call him JFKO"—reported the incident. The ripping of shirts was noted, except the press got it backward, saying it was John's shirt that was ripped instead of Michael's. One Hachette alumnus was told that John and Michael were both abashed at the fight. John sent an apology note with a new shirt a couple of days later, but Michael never spoke to John again. Eventually, Michael Berman negotiated a deal with Hachette to head their film and television development and stopped coming into the *George* offices.

On the surface, it seemed that Michael's departure should have widened the path for Carolyn to enter a more official role at *George*. She had become increasingly involved with the magazine, having been on the ground when it launched in September 1995. But instead, it was quite the opposite—the moment required John to display his independence. So, Carolyn stepped away from the magazine.

The dynamic at *George* was complicated, or at least influenced, by John's general reluctance to take orders. Gary Ginsberg explained, "Of course, John had an issue with male authority figures. If anything, he was initially too deferential, which led him into uncomfortable situations from which it could be hard to untangle."

In this struggle for independence, John realized it would no longer do to have his wife hanging around 1633 Broadway. John was famously unbothered by the meddling and accusations of the press, or the encumbrance of wannabes, when it came to his personal life. Perhaps it wouldn't have annoyed him if a friend was mentioned in the Style section because John had been strategically seated at their wedding. But when it came to his professional life, he was more protective of how his image was used. For instance, it upset him when Hachette Filipacchi CEO David Pecker, who would later run the *National Enquirer*, wanted to trot John and Carolyn out as show ponies for ad sales not just for *George* but their other holdings as well. One editor told Gillon, "He was like a toy. [John] was like a shiny object that [Pecker] could tout to these potential advertisers and people he wanted to rub elbows with." When John refused to be dragged out to endless dinners, Pecker would pressure him by noting *George* could not succeed without additional revenue.

Between the media's eyes locked on the fallout between John and Michael, and David Pecker's constant scrutiny of the magazine's numbers, *George* was in a state of crisis. He had to circle the wagons, alone. For her part, Carolyn understood. "For the moment, the directive at *George* became about the financial recovery, and that was not where Carolyn would have contributed," said MJ Bettenhausen. "She felt she needed to stay away while they were in crisis. But she would have returned once the crisis had passed."

WHILE THE STRESS MOUNTED at the office and in their public life, Carolyn and John's private life retained a warm glow. They invited Gary Ginsberg, his wife, Susanna Aaron, and their new baby up to visit them at Hyannis Port in March 1997.

"Carolyn was incredibly generous and sweet. She was great with children," Ginsberg remembered. "This was my first trip to Hyannis Port; my kid was two weeks old. We had arrived just before John and Carolyn, and John had forgotten to turn on the heat. My wife is crying, 'I can't believe we're up here with a two-week-old son and no heat.' Carolyn was on it as soon as she arrived. Until the heat kicked on, she was building fires and had brought up a sweater. She was incredibly nurturing."

When John walked in, she let him have it. "John, they have a *baby*. I cannot believe you never thought about the heat!"

Billy Noonan was also a houseguest in Hyannis Port that weekend, and he eyed Gary with suspicion. When Gary was understandably excited to see the presidential compound, Billy remarked to John, "He's a little too into it, don't you think?"

At one point, Gary asked John if he remembered any of the times with his father, either at the flagpole or where the helicopter landed.

John shook his head; he didn't remember.

"I do," Noonan, who was two years older than his friend, said.

"You do?" asked John. He had been friends with Noonan for decades, and Noonan had never said that before. It was an emotional subject for John, and those close to him were well aware of that fact. Billy used it as a weapon by throwing it at him now, in front of Gary.

"I told him about my experiences with Mary Ruane, my nanny, as a five-year-old," Billy wrote, "how she'd take me to see the President's helicopter land on the compound and how special it was. . . . I figured that enough time has passed for me to tell him about that, that if he was willing to tolerate Gary's enthusiasm, and bring presidential memorabilia into the house, it was time to start sharing my memories."

If the truth comes in blows, this was one of the first hits between John and Noonan. Noonan had been a friend whose large and loud persona had been a welcome deflection from a world often paying claustrophobic-making attention to John. But Noonan deflected perhaps too often. So when Noonan commented about someone else being "a little too into it"—"it" being the aura of fame, power, and wealth that surrounded John and his family—perhaps he doth protest too much. That Noonan crowed about his "special knowledge" of JFK in a game of one-upmanship in front of another friend, when he knew how painful it was for John that he did not have many memories of his father, was insensitive at best.

Noonan wrote, "[John] just dropped his head, didn't say anything, and walked away."

Whatever John thought about Carolyn's interventions in his communications with friends, he left no room for doubt. "Carolyn's my absolute best friend in the world," John had declared just weeks before this visit. "I've never had a better relationship with anybody. That stuff in the press is bullshit."

BULLSHIT OR NOT, THE "stuff in the press" was wearing on Carolyn. After a year of intense media scrutiny, she found it impossible to continue on in her previous profession, impossible to contribute in any meaningful and overt way to her husband's magazine—to which she had already contributed much—and impossible to leave her home without being physically chased. Feeling cornered, Carolyn went into a spiral of worry and anguish.

"She felt like a caged animal," said MJ Bettenhausen. "The situation devolved, and she was afraid to leave the house. We still took the dogs out, but that was about it. We stayed in our neighborhood; sometimes we would sit in front of Smith & Mills for a glass of wine." There, Carolyn didn't have to worry about people staring or a snarky news bite appearing the next day.

That spring of 1997, Carolyn tried to have a normal evening out with friends, including her former colleague Kim Vernon. They went to Raoul's, a restaurant in SoHo Carolyn frequented. They knew her and always sat her in a table in the back so she could have a little privacy. "There were a couple of us; I think Jessica [Weinstein] was there, and we were ready to have a fun evening, catching up and talking until one a.m. like we used to just a few years before. It was warm and they seated us in the back patio," Vernon recalled. "We were having an excellent time until a woman, a little tipsy, approached Carolyn. She asked her a question about dating, and while I don't remember the exact wording, it was meant to be intrusive and a little obnoxious."

Carolyn had smiled, hoping to get past the moment as quickly as possible, and gave her a kind answer, something like "You're beautiful, so I'm sure your boyfriend . . ."

"Eventually, the woman went back to her table, and we noticed a large group of men and women, still in work suits," said Vernon. "We tried to go on with our evening, but the spell had been broken. The table kept staring, and Carolyn felt on display. She calmly excused herself and left the restaurant.

"Afterward, Jessica and I went over to the table. We told them what they'd done was rude. The woman explained that the table dared her to do it. Again, Jessica and I explained to the table that even if they didn't have cameras, what they had done was not only unkind, it was an invasion of privacy," said Vernon. "Carolyn was so much fun and such a good friend. She deserved better."

It seemed that Carolyn could go nowhere without getting noticed, even outside of the city. Carolyn and John, along with Carole and Anthony Radziwill, visited Hamilton South at his house on Lake Waramaug, in Warren, Connecticut. "They came often to Connecticut, and we had a lovely, mellow time," South said. "I introduced them to friends, two New York City ballet dancers, who had recently relocated there from the city. Carolyn was fascinated by their lives and asking endless questions about dance. They talked for hours.

"Our house was right on the lake, and we would go out on the boat. It was serene and quiet," said South. "Until, of course, someone noticed Carolyn and John and then suddenly you'd see an uptick in boats near the house."

As was their custom, Carolyn and John went to the annual gala held by the Municipal Art Society on March 4, Carolyn suited up tight in a Yohji Yamamoto skirt suit from his fall 1996 collection with John by her side. The *Daily News* noted that she was pictured smiling with her husband—a rare moment of positive coverage.

That evening, John took to the podium at 40 Lafayette Street to award Robert De Niro the Jacqueline Kennedy Onassis Medal for his preservation of the Tribeca neighborhood. De Niro thanked the Municipal Art Society for holding the event downtown "because I really don't like to go above 14th St." Other guests included "uptown swells" Arie Kopelman, Duane Hampton, Brendan Gill, and Stephen Swid.

The *Daily News* always had a little bit of a backhand: "Carolyn . . . may not be ready for such arm twisting, but at least she was smiling, a switch from her recent public appearances," and she had "shocked onlookers Tuesday night by actually appearing happy at the side of hubby John Kennedy for the first time in months."

Carolyn was being noticed for more than her smile that spring. She was emerging as a fashionista of the times. The February 1997 issue of *Vogue* magazine had pronounced her style influence as "The Cult of Carolyn." The problem was that she didn't want to be a cult. "Although Carolyn Bessette-Kennedy shies away from the limelight, her naturally chic look is all the rage," wrote Kimberly Ryan. "Gianni Versace sees her as a major influence for his next couture collection. 'Her style and beauty represent the kind of woman that fashion requests now—angelic, virginal, but with a gutsy attitude that is absolutely modern.'"

But tabloids quickly weaponized Carolyn's style against her. If she's a fashion icon, then she also must be a vapid clotheshorse. The press noticed that she spent time shopping, but what is left out is that when she walked into a store, she was often visiting old friends. "After they were married Carolyn occasionally came by my shop on Fifth Avenue," Donatella Versace said. "I have never seen her more happy. I made fun of her. 'Carolyn,' I said, 'what do you do all day, sit at home just waiting for the next party? That's not like you.' She said, 'Just you wait and see.'"

But it wasn't that simple, as her next professional move had to be infallible given the scrutiny she was under. She had left her job just last spring, and had been married less than a year. Carolyn visited friends in their offices, at their homes, in the ateliers of designers whom she knew. She missed having her own career, but she still had her community—and even though she had jumped from one side of the fashion fence to the other, from a behind-the-scenes PR impresario to a front-and-center fashion figure, she still had her place among friends.

When she next went to Brad Johns's salon on Good Friday to have a color touch-up before spending Easter in Hyannis Port, she couldn't hang out chatting in the salon—it was necessary for them to whisk her into a back room. But once there, she relaxed and was her old self again. She talked up a storm, mothering everyone. Christopher Simonetti remembered her asking everyone what they were up to for Easter, and, even though he was just an assistant, "Carolyn remembered that I also worked at the Portofino tanning salon to make ends meet.

"'Oh, honey, what are you doing for Easter?' she asked.

"'I'm working,' Simonetti said with mock despair.

"'Here?!'" she asked, surprised. 'Or at Portofino?'

"That was my turn to be surprised. So I asked her, 'What are you doing for the holiday?'

"'Oh, just going to see family at the Cape,' Carolyn replied. She was unpretentious. Carolyn seemed tired, so I asked her how she was. She couldn't hold back.

"'Oh, you don't know!' she yelped. 'People ring our bell all night. They jump out of nowhere when you walk out the door. I don't know if they want to click or shoot!!' I felt so bad for her; she seemed exhausted by the whole thing. 'The journalists never let up; they are calling my sister in Asia, they're calling my grandmother, they're calling my father, and I don't even speak with him!' When she was ready to leave, Brad asked me to walk her out the door and make sure no one bothered her. I wanted to walk her all the way home. I could feel she was so nervous."

Yes, Carolyn was getting her roots retouched before Easter with her husband's extended family. The knowledge that her picture was likely to be taken anytime she stepped out the door and then examined for flaws was a driving force behind Carolyn's changes in style and demeanor. Her wardrobe was a way to further shield herself (more than just, as recently speculated, "a way to have a conversation with the public"). Her go-to choice of Yohji Yamamoto was a defensive measure, with the designer describing his work: "I make clothing like armour. I wanted to protect the clothes themselves from fashion, and at the same time protect the woman's body from something." Nothing could have suited her better at the time. In the face of her silence, the tabloids simply printed false rumors about the state of her marriage and her mental health to accompany the paparazzi shots.

"She became obsessed with not giving the press anything to find wrong—a hair out of place, the wrong color or fit of clothes, or having a scrap of dirt under her fingernails—and obsessed with trying control it," said a close friend. There was a muting of herself—in her hair, body, style of dress—to make herself less remarkable, less accessible, less newsworthy, both to the press and to the public, who were hounding her in increasingly intimidating ways. Where she was once just annoyed at the media and attention, now she seemed afraid of it.

The media environment was ever more ravenous, and Gustavo Paredes, house manager for the President's House in Hyannis Port and close family friend, pointed out, "Photographers chase celebrities every day now. But back then, they really only chased John and Carolyn on a daily basis. So, for Carolyn and John, there ended up being cameras everywhere, videos, you name it, it never let up."

Thus, Carolyn's self-inflicted regimen of muting gave her some control over the one thing that was spiraling beyond her control: her image. And while still eternally elegant and stylish, there was certainly a pulling back from the carefree, bohemian *je ne sais quoi* look of her earlier years in New York. The restraint, it seemed, was necessary. MJ Bettenhausen said, "If she had time to have gotten used to her role, all of that would have toned down a bit. She would have remained refined, but she would've let herself gain a little weight, soften up. . . . But for now, she was frightened."

The change in her appearance wasn't the only casualty of her new reality. Some friends suggested that her personality was also something she had muted, reined in except in the company of her nearest and dearest. What the tabloids often described as Carolyn's cold demeanor can now more accurately be understood as fear.

Yet Rob Littell remembered Carolyn as the opposite of cold. "When Carolyn let down her guard, which wasn't often, you could sense something wounded about her. I always chalked it up to the father who was so conspicuously absent from her life," he wrote. "But then again, maybe that's just who she was. Her vulnerability, well hidden beneath a tough, funny exterior, made her deeply empathetic to others. She saw herself as an underdog— unbelievable but true—and she went out of her way to protect anyone in whom she sensed unease or unhappiness."

Carolyn had been supportive of Rob's wife, Frannie, on several occasions, and the Littells, sensing her distress, now wanted to help her. They invited John and Carolyn out for dinner and got a limo specifically to "spare Carolyn from having to stand in the street while we hunted for cabs." They got to their apartment on North Moore Street, buzzed, and waited until John and Carolyn came downstairs.

"John started to climb into the limo," Littell recounted, but "Carolyn turned away and walked over to the stoop, where she sat down. She told John she just couldn't do it; she couldn't go. The limo was a mistake. It made her feel more ostentatiously 'famous.' I felt horrible. She began to sniffle, and I said to John that we could do it another time, no big deal. Carolyn sat there on that concrete, looking so alone. John put his arm around her shoulders and spoke quietly into her ear. Her face regained some color and she smiled a little. Still tentative, she stood up and climbed into the limo, looking physically drained from the effort."

What did he whisper to her to calm her down? That the Littells had gotten the limo to make her feel comfortable, not to be all glammed up? That they were looking forward to the night and would be disappointed if it was called off? That she was gorgeous, and why not go out and enjoy herself? That he wanted everyone to see his beautiful wife? If she hadn't gone, he might have pointed out, the Littells would have felt guilty about the limo for some time. Whatever it was, it worked.

"And then, to my surprise, we had a great time," Littell wrote. "Dinner was fun and easy, and by the end of it, Carolyn was her funny, smart-ass self, riffing about an encounter she had with Donald Trump's eyebrows."

On the way home, Littell tried to give her a pep talk, suggesting that by being preoccupied by the attention, she was "feeding the beast."

" 'No, *listen*, Rob,' she said vehemently. 'They're out there *every day*. It's horrible.' She seemed so tired. Tired of having to be on all the time . . . I think it was exhausting having to be beautiful twenty-four hours a day. She's gone from hanging out in their little pre-wedding sandbox to having to play in front of stadium-size crowds . . . I'm not sure why wanting to look good was something to criticize, since most of the women in my life spend time and money to improve what they see in the mirror. Carolyn felt she had to measure up to her image as John's gorgeous and glamorous wife, and she did."

"Carolyn truly wanted to be a good wife," MJ Bettenhausen said, "and always worried about letting him down. It was hard for her to accept that no matter how hard she tried, certain tabloids would never come around."

Her inability to process the media attention made her fear she was letting John down, which made her depressed, which in turn made her want to stay home, which made her more depressed. Catch-22.

BY THIS POINT, CAROLYN felt comfortable only with close friends and immediate family. The contrast in her ease between an event where she had close friends and where she was there as a "public person" was seen in two events in that April.

At a Badgley Mischka runway show on April 8, the "young Manhattan design team . . . scored the double whammy [of having a successful show and] of having the painfully shy Carolyn Bessette Kennedy as a front row guest at their runway show," reported the *Daily News*. The previous Thursday, with Narciso in tow, she appeared at the opening of Brad Johns's salon on Fifth Avenue, where, according to *Newsday*, she "electrified the official opening." Her ease among those she could trust brought back her open, warm manner. They went on to say, "Bessette, much lovelier and cheerier in person than she seems in most of her photographs, made a beeline for Brad, hugged and kissed him, and then with a graciousness that would have done Jackie-O proud, spent the next hour chatting with Brad's mom. The model-filled room (all sporting the colorist's famous buttery chunks) was desperate to get a really good look at Carolyn, but she stayed close to Brad's family—thrilling them and impressing us. A sweet girl."

But despite having access to the fashion shows, hair salons, and galas, despite having a supportive husband and a bevy of close friends, Carolyn needed to find her life's work. Calvin Klein was in the past, and, for now, so was *George*. The wedding was one and done. She needed to figure out what was next for *her*.

Carole Radziwill wrote in her memoir about getting her MBA at NYU's Stern School of Business and just returning from a class trip to China to study the emerging market that April. Carolyn called Carole and asked, conspiratorially, "What are you doin'?" She invited Carolyn to come by her office at ABC on Columbus Avenue and 67th Street. Once there, Carolyn spied a row of Emmy awards in her fourth-floor office. "'Oh my God, those are real?' she said. 'You have Emmys?' She grabbed me by the shoulder, so I faced her. 'Radziwill, why aren't you telling everyone?' She made me seem interesting."

Carolyn and Carole often talked about what Carolyn would do next. Carolyn was not planning on being a housewife. Still, she had not anticipated the need to factor the media's reaction into even her slightest professional move. The pressure tripped her up.

"'I'm thinking about going back to school to get a master's degree in psychology,' Carolyn said.

"'I think that's a great idea. You could probably teach the class.' We spend an hour discussing logistics. If she applied right away she could start in September. She wants to apply to NYU; it's close to her apartment. I suggest uptown, at Columbia University."

Carole said that "Carolyn was thinking about ways she could make a mark in the world and turn all the unwanted attention to something good, something bigger than herself. She had an innate talent at homing in on the heart of someone's troubles and uplifting them. I saw this firsthand when my husband was dying. She always seemed to know what to do and say, while others in my husband's family could be awkward. Where many people showed sympathy, Carolyn had empathy. There is a big difference between feeling sorry and having compassion which allows for the other person's feelings."

Anyone who had known Carolyn knew she had abundant gifts to share. It was now about finding the right place to share them. Carolyn had been "extremely creative," Carole said. Michelle Kessler remembered that "Carolyn had a strong point of view for our ready-to-wear shows, and a clear vision for every facet of staging, models, run-of-show, hair, makeup, and music. She weighed in on absolutely everything." It would take a while to not only find her footing as Mrs. Kennedy, but find her footing in a career in which she could be effective while also being everything the name Mrs. Kennedy entailed, especially as it related to the media attention.

Yet she had great examples, such as having been mentored by Lynn Tesoro at Calvin Klein. Following Lynn's example, Carolyn made helping other women a priority both professionally and personally. She had brought Michelle Kessler into Calvin Klein and promoted Monicka HanssenTéele to take over her position when she left. Monicka had taken over Carolyn's first position in VIP sales when Carolyn was promoted to PR, and they became close in Carolyn's last years at Calvin Klein. Carolyn mentored Monicka, teaching her the ropes of producing runway shows: casting, lighting, music, styling the models, no detail left undone, and HanssenTéele now has her own runway, event, and photoshoot production company, MHT.

Another consideration for Carolyn was how any career choice of hers would track with that of her husband. At an event for the JFK Library, Carolyn ran into her old friend from her days with the Lyons Group in Boston, Jonathan Soroff. Thrilled to see a familiar face, she walked straight over to him and gave him a big hug and a kiss.

"I was there covering the event for the *Improper Bostonian*, and we stood for a long while catching up on our days at the Paradise and 15 Landsdowne, laughing. John came over, and Carolyn introduced us with an enormous smile. We had a quick hello, but he was busy that evening and soon moved off. I wanted to know everything, how she was and what she was up to. I also apologized to her for speaking with the press after she married John. 'You were a friend,' Carolyn said. 'It's absolutely fine. I know there's nothing that you were going to say that's going to be nasty. I trust you.'

"I asked if she was working, and she said she couldn't any longer. I'd always known her to work. 'I would love to be working, but I can't. I can't make a move without the press making a circus. No one wants this scene.' I sympathized with her, saying how strange it was to take this on, having known her before.

"'Life has become a circus,' Carolyn said."

CHAPTER SEVENTEEN

CRUEL SUMMER

May 1997–August 1997

Later in May, Carolyn and John flew overseas again to Italy. When they first arrived in Milan, the *Daily News* noted that "the swarm of paparazzi made them switch hotels." The hope that the frantic attention they received would recede after marriage was slowly dissipating, as was the idea of anonymity. Attending an Italian fashion-industry dinner, John impressed both his hosts and his wife with a nod to his parents' history, and his commitment to theirs together: "Let me use the same phrase that my father did when he went to Paris with my mother 35 years ago," John said. "My name is John Kennedy, and I am the man who is accompanying Carolyn Bessette to Milan. I am honored to tell you she is my wife."

When the couple returned to New York a few weeks later in June, they were greeted with headlines speculating wildly about the possibility that Carolyn was pregnant: "JFK Jr.'s wife reportedly pregnant," "Carolyn 'Bassinet' Kennedy," and "A Kennedy bundle of joy?"

Invasive speculation over the domain of the female body is nothing new. But when a dynasty is part of the equation, there is pressure to produce an heir. Up-to-the-minute reporting—by town crier, by pamphlet, by carrier pigeon, and now by the *Daily News*—was the standard on any bulge of the belly, and whether or not the woman in question is taking proper care of said bulge. It continues until she has aged out of her childbearing years, at which point they begin to harp upon her aging.

The *Daily News* in June 1997 ran the insipid headline, "John-John to be da-da?" going on to say: "We wouldn't blame him if he dissembled a bit this time around. Kennedy does his best to keep media-aggravation of his sometimes-moody wife to a minimum. Following reports of the pregnancy rumor yesterday, camera crews were massed around his doorstep. The last thing Kennedy wants is for some kamikaze paparazzi to panic his beloved in the first trimester. But you can bet that, more than ever, people will be paying attention to what Carolyn wears—whether she starts moving toward a baggier look. You can also watch for Gianni Versace, who has anointed Carolyn as one of the women who inspires him as a designer, to start working on a line of maternity clothes."

Neither of those things came to be. Versace was not questioned when the maternity line did not come to pass, but Carolyn was hounded by cameras while coming out of her gynecologist's office at 300 West 72nd Street. Another frenzy began, as well as a breakdown of every single thing she wore that morning: "A Gap top, Selima Optique glasses, Jackie Kennedy's Cartier watch, and her Hermès Birkin bag." There was a debate over whether her jeans were JNCO or Calvin Klein carpenter jeans. (Calvin won the day, albeit on Instagram twenty-five years later.)

Carolyn lost her friend Gianni Versace within a month of that article, when serial killer Andrew Cunanan fatally shot the designer outside his Miami Beach home on July 15. Cunanan had been on a murder spree and targeted the fashion designer, although Versace was merely an acquaintance. Carolyn traveled back to Italy and was among the two thousand mourners at Versace's funeral liturgy at Milan Cathedral on July 22. A sad, bewildered-looking Carolyn sat behind Diana, Princess of Wales, Sting and Trudie Styler, and Elton John.

AFTER AN ELEVEN-MONTH REPRIEVE, Anthony Radziwill got tough news after his latest scan: The cancer had metastasized to his lungs and an operation was needed. So, after Milan, Carolyn flew to DC to be with Carole as Anthony checked into the NIH in DC. Carole recalled that Carolyn had, as always, brought a picture of her dog Friday, which she kissed and hung on the wall to cheer everyone up. Carolyn did this every time Anthony was in the hospital—it was cheering because it was funny that in her mind Friday was imbued with magical happy-making powers, like a canine good fairy. Unfortunately, despite Friday on the wall, there was a complication with the surgery, and Anthony had to remain in the hospital longer than expected.

Carolyn stayed, and when not rubbing Anthony's feet with a loofah and peppermint lotions, she hung out with Carole to keep her spirits up. "We drive to Tysons Corner in search of Hush Puppies," Radziwill wrote in her memoir. " 'It's all about a Hush Puppy,' [Carolyn] declares. 'You aren't leaving this town without them.' We stop at Bloomingdale's and give each other makeovers at the MAC counter. We order sticky rolls at Cinnabon."

John flew down to DC to pick up Carolyn; the two of them were due at a private reception and screening of *Air Force One* hosted by Bill and Hillary Clinton at the White House. Anthony was weak and swollen, with numerous wires hooking him up to machines, which shocked and frightened John. Carolyn apologized for leaving and said she would be back in the morning. "It's ridiculous, [Carolyn] thinks, to go to the White House to see a movie while [Anthony's] here in this room," Carole wrote. "Here is where she wants to be. But that is their life. Before they leave, she takes a makeup bag into the small hospital bathroom. She comes out with her hair up in a bun, clips it into place, and applies MAC Studio Fix powder on her face. 'Before . . . after,' she says, as she dots the circles under her eyes. She finishes up with Ruby Stain."

At the screening, John and Tommy Hilfiger shared treats, passing around Goobers, popcorn, and Tic Tacs. *Women's Wear Daily* reported that "Bessette Kennedy declined the Goobers, she told Hilfiger, because if she indulges, the press will think she's pregnant."

"Are you pregnant?" Hilfiger asked.

"Absolutely not," Carolyn responded.

Carolyn spoke at length with Chelsea Clinton, telling her it was ludicrous that people criticized Washington fashion as frumpy. "Washington women work in public service. They want to be judged on the issues, not on how they look or what they wear," Carolyn said. "Fashion takes a lot of time and energy. Sometimes, it can be a distraction."

THAT SUMMER, CAROLYN WAS shopping at the Ralph Lauren store on Madison Avenue at 72nd Street when she overheard two women approach the jewelry counter. The manager who was helping Carolyn had gone to find her something from another floor, so the women asked a young salesperson assigned to the jewelry counter, Mary Wade, for help.

"Carolyn came out of the dressing room and was looking for jewelry, some rings for her nieces. Suddenly two women began to insist that I go find a particular pair of pants immediately, demanding to be taken to find the pants in their size. They knew exactly who Carolyn was and were doing it because she was standing there. They were making a show of this."

Wade tried to explain that she could not leave the jewelry counter unattended. One of the woman began insulting Wade, even going so far as to say, "I bet she didn't even go to college."

"Suddenly, Carolyn slammed the rings down on the counter and said, 'Never mind.' I was worried she was upset with me. But she went back to the dressing room to call John, telling him, 'I can see my hand wrapped around these women's necks!' John convinced her not to go yell at the women, reminding her it would be all over the papers and definitely skewed to make Carolyn look deranged."

Carolyn could relate to this young woman, selling designer wares to clients who had an inflated sense of worth based on their spending power.

"She waited a few minutes and then came out to me and held my hands in hers," said Wade. "She told me to please not feel bad about people like that. She spent twenty minutes consoling me. She was incredibly kind, like an angel."

When Carolyn got home, she picked up the phone, called a florist in the neighborhood, and had an African violet delivered to the saleswoman. Betsy Reisinger and her fiancé, Kenan Siegel, were staying with John and Carolyn at the time. Reisinger recalled Carolyn's focus that afternoon when she came into the house, called the florist, and then told the story.

"She wanted to make sure that whatever damage those women had inflicted, that she invalidated it," Reisinger said. "This was the Carolyn I knew—her first response was always kindness and concern."

The summer weekends were spent at either at Martha's Vineyard or Hyannis Port, and were a mix of private time and socializing. On Memorial Day, they hosted Rob and Frannie Littell, and then for the Fourth of July, it was Sasha Chermayeff and her family.

Brown alum Billy Strauss, who says he didn't know the couple very well, once visited them in the Vineyard with his wife, newborn baby, and three-year-old daughter. "We were in that phase where our toddler was nonplussed at the new arrival, and she was going through a clingy phase. . . . For months, she wouldn't let another adult near her, but the moment we arrived at Red Gate, Carolyn said to her, 'Let's go down to the swings!' I couldn't believe it," Strauss said, "our daughter went with her immediately, with no fuss, and they stayed down there for well over an hour. If you've ever had a child in the clinging phase, even five minutes feels like a huge reprieve, so that she stayed with Carolyn for over an hour was shocking. When they came back, Carolyn kept her in her lap.

"Later that evening, Carolyn told us, 'Your wonderful girl is very articulate, and she knows what she likes. Loyalty is very important to her; she expects it from those she cares about, and she will certainly give it herself.' It's amazing twenty years later to look back; Carolyn was spot-on about our daughter. Within that hour, she had ascertained exactly who she was, and who she remained."

The former education major was always able to connect with kids. Ariel Paredes, the daughter of Gustavo Paredes (their house manager in Hyannis Port and son of Jackie's longtime aide Provi Paredes), spent summers in Martha's Vineyard with her mother's family and would visit Hyannis Port each summer. She looked at John as a friend and an annoying older brother. "I often rolled my eyes at things that John did," Ariel remembered, laughing. She thought of him as a typical guy's guy. "Watching him inhale his Raisin Bran cereal, I would just say, 'Take a breather.'

"I was so thrilled when Carolyn came along," Ariel said. "She was always so sweet to me. . . . She took me shopping and sat chatting with me for hours. Boys, school, grades, she always made me feel great about myself. She was the first person with whom I plucked my eyebrows. Hers were super thin, so I said, 'I love yours but maybe not as thin for me.'"

Gustavo said, "Yes, those two were always off together. Once in a while, John would say, 'Have you seen Carolyn?' 'Off with Ariel.' Or I would say, 'Have you seen Ariel?' 'Off with Carolyn.' We would just shrug."

"We would talk for hours at a time," Ariel said, "and she would take me to the mall in Hyannis Port, which had hardly anything in it. Maybe the Gap. She bought me a bunch of gray hoodies and said, 'In college, you'll need lounge pants.'

"We went for ice cream at Four Seas; she always liked butter pecan, which wasn't my flavor of choice," Ariel said, laughing. "Since I spent summers on Martha's Vineyard, I would see them there, too. Carolyn told me to use their beach whenever I wanted, which was beautiful."

That July, John attended the Experimental Aircraft Association Fly-In Convention in Oshkosh, Wisconsin, and became enamored with the Buckeye, a flying machine that "was essentially a steel cage with a motor attached to a parachute," also known as the Flying Lawnmower. John described himself as a "lapsed pilot" and told the assembled crowds that "he was an aviation enthusiast from his childhood." He had always sought out high adventure as a means of coping, whether it was helicopter skiing, playing chicken with the Staten Island Ferry on a kayak, or rollerblading in Manhattan traffic. As John had told Rob Littell, standing still, for him, would mean falling apart. It would make sense that John would eventually take to the skies himself, and despite Carolyn's initial misgivings, she couldn't deny that flying with John would afford an extra level of privacy and peace. And really, they were traveling all the time.

Naturally, behind closed doors, even friends and family wondered if Carolyn and John were thinking of having children. But Carolyn was not ready. She told friends she was already afraid to walk around New York City by herself, and she worried about protecting a baby under the circumstances. According to Billy Noonan in *Forever Young*, Carolyn told him: "How can I bring JFK III into this world? They'll never leave me alone. They treat John like a national treasure, so what are they going to do to his *son*?"

John was very eager for kids, though, and was not as worried about how to handle children in the spotlight. He had, after all, been raised there himself and had an excellent role model in his mother. Tammy Holloway, wife of football player and Kennedy family friend Brian, told biographer J. Randy Taraborrelli that John and Carolyn wanted to start a family and that they planned to be hands-on, just like Jackie had been. "She was there for us all the time, no exceptions," John said about his mother. "And she had a real code of behavior for us. I can still hear her voice . . . 'Just because you are a Kennedy doesn't give you license to be unkind to others. I don't care whether he is rich or poor, black, white, whatever . . . Every single person deserves your respect.' That's what she used to tell us and I daydream about telling my kids that."

In the meantime, they had just as much fun hanging out, kid-free, with their grown-up friends. Hamilton South remembered all of them going to Mike Nichols and Diane Sawyer's house when they were in the Vineyard. "Diane and Mike loved Carolyn. We used to have so much fun, with long dinners. We would play Bartlett's, or sometimes a made-up version of it called Novel," South said. "One person went to pick a novel from their bookshelves, and then chose the first two lines from the book and wrote them down. They would show everyone the novel but not the lines. Everyone had to make up two lines, and we then mixed all the papers. Finally, everyone had to guess which were the real lines. Carolyn *always* won. . . . She was such a bright light, so erudite.

"And she and John were happy," South added. "She just needed time to adjust to the craziness around them, of which there was a lot."

In August, when Caroline and Ed had Red Gate Farm on Martha's Vineyard, Carolyn and John would spend most of their time in Hyannis Port.

"Carolyn was so laid-back when on the Cape," Ariel said. "It was only when she had to worry about being papped that she dressed to perfection. She would often walk around in a sarong and wild hair. I would say to her, 'Are we not brushing our hair today?' She would just laugh at me.

"Carolyn was really lovely with me," Ariel continued. "We would stay up late on the couch talking. That summer was their first whole summer as a married couple. Carolyn and I would yammer well past midnight, until we'd hear John trudging down the stairs.

"'Carolyn?'" Ariel remembered him shouting. "Carolyn would say, 'Oh, I'd better get upstairs.' I didn't really get the marriage dynamic yet and I'd roll my eyes and say, 'Why do you have to go up there?'

"'You'll understand when you're married,' she'd say."

Carolyn and John didn't stay in Hyannis Port that August, as there had been trouble brewing at RFK's next door. Sheila Rauch, the former wife of Joe Kennedy, a Massachusetts congressman currently running for governor, was soon to publish *Shattered Faith: A Woman's Struggle to Stop the Catholic Church from Annulling Her Marriage*, in which she took Joe and the Catholic Church to task for annulling their marriage so that he could remarry and still take Communion. The press was having a field day over the hypocrisy of annulling a twelve-year marriage that had produced two children. At the same time, Joe's younger brother Michael was in even hotter water. Michael had been caught having an affair with the family's underage babysitter, Marisa Verrochi, whose parents lived down the street and had contributed $50,000 to one of Michael's campaigns for gun control.

John came up with the idea of writing about temptation—both his own and that of his cousins—in his editor's letter for *George* magazine, which would come out in late August. It was an unusual choice, some of his editors noted, to write after only one year of marriage, "I've learned a lot about temptation recently. But that doesn't make me desire any less. If anything, to be reminded of the possible perils of succumbing to what's forbidden only makes it more alluring." John took special notice of how the public delighted in the "distraction of gawking at the travails of those who just couldn't resist. We can all gather, like urchins at a hanging, to watch those poor souls who took a chance on fantasy and came up empty-handed—to remind ourselves to keep to the safety of the middle path . . . Two members of my family chased an idealized alternative to their life. One left behind an embittered wife, and another, in what looked to be a hedge against morality, fell in love with youth and surrendered his judgment in the process. Both became poster boys for bad behavior."

According to friends, Carolyn did not take umbrage that John wrote about temptation. They had been married a year, and she felt sure of his love. In fact, the endless press speculation about John and other women and/or Carolyn's jealousy became a joke between them. A friend said Carolyn "once had posters of nearly every supermodel working on which she had written mock notes of love and adoration sent to his office. You know, 'Dear John, I think you are still the sexiest man alive. Love, Claudia.' John thought it was hilarious, and you could hear him roaring with laughter in his office."

While John was essentially defending his cousins' behavior, his cousins did not see it that way. Joe, in particular, hit back by stating, "Ask not what you can do for your cousin but what you can do for your cousin's magazine." John was flummoxed that they didn't understand his meaning. "But if they're too stupid to get the point," John said to Billy Noonan, "who needs them?"

John might have needed them. He was pilloried in the press for his essay and the accompanying picture: John, crouched, knees to his chin, looking up at an apple hovering above, and as far as the viewer could tell, naked. Was this the first "Felt cute, might delete later"? If only he could have. The *Washington Post* called it "so innocuous, so mundane, that it comes as something of a disappointment," while Maureen Dowd wrote in the *New York Times*: "[T]he Kennedys always embraced hypocrisy as a family value. Now they have embraced stupidity." *Newsday* noted that Jackie had had her children keep their distance from the RFKs, but the newspaper still called *George* a "*People*-ized approach to politics," and called John a "himbo."

As if *Newsday* didn't have enough to say against John, they went on to attack Carolyn, for good measure, but not for any editor's letter or defense of the RFK cousins, but, of course, for her body. Carolyn "resembles in many ways Princess Diana," wrote James Pinkerton. "Carolyn also is a lissome and somewhat beaky blonde. And if the tabloids are to be believed, she is also high-maintenance, prone to depression and flakiness."

The implication was that Carolyn was simultaneously holding John back and making waves with the extended family, whom Jackie may have avoided, but had never broken ranks with. This was a moment where John was going against the grain, yet the hammer still came down on his wife for it, if by association.

EAGER TO NOT BE in the Hyannis Port vicinity after the fallout from the editor's letter, in August John headed to Iceland to go kayaking. And Carolyn spent much time in the city with her sister Lauren, who was visiting from Asia. Lauren's close friend Chip Arndt recalled seeing the sisters for lunches and dinners that summer. "[John] was gone for about two weeks, during which time, tabloids began printing rumors that Carolyn had begun an affair with Michael Bergin," Arndt said. It was a claim that Bergin himself corroborated, writing in his 2004 memoir that Carolyn came to Los Angeles in July, begging him to "save her."

"The idea that Carolyn would have flown to Los Angeles to go see Michael Bergin after her marriage is ludicrous," said Jack Merrill. "There was no way she would have been getting on a plane herself at that point. She was so fearful of the press that she wasn't leaving the house, much less to go see Bergin. We had last run into him at The Bowery Bar around six months earlier. He came over and sat with us, but Carolyn had wished he wouldn't.

"She was polite and nice, but by that point, he had been chasing her for years, and she had made it very clear that she had no interest. Even before John, she had very little interest. Carolyn, by that time, found him creepy."

That summer, Carolyn rarely left the loft, much less New York City, without John. MJ Bettenhausen explained that their compromise "was to stick in the neighborhood," spending time with the dogs at their makeshift parking lot/dog run.

"We had a few other friends who brought their dogs, and we did this every day. On the day John returned from Iceland, he was expecting a welcome home party from Carolyn, with her waiting at the airport for his arrival, which she sometimes did. But this time it was one of the dogs' birthday—a huge, beautiful Malamute named Star. We had cake, dog toys, the works. Carolyn told him she couldn't miss Star's birthday. When John drove up and saw us, he just laughed."

Upon John's return, the couple flew to Martha's Vineyard to join Caroline and Ed at a dinner party for Hillary and Bill Clinton. They went on to Hyannis Port a couple of days later, at the behest of Ted, who had arranged a family summit as a show of unity after the "poster boys" moment in *George*, and to play some touch football, naturally.

AT THE VERY END of August, Princess Diana was killed in a car accident at Pont de l'Alma Tunnel in Paris as the result of her driver trying to outrun the paparazzi. John told Billy Noonan, "[Carolyn's] really spooked now." Just a month earlier, Carolyn had sat behind Diana at Gianni Versace's funeral, whose death, it could be argued, was also a result of his fame. She couldn't help but wonder if a similar fate would befall her. Carolyn was terrified.

Less than a week later, Carolyn and John had dinner in Hyannis Port, on the evening of Diana's funeral, with Kathy McKeon, Jackie's former assistant and occasional babysitter to John and Caroline. She was meeting Carolyn for the first time and later wrote in her memoir, *Jackie's Girl*, that Carolyn's skin "was almost as white and translucent as fine porcelain. She was chic in beige shorts and a short-sleeved black cashmere sweater, with a cardigan tied at her waist. She was holding a fluffy tuxedo cat and kissing him as he shed all over her expensive sweater. She'd just arrived herself, she explained, and she hadn't seen her cat in a whole week."

When they sat down to dinner with Provi Paredes and McKeon, the subject of Diana and the scourge of the paparazzi came up, and McKeon described Carolyn's strong reaction:

Carolyn, who had seemed shy and reserved until then, opened up. She had gotten into some well-publicized fights with the photographers who chased her as she walked the streets of Manhattan, even kicking one. She felt besieged. John was clearly worried about his high-strung bride.

"Kath, tell Carolyn how Mom used to handle them," he prompted me. Provi Paredes jumped in to answer first, but John cut her off.

"No, wait, I want to hear from Kathy," he said.

"When she was up here, she'd leave the gate smiling, give them one good picture, and they'd let her go," I remembered.

"No!" Carolyn nearly shouted. "I hate those bastards! I'd rather just scream and curse at them."

"That's exactly what they want you to do," I argued. "They'll get great pictures."

She described how she had gotten chased down the sidewalk by a wolf pack of photographers and ducked into a building to escape them. They cornered her by the elevator as she frantically pushed the button. "They were grunting and groaning and pushing each other. They were almost on top of me," she recounted. "It was just awful. I can't take it!"

John interjected. "You gotta just take it easy," he insisted. "Relax."

While Carolyn was forthcoming about her despair concerning the circumstances of Diana's death, John remained quiet for the most part, though he was also affected.

"When Diana died," Biz Mitchell, executive editor of *George* at the time, told the *Hollywood Reporter*, "I remember calling him at home and saying, 'We're going to have to do something.' And he said, 'Yeah, OK, we'll talk about it.' So I called a meeting to discuss it. He just didn't come—he wasn't showing up on time, which he normally would never do. We kept delaying, and finally he came in and said, 'I can't do it right now, I need to clean my office.' It was obvious he was having an emotional response to the tragedy and finding it difficult. He kept saying, 'I don't see why this needs to be a story.'

In the end, we did this incredible photo essay of the mourning going on in London."

Carolyn tried to get John to call Princes William and Harry to give his condolences when it came out that Diana had hoped for her sons to emulate John's modesty in the face of media obsession. "'Those poor boys,' Carolyn said, shaking her head as she scanned the newspapers at Bubby's," Christopher Andersen later wrote.

He demurred as he didn't know them and thought, perhaps incorrectly, that their situations greatly differed. "I was able to lead a normal life from about the age of five," he said. Carolyn, as ever, was acutely aware of those who were left behind. Between the loss of her friend Gianni and the horrific circumstances of Diana's death, it was a difficult summer. There were, however, reasons to look ahead with optimism. Number one was that Carolyn's sister Lauren was planning to return to the United States.

CHAPTER EIGHTEEN

BURNING AT BOTH ENDS

September 1997–December 1997

Carolyn and John celebrated their first anniversary in September in San Francisco and managed to do so with a modicum of privacy. They canoodled in the Huntington Hotel's lobby bar before attending a dinner at the Saks Fifth Avenue men's store for the Delancey Street Foundation, a residential rehabilitation program. Carolyn looked bright and happy, in an unusually non-black, or rather black-and-white, houndstooth Yohji Yamamoto skirt suit from the 1997 autumn/winter collection, and seemed to not only find comfort in being away from New York but also in being with her husband.

The *San Francisco Examiner* asked her about her first year of marriage. "Describing what it's like to be a new bride, especially one who's hitched to the world's most publicized man alive, Bessette-Kennedy mused on 'this profound metamorphosis in nine or 10 minutes of shared vows, and all of a sudden your life is completely different. It's important to have people around who love and understand you, so you don't feel you're the only ones invested in your future.' A pretty good description of marriage, whether to a Kennedy or not. Contrary to the rumor mill, her husband seemed to be in her thrall as he grabbed her arm affectionately and fixed the curve of her shawl collar." Carolyn also mused, "It doesn't seem like a year."

From San Francisco, they drove south to Big Sur, where they stayed at the rustic Ventana Inn. With "tent cabins," it was essentially glamping before

the term was coined, the accommodations overlooking a twenty-acre can-
yon. Guests had choices of going falconing, hiking among the redwoods, or
even relaxing in the Japanese baths under the stars.

Carolyn's outlook had vastly improved on the trip, and John was invested
in keeping it that way. Christopher Andersen wrote, "When they returned
to New York, John was determined to keep Carolyn from sinking back into
a state of depression. He set aside two lunch dates per week for Carolyn and
instructed the staff to interrupt him whenever she called. 'I don't care if I'm in
a meeting or on the phone to the White House,' he said. 'Put Carolyn straight
through.' But Carolyn, still forced to run the gauntlet of photographers every
time she left their apartment, again became bored and withdrawn."

She still couldn't go into the *George* offices, because everything had gotten tense at the struggling magazine, and the paparazzi had gotten into the
habit of not merely swarming her when she walked down the street, but also
calling her vile names. "They called her a whore," said one friend, "and they
called her a cunt." An intensely unhealthy feedback loop developed.

"The more mysterious she became," Steve Gillon wrote in *America's
Reluctant Prince*, "the more the public yearned to know more about her. For
the paparazzi, money drove the entire operation. Victor Malafronte, who
stalked John for years, claimed they could demand $500 to $1,000 for an
exclusive picture of John and Carolyn. While that amount may not sound
like much, a photographer could sell a photo to multiple newspapers and
magazines, both in the United States and around the world. Therefore, he
could end up making between $15,000 and $20,000 with a single picture.
Malafronte remained unapologetic about hunting John and later Carolyn.
'It's hard to feel sorry for a guy who is so rich, good-looking, and a Kennedy,'
he said matter-of-factly."

And it became well-known that a picture of Carolyn looking angry, sad,
or terrified would yield a bigger payday than if she looked content or smiled.

Just as photos of Carolyn looking unhappy sold more, so did stories that
the couple was unhappy, fighting, and on the brink of divorce. John cut his
hand in a kitchen accident, and the tabloids insinuated that the injury was
a result of a violent fight and that Carolyn had inflicted the damage. Close
friend Dan Samson truly felt for Carolyn. "At first blush it seems naïve to
think Carolyn didn't know what she was getting into when she married
John, but I really don't think she expected that every day she walked out the

front door of their Tribeca apartment the paparazzi would jump out of cars and scatter out of alleys and up the street like rats to catch her walking from the building to a waiting car out front," Samson said. "She didn't ask to be a style icon or an American princess—it was thrust upon her, and then people seemed to be critical of her at every turn. I think women were literally mad at her for taking John off the market."

John's interviews and meetings could take him pretty far afield, leaving Carolyn on her own back in New York. On October 23, John flew to Cuba with *George* writer Inigo Thomas to meet with Fidel Castro.

"John spent months laying the groundwork for the trip," wrote Gillon. "The magazine sold extra ads knowing that a face-to-face encounter between the son of the American president and Castro would generate loads of buzz. It was JFK who had helped neutralize Cuba and the Soviet Union in the most dangerous confrontation of the nuclear age."

Castro kept John dangling for four days. "He will see you for dinner tonight, and we will contact you," John was told every morning when he called. Then every night, during the hour that had been appointed for dinner, he would get a phone call back saying, "El Presidente cannot meet you this evening. Perhaps tomorrow."

Inigo Thomas remembered, "We spent four days aimlessly popping around Havana in a van driven by some governmental aide. We were close to giving up."

But Carolyn let John know, in no uncertain terms, that giving up was unacceptable.

Gillon wrote that during one of their nightly calls, Carolyn told John, "You get on that fucking phone to whomever you need to, whether it's a US diplomat or Castro's guys, and you tell him that you are not going to sit around taking this shit. You came to see him, you are a Kennedy, you are a journalist with staff here, and if his office promised an interview, goddamnit, you're not leaving until you get one."

John stayed, and he and Inigo finally got to meet with Castro. According to Gillon, one of the first questions Castro asked of John was, "Are you the same height as your father?"

John replied, "He was a little taller, and a little thinner."

For the next five hours, Castro regaled John with "little more than plati- tudes, self-serving blandishments, and a scattering of banal observations about nothing in particular." Castro kept an uneaten shrimp on the edge of his fork as he held forth forever, essentially wasting John's time, though he did say he was an admirer of JFK, and "seemed to apologize for refusing Lee Harvey Oswald an entry visa into Cuba in October 1963," wrote Andersen, "an act that almost certainly would've prevented Oswald from being in Dallas one month later."

When John returned to New York, he professed to dislike the guy too much to put him in *George*. Pecker begged him to include the interview, but John refused. It would have been better for the magazine if John had relented, but John's feelings on the matter can best be understood by the diabolical parting Castro gave to his nemesis's son. Just before being driven off into the night, Castro rolled down the window to his car, and motioned John to come close and lean down to hear him. "I didn't do it," Castro said.

IN THE FALL AND early winter of '97, Carolyn and John were stuck in a vicious loop: They would have troubles and the media would report on it, which, in turn, would cause even more relationship troubles.

In October, the *Daily News* ran an item about a fight John and Carolyn purportedly had the previous summer. "In-flight turbulence for JFK Jr. and Carolyn" ran the headline. It went on to say, "John Kennedy Jr. and Carolyn Bessette reportedly have been talking—make that shouting—about divorce. The bickering pair began to generate turbulence aboard a 12-seater plane even before it took off from Newark airport on its way to Martha's Vineyard back in the summer. . . . [T]he couple argued through most of the hour-long Continental Express flight, but . . . the quarrel reached its highest altitude when John yelled: 'Maybe we should get divorced. We fucking talk about it enough!' Carolyn reportedly shot back, 'Oh no. We waited for your mother to die to get married. We're waiting for my mother to die to get a divorce.'"

The *Daily News* went on to say that they headed to Red Gate Farm after the flight, but Carolyn soon left on a private charter plane, while John "spent the entire next day frantically bicycling around the island."

George Plimpton said the stories about an impending divorce were not true, nor were the stories about either of them hiring private detectives to follow each other—"but each story only added to Carolyn's fear and loathing of the media."

Plimpton suggested to John that Carolyn seek counseling, but not as a referendum on her as a person, or in the way that the nineties press implied mental health issues were due to a character flaw. "The temptation to say, 'Get over it—get past it' is far too simplistic," said Plimpton. "Her fear of the media as well as crowds impacted her desire to have children. So I recommended John send her to a shrink. Is there anyone in New York who hasn't at one time or another been in therapy? John went to the same shrink I'd seen for a while. And he was still in therapy, though with somebody else. Carolyn began therapy in the summer of 1997 and continued for two years, until the end of her life. The psychiatrist put her on antidepressants. She wasn't really depressive. What saddened her, I believe, was her sense that she was letting John down . . . Had they lived, I have no doubt she would've learned to cope. They would have had children."

As Anthony Radziwill's health continued to decline, both Carolyn and John were heartsick. Carolyn accompanied Carole and Anthony to DC to the NIH again, and the friends again found humor in the absurd together. Al Gore's mother-in-law, Margaret Aitcheson, was also a patient at the NIH there, and she mistook Carole and Carolyn for nurses. They first spied her wandering around the hallways looking for cigarettes. "Where are my cigarettes? Someone stole my cigarettes!" So while Hamilton came down to break Anthony out of hospital jail to go shopping for shirts, Carolyn and Carole happily ran errands for Mrs. Aitcheson. "It is funny, hilarious to them in the retelling," Carole wrote in *What Remains*, "Anthony prodding Hamilton along as if this is just a fun weekend away with friends."

In late October, Carolyn and John attended a Halloween party at the home of artist Terry Fugate-Wilcox and his wife, art dealer Valerie Monroe Shakespeare, who told C. David Heymann that John and Carolyn had dressed as George and Martha Washington in honor of the magazine. "They dressed [Friday] in orange—he came with them—and they called him 'Pumpkin' all night. John seemed a bit shy at first. He was polite and gracious. I asked him, 'How is it all Kennedys look alike?' 'Same hairdresser, same dentist,' he answered. . . . Neither John nor Carolyn said anything of a highly personal nature. They laughed and joked a lot, but they also erected a kind of wall beyond which you knew not to tread," Fugate-Wilcox said. "They usually let down their hair only in the presence of trusted friends. Once we grew closer, they began to relax."

Carolyn always sent a thank-you note, bordered in Tiffany pale blue, and she sent one to Fugate-Wilcox and Shakespeare after their Halloween party. But for her own parties where she was the host or had to be "on," Carolyn, at this point, wanted backup. For the second-anniversary party of *George* magazine, she brought her mother along. *Women's Wear Daily* reported that she stood for two hours at the door, meeting and greeting people from Ian and Rita Schrager to Ted Nugent, who wore a Ducks Unlimited baseball cap. "Don't be too hard on those ducks," she said to Nugent, with no idea how prescient her words to the pro-NRA gun-toting Nugent would be.

Lee Radziwill was there with her husband, director and producer Herbert Ross, and Ellen DeGeneres and Anne Heche also showed. When the crowd around his wife got heavy, John came up to her to check in.

"How're you doing, honey-bunny?" he asked, giving Carolyn's shoulder a quick squeeze.

Michael Musto told the *Daily News* that Carolyn looked "gloriously happy. . . . She was radiant and smiling and acting affectionate with John-John. She was rubbing his back. I was amazed—she looks so happy."

Women's Wear Daily reported, "On her way upstairs for a break, Bessette-Kennedy stopped to commiserate with *George* staffers about a recent wilderness retreat they took in the Catskills with her very fit husband. 'You could be hanging from a cliff by your fingernails, and John would say, *Come on, let's go! What are you waiting for?*' she said later with a laugh. 'I told one of the editors, *Now you know what I go through every weekend.*'"

Eventually, the conversation turned toward *George*. Carolyn's favorite piece in the magazine was a November 1997 profile John wrote on the late Mother Teresa. "Through her great need to be vigilant for the disenfranchised," she explained to *Women's Wear Daily*, "Mother Teresa was an extraordinary departure from the values of media culture. And any figure who challenges that is a powerful political figure."

As Carolyn left the party with her mother, Ann was heard exclaiming, "I don't know how you put up with this. I don't care how much you love him—it's just not worth it."

Carolyn's circle tightened, and she enlisted family and close, trusted friends to help her cope with the glare of the spotlight. Carolyn found solace in having her sister Lisa with her at the November 6 Whitney gala for the opening of its Andy Warhol exhibition. The previous year's boos from the phalanx of press lining the entrance because she hadn't paused to give a quote were likely well remembered as she traversed the steps into the building.

Later in the month, during the twenty-fourth anniversary of the JFK assassination, Carolyn and John left town, as was John's ritual during that sensitive time. They went to investigate buying a two-seater Buckeye in Argos, Indiana, where they spent time with Ralph Howard, who owned Buckeye Industries, and his family. Ralph said Carolyn "talked a mile a minute, and we could tell it was a relief for her to be out here, away from the attention, where she and her husband could be together and not worry."

He added that she "babied John. She treated him like he was her child—always asking him how he felt, reminding him to wear a scarf, that sort of thing." On the trip, it was clear that John was vulnerable that week. He had misplaced his hat and had an outsized reaction. A surprised Howard remembers, "It was pretty odd; he was quite upset and starting to get angry at my employees, thinking for a moment that one of them had taken it for a token of Kennedy memorabilia. Carolyn calmed him down and found the hat in the backseat of the car they had come in. She later explained that he was upset because it was the last gift his mother had given him."

Howard brought up the tabloid rumors about their marriage, and asked if all was indeed well. The couple reassured him that it was. Then he asked if they were planning to have children. "They looked at each other. 'Oh yes,' Carolyn told me, smiling at John."

Carolyn and John spent Thanksgiving that year in Hyannis Port with Narciso Rodriguez; Provi, Gustavo, and Ariel Paredes; and Billy and Kathleen Noonan and their son, TJ. Even Noonan, who was not particularly kind to Carolyn in his memoir of his friendship with John, admitted she was wonderful with children, babies, and animals. There are pictures of Carolyn cradling their baby and putting the pacifier in his mouth while John regaled everyone with the story of Castro's shrimp. "That fucking shrimp," John called it. John, with training from his days in the theater, imitated Castro's gestures and accent perfectly. " 'God, it seemed like hours,' John told us. But, thanks to Carolyn, he got his interview," Noonan wrote.

ITALY WAS CLEARLY A happy place for the couple. On December 7 they were once again in Milan and attended the Teatro alla Scala to see Giuseppe Verdi's *Macbeth*. It was their third trip to Italy in a year, and Carolyn left the opera looking like a 1920s screen siren, wearing a black beret and what had become her signature look: Bobbi Brown Sheer Lipstick in Ruby.

Italy had been a beautiful escape, and the couple planned for more respite. They went south to Vero Beach, Florida, for several weeks in December, where John would take flying lessons at the FlightSafety Academy. Carolyn was not happy about this development. The Buckeye flights had been brief, up and down again in minutes, like playing with a toy. An actual airplane was another matter altogether. Carolyn, like Jackie, sensed that this was not a good idea.

Christopher Andersen later wrote that Carolyn said, "I mean it, John. I have a bad feeling about this. I don't want you taking flying lessons."

Yet she could not dissuade him. The couple had a beautiful time together, finding happiness in privacy, but Carolyn was frightened. As if she had tapped into the truth of a larger-scale worry of being a Kennedy, they got the news on January 1 that John's cousin Michael Kennedy had died in a skiing accident in Aspen on New Year's Eve. The RFKs had been playing football with a snow-filled frozen water bottle for a football while skiing down the mountain on the last run of the day, and Michael hit a tree.

John and Carolyn rushed to Hyannis Port for the funeral. John was heartbroken, and everyone's nerves were frayed. Despite the time they had spent with his cousins in the summer and over Thanksgiving, there was still tension due to John's editor's letter about Michael and Joe earlier that fall. John tightly hugged Douglas Kennedy, Michael's youngest brother, and displayed more emotion than he had at other funerals, including Jackie's. The *Daily News* ran photographs of John standing next to his cousins, trying to make eye contact with Joe, to no avail.

"At the funeral in Centerville, Massachusetts, Joe whispered comforting words to mourners but greeted John with stony silence," wrote Andersen.

"It was difficult," a family member recalled to Andersen. "Everyone was still in shock. . . . It didn't help that John's attack on Michael came so close to his death."

While Carolyn and John waited for the flight home at the small Hyannis Port airport, a couple of familiar photographers cornered the couple, including Laura Cavanaugh, who frequently lurked on North Moore Street and probably spent more time than Ted Kennedy on the pier in Hyannis Port.

"Why can't you just leave us alone?" John asked. He produced his own camera and began taking pictures of the photographers, to use for a potential lawsuit against these people who hounded them every day of their lives. As the photographers began to leave, Carolyn grabbed John's camera and trotted after them. They had finally pushed too far. Carolyn, who had always been physically expressive with those she loved, platonic or romantic—touching feet in taxis, twirling hair, and cupping faces with her hands—was no longer able to contain the emotion she felt toward the paparazzi. She approached Laura Cavanaugh and spat in her face.

CHAPTER NINETEEN

MRS. KENNEDY AND
THE VICIOUS CIRCLE

January 1998–March 1998

Carolyn dreaded any potential fallout from the spitting incident, but in some ways, she felt justified. Cavanaugh had, after all, displayed an astonishing lack of boundaries, coming up close with the hulking camera at a time when the Kennedy family had suffered another tragic loss. Yet Carolyn had been cast as a banshee since that pre-wedding fight nearly two years earlier and had never quite been able to overcome the portrait. This could do her in. Thinking of how this would play out worried Carolyn. "While she might have played it lightly, she would be worried about what the family would think if this had come to light," said MJ Bettenhausen.

Somehow, Cavanaugh's employer, the *Globe*, decided to play down the incident. Perhaps they had a moment of humanity. More likely, they realized that advertising Carolyn's spiral of fear, anger, and disgust that culminated in sputum in their eye might lead to a discussion of why she was in such a state. The paparazzi had hounded a family in a moment of crisis, time and time again.

Carolyn was afraid to venture outside of North Moore Street unless she was shielded by family or trusted friends, such as Dan Samson, who recalled, "Carolyn always wore simple black clothes and tried to keep a neutral face in public. She knew if she gave the press anything, they would turn it into something negative. The best way to prevent that was to give them as little as possible."

"To Carolyn, that meant the black clothes and an inexpressive face," Samson said. "Which makes it all the more ironic that, by contrast, my lasting vision of Carolyn is as a loud, boisterous, smiling, and incredibly engaging person. That's why John married her.

"If you were Carolyn's friend, you were made," he continued. "She cared deeply for her close friends and demonstrated it with heartwarming support for all of them, and she got it back in return. I think Carolyn knew she was that person to those people, so as biting as some of the media attention she received might have been, deep down, I'd like to believe she was content, even though the simple act of walking to a waiting car had become a chore for her."

Carolyn spent her thirty-second birthday on January 7, 1998, at their loft with just a few friends and family members, according to Andersen. As she blew out the candles on the buttercream-frosted cake, John asked her what she wished, and Carolyn said, "All I want for my birthday is to know you'll always be around."

Michael Kennedy's death was very present in their minds and would be so for a long time. John was not close to Michael like he was with other cousins such as Bobby Jr., Tim Shriver, or Anthony Radziwill, but he loved his family. It was a reminder of the havoc that playing fast and hard had wreaked on the Kennedy family for generations. On top of this, Anthony's condition had worsened. These were young men, so this was all the more painful to process.

Carolyn lobbied John to stop taking flying lessons. According to Andersen, she lamented to a former colleague at Calvin Klein, "With this family's history, John is the last person on earth who should be piloting his own plane . . . I can't stop thinking John could be the next to go."

She conscripted his uncle Ted Kennedy to join her campaign. John's sister, Caroline, also asked her brother to stop the lessons. Andersen quotes her as saying: "You know Mummy didn't want you to fly. I think you know how angry she'd be with you right now—and how worried she would be. . . ."

Carolyn begged John, "Walk away now, while you still can—please, for my sake."

Rattled by Michael's death in a way that he had never been rattled, John complied. But not for long. For her part, Carolyn would not acknowledge anything but the grief of her new relatives. "Though she never expressly said so, she most likely wished John hadn't written about his cousins," said MJ Bettenhausen, "or at least been clearer that rather than shaming them, he was calling out the public for doing so with plenty of schadenfreude."

The Kennedys are a large family, however, and Carolyn had allies. She had grown close not just with the Bouvier side of the family—Lee, Anthony, and Carole Radziwill—but also with Bobby Jr. and his wife, Mary; Timmy and Linda Shriver; as well as Maria Shriver and her husband, Arnold Schwarzenegger.

Carolyn still frequented the dog run, but going out in public for groceries, to a shop, or to dine out was something she avoided if she could. She would have friends over to the loft. It sounds like she may have been depressed, and no wonder. One of the few times Carolyn left North Moore Street was to celebrate Bobby Kennedy Jr.'s birthday at his home in Bedford, New York. Carolyn and Carole spent much of the evening close together. "It was very crowded but Mary Richardson, Bobby's wife, always gave wonderful dinners," said Carole. "She was so lovely and made everyone feel at home. It was one of Mary's superpowers."

Carolyn had also grown more comfortable in Hyannis Port. She enjoyed her time at the compound, even if sometimes, according to Matt Berman, "she would rather stay in bed with the dogs and snack" while they went dragging.

As much as she appreciated spending weekends with thirty-some cousins, Carolyn wanted to have a nuclear family of her own, just her and John. Build their own clan. She craved a level of stability from which they could continue to grow, telling RoseMarie Terenzio, "I just want some normal married time. I'm exhausted."

Carolyn was welcoming and even loving with most of his many friends, but, as she confided to a friend, she felt a strong marriage needed to be cultivated by learning how best to live together, help each other, and give intentional thought to their future. Would they stay in New York, where they couldn't make a move without the paparazzi in their face? Would John continue with *George* or move on to another venture? Would he launch a political career? They needed to plan together, with careful consideration, how each would thrive under the circumstances.

"She first wanted quiet, quality time with her husband," said MJ Bettenhausen. But envisioning a life that could work for both of them seemed impossible at the time.

As Billy Noonan learned, Carolyn felt like she had few options and little guidance. He wrote about taking her out to lunch one day—he was in town from Boston for work, and so he went to pick her up, as his office wasn't far from the North Moore apartment. Noonan wondered if she was being neurotic about the paparazzi when she looked out the window to check for the telltale telephoto lenses before stepping outside. They went to Bubby's and were seated in the back because the host understood Carolyn's need for protection.

"They're all staring at me," Carolyn said.

"Carolyn, for God's sake," said Noonan, "I'll protect you."

"See that guy going to the bathroom? He just stopped to look in the mirror," said Carolyn, "and I saw him looking at me."

Noonan got frustrated.

"Carolyn, you're beautiful, you're the envy of every woman in New York, and you're the dream girl for men. Why not enjoy this?"

But eventually Noonan understood.

"I looked in the mirror, and of course she was right—people were staring at her in its reflection."

When they went back to North Moore, Carolyn confided in Noonan that it was difficult to live in Tribeca, which, while up-and-coming, was still pretty desolate. There is safety in numbers, and Tribeca didn't have numbers. There were too few neighbors and too many photographers. She wanted to have something that was *theirs*.

"Our other house is his father's, and the Vineyard house is his mother's," Carolyn explained. "I have no place of my own."

"Would you move to some bedroom community nearby?"

"No, [John would] never do it—he thrives off the energy of the city," Carolyn said.

"How about uptown?"

"He grew up there," Carolyn said, which apparently meant John would not want to live there. "And I'd still get chased by photographers every time I went out."

Noonan later wrote, "I could see where this was going. She was in a spot, psychologically, where she could see no solution."

It is curious why this was taken as simply psychological, since she was indeed chased by photographers in New York—and John wanted to stay in the city.

"Carolyn," Noonan told her, "there are more of them than you, and you're going to have to get used to it. They did the same thing to Jackie."

"Yeah, well, I need her now, but she's not here. The only one that can help me is Caroline, and she hasn't been helpful."

"Why do you think that is?" Noonan asked.

Later, he answered his own rhetorical question with the following dubious assertion: "In fact, I knew why, and I hoped we didn't have to get into it. They were from utterly different backgrounds." This reads more like Noonan projecting his own issues: He was intensely protective of his relationship with John, which went back to their childhoods, and he was also acutely aware of the myriad ways in which they came from different worlds.

But it is interesting to ponder why Caroline was not able to intervene in this crisis given that she had just written a book focused on the exact issue at hand. *The Right to Privacy*, published in 1997, is a collection of legal essays, not a memoir, but she writes in a distinctly impersonal voice, no doubt in the interest of protecting her own privacy. Chapter titles such as "Privacy and Yourself" and, in particular, "Privacy and the Press" suggest an intimate understanding of what it means to have a continuous waterfall of camera clicks and flashbulbs as the backdrop to a life. It was Jackie who, in 1972, filed one of the first lawsuits against the paparazzo Ron Galella, whose entire professional career and livelihood were built around stalking her. Jackie claimed Galella made her life "intolerable, almost unlivable, with his constant surveillance." She won a restraining order that required him to stay twenty-five feet away from her, and thirty feet from her children. Caroline's language is less vivid, less personal, but makes the same point: "Private individuals join public figures in decrying 'tabloid journalism' and complaining that the press can invade lives with impunity," she wrote. Given her familiarity with the subject, might she have had some thoughts to share, if only by way of commiseration, with her new sister-in-law?

Additionally, like John, Caroline's ability to handle the press invasion had been learned by osmosis. Yet her personality was vastly different from that of extrovert John. A mother who had children around the same age as Caroline's remembered seeing her waiting for them while they took dance lessons at Ballet Academy East on Third Avenue. "She was lovely but wasn't one to mingle. She quietly read in the corner until class was over."

Those close to Caroline saw her reticence to engage as rooted more in basic facts of life. "If Caroline was preoccupied and unable to reach out, it had more to do with the fact that she was in mourning," observed a close family friend of John's sister. "She had recently lost her mother, and she was extremely worried about Anthony. Once you factor in having three small children, she was understandably already overloaded."

Carolyn could have used a new friend that February when she lost an old one through no doing of her own. Suddenly, there was a problem with Brad Johns. He had spoken to the press about coloring her hair, with Carolyn's blessing. She had told Brad and his staff that if it helped the salon to say they did her hair, to please do so. But suddenly, the press reported that John Kennedy Jr. was upset with the salon for talking. Columnist Liz Smith was perplexed over why John's office would make a statement asking Carolyn's hair salon to stop speaking of her patronage when they had a policy of no comment on most else: "Well, now we know what bothers Mr. and Mrs. JFK Junior. Not the endless, sordid rumors of vicious battling, divorce rumblings, mysterious injuries, speculation about why they don't have kids yet. Nope, that's all OK. But a hairdresser who treats Carolyn's blonde tresses, and talks about those treatments, is presented with threats from JFK's lawyer. Amazing."

Carolyn, however, was just as amazed. She had no idea where any of these statements had come from. The "objection," it turns out, came from a press release faxed by a disgruntled former employee of Brad's who had a close mutual friend with John. It was a sticky situation for Carolyn. "It took a couple of weeks for Carolyn to agree to leave the salon, but she finally relented," a source said. "The now-fired friend made John feel that he, and by extension Carolyn, had to choose sides. For all the claims about Carolyn's pushiness, it was not she who won this battle."

ON FEBRUARY 5, CAROLYN and John went to DC to attend a state dinner at the White House given for UK prime minister Tony Blair. Unlike the usual classical musicians providing entertainment for past dinners, Stevie Wonder and Elton John performed. Harrison Ford, Barbra Streisand, and Tom Hanks were also there. Blair asked to meet Steven Spielberg. It was such a sought-after ticket that they had to put up a tent on the West Terrace, and social secretary Capricia Marshall said the 240 invitations meant "We were playing a sort of numbers game." The event was so "white hot" that people changed their *regrets* to *attending* at the last minute.

The Bill Clinton/Monica Lewinsky scandal had broken just a couple of weeks earlier and the administration was in the throes of it. Reporters who had been covering the scandal, such as Peter Jennings, were in attendance, "But the president just laughed his way through the evening."

Newsday erroneously reported that it was John's sister, Caroline, not his wife, who "wore black arm-length gloves."

Carolyn, meanwhile, was able to muster up some of her former vitality. Old Hollywood legend Carol Channing enthused to the *Palm Beach Post*: "[John] and Carolyn were at my table, and she just eats everybody up. She was just so attentive and so interested in everyone, and she knew something about each person at the table. She's the best thing that ever happened to John."

Anna Wintour also attended the dinner and later assigned writer Julia Reed to find out "what constituted appropriate dress in Washington." Wintour wrote of her surprise that Reed reported the mandate in DC was the "'trailing after' phenomenon—the good wife that doesn't want to upstage her husband," and went on to say that the effect was "certainly in evidence at the White House dinner for Prime Minister Blair that I attended, where fashion statements were generally plain, somber, and shapeless." She named Carolyn as one of the "only exceptions," as she was "striking as always in what I think was a Yohji dress."

Also striking is that even Anna Wintour couldn't place the make of her dress, which was intentional on Carolyn's part. Her restraint—exemplified by understated yet perfectly cut, luxurious material, and refined, barely there makeup—was the essence of her singular style.

From Washington, Carolyn and John headed to Utah for a ski trip, followed by the American Association of Advertising Agencies media conference in Anaheim, California. That they traveled to the conference indicated just how worried John was about the ad sales for *George*. While there, John defended Clinton, saying, "I was under that very desk 35 years ago, and I can tell you there's barely room for a three-year-old." Carolyn was a Democrat and had been pleased by many of the accomplishments in Clinton's presidency, "but she found aspects of his affairs with Lewinsky and Paula Jones pretty unsavory," said MJ Bettenhausen.

Carolyn and John returned east in time for Uncle Ted's sixty-sixth birthday party held on February 17 at the St. Regis hotel in New York City.

Guests paid $1,000 each to wish the senator well, and the proceeds went to his reelection campaign committee.

As for John, a run for political office was not only manifest destiny, but also the rip cord that steered him away from *George*'s declining fortunes. It had always been on the table. "The worst thing that could've happened was a bad disposition of the asset, and he wouldn't have let it happen," Ginsberg explained. "John was confident he could find the right way to keep *George* going. It was going to be tough, but it was salvageable."

Yet Carolyn, despite being on John's arm for as many events and appearances as she could, was falling apart in those first months of 1998. Lauren knew her sister needed help and returned from Hong Kong. "Not in any kind of 'I'll sit beside you all day and hold your hand' way, but Carolyn needed an ally in the midst of several crises," said Jack Merrill. There was the onslaught of the paparazzi, the precarious state of John's magazine, Anthony Radziwill's declining health, and a world constantly seeking her husband's attention. Put it all together, and it was hard for Carolyn to have open, easy communication with her husband, and sometimes to even hear herself think.

"Lauren kept a busy life and dove into her work in the New York offices of Morgan Stanley," said Merrill. "She bought an apartment at 17 White Street, just a few blocks away from the loft on North Moore. Carolyn and Lauren were already close, but they became closer than ever."

Lauren had been promoted to principal from vice president and was now on track to be managing director. Adam Clammer, who had worked with her overseas, told *Town & Country* that Lauren "would walk into a room and people would think, 'Okay, somebody brought their assistant.' And then she'd get up and present the IPO pitch in Mandarin, and people would be like, 'What? I've never seen anything like this!' She was so humble yet so smart and poised."

A lawyer for another investment bank who worked with her on deals in Hong Kong put it more bluntly: "She was a badass."

Back in New York, Chip Arndt said, "Lauren was concerned for her sister; they were best friends, really. But whatever Carolyn was dealing with was all kept close to the chest. The most Lauren ever said was, 'Carolyn is going through some things.'"

In truth, both Carolyn and Lauren were going through some things. John had urged both of them to reach out to their father and try to make a little room for him in their lives. If there is anyone who could see the value of forgiveness toward a father, it is someone who doesn't have a father to forgive. Maybe doing it together would make it easier for the sisters. Talking to William as an adult, Carolyn learned that the reason her father had seen her so infrequently wasn't because he didn't love and care for her. Sometimes, life just got in the way. William's weekend with the girls might have fallen on one with a wedding or baby shower on the Messina or Freeman side of the family, or his work as an engineer would take him out of town, often for months at a time. And then the girls were teenagers. Friends, boyfriends, football games, and French fries at Tod's Point took precedence over time with him.

Carolyn's friend from Greenwich Dr. Deena Manion, an addiction recovery specialist, said, "My husband worked with William Bessette on a few homebuilding projects. Mr. Bessette was a tall, handsome, and soft-spoken man, and they became friendly. He spoke of how it had been hard not to see his daughters in previous years and that he loved his girls and had always wanted to be part of their lives, but their lives 'just sort of got busy and he didn't want to make waves.' Then he said, 'It's okay; we're in touch now.'"

In earlier years at Calvin Klein, Carolyn had told a few friends that she "hated him." And MJ Bettenhausen recalled, "Once in a while, if we had a couple of drinks, which was rare for Carolyn, she would pour her heart out about her father. That he wasn't there, that she didn't know if he cared."

But later, her perspective shifted. "For a long time, Carolyn didn't mention her father, but around 1998 she began to talk about him, remembering some of the good times, even expressing regret they hadn't been close," said Bettenhausen.

Carolyn started to spend more and more time at her sister's apartment. Lauren's new loft on White Street, located in a six-story building that had once been a leather and garment factory, provided an escape.

Carolyn may have felt up a creek, but at least now her sister was there with a paddle—a job previously held only by John.

"As 1998 progressed, John grew more frustrated with Carolyn's troubled transition," Rob Littell wrote, "but he also felt an enormous responsibility for her happiness. They lived out a complicated dynamic, resenting the demands each placed on the other while at the same time empathizing with the other's frustrations. John felt hog-tied by not being able to solve Carolyn's problems, though he had to live with them. We talked a lot about this during the second year of their marriage. He hated the illogic of the whole thing: in his mind, they had so much. There were so many reasons to be happy. But he also knew that Carolyn's coping mechanisms had been overwhelmed. I listened and felt bad for both of them."

IN EARLY MARCH OF 1998, Anthony Radziwill went back to the NIH for surgery, and this time the recovery took much longer. Carolyn went down to DC again to be with Carole. The two women were driving to visit Anthony the day after the surgery when Carole remembered last minute that it was Lee's birthday. Carolyn stopped the car. "Are you kidding? We can't just ignore her birthday." As Carole wrote, "She turns the car around, and we go to the florist in Bethesda and pick out arrangements of oriental lilies. Big, bright flowers. 'These look like her,' she says. We spend an hour with the florist getting them just right, and take them back to the hotel and put them in her room. Carolyn signed the card from the four of us."

Carolyn maintained her close friendship with Betsy Reisinger, soon to be married to John's friend Kenan Siegel on March 21, 1998, in Miami. "Carolyn came down a week early to help me get ready for the wedding," Betsy remembered. "She took me shopping in Bal Harbour and guided me toward the perfect shoes and dress for the rehearsal dinner. There was a particular pair of white satin Manolo Blahniks she had that she also wanted me to have for the wedding. She called everywhere she could think of to get them for me, but they were sold out.

"Carolyn's solution was to buy me this gorgeous pair of rhinestone and velvet Dolce & Gabbana shoes. They were absolutely gorgeous—except that I couldn't walk in them. We tried to see if I could take a couple of steps, and it was clear I couldn't. Carolyn laughed and told me, 'Well, at least you'll always have them.' "

John and Carolyn had a good time at the wedding, and asked their friend Robert Curran, who was shooting photographs, to take a few of them. That's how he got the picture with Carolyn's head thrown back in laughter while John embraces her. "He was singing a song into her ear," Curran recalled.

In another, Carolyn and Betsy hug tightly while Carolyn gives Betsy a big, clutching, grandma smooch.

"Our wedding was such a happy day," Betsy said. "For us, but for our friends as well. You can see from the pictures our friend Robert Curran took, Carolyn and John were deeply in love, and in love with life. That is how I remember them, when they felt safe."

These were the moments when Carolyn seemed to be able to step out of what could possibly be called depression, though that was a word not often spoken at that time. These moments often occurred outside the familiar places of her life. That she had such a blast at a wedding in Miami, far from what had become the routine rounds of fabulousness—the galas and dinners that populated their New York social life—may speak to a subtler disappointment at play in Carolyn after she married. She had crossed over from being the person who greeted celebrities to being a celebrity herself. That's the Cinderella part of the fairy tale: The slipper fit. We need to think more about the difficulties of getting what you want. Maybe her mortification wasn't just about the paparazzi staring at her, bullying her, but what it was like to be on the inside of those special events with all the fabulous people— the movie stars, the bankers, the famous politicians. Perhaps that world was a lot less interesting and fun than she had thought it would be.

THE PREVIOUS YEAR, JOHN had wanted to commission photographs of his wife where she was smiling and at ease—perhaps to stop time, which seemed to be moving at a breakneck pace. Bruce Weber, who took the memorable portraits of Carolyn romping on the lawn of a friend's home in Glen Cove, Long Island, remembered a story Carolyn had told him about Lee. "Early on, Lee once sent her a box of hair bleach and a set of curlers as a gift," Weber said, laughing. "Carolyn thought it was wildly funny. She said, 'I couldn't figure out whether I should write a thank-you note or not.'"

"She was so incredibly beautiful; it was a pleasure to shoot her," Weber added. "Unlike many famous beauties, she didn't ask for touching up, nor did she have a 'preferred angle.' She was unconcerned and truly focused on our chat and the animals, especially her beautiful Canaan dog, Friday. She herself was like a jumping colt."

Carolyn also told Weber how much she loved her husband. "She spoke so highly of John," Weber said, "and was thrilled with him and loved watching his dedication to making *George* a must-read."

And yet, making *George* a "must-read" meant longer hours in the office. John had also been showing up for as many Kennedy family events as possible and factoring the press into his long-term goals. If he wanted *George* to succeed, he had to court the press, and if he wanted to finally enter the family business, *George* first had to succeed.

Carolyn continued to join John at numerous events that spring, including on March 25 to celebrate HBO's *From the Earth to the Moon*, a twelve-part miniseries chronicling the US race to the moon. The crowd included Bryan Cranston, who portrayed Buzz Aldrin, as well as Aldrin himself, and fellow explorer Al Worden from Apollo 15. In many ways, it was an odd replay, another moment in which JFK's work and enormous ambitions paved the way for achievements that he didn't live to see. The screening was held at the White House, and John was asked to speak.

John flew in separately with an instructor to earn more hours toward his pilot's license, a day or so later than Carolyn, who had flown commercial and was visiting with Carole and Anthony at the hospital. Chauffeur Jefferson Arrington picked up John from Signature Aviation, a private section of Reagan Airport. John asked to be taken first to Arlington Cemetery, where he visited his parents' graves, and then to his hotel. After John changed for the evening, Arrington took him to pick up Carolyn at the NIH.

"'Jefferson, this is my wife, Carolyn,' he said," Arrington recalled. "My impression at the time was how very nice, how normal, these people were. She was lovely and dressed in a classic way. I remember thinking she was not a raving beauty in the traditional sense, but a very pretty woman, and she was exceptionally nice. As we drove back to the hotel, the two of them talked and held hands. John took the opportunity of this twenty-minute drive to read his speech to Carolyn. As you might imagine, the speech was very well written, with some quotes from President Kennedy woven in. When John finished reading, Carolyn leaned forward and kissed him, telling him how much she liked it.

"There was a slight pause," remembered Arrington, "and John finally spoke. 'Now when I quote my father, I hear his voice.' Again, Carolyn gave him a warm hug and kiss. I felt as if I had been in on a very personal, wonderful moment."

The couple arrived at the White House and got out of the car. Carolyn, who had exited on Arrington's side, had a slight wardrobe malfunction as she rose, static cling making the lower half of the dress ride up, as she stepped out from the passenger door. Jefferson stood to block her as she quickly recovered herself, laughing. The moment was brief, but just long enough for the cold to envelop Carolyn, who was without a coat. On the east side of the White House, there was a long line funneling into a security check at the entrance.

"Uh-oh." Carolyn was giggling by this point. "Look at that line. I'm already shivering."

Since John looked concerned, Arrington told them, "I don't think you have to wait in line. You used to live here.

"Carolyn looked at John, surprised, and John looked back at her and smiled. He took her hand, and they walked right in—security didn't stop them for one second.

"When you work in the Secret Service, part of your training is to study the Zapruder film," Arrington explained, referring to the footage of the assassination of JFK in 1963. "You learn how quickly things can happen, and you've got to cover every angle. There must have been a feeling that evening to let that young man and his beautiful wife in right away; we let them down before, and we will not let it happen again."

"They arrived like royalty, gliding through the crowd as if on air, he, confident and purposeful—she, shy and demure, both of them gracing the presence of those who strained on tiptoes for a look," cooed Andrea Shea King of *Florida Today*. Carolyn and John sat in the front row, whispering in each other's ears before the film began.

In his speech, John quoted his father's 1961 pledge: "I believe this nation should commit itself to achieving the goal before the decade is out of landing a man on the moon and returning him safely to Earth."

Then he continued, "Thank you for fulfilling that pledge that was made twenty-seven years ago. Some people thought $65 million was a bit steep for a television series. But I remind all of you that HBO put twelve men on the moon for less than one-fourth of what it cost [*Titanic* director] James Cameron to sink one old boat."

Arrington picked the couple up later that evening. "Despite a large exodus at around 11:15 p.m., the Kennedys did not emerge until well after midnight," Arrington said. "On our short trip back to the hotel, the couple spoke of what a great evening it had been. I realized that the late hour was because President Clinton had given John and Carolyn a tour of the White House."

The next day, Arrington drove John back to the airport. "I arrived at the hotel at about 5:20 a.m. to pick John up for an early flight. When we arrived at [Reagan] National Airport, John hopped out of the car and grabbed his small bag. He made a point to stop, shake my hand, and thank me," said Arrington. "He also took an envelope out of his pocket and said, 'My wife and I would like you to have this.' I thanked him, and he was off. I really hoped the envelope would hold a simple signed note. But instead, it held a very generous, very thoughtful tip. He had taken the time to give me an envelope, which seemed so in character for this fellow. After all, he had been John Kennedy all his life, and he was very good at it."

Despite his skill at being a Kennedy, John also needed the résumé if he was ever to run for office. He'd gotten his law degree, worked for the DA, and launched a political magazine, however fledgling, that he planned on making solvent. John was a long way past just being the Sexiest Man Alive.

CHAPTER TWENTY

THE RUMOR MILL

April 1998–August 1998

It seemed that, when on his own terms, John could step into his own legacy quite easily. But where did that leave Carolyn? The very things he loved about her—her empathy and sensitivity and bullshit radar—were the same qualities that would make it challenging for her to remain by his side if he became a politician. He was working toward a political career, but she had no interest in playing nice with those she mistrusted. And she could hardly tolerate it when John did so in the name of diplomacy, for the magazine or otherwise.

Did John feel held back politically if Carolyn wasn't ready for him to run? Conversely, was Carolyn increasingly frustrated at *George*'s troubles and the sense that John was digging himself into a hole? Did she feel her like their marriage was on hold until the situation resolved?

That spring, the tabloid press began milling rumors of an extra-personal sort, and it destabilized Carolyn even more. "A strange thing happens when the press is writing all these things about you. After a while, it becomes confusing," said Carole Radziwill. "A family member or an old friend might call and ask you, 'Is this rumor true? Are you okay?' You say, 'No, all is well,' and go on. But after a while, it interrupts the navigation of these relationships with people who you know have read about you, and you can find yourself as confused as the tabloids are. It's a form of gaslighting. You think, *Wait, that's not true, right?* It can seep into your own life; mess with your mind. I can see it so much more clearly in retrospect, and I think that happened to her."

Carolyn once walked into her grandmother's house and heard her on the phone chatting away. "She was on the phone talking to someone called Bambi," Carolyn told *Women's Wear Daily*. "My grandmother is pretty old, and I know most of the people she knows, and I couldn't figure out who this Bambi was. 'Oh, Bambi, I don't think that's true,' she was saying, and 'Oh, Bambi, that's so funny.' And 'Sure, anytime you want, Bambi.' Finally she got off the phone, and I said 'Who's Bambi?' And she said, 'Oh, Bambi is my friend from *Hard Copy*.' And, of course, she had no idea what *Hard Copy* was.

"If I don't do something soon," Carolyn joked, "I'm going to end up in a trailer park screaming, 'I used to be married to JFK Jr.!'"

Popular fictions about Carolyn were that she was having numerous affairs and was a cocaine addict. There had been the "raging party girl" claims by the *Washington Post*, and as early as March 1995, the *Daily News* accused her of hanging on to Michael Bergin as "her ammunition to remain equal to John." The specter of an affair with Bergin would follow them their entire marriage, and beyond. No one who knew her well—Carole Radziwill, MJ Bettenhausen, Hamilton South, Betsy Reisinger Siegel, Michelle Kessler—gave credence to these rumors.

MJ Bettenhausen said, "People loved to mistake male friends as a lover. Many of her friends were gay, such as Narciso and Gordon, and she was as physically affectionate with them as she was with her girlfriends and platonic male friends. She was affectionate with everyone; the press just loved to conjure up a story."

Reisinger said, "Carolyn barely drank wine, and she was head over heels for John." And Michelle reflected, "Carolyn would have *never* jeopardized her marriage by an affair, she was way too smart for that." Radziwill and South just laughed at all of it. No way.

What Carolyn knew—now more than ever—was that there were people who could be trusted and those who could not. And if John wasn't going to be the keeper of the gates, she would have to be.

She was vehemently careful about their inner circle. "Carolyn had a bullshit detector," said Sasha Chermayeff, "and if someone was in any way full of it, she didn't like it; she was all over it. It was truly fun for me when Carolyn came along, and one of the reasons she and I bonded was because she loved that whole psychological take on life. Because she could feel all the energy out, too. So as soon as we met, we would go into discussions about what people were really feeling. She was psychologically driven, and psychologically astute."

Noonan accused Carolyn of taking things too far. "But now I was watching Carolyn, in becoming isolated herself, trying to isolate him, too, whittling down his friendships," Noonan wrote. "She'd speculate about how some of his friends didn't trust other friends. It was classic, playing both ends against the middle so that she'd have more control."

But then, Noonan was a friend from John's wilder, unencumbered teenage years, when no one was the boss but John. William D. Cohan remembers Noonan showing up every weekend or even more at Andover, enjoying John's privileged access to parties, girls, music . . . living the good life. Perhaps this made it harder for Noonan to accept that John's grown-up life held new priorities—a wife, a magazine, maybe a run for office, maybe starting a family. And this life had a new gatekeeper, or rather partner, in Carolyn.

Billy wrote that he had taken issue with John flying solo to Hyannis Port without him, accusing John of making him "so pissed off that I yelled at [my wife]."

The ensuing fight between the two men, Noonan wrote later, was a result of people who "would have gladly seen me out of the way—a few who were trying to step into John's world, to benefit from a closer relationship, always to better themselves. This played into Carolyn's hands as she looked for allies against enemies. I was, for now, a convenient enemy."

Rob Littell had a different take. "If Carolyn perceived that someone was using John, she went into battle mode," he wrote. "As a result, she made some enemies. I'd hear about it when a banished friend would call me, trying to figure out why he'd been tossed aside. . . . I also know that she was eerily empathetic, so it's entirely possible that she was right in her judgments. . . . I do think that some of the ugly stories about Carolyn that emerged later were the result of her war against those she considered false friends.

"Carolyn used to divide people into three categories regarding their behavior around John," Littell continued. "The 'regular Joes' who remained essentially unaffected by his fame; the 'windblown,' who were good eggs but were visibly influenced by John's celebrity; and finally, the 'freaks,' who lost all self-respect in their effort to suck up to John and get whatever they thought he could give them. The 'freaks' didn't last long."

John was also promoting the upcoming release of *The Book of Political Lists*, compiled by the editors of *George*. One of the best inclusions was the Secret Service code names for the Kennedy family: JFK was Lancer, Jackie was Lace, Caroline was Lyric, and John, fittingly, was Lark, a nod to the carefree child he had been. And perhaps still wanted to be. He told *USA Today* that Carolyn joined him on his plane "the second it was legal," which was three weeks prior to the *USA Today* interview, in late April, when he earned his pilot's license from the FlightSafety Academy in Vero Beach, Florida—against advice from many friends and most of his family.

It was as if all the pressures building up in life demanded a release, and flying gave that to him. "The only person I've been able to get up to go with me, who looks forward to it as much as I do, is my wife," he said. "Whenever we want to get away, we can just get in a plane and fly off."

That she loved flying was probably a reach. Bruce Weber remembered talking to Carolyn about planes. "We both spoke of our dread of flying, especially over those islands off the coast of Massachusetts, because the weather can change so quickly," Weber said. "I had a bad experience once, where the flight was so bumpy our heads were hitting the top of the plane. The pilot was trying to land, but no one would take us because the visibility was so bad. Eventually, we made it, and the pilot told me, 'For the first time, I was really nervous.' Thank goodness he didn't show it in-flight because I was already frightened enough. It was crazy; you couldn't see a thing below you."

Despite Carolyn's feelings about flying, she would likely have appreciated the chance it afforded her to be alone with John. After Kenan and Betsy's wedding in Miami, she had kept herself tucked away, abstaining from most public events. One exception was an appearance at the Parsons Dance premiere of "Anthem" with Lee Radziwill, Herbert Ross, and Hamilton South. Entering the theater in a black satin Yohji Yamamoto wrap dress, Carolyn held tightly to Lee, who shared her sharp sense of humor. Carolyn's hair was darker than usual and pulled back stark and straight. There is a photograph of the evening in which Carolyn, with Hamilton on her left, is leaning across André Balazs, pointing her finger at her aunt-in-law. "Everyone was very young, and we lived very much in the present, so exact words are sometimes beyond reach almost thirty years later," said South. "Since Carolyn was like a mother lion to her many friends, this could have been a moment where she was describing what she called 'deal-breakers,' that moment when someone or something outside our close circle is not worthy of a friend. Lee had her own version of deal-breakers, and the two of them always had a witty repartee."

Carolyn had, by then, found a new colorist, André Vivieros. In early June, she paid him a visit to prepare for the Council of Fashion Designers of America Fashion Awards, which was honoring Calvin Klein as Menswear Designer of the Year. Vivieros had come to know the couple quite well and got a pretty good snapshot of everything Carolyn was dealing with at the time.

"Carolyn was one of the most authentic people I'd ever met," he said. "I ran into her on the street, and she introduced me to John. They both stood and chatted for a lengthy time as friends do, not the quick, fake air kiss that some clients give when they saw me outside the salon. They invited me to drinks; we went to coffee. Every conversation was about the world around her: the embassy bombing in Kenya and Tanzania, the FDA approval of Viagra, the Iraq disarmament crisis, the murder of James Byrd by white supremacists, and of course, her worry for Anthony, Carole, and John in the face of Anthony's illness. Not herself or other gossip. She could not tolerate pretense. Other than her hair color, which I would not allow her to bleach white blonde when she asked because I was not going to be the 'colorist who ruined Carolyn Bessette's hair,' everything she did and said was authentic. If I was her friend when she was in my chair, I was her friend everywhere."

Carolyn had one more event left on her calendar that spring: the Profile in Courage Award, held at the Kennedy Library in Boston on May 28. The morning ceremony, followed by a luncheon, included hours of mingling. John gave interviews alongside Caroline on *Today* and *Good Morning America* for award recipient Garfield County attorney Nickolas C. Murnion.

According to two different friends of the family, the energy in the room completely changed when John and Carolyn arrived. "We were just making our way into the room when suddenly the whole room shifted," said a longtime family friend. "What had been our beeline toward the bar was blocked by a wall of people thronging toward Carolyn and John. It was unbelievable . . . 'Hi, how are you guys doing? Long time, no see,' John said. He and Carolyn were laughing because the mere attempt at having a normal hello amid this stampede was a joke. I'd never seen anything like it."

The *Billings Gazette* described the couple's entrance, as they held tightly to each other's hand, as "profiles in glamour." Carolyn was clad in her usual Yohji Yamamoto, this time a jacket and ankle-skimming skirt from the spring/summer 1998 collection that highlighted her graceful height.

Another close family friend said, "Everything changed the minute they walked in. It was as if lightning struck the room. One couldn't help but wonder what the other family members thought about it, just because it was such a stark change."

AS SUMMER KICKED IN, everyone gathered in Hyannis Port for the Fourth of July. It was a major family celebration. The Shrivers held a mass under a tent in their yard, and after Communion, it became the usual mayhem: The cousins ran around the property, some playing football, some swimming.

There was a videographer present, and with ninety members of the family in attendance, there were constant activities afoot on the expanse of lawn. Carolyn was teaching the children how to do handstands, handsprings, and cartwheels. Groups huddled together to have pictures taken, while footballs flew by, as did cousins. Carolyn and John happily posed with Bobby Jr. and his wife, Mary Richardson.

Then the family gathered for a big photo op, the ladies sitting with the men standing behind them. John suddenly comes into view, dragging Carolyn, in jeans and a black top, to the front of the group. Carolyn was embarrassed to be getting in front of the children. Still, John insisted and pulled her down on the ground, and they lay with their feet toward the camera, lowering themselves enough to avoid blocking the camera's view of the children. Everyone is smiling, laughing; Carolyn looks relaxed and happy.

Later, she goes back to her handstands, coming up from a third handstand only to find John, braced to jump toward her, arms ready to enclose her. Carolyn laughs, and pulls her arms tight in front of her as if she worries he will tackle her just as his cousins are doing to one another a few yards away. But he pulls her in for an embrace. Uncle Ted could be found under the tent, drink in hand, chasing a toddler in circles, the two with similar shapes and gaits. The sheer number of them, all at play and by their mere presence clearly in support of one another, created a safe space.

Carolyn felt less safe about John's purchase of his own plane that April of 1998—it was a 1977 Cessna 182Q Skylane, which he bought as soon as he earned his pilot's license. Geoffrey Freeman, now director of Martha's Vineyard Airport, was a runway attendant at the time and remembered that Carolyn "always either drove the five hours to Hyannis Port, and if they were going to the Vineyard, it was five hours plus the ferry. Otherwise, she took the shuttle. Sometimes the shuttle would leave before John, and sometimes she waited after John took off, sitting quietly on a bench in the waiting area. No one bothered her; at the time Martha's Vineyard was a very laid-back, quiet place. She would've been pestered all the time if it were today."

For what it is worth, Freeman also said, "In all the times I saw John and Carolyn at the airport, which was often, I never saw them fight. I saw John fight with Daryl Hannah, but never Carolyn.

"John was always very careful," Freeman remembered. "Many pilots who flew their own private planes would arrive at the airport, just hop in their plane, and go. He meticulously checked everything on the plane."

On the rare occasion that Carolyn did fly with him, there was always an instructor on board. "Carolyn's misgivings may have had less to do with John's supposed penchant for risk-taking than what even he conceded was his chronic absentmindedness," wrote Christopher Andersen. "And even though he kept his keys on a chain fastened to his belt loop, he still somehow managed to misplace them. This happened so often that he kept a spare set of keys to his apartment at 20 North Moore Street tucked in a hiding place under the front stoop."

There was a café at the airport that Carolyn and John frequented, often ordering coffee and clam chowder. Joan Ford, who worked at the café there, told Andersen that she once asked Carolyn why she and John came and went separately. "I don't trust him," Carolyn told her, point-blank.

Uncle Ted and Maurice Tempelsman didn't love flying with John, either. Andersen noted, "Not everyone shared young Kennedy's enthusiasm for flying—at least not with him in the pilot's seat. After he got his license in April 1998, John joked often and openly about how family and friends simply refused to fly with him. Uncle Ted, remembering how Jackie feared for her son's safety, not only declined every invitation to fly with his nephew, but tried to talk John out of it every chance he got."

⚬≈

UNLESS SHE AND JOHN were in Hyannis Port or at Red Gate Farm, Carolyn spent a lot of the summer of 1998 at the North Moore loft. In July, she accompanied John to a London party hosted by Prince Charles to honor the top donors of the Washington-based Prince of Wales Foundation. Carolyn tried to get an appointment with her new colorist, André Vivieros, the day before their scheduled evening flight, but André was all booked up. Never one to demand special treatment, Carolyn shrugged and prepared to go to the UK with a few roots showing. But then, the very evening she was supposed to fly overseas, Carolyn showed up at his salon to see if he had any last-minute cancellations.

"'What are you doing here?! I thought you had left!' Vivieros said.

"'John couldn't find his passport, so he had to run down to Centre Street. We'll fly tomorrow.' She laughed, rolling her eyes. She was so easygoing about it all," Vivieros said. "We spent her time in my chair laughing about all the things he constantly forgot. It was quite the list."

According to a report that appeared in the *Wichita Eagle*, Carolyn and John "buzzed over on the Concorde, partied down, and then flew home the next morning. Carolyn, who dresses a touch conservatively, wore a navy silk dress with a full skirt and strapless bodice. Wouldn't you know it, she's thin as a bone, married to John Kennedy *and* has good arms to boot." The dress was a Yohji Yamamoto, of course.

Carolyn was a little more relaxed about leaving the shelter of home when in Hyannis Port and Martha's Vineyard. Ariel Paredes, who saw Carolyn and John in both places during the summers, said, "Carolyn liked to come and meet me for lunch on the Vineyard. I worked at the Black Dog and had a specific time for lunch, but she would always get lost. She'd call me and say, 'I'm lost! I'm at Cronig's Market, I don't really know where I am.' There were two Cronig's, one up island and one down island, and if you weren't used to it, including which way was up island and which was down, it could get very confusing. She'd finally show up in a hastily wrapped sarong with her hair everywhere, and my lunch hour would be over. My coworkers were all over it.

"'Who is that?' they'd ask. We'd scurry off to Rocco's pizza and have only fifteen minutes to actually catch up since she was so late! Between me teasing her, my coworkers' curiosity, and people stealing glances, she would get flustered. I'd say, 'Take three deep breaths . . .' And she would calm down. She would laugh and say, 'This is ridiculous, but look at you helping me out!'

"But Carolyn was always being chased. And people were always staring at her. Anyone in that situation needs an assist from time to time."

SHE HAD A BRIEF respite from the chronic chasing that August, when Carolyn and John traveled to Italy for Christiane Amanpour's wedding to Jamie Rubin held in Bracciano. The groom was serving in the Clinton administration as assistant secretary of state for public affairs, and Amanpour had been reporting on Iran's crackdown in the 1990s on women's rights, bringing to light their deadly use of force against protestors.

Bracciano is a small, tenth-century medieval town on a steep hillside above a volcanic lake in the region of Lazio, just under thirty miles northeast of Rome. Two ceremonies were held: one in the Basilica of Santo Stefano, and later, a Jewish ceremony at Castello Orsini-Odescalchi. Andersen wrote that "when the priest told the groom to kiss the bride, John leaned over and kissed Carolyn tenderly."

Perhaps it was the break from the bustle of New York that gave them such a romantic flush, or the light in Italy that highlighted Carolyn's and John's beauty, but they both glowed at this wedding. Carolyn wore a black Yohji Yamamoto cocktail dress with barely there black ruffles at the top of the bodice, and minimal jewelry—just pearl earrings. Her hair, at its brightest blonde, was pulled back into a low chignon, and she finished the look with black patent Manolo Blahnik heels and a black leather clutch.

Carolyn and John seemed at one of their happiest moments as they watched their friends marry. Later, in the twilight at the reception, Carolyn stood behind John, her arms wrapped around his upper arms, and his hands reaching up to hold hers in front of him.

After the Rubin-Amanpour wedding, John, accompanied by photojournalist Robert Curran, went to Vietnam to interview General Võ Nguyên Giáp for *George*'s November issue. After a trek to Điện Biên Phủ, and a four-day kayaking trip on Hạ Long Bay in the Gulf of Tonkin, they finally received word that the general had agreed to an interview time, though with the bizarre stipulation that John be photographed with a newborn baby. (A couple close to the general believed it would be good luck to be photographed with John.) He agreed, the photo was taken, and the interview, which occurred on Giáp's eighty-seventh birthday, was fruitful.

BACK IN NEW YORK, Carolyn bided her time until John got home. She had friends over to the loft but rarely ventured out. Even her beloved dog run had ceased being a sanctuary: "Carolyn quit going to the run that spring when P.S. 234 took part of it as a playground," MJ Bettenhausen said. "There had been two exits; if people or photographers gathered, she had an escape. But now there was only one exit, and she felt she couldn't get away if she needed to." The feeling of being alone in the city in late July, with John's frequent absences—either traveling for work or just at work—and the bright days of summer mostly behind them, was hard for Carolyn. She felt left behind. John was a man with a mission—he was preoccupied with *George* and may have developed a blind spot to the needs of his wife. Maybe he couldn't understand the newfound fragility in the strong, vibrant woman he had married. But Carolyn was being worn down. Photographers were always outside her apartment in wait, and without the goodwill they had for John.

Carolyn's description to Kathy McKeon about the photographers, "They were grunting and groaning and pushing each other. They were almost on top of me," makes it clear that she was physically frightened, not just angry that she felt caged in a Tribeca warehouse. Adding to the problem: the pressure to have kids when she felt like her husband wasn't making her a priority. In *America's Reluctant Prince*, Steve Gillon wrote that Carolyn said, "If I'm going to have a kid at some point, I'm not walking around by myself in the streets of New York City with a stroller with every psycho in the world. They barely let me get across the street now."

As the pressure ramped up, so did Carolyn's inability to cope with a life over which she felt she had no control. She'd had to put her career ambitions on hold until John's evolved. His outsized fame was as much as, or more of, an intrusion in her life as his, but without the affection the media held for her husband, while she was perceived as an icy witch. Altogether worse, unable as people are to stand in another's shoes, even those who loved her could not quite grasp why she could not just rise above it all, which furthered her isolation. Carolyn began to unravel.

CHAPTER TWENTY-ONE

ALL THE WORLD'S A STAGE

September 1998–December 1998

U nfortunately, John didn't understand why the paparazzi made Carolyn so upset or why I was neurotic," RoseMarie Terenzio wrote in
Fairy Tale Interrupted. " 'It's no big deal,' he said to Carolyn over the phone
in response to her complaint about a particularly vicious incident. 'Just don't
pay attention to it. I don't.' I cringed. 'There are worse things that could happen than a few photographers following you around . . .' he said."

Terenzio clarified, "I knew that John's dismissive attitude was due to
his frustration. He had no control over the situation and was angry that he
couldn't protect his wife from it. He should have told her as much—I know
she really wanted to hear it—but instead he was flippant."

Even though Terenzio was John's assistant, she was a confidante and sup-
porter to Carolyn and John both. "And I had to appease both sides," Terenzio
wrote. "I couldn't tell John off or dismiss Carolyn's complaints. Instead, I
acted as a mediator. . . . To John, I would say, 'Give her a break'; to Carolyn,
'He doesn't get it.'"

Eventually the paparazzi even found Carolyn and MJ Bettenhausen's
dog run. "She came less and less because she felt that people standing on
the other side of the fence would be a bother to other dog owners," Bettenhausen said.

"She got depressed," Carole Radziwill said.

John's experience of the press simply wasn't the same. Photo editors did not clamor for a shot of him looking sad or upset in the way they did Carolyn, knowing catching her at loose ends was of greater interest, and, by extension, of greater value. According to friends, she was indeed surprised and pained at how caustic they were with her, and again when getting married did not change the dynamic in a positive way. She was still vilified in tabloids, and she could feel that public opinion still clung to the images of her sparring with John in Washington Square Park. Yet it was important to Carolyn to be a good wife, and she worked at it. She showed up: at Municipal Art Society galas, Profile in Courage Awards, *George* events, and romping on the lawn in Hyannis Port in front of family photographers. She felt like she was there for John in every way: as a wife, as a colleague, as a member of the Kennedy dynasty. To endure the crises surrounding each of these imperatives, she wanted her husband's time and attention. And most likely reassurance.

Thus, Carolyn craved more time when it was just she and John, wanting to know "he would always be there" so that she could feel safe enough to give him the children they both wanted. As Pam Thur observed, "She was asking him to slow down to be with her."

But John was not built to slow down. John felt the crises and, by rote, thought the best way to survive was to keep moving—make the magazine a success, position himself for office both in the public sphere and in the Kennedy hierarchy. They had opposite reactions to the same set of issues. What Carolyn hoped for in John was care and attention reciprocal to what she had been giving him. Instead, John's tunneling forward very well could have felt like the abandonment she had always feared. As a response to that fear, she not only withdrew from the world, she withdrew from John.

John would have felt it had Carolyn been pulling away. In *Four Friends*, William D. Cohan wrote that "John seemed quite stymied by Carolyn and how poorly they were getting along." Carolyn was not a quiet, undemonstrative person. If she loved someone, if she was happy with them, she would show it. She asked questions, tended to someone's concerns, and never left one in doubt of her feelings. The absence of that would have left a huge void.

It was not only the press trying to drive them apart with false stories and conjured dramas. There were a few people in their circle—really friends of John's—who were perhaps hoping for the downfall of Carolyn and John's marriage. Maybe some wanted their buddy back in the proverbial playground, and maybe some hoped to be the second Mrs. Kennedy. It exacerbated a rough patch in their marriage, and both spoke to friends of the predicament.

Carolyn had long witnessed women throw themselves at John, even as he held her hand. He had many female friends, which was usually fine. Until it wasn't. John had lunch with Julie Baker once a month, and Carolyn did not object. Yet, she drew the line after Julie Baker climbed into his lap during a party at the loft. Understandably, Baker was then banned. But John still kept his monthly lunch with her.

John, by now, was unlikely to be bothered by rumors about Michael Bergin. Yet in her distress and hiding in Tribeca, she had befriended John Birch, who owned Wyeth Antiques, then located a walk around the corner at 151 Franklin Street. Birch specialized in the mid-century modern furniture that Carolyn loved, such as her Dunbar desk and dining table, the few pieces of her choosing that would fit in a loft full of Kennedy history. Visiting Wyeth was a way to get out of the house without exposing herself to a phalanx of photographers. "Carolyn had always had male friends," said MJ Bettenhausen, "and that's what John Birch was to her. A friend and confidant during a difficult time."

John Kennedy had kept a journal most of his life. As with many of his belongings—no matter how valuable or personal—he was careless about keeping track of it. As Cohan recounted, John once left his journal on an outdoor table at a Greenwich Village café. A friend took a peek when he went to the bathroom. This same friend again "happened upon one of John's journals on the coffee table" at North Moore Street. On this occasion, the friend read an entry in which: "John had written that he suspected Carolyn of having an affair with a friend who was a married antique dealer: 'I can't believe she's doing this to me.'"

"When John discovered that his friend had read [the] journal entry, he didn't seem upset. 'My life is a mess and it's all because of Carolyn,' he apparently had told the friend. 'The only question is how do I get myself out of it.'"

The friend who read John's journals told Cohan that Carolyn was "snorting more and more cocaine" and revealed information that John had shared about a lack of physical intimacy in his marriage. This friend remains unnamed, as do his or her motives in making these statements.

While a few accounts include Sasha Chermayeff as confirming some of these rumors that swirled around Carolyn, she takes issue with the misrepresentation of her words. "I never saw her do drugs, and I never concluded, at the time, it as a given she was having an affair with the antiques dealer or Bergin," she stated firmly. (She wrote an email on the Andover alumni page contesting her quotes in Cohan's book, also stating that it was "sad and painful to see Carolyn once again characterized as a shallow, selfish bitch, by someone who never knew her.")

The strain of a rumor mill in overdrive was taking a toll. Chermayeff recalled, "One evening when John convinced me to get Carolyn out of the loft for a glass of wine, she asked me how long-term couples keep passion in their relationship, which I found odd as they hadn't been married for yet three years."

Chermayeff wasn't the only friend to notice the visible toll on Carolyn. "The last time I saw her we had lunch at Bubby's with Effie in the early fall of 1998," MJ Bettenhausen said. "Carolyn was subdued, but there were traces of the old, joyful Carolyn. At the end, she gave me her new cell phone number, saying, 'Call this new number, honey.' It seems they had to change their numbers often. I spent the next six or seven months in California, as my husband's mother needed help, so I didn't get to see her. But I feel she would've pulled through this difficult time."

John's college friend Chris Oberbeck saw the issue as having several complicating factors. "One, it was the beginning of the degradation of the media where they increasingly lowered their standards, sort of the beginning of the 'post-truth.' Therefore, they were willing to print anything about her as long as it sold, and Carolyn sold," he said. "The further she retreated, the more ferocious they became. And then Carolyn, stuck at home, was like a tiger in its cage; pacing back and forth and understandably angry."

Oberbeck illustrated a secondary factor with a memory from rooming with John at Brown. "At a certain point, I became fed up with the dynamic in the house. I felt everyone always deferred to John," Oberbeck said. "I wanted to be friends with him, but only if we were going to remain on equal footing. 'I used to think we were pretty good friends, but now I'm not so sure,' I told John. I gave him a list of reasons why I was questioning the friendship. He was so used to getting his way that he began to walk with a swagger. I don't think he was even aware of it. My comments took him by surprise. His entire face dropped as if to say, 'Oh, that's not true.' But he listened, and he took my feelings to heart. Then he changed—he worked on it. He could be selfish, but he was never malicious. It was natural selfishness, because he was who he was."

Yet the positive changes John needed to make in his friendship with Ober-beck were of a more concrete nature. It was easier to step up on one's share of chores and not eat the last of the cereal than it was to convince the media to leave his wife alone and convince his wife the media didn't figure in their lives.

"Additionally, now that John was running *George* and eyeing political seats, the media actually did matter," Oberbeck said. "John and Carolyn were woefully under-managed for their outsize life. They needed aides-de-camp. They needed security. And they should have probably moved away from that building where there was only one entrance that stepped out onto the stage that North Moore had become." The remark wasn't purely figurative—the front door to their building literally opened onto a low platform that was a step above the sidewalk. A stage.

FOR LABOR DAY WEEKEND, once again there was a big Kennedy fam-ily gathering. Rather than flying with John, Carolyn drove to Hyannis Port. When flying above the Vineyard, John would "buzz" Jackie's house, a neigh-bor told Andersen. John would swoop down close enough so everyone below could clearly see N529JK, a reference to his father's birthday, on the fuselage. Then, at the last minute he would pull up after having made sure to show whoever was in the plane with him an aerial view of Red Gate Farm. However, none of his family would go up in the air with him—not Ted, not the Shrivers, not even the RFKs. At the close of Labor Day weekend, the *Philadelphia Daily News* reported that John had "made a perfect approach and touchdown" at the airfield in Hyannis Port but noted that Carolyn "met her hubbo" there, and that "the two were expected to return home to Manhattan—again, traveling separately."

Caroline was concerned that her brother was flying again and urged him to be cautious, saying, "After all, you're no longer alone—you have a wife to worry about." Caroline didn't take lightly the value Carolyn brought to her brother's life. "Whenever she's around, he's got that goofy, fool-in-love expression on his face," Caroline once told a friend soon after he'd earned his pilot's license in April.

On September 18, Carolyn and John stole a few moments alone on a trip to the Caribbean. As they were flying commercial, they were "under surveillance." A Rush and Molloy gossip column reported that "John Kennedy Jr. and wife Carolyn Bessette looked quite affectionate on Friday aboard an American Airlines flight bound for the island of Dominica. In between smooches, John had his nose in an aviation textbook." It was a quick weekend trip, however, and then it was back to business.

Carolyn continued to be discerning about the events she attended with John. The Municipal Art Society gala made the cut, as it was closely associated with John's mother and the award was in Jackie's name. It was a family affair, so Carolyn had safety in numbers. She was seated next to Lee Radziwill, with co-chair Caroline, Patricia Kennedy Lawford, and Eunice Kennedy Shriver in attendance. Carolyn also had John. The *Times Herald* described how he "drooled over his wife Carolyn Bessette Kennedy's stunning black strapless gown, worn with long black gloves and the spikiest heels. He had a surprising revelation about the designer: 'It's by me! You gotta to see the back. The back is the best part.' Actually, Carolyn said, it was by Yohji Yamamoto, a favorite designer of hers. The back featured a sort of derriere wrap around."

Condé Nast CEO Steve Florio made the announcement that the event had raised more than $1 million for the art society. Also there were UN Secretary-General Kofi Annan, musician Bobby Short, writer Dominick Dunne, and *Vanity Fair* editor Graydon Carter.

Later that month, Carolyn made another public appearance, albeit in a less glamorous setting. She appeared at a Tribeca Community Board 1 meeting, where she spoke out against a proposed installation of a cooling tower for the nearby Holland Tunnel, which would have made a deafening noise. To have their one safe space in New York City become a cacophony of hissing engines would've been a stressor they didn't want to add to the already long list. (They eventually lost the battle, but they would not be around to know—the cooling towers were erected in 2000, with the *New York Times* claiming that Tribeca, "the old butter-and-eggs district of Lower Manhattan, isn't sizzling any longer. It's deafening.")

Carolyn stepped out once more that fall, at the Foreign Policy Association Dinner at the New York Hilton, where First Lady Hillary Clinton made a thirty-seven-minute speech about the United States' responsibility to the United Nations.

It seemed that Carolyn was very intentional about which events would bring her out of the apartment—in particular, those that might be important to John's future in politics. It was clear where he was heading. *George* was an Act I.

He spoke with several trusted friends about running for the seat of New York senator Daniel Patrick Moynihan, who John had heard was not planning to run when his term ended in 2000. He told Gary Ginsberg that he was seriously considering running. John was also approached by Democratic leaders to gauge his interest. He told Judith Hope, Democratic chairwoman of New York State, that he was in.

"His next goal was to be New York senator, or possibly governor. And then he would've run for President," wrote Littell. "He'd already been offered the opportunity to run for Senator Lautenberg's seat in New Jersey, presumably using his mom's Peapack address as his home base. He rejected the idea and began to put a team together to develop a roadmap for his political future. John was intensely dedicated to destiny, and he had his nose quietly to the grindstone."

John threw himself even further into his work that fall. While Carolyn intellectually knew that he had to do everything he could to save *George*, emotionally, she would have liked more of his time. He was turning thirty-eight that year, and one can't help but wonder if he compared himself to his father at that age: JFK received a Purple Heart at twenty-six after his PT boat was torpedoed and he led his crew to safety, where most were rescued; by twenty-nine, he was elected to the House of Representatives; by thirty-five, he was in the Senate; and he married Jackie at thirty-six. He wrote *Profiles in Courage* at thirty-nine, at once contributing to the mythology of those he celebrated and putting himself in their company, for which he won the Pulitzer Prize, the same year Caroline Bouvier Kennedy was born. He became president at the age of forty-three.

John's accelerated trajectory toward his future was both profound and a little frightening for those close to him. Gillon noted that even Caroline's husband, Ed Schlossberg, fumbled around the intensity of his brother-in-law's path. That fall, John got a call from HBO asking if he would narrate a documentary about his father's assassination, executive-produced by Edwin Schlossberg. John was livid. Not only had John never commemorated his father's assassination, he actively avoided all mention of it. That

Ed would begin such a project and then not call his brother-in-law himself but have HBO call to see if John wanted to participate was way out of bounds. It was the second time Ed had started a film project on JFK without telling John.

"Who the fuck is he to tell me how to honor my dad's death?" John yelled.

Another friend said, "I've never seen him so mad, and I'd never heard him expel a string of expletives like that in all the years I'd known him."

At the end of October, Carolyn and John were planning on attending a Halloween party given by Women Model Management of New York. Easily enough, they would wear their George and Martha Washington costumes, still on hand from the previous Halloween. But Carolyn and Lauren got a call that their grandmother Jennie, Ann's mother, had fallen ill while on vacation in Florida. So, John attended solo while Carolyn and Lauren flew to be with Jennie.

The press saw an opening and pounced, with the *New York Post* announcing: "JFK Jr.'s marriage is falling apart because John is spending time with other women. On Halloween, he left Carolyn at home while he dressed up as George Washington and went to a party attended by Naomi Campbell, Kate Moss, and other leading supermodels. Indications are that his marriage is in trouble."

This snippet was catnip for all the tabloids, who went on a snarking spree. "Do you think the hunk showed Naomi Campbell and Kate Moss his Declaration of Independence?" asked one paper.

In November, *Manhattan File* published the first of what was to be a series titled "Diary of a Bitch," a new column by Candace Bushnell of *Sex and the City* fame. The portrait was ruthless. The subtitle was "Spoiled in the City. She married the world's most eligible bachelor, and inherited way more than she bargained for: an unreformed husband, a paparazzi conspiracy, and a nasty habit for popping pills. Is something rotten in SoHo? Introducing the diaries of CKB."

"CKB" was portrayed with less nuance than a Disney villain: pouting for attention, pretending to be pregnant. Written in the first person, CKB says, "And then I did what I trained myself to do when I was kid. I started the cry."

Carolyn felt pummeled. So, she stepped out of the ring, just as her sister Lauren was stepping in.

"Carolyn asked me to show Lauren around town," Jack Merrill remembered. "Lauren was smart. She was bright and funny like Carolyn, but more subdued.

"But the reason I was showing her around instead of Carolyn," Merrill continued, "was because Carolyn was not leaving the house."

"This was not the Carolyn I knew, and I have no doubt that eventually, she would pull out of this and bounce back," said MJ Bettenhausen. "All of it, the white-blonde hair, the eyebrows, the rail-thin figure; eventually, she would have centered. She was always fit and had a beautiful figure, but she became so thin and pale. Carolyn was an Italian girl who used to laugh so hard she couldn't breathe. I think she felt she had to fit in, to be what she thought people expected a Kennedy to be. So . . . blonder, thinner. It was exhausting. But I know she would have bounced back."

Carolyn took solace in her animals. "Yet even that was disrupted, albeit temporarily. John didn't want it known that he hunted deer with his cousins—Carolyn hated it," Bettenhausen remembered. "John tried to bring Friday, who was not a hunting dog, a few times. Friday was an already high-strung breed, and the sounds of the gunshots terrified him. Poor Friday suffered from some high anxiety after a few trips. Carolyn was furious. It took a while to get him settled back down enough to walk outside for longer than a bathroom break.

"Once, he even got skunked, and John had to give him a tomato juice bath to get the scent off. Friday was pink for a week," Bettenhausen said. "Some friends from the dog run asked her, 'Why did you dye Friday pink?' Carolyn deadpanned right back, 'Ask John; it was his idea.'"

Although she was pulling back from the public eye, her sense of humor remained intact.

Bettenhausen recalled when "Carolyn once accidentally introduced herself as Caroline Kennedy. She immediately realized her slip and doubled over laughing at the mistake. The thought of the two of them being interchangeable was preposterous."

Carolyn would spend hours on the phone, calling to check in with those she cared about. "I knew when Carolyn called I would need to put time aside from my day," said Hamilton South.

She was "an incredible conversationalist and her humor was generous of spirit," South reminisced. "Carolyn was the first person to be up and reading the entire paper. We would go over everything. News, politics, arts, she had something bright and witty to say about it all. But she wasn't really leaving the house, at least not when in the city. The intrusion of the press and the subsequent feeling of being trapped was still there; always there."

"Even though she was having a difficult time, she was still a caretaker," recalled Ariel Paredes, who was then at Boston College. "She would buy clothes and beauty products for me and send packages wrapped in so much *George* packaging that my eyes would bleed. I would call to thank her and laugh about all the *George* paraphernalia. 'You're the only one I can use this crazy packaging for,' Carolyn laughed. 'Your friends in Boston won't care or even know what *George* is.'"

Staying at Lauren's may have been Carolyn's nonverbal communication to John that she was not pleased with the excessive demands the outside world made on their lives. RoseMarie Terenzio wrote that John had, at times, a blind spot about other people's time. "Carolyn would decline invitations from friends because John said he was coming home for dinner. So she would wait and wait and wait, while he worked late and went to the gym (without letting her know), and then waltz into to the apartment way past dinner time. . . . Another classic scenario was when he would spring important information on her at the last minute, such as 'Oh, by the way, the Whitney benefit is in two days' or 'I'm bringing a friend home for dinner . . . right now.' She wanted to know why the hell he didn't tell her sooner. It wasn't mean-spiritedness on his part. He was simply as disorganized and clueless as a kid. Still, it didn't make scrambling to accommodate him any less frustrating."

So Carolyn retaliated. "[She] used to hang out at her sister Lauren's house in Tribeca and bitch about the invasion of her privacy," said longtime Bessette family friend William Peter Owen. "She'd stay late. John would return to 20 North Moore Street, and she wouldn't be there for him. This happened on several occasions." She would often stay at Lauren's until the early hours of the morning. Sometimes, she would stay the night. The message seemed to be: *I still have my own life. Take me for granted, and I won't be there.*

To further aggravate matters, Carolyn declined to accompany John on outings and trips that fall, exhausted by the strain of worrying about her husband's career, the declining health of beloved Anthony, and having to nonetheless appear happy in pictures or be faced with another tabloid story. On a trip to Rome to sell ads for *George*, John strolled through Piazza Navona on his own. Carolyn had skipped Italy.

When it came time for his annual trek out of town to avoid the anniversary of his father's assassination in November, she passed on camping in Maine. On Thanksgiving, John and Carolyn went to Hyannis Port for the holiday, and, while Carolyn went to the Thursday dinner, she skipped Ted's Friday-night cocktail party as well as his Saturday brunch of leftovers. John was alone for the family football huddles, beach walks, and sailing, looking, according to the *Detroit Free Press*, "lost and dour."

Picking and choosing carefully, Carolyn attended just a few events in December—she went with John to the Robin Hood foundation breakfast on the 2nd, with Lauren in tow. Diane Sawyer and Mike Nichols were there, and there is a video clip of Carolyn's delight at speaking with Sawyer, whom she adored. Carolyn would remain circumspect in her appearances and usually dressed that way as well, with black, midi-length dresses by Yamamoto.

A sea change came on December 11 when she attended Revlon's Fire and Ice Ball at Universal Studios in Los Angeles in a bright-white Versace evening dress. Was this a willing return to public life? It would depend. It isn't easy to pull out of a cycle of fear, especially when accompanied by real threats. As recently as 1995 the FBI had received kidnapping threats against John by Colombian drug cartels, so Carolyn's concerns for their physical safety were not unfounded. But that evening in December, attending the Fire and Ice Ball with Maria Shriver and her brother Bobby, Carolyn seemed carefree, although bashful. She joked with the reporters outside, saying, "I've been waiting a long time for a date with my cousin Bobby." When asked what her favorite part of the evening was, she said, "I had no favorite part. The whole evening was spectacular."

In their troublemaking manner, what the papers took away from the event was that Carolyn "really hit it off" with John Enos, an ex-boyfriend of Madonna's, and that she was "unaccompanied by her husband."

Carolyn and John spent Christmas Eve at the Freemans' in Greenwich, bringing Marta Sgubin and, of course, Friday with them, then had a very quiet Christmas dinner with Anthony and Carole Radziwill. "There is nervous energy around all of us," Radziwill wrote in *What Remains*. "We plan a trip to Cuba and Greece. We are trying to ramp a lifetime into a few short years."

After Christmas, Carolyn and John headed to visit cousins Maria Shriver and Arnold Schwarzenegger in Sun Valley, where they had a large home and often hosted parties. Liz Smith, informed that the couple was there, duly reported that "John Kennedy Jr. was out on the slopes skiing or snowboarding every day, and lunching with his guy pals. Carolyn Bessette appeared on the mountain once before she decided to head down an easier run with Ralph Lauren exec Hamilton South." The press would not give them peace in Istanbul nor Idaho, it seems.

No matter. Carolyn was not a strong skier, but she and Hamilton found a way to have an excellent time together. "She looked great in all black—ski pants, coat, and a black headband. She lectured me on skiwear as she felt I needed to up my sports attire." South laughed. "Neither of us were advanced skiers. We only did one run, and then it was down to the lodge for après ski for us, or back to the place we had rented near Maria and Arnold's."

Finishing out 1998 with laughter and friends and family seemed like a hopeful end to a really tough year. Lauren was now just blocks away, and they were closer than ever. With newfound strength from the proximity of her sister, Carolyn readied for the days to come.

CHAPTER TWENTY-TWO

GREY GARDENS IN MANHATTAN

January 1999–March 1999

The New Year began in the company of friends. In early January, Carolyn and John went to Rob and Frannie Littell's East Village apartment to catch some of the NFL playoffs on TV. "While John and I screamed at the TV," Littell wrote, "Carolyn played with Coco and Tate and eventually fell asleep on the couch. She awoke as the final whistle blew. John started needling her before she could rub her eyes. 'Yo, Carolyn, honey, you were snoring. What kind of person falls asleep at a football party?'" He then jokingly apologized to Frannie for his wife's less than scintillating presence, attempting to get a rise out of Carolyn.

Always up for teasing banter, Carolyn thanked Rob and Frannie for "making her feel so comfortable that she could just fall asleep and apologized for her husband's inability to recognize true hospitality when he saw it. We all laughed," wrote Littell, "and the two lovers soon went arm in arm into the night." If only Carolyn and John could have stayed in that cozy living room.

In the first days of 1999, John went to a meeting with Barry Diller's USA Network in Los Angeles, arranged by Hachette. It became clear that David Pecker had indicated that John would play a large role, likely pushing for him to host.

"Fuck this!" John yelled, and left the room.

Steve Gillon wrote that John then phoned Pecker, and the two engaged in what staffers called "a fiery phone call." At that point, John's relationship with Pecker had devolved into war.

John tasked executive editor Biz Mitchell with hiring a forensic accountant, because, according to Gillon, "John was suspicious that Pecker was running John out to every dinner in town to attract advertisers, and then funneled the money into other titles at Hachette." John wanted Biz to find out where the money was really going, because it wasn't going to *George* editorial budgets nor toward the magazine's profits. The move ramped up the vitriol with Pecker, and he let John know that, barring making a profit, Hachette would not renew their contract, which was expiring at the end of 1999.

"Pecker was comparing current sales, which was not unusual for a magazine that had just gone monthly three years earlier," said Gillon. "The enormous success of the first couple of issues were unusual, and the comparison shouldn't have held."

But the antagonizers had gotten to John. It had been Michael Berman, and now it was David Pecker.

And then there was Anthony. Until this moment, John would not accept that he could not save Anthony, but this facade was becoming harder and harder to uphold. It was painful to watch someone under this much pressure, and perhaps Carolyn's instinct to nurture brought her slowly but surely out of her isolation.

Carolyn had remained a lifeline for Carole and Anthony, accompanying them to nearly every hospital stay. John acknowledged as much, telling Billy Noonan, "I just worry about Carole . . . Carolyn has been really great to her. She does these little sweet things, like buy her friendship rings . . . I keep losing everyone. I really need to start thinking about having a family. [Losing Anthony] is going to suck."

As the problems at *George* escalated in 1999, Carolyn started coming to the office once more. She would also accompany John in the search for new investors. On January 27, they were spotted coming out of the David Hare play *The Blue Room* at the Cort Theatre, which starred Nicole Kidman. Carolyn, while still in her signature black, had let her hair loose from the severe chignon and ponytail she had lately favored, her hair blowing wildly in the wind, much like she had worn it before the days when her every move was caught on camera.

Later in the month, Carolyn invited herself to Carole Radziwill's parents' house in Suffern, New York, to watch the Super Bowl. "'I can't believe you never invited me there,' she says, indignant. 'I want to see where you grew up. I'm coming,'" Carole wrote in *What Remains*. "After dinner, Carolyn looked through all of the wedding albums. 'You look like Cary Grant!' she says to my brother. She has all of them tell their stories. Jeff, my brother-in-law, just got his pilot's license, and they talk about John's plane. 'I don't know if I want him to fly when we have kids,' she says."

On Presidents' Day weekend, Carolyn was supposed to go skiing with John in Utah but canceled. It's unknown if this change in plans was the result of a fight, but, more likely, once Carolyn heard where they were staying—a place in Alta called the Peruvian Lodge, where the rooms were like dorms with shared bathrooms at the end of the hall—she took a pass. John called Chris Oberbeck last minute to see if he would join. Chris knew that John was having a rough time, and after checking with his own wife, he bent over backward to make the trip happen.

"About two years into their marriage, Carolyn seemed to be regaining her balance," wrote Littell. "Which isn't to say all was rosy—in fact, the two of them spent a fair amount of time locking horns."

"They had an intense passion," said Chris Oberbeck. "That passion was manifested in loving each other and really having a great time together, and it was also manifested in unbelievable fights."

What Carolyn wanted from the marriage naturally put pressure on John, because she was asking for a full partnership in a way he had not been asked before. "Carolyn was not afraid to say no to John, or to get him angry," Carole Radziwill said. "And he needed that."

"Most women sort of became tongue-tied around John. But not Carolyn," said Richard Wiese. "She was very strong-minded, knew what she wanted, and had absolutely no difficulty speaking her mind."

But still, many tabloids could only focus on her employment—or lack thereof. "What does she do with her days?" was the query that the *Washington Post* felt entitled to ask the previous September.

It was a question that kept coming up. For the public, but no doubt for Carolyn herself as well. Carolyn was a woman whose energy and time had always been taken up with work. She wanted and *needed* to work. But the perennial question, since she had linked her life to John's, was: What would that look like?

"She still hopes to return to a career. But what? There were a lot of stipulations. She couldn't go near fashion because of John's magazine, and she also had to be available to him and his unpredictable life," wrote RoseMarie Terenzio. She traveled with him incessantly, recently especially so, looking for new backers. There were those who shouted she should be taking up charity work, to which she did give her time and support, albeit quietly. But officially putting her name to any of the many nonprofits that approached her had to wait. Given that their public life was primed to become even more public if John held office, Carolyn wanted to be cautious, not least because every move she made was being picked apart.

"Not to mention," Terenzio continued, "that Carolyn's high-profile presence would have disrupted most offices." It would have, and sometimes did. Carolyn had become very close to Hamilton South, and if they didn't spend an hour on the phone, she would sometimes pop over to his workplace. "But then everything just stopped. Everyone wanted to glimpse her, and it was mayhem," he said. "Eventually, I moved closer to Tribeca, and we all had our evenings together so that we could spend time without my work life coming to a halt!"

"Carolyn and John had home routines," said South. "When Effie didn't cook—and usually he did—Carolyn had one recipe, roast chicken with lemon and garlic. If it wasn't one of those two then they ordered in, sometimes even from Kentucky Fried Chicken. I would come over, and Carolyn was always at the Dunbar desk in the side room as you walk in, that she had made her base. At home, Carolyn dressed casually, jeans and a T-shirt, and I would walk in to see her at the desk poring over the papers. The moment I entered, with her hands fluttering about her for emphasis, 'You will *not* believe what is going on!' And it was always about the world, never about her.

"When she wasn't at that beautiful desk, she was on the couch, making phone calls to friends. Again, it was about them. Their lives, the world, a new film, or ballet on at Lincoln Center."

Carole Radziwill said that, in the spring of 1999, she had spoken with Carolyn a good deal about getting into documentary filmmaking. "I was doing docs at ABC News, and she was always interested in illuminating other people's stories." She added, "I think, because of her upbringing, being raised by a single mom, she identified with the underdog, and now she was in a position to provide insight into the struggles and victories of ordinary people. That really appealed to her."

Another complication to launching a career was the onus to have children—not just any children, but the JFK IIIs. "John was eager to start a family," wrote Rob Littell. Carolyn was not. "She would, with a bit of bluster, say that she could never subject a baby to the weird, public spectacle of their life . . . I think she was frightened that she wouldn't be a good mother, that she wasn't strong enough to care for another human being."

Everyone, if they are honest with themselves, is daunted by the idea of being a first-time parent. If you add all the poison from the paparazzi, it's even more frightening. This brings to mind Carole Radziwill's earlier comment that Carolyn's fashion friends couldn't comprehend "that this unusual blitz was an entirely different beast." When Jackie Kennedy said that Ron Galella's stalking made life "intolerable," she was talking about the work of one man. Carolyn was dealing with Galella's progeny: a voracious mob.

Also, "she had seen firsthand how one family can sort of become central, and slowly the other side loses touch and barely has contact at all," said a close friend. "This was hitting home for Carolyn, now that she was beginning to understand that not seeing her father wasn't what he *preferred*. It was just how time and life played out. Carolyn realized it was one family being closer and busier than another. And if any family in the world was close and busy, it was the Kennedys. She worried she could lose her children she had with John in the same way her father had lost her. It was an unbearable thought."

Littell, writing about Carolyn in the spring of 1999, noted that she hadn't given up: "Carolyn seemed more lively, more engaged. I think she was literally fighting her way out of her depression. She often went to La Palestra, the gym owned by John's friend Pat Manocchia, spent time with her friends, and started to carve out her own space in the marriage. And, yes, as widely reported, John stayed at the Stanhope several nights over their years of marriage. . . . I've spent a night or two out of the house in anger, too. The thing that's most poignant to me is John's choice of the Stanhope, located quite near the apartment he grew up in. It's as if he tried to go 'home' in his darker moments."

John admired his aunt Eunice and uncle Sarge's marriage, in which the wife had her own professional goals. Eunice had to push past her own father's belief that women should not work, and began on day one of her brother's presidency to push him to put physical and intellectual disabilities on the agenda. Eunice was tireless, driven, and devoted, eventually founding the Special Olympics. Part of what drew John to Carolyn was exactly that kind of potential in her, and part of what made her happy as an individual was putting that energy and drive to use. Yet for the last year she had been sapped of power, paralyzed by the sting of the press and the need to lie low while *George* struggled.

Carolyn, by refusing the Peruvian Lodge and Maine camping trips, was recovering herself. *I am in this, too*, she seemed to be saying. *You have to begin to consider me in these things. I am not simply a Kennedy accessory.*

Carving out her space inside the marriage needn't have meant an affair. Here we enter a bit of a meta moment, because much of what has thus far shaped our knowledge of Carolyn has been history written by men. Some of this can be put down to sensationalizing. But is it fair to ask if some other hostility was playing out in these men? Some knew her, but many who did not were possessive of John both in life and death, and several wrote as if it were common knowledge that she was having an affair. Among them was Edward Klein, who wrote in his 2003 book, *The Kennedy Curse*, that Carolyn was having an affair with Michael Bergin. Klein had written numerous books about the Kennedys, all with the breathless voice of an insider, though John told RoseMarie that he was "a guy who had lunch with my mother once at someone else's house and dined out on that the rest of his life."

MJ Bettenhausen put it quite succinctly: "She didn't have an affair with Bergin, nor the antiques dealer. She would not have jeopardized her marriage to John. Crying on a shoulder, perhaps, but she would not have strayed."

Clifford Streit, Bergin's former manager and the inspiration for *Sex and the City's* beloved Stanford Blatch, said that "the part about his having an affair with her after she married John Jr. was total horsecrap. Michael and I often discussed Carolyn after she married John, and it's simply not true that he slept with her after she got married. They may have spoken on the phone a few times, but that was it."

Carolyn and John began couples therapy in March. "By 1999, the Kennedys have reached a pivotal moment in their relationship," wrote Christopher Andersen. "John was telling friends that for months, Carolyn, unhappy, despite a steady diet of prescription antidepressants, had simply refused to sleep with him. Frustrated and confused, the couple began seeing a marriage counselor in March." This accords with Sasha Chermayeff's observation that "prescriptions are doled out like candy, and they don't tell you about the side effects, which for antidepressants can be a severely decreased libido."

At the same time, John had been successful in his efforts to encourage Carolyn to begin a rapprochement with her father. John held the belief, gained from firsthand experience, that even problematic family members were better tolerated than cast away. John helped Carolyn, and Carolyn helped John. That had not changed. In those last months, she traveled with him, looking for new backers to hopefully save the magazine. But she was also instrumental in getting him to consider the next steps in his career, which likely included political service.

Things could be terrible one moment, and bliss the next.

"They were talking about kids, and they were talking about him becoming a senator," Littell said in the JFK Jr. documentary *Final 24*. "She'd smoothed out."

On March 9, the Whitney Museum hosted its Brite Nite fundraiser, where, according to the Rush and Molloy, "some of the museum swells [were] reportedly a little nervous about the evening's sexy entertainer, Foxy Brown. So they are relieved Miss Brown wore a tasteful blue dress when she spouted rhymes for the likes of Leonard Lauder, Ron Perelman and Claudia Cohen, Martha Stewart, Russell, Kimora Lee Simmons, and Tommy Hilfiger. Kennedy and a happier-looking Carolyn Bessette stayed to dance into the wee hours as the party filled with fragrant smoke." Perhaps Carolyn was amused enough by the "swells" looking worried to make it a long night. *Vogue* observed that the downtown crowd, "including its most famous couple," came uptown.

Was Carolyn's happiness due to John's newfound understanding of the need to create a lifestyle conducive to building a nuclear family or to Lauren's presence in New York City?

Carolyn and Lauren were pleasantly surprised that the more time they spent with their birth father, the more comfortable they became with him. Like all relationships, this, too, was not a simple matter of "one day the girls and their father were estranged" and the next "as if he hadn't missed a day of their lives." It was a process, and it was healing. Healing, too, for John to watch, as he actually *did* have the trauma of his father here one day and gone the next.

Now he was facing a profound loss again with his best friend and cousin, Anthony, who had spent New Year's having emergency surgery at NIH. He began chemotherapy at Columbia-Presbyterian. The proximity to his loved ones was a good thing, but it felt like moving backward: Surgery had not worked, so now they were trying chemo.

When things felt very dire, Carolyn and Carole played a game they called Townhouse. It was a grown-up version of a child's game of make-believe. "The townhouse as we know it is straight from Edith Wharton—a tottering mansion in Gramercy Park sitting remote and dreamy on an empty lot, towering over the neighborhood," Carole wrote in *What Remains*. "There are four floors and sixteen-foot ceilings and a wrought-iron gate. Heavy velvet drapes cross the windows, and we sometimes peek out from them." Radziwill called it "*Grey Gardens* in Manhattan," a tip to the estate on Long Island where Jackie's cousins Big Edie and Little Edie Beale infamously sequestered themselves after Phelan Beale, Little Edie's father, left them destitute. The mother and daughter lived for decades hidden in the East Hampton mansion, which fell into complete disarray. Jackie stepped in to help, giving them $25,000 to bring the house back up to code after the Suffolk County Department of Health Services gave them countless violations.

"'I'll be Big Edie,' Carolyn says. 'No, Little Edie, with a sun hat and halter, reading the *National Enquirer*. Oh my God, that will be us, the Beales! People will say, "Whatever happened to Carole and Carolyn? They had so much promise." And we will be locked up behind our gate ordering takeout and dressed in vintage Dior gowns,'" Carole wrote. The irony was that, while the Beales were reclusive shut-ins, living out of sight and out of mind of the world until the Maysles brothers showed up with their cameras, Carolyn was a recluse *because* of the cameras that were certainly not invited into her life.

CHAPTER TWENTY-THREE

PRESENT TENSE

April 1999–June 1999

Carolyn and John finished out the month of March with a brief trip to Italy. Upon their return, Carolyn's outlook seemed much improved. In mid-April, she was seemingly unbothered by the stares when she and John had breakfast at Bubby's. The couple was all happy smiles. Earlier that week, she had gone—without John—to the Krizia exhibition at NYU's Grey Art Gallery. Carolyn was seen entering the gallery in a videotape proving everyone wrong that she never smiled at photographers as, once she passed the corral outside and made it through the doors, she beamed brightly at photographer Patrick McMullan.

"Hi, Patrick! You know, I so appreciate what you do and how you are as opposed to the paparazzi," Carolyn said. "You won't believe it. Every time I leave my house there they are, trying to get pictures of me cleaning up after my dog, or looking angry. I never see you do that."

"I don't have time," Patrick said with a smile.

The evening highlighting the work of Krizia's Italian designer, Mariuccia Mandelli, celebrated the shifting boundaries between art and fashion and was a benefit for the Community Research Initiative on AIDS. Carolyn got to catch up with Kelly Klein while milling about with playwright Terrence McNally, director Julie Taymor, and actors Julia Ormond and Annabella Sciorra.

Maybe Carolyn was cheerful that night because her sister Lauren was there with her. "Lauren was so creative and spontaneous," said Chip Arndt. "She was such good company. She was always eager to try new things, maybe because in finance the days can become predictable. Lauren was so good at finding the balance between being 100 percent on top of everything in a conference room and living an exciting life. The times I saw Carolyn and John with her, usually at a lunch where the location remained secret until we arrived, they were also great company, people who enjoyed their life. They both loved what they were doing with *George*.

Meanwhile, Carole had been caring for Anthony for several years, and she was beginning to need care herself. So, when there were emergency room visits or overnight stays, Carolyn and Carole checked into the guest rooms available at the hospital's McKeen Pavilion. When Carole showered the next morning, Carolyn laid out her clothes and blow-dried her hair for her.

Carolyn was always there. As one of Anthony's doctors, Dr. Gil Lederman at Staten Island University Hospital, described to Andersen, "Carolyn sat shoulder to shoulder with the patient's spouse, their pinky fingers intertwined. Carolyn was with Tony when he arrived for each treatment and stayed to take him home afterward. Her bright eyes and loving way gave him tremendous confidence. She was soothing and reassuring," Lederman said. "While she sat in the waiting room, Carolyn called John on her cell phone to keep him informed concerning his cousin's condition."

John, too, was vigilant when it came to Anthony, as an anecdote from a few months earlier, around Christmastime, poignantly shows. One night, when Anthony's health took a frightening turn, Carole and Carolyn were still there when John turned up at the hospital late, still in his tux after an event. John sat down next to Anthony and held his hand, and began humming "The Teddy Bears' Picnic." "Anthony's eyes are still closed, but they seem more relaxed when he smiles," wrote Carole. "They sing together softly, this children's song . . . The doctors think Anthony will die tonight, and John takes him to the safest place he knows."

By Easter, Anthony mustered enough strength to travel, so he and Carole met Carolyn and John at the Vineyard to spend the holiday together. Carolyn, Anthony, and John went to church on Easter morning, and in the afternoon, they visited Diane Sawyer and Mike Nichols at their home on

Lake Tashmoo. Hawk nests are perched like sentries on trees around the house, which sits near the narrow strip of sand that makes up the Lake Tashmoo Town Beach, with the expanse of the Vineyard Sound just beyond. "Diane has hidden colored plastic eggs with gifts inside," wrote Carole in *What Remains*. "Press-on earrings, peel-off tattoos, fake eyelashes—and we run around the house, shrieking, to collect them. We have dinner and play parlor games until late in the evening."

It was spring and they were hopeful. By May 1, all was well as Carolyn flew from New York to Washington, DC, with John in his new Piper Saratoga. They were going to the 1999 White House Correspondents' dinner, a clubby kind of roast where a who's who of national political media get together to listen to jokes about and by presidents. Carolyn chatted with actress Claire Danes, who had grown up on Crosby Street, not too far away from North Moore Street. John reveled in hosting at his table *Hustler*'s Larry Flynt, who had pledged a million dollars to anyone who had dirt on the Republicans going after Bill Clinton.

Carolyn glowed in a black Jean Paul Gaultier dress from the current spring/summer haute couture collection, with its beautiful clamshell neckline and her by-now iconic red lipstick. She had no problem with Flynt at the table, though she spent most of her time talking with Danes. Later, at the *Vanity Fair* after-party, she found time to sit in John's lap and whisper something in his ear that made him throw his head back, roaring with laughter.

White House reporter Helen Thomas said, "They never looked more content and in love than they did that evening. I thought, *My God, this is Jack and Jackie all over again, isn't it?* They were so compelling; you actually couldn't take your eyes off them. The way photographers swarmed them, it really reminded me of the old days, the so-called Camelot days."

At the after-party, John also introduced Carolyn to Diane von Furstenberg, who had just two years earlier reintroduced the wildly popular wrap dress she had first created in the seventies.

"We exchanged emails and made a plan about a month later to have lunch together, which we did," said von Furstenberg. "She came to my office in the West Village, and we had an excellent time. I would have loved to have known her better, but I never got the chance."

A few days later, Carolyn and John flew to London to meet with possible new investors for *George*. They attended the celebration of a London Ralph

Lauren store opening at Mirabelle restaurant, looking relaxed and happy despite the immense duress they were under.

After a couple of days of meetings in London, they both needed a respite. But what would respite mean to them? For John, that meant a visit to Runnymede, the water meadow along the Thames where King John and his barons signed the Magna Carta. More important to John, the UK had built a memorial to his father there. When it was unveiled in 1965, Jackie, Caroline, and John attended the ceremony with Queen Elizabeth and Prince Philip, who held young John's hand.

Hamilton South, who was traveling with the couple, said Carolyn "was more excited about a private tour of Windsor Castle. Besides the exquisite beauty of the castle and surrounding grounds, we got to see the royal family's breathtaking collection of art, such as Lucas Cranach the Elder's *Apollo and Diana*, and Antonio Verrio's *The Apotheosis of Catherine of Braganza*. To view such masterpieces without the crowds that would have hindered not only their ability to enjoy, but to have enough time to view the art without being approached, was a spectacular treat. Carolyn was so grateful and thanked them profusely for allowing this special moment. It was dreamlike.

"We were staying at the Dorchester," said South, "and when back in London it was back to the paparazzi. Back to reality. Just a scene everywhere Carolyn and John went."

Yet Christa D'Souza, a friend of John's from Brown and a reporter for the *London Telegraph*, told Andersen that "Carolyn was rapidly improving after the couple had begun marriage counseling. Carolyn made tremendous progress in her personal life and was coming around to the idea of starting a family."

On May 19, *George* held a fundraiser in conjunction with Paul Newman and his Newman's Own Foundation. The event was held at the U.S. Custom House at 1 Bowling Green on the southern tip of Manhattan. When John and Carolyn stepped into the room, the crowd broke out into applause. Senator Alfonse D'Amato and Sean (then known as Puffy) Combs sat at their table while $250,000 was awarded to a charity called Idyll. Carolyn was comfortable and at ease, in a playful, ruffled Yohji Yamamoto jacket and pants. She even spoke to gossip columnist Mitchell Fink, saying that, when it came to all the gossip, "I choose not to make it an issue. It only becomes a problem for me when it's thrust in my face, or on my doorstep."

Photographer Patrick McMullan, who covered the party, said, "I could see that Carolyn had finally reckoned with becoming a public figure. She was at ease, and she and John looked as happy as they'd ever been. They both also had an excellent rapport with Paul Newman and Joanne Woodward, and they delighted in each other's company."

Fink later wrote, "Gone were the fearful looks she often displayed when encountering large crowds and the media, the icy apprehensiveness that had come to define her public persona."

John had seated Republican Senator D'Amato next to his liberal friend John Perry Barlow, excited at the prospect of a verbal brawl between the two. Barlow and D'Amato hit it off, though, as opposites sometimes do. The senator was especially enthusiastic about Carolyn. "What spirit, what confidence, what zest to her," he later recalled. "She talked to me about her Italian grandmother—'Nana' was what she called her. She talked about her grandmother's spirit and her cooking. I talked about Mama D'Amato. And a sense of humor, boy, Carolyn's got it."

Carolyn and John saw the Noonans for the first time in almost a year on May 24, at the Profiles in Courage dinner at the Kennedy Library in Boston. Noonan later said of Carolyn's distance, "Either John told her to keep quiet, or she was seeing a psychiatrist, or she was medicated. Or a combination of all three." This litany fails to consider the possibility that she simply did not like or trust him.

Laura Raposa, a journalist for the *Boston Herald*, remembered her much differently that night: "Something had changed. . . . We have pictures of her smiling. She even tweaked John on the ass. They were being very physically playful with each other. I've heard that they were seeing a marriage counselor. It evidently worked."

IT WAS JOHN'S TURN at Red Gate Farm on Memorial Day weekend, and he flew the Littells up in his Saratoga. Sasha Chermayeff and her husband, Phil Howie, along with their two children, met them on the Vineyard. It was the usual ritual of physical activities—waterskiing, hiking, Frisbee, swimming, and biking. Anthony and Carole began the summer at Diane Sawyer and Mike Nichols's nearby estate, but the plan was for them to come to Red Gate by mid-July and remain there for the rest of the summer. The part of the plan left unsaid was that Anthony would likely not leave Red Gate Farm.

On Sunday, they watched the basketball Eastern Conference finals. John was a long-time Knicks fan, with season tickets on the baseline of Madison Square Garden. Littell recounted that at some point in the fourth quarter of a close game, John, not so much out of pessimism as from the self-preserving instinct of someone who had watched the Knicks lose leads in the fourth quarter too many times, decided he needed a break. He walked outside to take a spin in the Buckeye. Rob helped John get the machine out and prepare it for flight. While the Knicks pulled out a close game, John took off. Everything went according to plan, until a gust of wind blew John and the Buckeye "a good fifteen feet to the right and into a gnarly-looking shrub."

All the children, Rob's and Sasha's, ran to the crumpled machine, yelling, "John got hurt!" John had broken his ankle. Carolyn and Rob took John to the hospital, where he was told he would need surgery to repair his ankle and six weeks in a cast to heal. That evening John, upset with himself, tried to make the best of it. He told Sasha, "I am literally going to be sitting in a rocking chair next to Anthony for the next six weeks. And that is exactly where I belong."

As is the case with many major moments and events in our lives, we look back later and see certain numbers collide. John broke his ankle five years and twelve days after his mother died. Sometimes, without knowing, our bodies react to a loss, pumping increased adrenaline that we cannot account for, and maybe we blame the Knicks or a stressful week at work.

John was very quiet at dinner that night. Efigenio had prepared swordfish. But a different menu was prepared for Rob Littell.

"I was served my usual big, luscious burned burger and noticed Carolyn, who was sitting to my right, eyeing it greedily," Littell wrote in his memoir. "I moved it to the left side of my plate. But as soon as I looked away, she grabbed it and took a big bite. Secretly pleased to have another culinary misfit on the island, I offered her the rest. But no, she handed it back to me and called out politely to Efigenio. I rarely saw Carolyn ask for anything, but that night, she said, 'Effie, would you mind making me one of those delicious hamburgers?' Efigenio, surprised but amused, replied, 'Of course not, how would you like it cooked?' 'Rare,' said Carolyn. 'Bloody. Please.' I'm proud to say that on our next visit, a month later, Carolyn had dispensed with the gourmet menu entirely and was subsisting on pink burgers each night. She wolfed them down with the appetite of a linebacker."

Carolyn and John returned to New York, and John had surgery on June 2 at Lenox Hill Hospital on Manhattan's East Side. Carolyn called Carole Radziwill and said, "I don't know if we can survive a broken ankle. It's such a goddamn bad time for this."

Something in Carolyn had broken as well.

"She is angry, exhausted," wrote Carole. " 'We can't afford to be careless now. We simply can't manage anything else. Six weeks in a cast!' Carolyn said. 'No kayaking, no waterskiing. No physical activity of any kind.' "

Given that Carole's husband was dying of cancer, it could be said that Carolyn was making too much of a broken ankle. But the two women were so involved in each other's lives at this point, and this was Carolyn being honest with one of the few people in her life who would understand.

The bubble of optimism had been popped. The summer had been, by design, split into the first half and the second half, the latter involving Anthony Radziwill's arrival in Red Gate Farm for a hoped-for recuperation. But there was the fear, a likelihood, that there would only be a decline.

Carole flew to New York for a party in honor of Tina Radziwill's engagement to medical professor Ottavio Arancio, at Caroline's apartment. Anthony was too weak to attend his sister's engagement party, so Carolyn picked Carole up and they went together. "She calls from the taxi on her way uptown," Carole wrote in *What Remains*, and when Carole asked Carolyn whether she should wear strappy sandals or flats, Carolyn replied, "Strappy sandals, of course." Yet when Carolyn arrived, she changed tack.

"Uh, Lamb, what's up with the dress . . . it's a little *The Postman Rings Twice*," she told Carole. Carolyn gave Carole a gift from Tiffany's, a toe ring that matched her own. Carole spun in her dress, laughing, and Carolyn said, "Okay, Lana Turner."

BY JUNE 6, THE tabloids had learned of John's broken ankle. The *New York Post* piece that opened with "JFK Jr. is one hobbled hunk" made a point of mentioning, "Two years ago, he seriously injured his right wrist in a mysterious accident that some blamed on a fight with his wife, Carolyn Bessette Kennedy."

Photographer Jacques Lowe had sympathy for her. "You had to feel sorry for the girl," he said. "Every move she made—and every move she didn't make—provided the press with another story. You wondered how and when it would ever end."

At this point, Sasha Chermayeff remarked, "Emotionally, there was some distance that hadn't been there before, but that happens with couples. They were going through the first five or so years when you learn what you're getting yourself into, when you're no longer blinded by love. And then it gets intense. It was difficult, but they were deeply connected. What was going to happen, we'll never know."

IN MID-JUNE, SHE TOOK a solo trip to London to "pitch *George* to publishers." It's possible they were looking overseas for new financing. Afterward, she attended a dinner at Ralph Lauren's London town house. *Women's Wear Daily* quoted her as "urging her tablemates to go out" for more fun after the dinner. " 'You can be boring at home,' she implored. 'Let's hit the road.' "

When she returned, John flew the Littells up again in the Piper Saratoga with a copilot, as Carolyn had told him that she'd had so much fun on Memorial Day that she wanted to have a repeat house party. Littell described Carolyn as an attentive hostess, and she often called ahead of a "planned weekend at the Vineyard to make a shopping list for our diet-deranged family. Talking fast and low, without any opening small talk, she'd say, 'Frannie, it's Carolyn. Which Cheerios does Colette [Rob and Frannie's daughter] eat, regular or Honey Nut? Will Rob eat steak?' "

At the end of the weekend, John flew the Littells back to Essex County Airport, in New Jersey. When they landed, they all agreed, "This is as good as it gets."

CHAPTER TWENTY-FOUR

REFERENCE POINTS

July 1, 1999–July 16, 1999

The press continued to play its background music to Carolyn's and John's lives, singing of their every move. Rumors were flying that John had moved into the Stanhope and was seeing his former flame Julie Baker; that his magazine *George* was failing; that Carolyn was doing cocaine and spending nights away from the apartment; that their marriage was in shambles. The Kennedys had been through worse, though this was up there in the ranks of the many circles of hell. The headlines were almost comical: "JFK Jr. Love Child" and "Secret Affair!"

John had been lamenting to some friends the couple's lack of physical intimacy in those last months, which, if true, was likely due to what Sasha termed as Carolyn's "justifiable anger" at being constant tabloid fodder.

"She was pretty angry," Sasha observed. "About a lot of things, and it was understandable. But at a certain point, you have to slow down and ask yourself, 'Do I want to be in constant outrage?' Because you can't grow in that state. And like all of us, she had to grow. Although John could have been more patient with her feelings of being overwhelmed with press attention, at some point, you do have to try to move past it and get on with life. And he was looking at this beautiful woman that he loved dearly, thinking, *When will she get there?*"

Michelle Kessler found it incredible that anyone "would ever think that John F. Kennedy Jr. would marry someone who was a bitch. He married her for the opposite reason—she was a super empath. And super empaths are also supersensitive. She was simply going to make sure that things were aboveboard and was never afraid to speak candidly."

ANTHONY AND CAROLE WERE still on Martha's Vineyard at Mike Nichols and Diane Sawyer's place. During Anthony's illness, Carolyn had encouraged Carole to see a therapist, as she knew the difference it could make in someone's life. "On the other hand, she has stopped seeing her therapist this summer—even if she is thrilled that now I have one," wrote Carole. "She has stopped going to the gym. She has given up, for the time, the idea of going back to school. We talk about making documentary films, but she seems to have lost her footing. I want to tell her it will be okay, but I think it can wait."

Carolyn had been ruminating on her career options, and a way forward was not yet clear. A friend with whom Carolyn discussed the possibility of documentary filmmaking explained: "It wasn't as simple as just jumping in and going for it. Creating a production company, studying the subject, as well as hiring crew is a labor-intensive job as it is. Carolyn, who was a perfectionist anyway, would need to be very deliberate indeed to actually begin the process of bringing light to stories of humanity that would teach us to not only think about others, but to put ourselves in their shoes—something at which she already specialized. To actually put her toe in the water would have required much more than the usual preparation. For her to even begin, she would've had to have everything one hundred percent locked down at the word *go*, every *i* dotted, and every *t* crossed, or the press would've torn her to shreds. She had only left her job at Calvin Klein two years prior. Add to that, she was on the tour to help save *George*, traveling constantly to secure ad sales and possibly new investors. For the time being, Carolyn's project would have to be put on ice."

It was known that Carolyn and John were still struggling, but to what extent seems up for debate. That week, John had told several friends and colleagues that he and Carolyn were splitting up. Yet, other friends and colleagues noted that they seemed very happy together, even just the weekend before. Gillon also quotes Carole Radziwill as saying, "There was nothing, not one conversation to indicate that there was an impending divorce."

Sasha recalled a conversation from that Fourth of July weekend, which she relayed to Steve Gillon, who wrote: "John was lying on the lawn of Red

Gate Farm, gazing up at the sky. Sasha, who was also part of the weekend group, was standing next to him. 'He told me how fucked up it had gotten with Carolyn, and that they were emotionally very distant,' she recalled. 'Carolyn refused to have sex with him, and they seemed to be leading entirely separate lives.' He never used the word divorce, but it was clear to Sasha that that was what he was alluding to. *Oh my God, this is it*, Sasha thought. *Carolyn*, she realized, *has no idea how badly this is going to take her out, because her whole life revolves around the fact that she is this important person who is JFK Jr.'s wife, and when he tells her that this marriage is falling apart and he's done, it's going to be so hard for her.* Sasha predicted that while divorce would be difficult for both, John would recover more quickly."

John would say to his friends what he felt in the moment, in keeping with his need for forward motion. One minute, he may have felt like his marriage was done; the next, he didn't and still wanted his wife to come to Rory's wedding that very weekend. Some information, given on background after their death to several authors, seemingly manipulated a lot of that narrative toward the negative.

As Carolyn and John knew from the stops and starts when they met, two things can be true at once. You can be in love with someone but need an escape. You can want to make something work but have no idea how to do so—you can have so much on your mind and be so overwhelmed that sometimes you need to not think about how to make it work.

"As far as what would have happened in their marriage, anyone who makes a claim one way or another is speculating," Sasha concluded. "There were problems, but they'd loved one another passionately."

ON JULY 10, THERE was a long-scheduled dinner planned with all the Bessette women, including Lauren, Carolyn, Lisa, their aunts, and their cousins, at a restaurant in downtown Manhattan. The gathering took place, but Carolyn had to cancel at the last minute, explaining that they were moving Anthony into Red Gate Farm on the Vineyard at the end of that weekend.

Carolyn and John arrived at Martha's Vineyard, where Christiane Amanpour and Jamie Rubin joined them at Red Gate Farm. The guests went waterskiing, and they all shared quiet dinners and drove around the lush island in what John called "The Goat," a black 1969 Pontiac GTO convertible. After dinner one evening, the two couples went for margaritas at the Lampost, a dive bar in Oak Bluffs. Since Christiane and Jamie had been married just about a year, John inquired if they were planning to have children soon.

"We are," Christiane told him. "We've been trying to get pregnant."

"Oh, please don't say that," Carolyn said. "If you get pregnant, John will want us to get pregnant, too."

When they left, Carolyn rushed back in to give the waitress an extra tip, saying, "I know how expensive rents are here on the island."

JOHN LEFT BRIGHT AND early Monday morning, work already on his mind. Carole wrote in *What Remains* that Carolyn stayed behind to help her and Anthony settle into Red Gate Farm, moving a bed to the first floor for Anthony so that he could avoid climbing stairs. She got ready to leave, blow-drying her hair and hanging out with Carole and family friend Holly Peterson in the upstairs bathroom. As Carole recounted, Carolyn gave Carole a sage-green sari. She pulled out a leopard-print sarong and turned to Peterson. "'Here, try this on,' Carolyn said to Holly. 'You'll look great in it.'

"She says goodbye and kisses me at the door. Friday is lying on the porch, and she scoops him up in her arms like a baby, kisses him on the mouth, puts him down, and runs toward the car," Radziwill later wrote. "She stops suddenly, then turns around and runs back. 'Here, take this, it gets cold at night. I love you.' She takes the peach pashmina scarf she is wearing and wraps it around me and squeezes me tight. 'I'll call you later.'"

Carolyn returned to New York on a commercial flight and called Hamilton South soon after her arrival. South was initially supposed to have come to the Vineyard that weekend as well but stayed behind because he had met someone. "When Carolyn came back to town, she called me immediately and asked what the date was like," he said. "I told her, 'It was great.' She wanted the entire rundown of the evening."

The afternoon of Monday, July 12, John flew the Piper Saratoga to Toronto, with instructor Jay Biederman on board, to meet with potential investors Keith Stein and Belinda Stronach. The meeting, arranged by their friend Leslie Marshall, an editor at *InStyle* magazine, lasted for several hours. Keith Stein emerged from the conference convinced that it had "gone well." Even though it was a business meeting, John also mentioned his and Carolyn's desire to have children. "He talked about having kids as if it were imminent in their future," Stein said. "He mentioned his wife a lot. She was a real reference point. It was clear they had a very strong relationship."

Yet despite the magazine's accomplishments or cultural relevance, John worried that any new investors would be signing on because of him and the last name of Kennedy, rather than the magazine. It was the same conundrum Carolyn faced finding meaningful work once they were married. The issue of his fame and last name was what he felt had aggravated things with Hachette, and he didn't want to make the same mistake twice.

Rob Littell noted that John "hated flying around the globe with his hat in his hand," and that the stress was beginning to physically show. "He gained weight, he looked tired, his hair was noticeably grayer."

Sasha told Kennedy biographer Lawrence Leamer what she saw at the time: "There were great things in their love, regardless of what anyone says. She was strong, and she had some wonderful qualities, but the question was whether she was going to get beyond this obsession with the paparazzi. Get over it. Move on. Smile for them. Frown to them. Give them the finger. Be the world's biggest bitch, Leona Helmsley with blond hair and a ponytail. Or be Lady Di. Who cares? Fill up your soul. This is not a dress rehearsal. Wake up. Wake up, and you better do it soon."

What's fascinating is the evolution of how Sasha sees it now: "In the moment, at the time, I didn't have sufficient understanding of the stress Carolyn had to deal with," Sasha said. "I see it now. At the time, it could seem like she was blowing it out of proportion. Even her closest friends and husband sometimes couldn't see it for what it was.

"Everyone thought, *Come on, figure this out.* . . . Only in hindsight, from this perspective now, I see that no one was really fully there for her in that way. That proved to be further isolating for her, compounding her fear and anger, but her anger was healthy given the situation. I want to express that now. I wish I'd been able to be more compassionate and supportive to her in how alone she felt, or anyone would, in her position, and I wish I'd seen the intensity."

JOHN'S COUSIN RORY KENNEDY'S wedding in Hyannis Port was scheduled for the following Saturday, July 17. On Tuesday, July 13, John and Carolyn had a heated fight about whether or not she would attend; Carolyn didn't want to go. She was exhausted by it all—flying, the crash of the Buckeye, a declining magazine, ankle surgery, cancer surgery, and the endless requirements to keep up appearances amid all of it. She needed a break; she felt she'd done her share of Kennedy events for the time being. John felt obligated to show up to family events and he was distraught at the prospect of going solo. Carolyn's absence would lead to yet another media blitz of speculation over the state of their marriage, and he just wanted her there with him. Carolyn and John's fight turned into an enormous blowup, with John losing ever more patience, and Carolyn feeling ever more like an afterthought.

Earlier that evening, John had gone on his own to a party thrown by *Dazed & Confused* magazine, in Tribeca. He had dinner afterward with photographer Jacques Lowe, whom he told that Keith Stein was interested in *George*, but "only if they can run the show. I'm not about to relinquish my role in the venture. I'll shut it down before I do that," John said.

Carolyn was spotted by a neighborhood friend sitting alone at the bar at the Independent, on Broadway and Worth Street, three blocks from her apartment. Picturing her in this solitary moment, one wishes she had had the boisterous company of all the Bessette women the previous weekend. John's party was only a few blocks away. Perhaps he was coming to meet her. Perhaps he wasn't. "All I remember is that she just looked so very sad," the friend said.

APPEARANCES WERE KEPT UP on Wednesday morning when Carolyn and John hosted a breakfast for the Robin Hood foundation at the offices of *George*. Andersen reported that the two of them were radiant, and when John was again asked if he was going to run for Senate, he told the crowd that for now he was putting everything into the magazine. "I like things as they are now," John said as Carolyn beamed. "I love my life."

Yet the air was rife with tension as Carolyn still resisted the weekend in Hyannis Port.

Lauren stepped in. That same afternoon, the two sisters got in a car in Tribeca and went up to meet John at Café M in the Stanhope, where he had rented a conference room as a sort of "war room" in an attempt to create some space between himself and David Pecker, who was always hovering at Hachette. Witnesses of the trio at lunch said that things seemed tense at first but that at some point, all three of them, at Lauren's encouragement, held hands. Carolyn agreed to go to the wedding. John and Carolyn would give Lauren a ride to Martha's Vineyard on the way to Hyannis Port on Friday. Lauren had begun seeing Bobby Shriver, who would be on the Vineyard, and she was meeting some friends there. Then, Carolyn and John would hop over to Hyannis Port and catch the tail end of Rory's rehearsal dinner.

Even though John had stayed at the Stanhope the night before and would stay Thursday evening again, it seemed that this lunch signified a truce of sorts. Martin Nordquist, an engineering consultant from Georgia who was dining at the restaurant that afternoon, told Heymann that Carolyn and John even began to kiss while still seated at the table. But toward the end of the meal, there was a squabble about an appointment Carolyn had made, in the hope of finding a place of their own, with a Cape Cod real estate agent to look at properties.

"'Not this weekend,' said John. 'We're going up there to attend a wedding, and then we're supposed to join Anthony and Carole at Gay Head.' Carolyn responded, 'There's plenty of time to look at real estate.' They were still haggling when they stood up to leave," Nordquist said. The disagreement continued into the afternoon, and on Wednesday evening, John checked into the Stanhope, a mere four blocks from what had been his mother's apartment, his childhood home.

Later that Wednesday afternoon, when Carolyn dropped by to see her old Greenwich Village landlady Marlaine Selip's daughter, Erin, there was no indication of marital trouble. Carolyn was all smiles, arriving with an armload of clothes, as she often did. Speaking of that last visit on July 14, Erin recalled, "She was full of light and happy."

And perhaps she was. Yet life is full of contradictions, as are people, and things can change on a dime. After John returned to the office, Richard Bradley heard him arguing with Carolyn on the phone. "In startling, staccato bursts of rage, John was yelling. His yell would be followed by silence, then John's fury would resume. At first, I couldn't make out the words. Then after a particularly long pause, I heard John shout, 'Well, goddammit, Carolyn, you're the reason I was up at three o'clock last night!'"

John had recently told a friend, "Given that I can get bored easily, I realize I'm often drawn to challenging women."

THAT SAME EVENING, JOHN'S former girlfriend, the model Julie Baker, was spotted walking into the Stanhope just after midnight. The story goes that Julie left the hotel a couple of hours later.

Yet she and John were also spotted having breakfast Thursday morning at the hotel. It has been said that it was just a friendly visit, for John to have someone with him, someone in whom he could confide his troubles. "I knew Julie was a lover from the past, and I assumed it was a sexually intimate encounter, but that was only what I assumed," said Sasha. "I was aware of the struggles in his marriage and of his past with Julie, so I presumed. But I never spoke to John about it."

Sasha explained that John's actions were about only the moment: "There are people who you love as a friend, and you haven't had sex in a while, so you go get laid. John was not going to date Julie. He wasn't going to break up with Carolyn and marry Julie."

Sasha was thoughtful and circumspect about that time, sympathetic to both Carolyn's and John's predicaments. "Marriage can be hard and complicated, and sometimes people aren't faithful. It doesn't mean they are bad people; it means they were going through a bad moment," she explained.

If John was unfaithful, his infidelity came from pain. Had they lived, this would have added to the challenges they would have to overcome. And thus more pain. But John, without his usual outlet of physical activity, perhaps couldn't tolerate it all: *George*, Anthony, feeling estranged from Carolyn. Both Carolyn and John were aggrieved.

Later that afternoon, John met with Hachette's new CEO, Jack Kliger. Before discussing *George's* future, they both recalled how John could have taken the magazine to Condé Nast, which had wanted to work with him when he shopped it in 1994. "But at Condé Nast," John said, "I would be a bird in a gilded cage." He still refused to be caged. From there, recollections differ.

Kliger, now president and CEO of the Museum of Jewish Heritage, said he told John it was a possibility that Hachette would keep *George* on. But John came out of that meeting with a different story. He told his staffers that Kliger had said they were dropping the magazine at the end of the year. John seemed amused, and his colleagues couldn't figure out why, until John explained that he was watching Kliger the whole time, and he could tell Kliger had bad news and was nervous because he picked up John's water bottle and drank from it before saying, "We're out."

Thursday evening, John went with Gary Ginsberg to a baseball game at Yankee Stadium, the Yankees versus the Atlanta Braves. They sat in box seats at field level beside the Yankees dugout with James and Lachlan Murdoch of News Corp, for which Gary had been president of global marketing and corporate affairs. They spoke at length about *George*, and John was even cautiously optimistic that the Murdochs might invest in the magazine. Gary and John also spoke about John's ill-fitting suit after Gary laughed at what he was wearing. John told Gary he bought his suits from Julie Baker, who had been selling menswear. Gary told John, "Well, then you better tell her to get into another line of work." John called Julie and jokingly gave her Gary's advice.

Ginsberg added that "the pressure on John by July was immense, especially while in New York City. The work, the incessant attention, the family issues. Normally he had a physical outlet to blow off some of the steam—any one of the many sports he played. But that summer he felt trapped in his own body. So the best outlet was flying. Having that solitude, up in the clouds, was a form of escape that was deeply important to him. It was a form of emotional and psychological escape, as well as an easy way to get to Hyannis Port and the Vineyard."

As for Carolyn, after their fight, had she reconciled herself to giving up her own needs to be married to a high-profile Kennedy? To once again take John's arm, despite how she was feeling? As Ariel Paredes noted (and countless friends concurred) about Carolyn and John: "They would love hard and they would fight hard but they were very much a couple."

Or perhaps, as Richard Bradley wrote about that fight, "That didn't mean they were headed for divorce, as would be reported in the tabloids, just the two of them had a fight hurtful enough for John to sleep out somewhere. If you would ever see John's temper or Carolyn's determination, you knew that wasn't so unthinkable. And if you'd ever seen John and Carolyn make up after a fight, you also knew how temporary those rifts could be."

Passionate, loud fights would suddenly resolve, and they would return seamlessly to being affectionate spouses. When John talked about a split that week, he may have spoken his thoughts out loud before he was sure he wanted to act upon them.

Carolyn was more circumspect, confiding in few about her feelings and disinclined to make pronouncements before making a decision. While his uncle and some of the RFK side of the family had been through divorces, the JFKs had not. Jackie remained by Jack's side through marital challenges. When they first met, John intentionally kept a very low profile while he hashed out the business and editorial plans for the creation of *George*. She was in the trenches right there with him, in it together. Life was a different beast now that he was the public face of a magazine. John often said if he slowed down he'd fall apart. Part of him wanted the speed, wanted the mayhem. As he matured, he probably would have grown past this. But for now, he was so used to getting himself out of scrapes and close calls, he found it necessary to feel the thin edge between thrill and destruction to lessen the weight of that which had been placed on him by the world. Carolyn, however, was encouraging him to change how he responded to pressure. But he was not yet able to, in the same way she was not yet able to wave away the paparazzi's hostile gaze with a smile.

John adamantly wanted Carolyn to be at the wedding. It was about her commitment. He wanted the commitment. He wasn't willing to go without her.

RoseMarie Terenzio, who understood the stakes, wrote that she had explained to John that he had to stop putting everything else before Carolyn if he wanted his marriage to succeed. But she also knew that the press would have a field day if John showed up stag to the wedding.

"I picked up the phone to call Carolyn and got right to the heart of the matter," RoseMarie recounted. " 'Carolyn, are you fucking kidding me?' I said. 'What are you doing? You're smarter than this.' "

"I'm not a priority. It's always something else. *George*," Carolyn bemoaned. "Somebody getting fired. An event. A trip to Italy to meet advertisers."

"I know," RoseMarie wrote. "But now's not the time to take a stand. His whole family's going to be at this wedding, and you need to go with him." Rose continued that she "readied herself for an argument, but Carolyn didn't offer one. Instead of getting angry, she softened." Rose expressed a huge sense of relief, and she booked a car for Carolyn to be driven to the airport.

FRIDAY AT THE OFFICE, John had another meeting with Jack Kliger. "My focus with John in that meeting was about how the magazine had been prematurely pushed up in terms of frequency and circulation," said Kliger. "I was willing to look at a reduction in terms of productions and circulation that would've given him freedom to do more, perhaps move the magazine online and have time to go into politics. The last thing Hachette was going to do was to shut down John Kennedy's magazine. Worst-case scenario we would have made sure *George* found other backers. We wrapped the meeting with the deal that he was going to come up with that business plan and get back to me later that day."

John had lunch with Richard Bradley at Trionfo, located on the ground floor of Hachette's offices. John had spoken of a personal family problem in a meeting the day before, apologizing for having been so preoccupied. Bradley asked John, "That personal problem you were talking about in the meeting yesterday—you okay?"

"I am," John replied.

In preparation for their flight, John got a report of clear visibility to Martha's Vineyard that afternoon, where he would land the plane to drop off Lauren before continuing to Hyannis Port for the wedding. The ASOS, or Automated Surface Observing Systems, equipment at the Martha's Vineyard airport, which John logged on to before he left his office, only checked the airspace directly overhead.

Before she left the office that Friday, RoseMarie left a note on John's phone, reminding him to meet Lauren in the lobby at 5:30. John checked several weather systems from his computer and then went to the gym. He met up with Lauren in the building's lobby, and he took her upstairs to show her around. Inigo Thomas saw them when they came into his office asking for reading recommendations for the weekend. Surveying the stack of galleys and hardcovers piled all over the place, Lauren grabbed John McCain's memoir *Faith of My Fathers*, and John, somewhat improbably, chose Stephen Fry's *Moab Is My Washpot*, the wry English actor's autobiography. They were soon off to the airport in the sticky July heat. Even for a Friday afternoon in New York City, the traffic was miserable.

Tabloids put forth an alleged timeline in which Carolyn lingered for hours getting a pedicure, where she insisted the color be changed three times. Yet an eyewitness report has her leaving the pedicurist by 5:00 p.m. She went to Saks to buy a dress for the wedding the same day she was leaving, because she hadn't planned on going. Carolyn was sweet to the salesgirl on the third-floor designer section who recognized her, and they chatted about her plans as she picked out a black silk crepe Yves Saint Laurent evening dress from the fall/winter collection of Rive Gauche, their ready-to-wear line. As the *New York Post* reported, the dress had a "full, gathered bodice cinched in the back of the neck with a wide satin bow."

The salesgirl remembers Carolyn saying, "He just had the cast taken off his leg. I don't know if he's ready yet to fly again." After the purchase, the salesgirl wished Carolyn good luck. "Thanks," Carolyn replied. "I'm going to need it."

Carolyn was in a car headed for the airport at the same time as John and Lauren, 6:30 p.m. Normally, it takes forty-five minutes to get to Essex County Airport, known informally as Caldwell. They all thought that they would've arrived by 7:15 and taken off at 7:30, plenty of time to land before it got dark at 8:40. But as hard as New York City is to get into, it's even harder to leave on a summer Friday. They were stuck in traffic and didn't make it to the airport until after 8:00 p.m.

Stephen Meister, a pilot who kept his plane at Caldwell, said, "Pilots usually have one job. Certainly commercial pilots. And if I'm flying, that is all I do that day. John had way too much on his plate."

"One very important reason she agreed to go back that weekend," said Hamilton South, "was to be with Carole and Anthony. Both Carolyn and John loved them and wanted to be with them as much as possible, particularly as Anthony was so sick and was at that point staying full-time on the Vineyard." Before they took off, Carolyn called Carole, and they talked about what they would have for Sunday-night dinner. "The plan," Carole wrote, "was grilled steaks and peach pie."

Kyle Bailey, another pilot who was at Caldwell that evening, reiterated that all three of them arrived within minutes of one another. He said that John then called a pilot information number for a weather briefing, which at 7:53 p.m. reported eight miles of visibility and clear skies. John's license allowed him to fly at night as long as there were at least five miles of visibility.

Jackie Kennedy once said, "Even though people may be well known, they hold in their hearts the emotions of a simple person for the moments that are the most important of those we know on earth: birth, marriage, and death."

The plane took off at 8:38 p.m. Sunset on July 16, 1999, was 8:26 p.m. Dusk was at 8:58. Carolyn, John, and Lauren had twenty minutes of crepuscular blue and then darkness.

CHAPTER TWENTY-FIVE

THE OTHER SIDE

July 16, 1999–July 24, 1999

L oved ones were waiting for them. They waited on the other side—of that blue, of the sky, and of the water. At 10:00 p.m. on Friday, July 16, a couple and their young daughter were waiting at the Martha's Vineyard Airport for Lauren's plane to arrive, after which they would all head back to their house.

Dan Samson was waiting to meet John and Carolyn at the Hyannis Port airport. John had asked Samson to head east from his home in Seattle to hash out a plan that weekend for a new business venture. Whether it was to transform *George* into an online magazine or perhaps even revive Random Ventures' mass production of handmade kayaks, Samson was not sure. All he knew was that he was supposed to pick the couple up and bring them to the Kennedy compound, where the celebrations for Rory Kennedy's wedding to writer Mark Bailey were already underway.

Outside the main house was an enormous white tent for Saturday's ceremony. Inside, there was laughter, toasts, and gifts, including a large quilt with something representing a member of the Kennedy family stitched onto each square. Everyone was cheerful and happy for Rory and Mark, who had just worked together on her recently completed documentary, *American Hollow*. There were 275 guests at the gathering, and the mood rose with the volume throughout the night. Some knew that Carolyn and John were dropping

Lauren off first and that they'd gotten a late start. Maybe they had grabbed dinner before heading over. No one there was worried yet.

However, the couple waiting for Lauren began to worry, and asked a Martha's Vineyard Airport operations employee if he knew where the plane was, who in turn inquired at the control tower about whether there had been a flight plan filed for the Piper Saratoga. There was none. They waited some more and asked again, as the airport was closing soon at ten p.m. A few minutes after closing, at the couple's request, a maintenance worker called the Bridgeport, Connecticut, Federal Aviation Agency station.

Dan Samson called Carole Radziwill, who was at Red Gate Farm with Anthony for the summer, where Carolyn and John would help take care of him—them both, really—over Anthony's last weeks. It was now midnight, and Anthony wordlessly handed Carole the phone; she initially thought it was John.

Samson apologized for calling so late and said he was supposed to pick up Carolyn and John from the airport, but they hadn't arrived. He asked if they were there.

"It is midnight, past the time when people call," Carole later wrote. "It is the wrong voice, and I know everything now."

Carole walked down the hall into the kitchen, and Friday was right behind her. She saw a wetsuit Carolyn had draped over a chair to dry the previous weekend and calculated that it had been four hours since Carolyn had called her, just before they took off.

Carole called the Hyannis Port airport. She waited for a return call while a maintenance worker looked for John's plane. He called back; it was not there. Carole reminded him it was a new plane. Was he sure?

He said, "Uh, I'm sorry, but John definitely didn't land here tonight," Carole later wrote.

Next, she called Caldwell Airport. Yes, they took off around 8:30; John's car was still there. Then she tried Bridgeport, where there was no record because there was no flight plan. Carole called Martha's Vineyard Airport next. At first there was no answer, but a man called back and read her the note Lauren's friends had left her. They had waited, but had gone home . . . "Call when you get in. I'll come get you. Daniel."

Carole called Daniel, who had been hoping she was Lauren. She kept calling Dan Samson, too, who was trying to reach Ted Kennedy. Carole tried

Carolyn and John's apartment, where at first she thought RoseMarie, who was staying there because her air-conditioning had broken and had answered the phone, was Carolyn. Rose, too, joined the vigil of anxious phone calls and torment.

Carole found the number for John's flight instructor, Jay Biederman. Jay had not been with them, and another sliver of hope was gone. Eventually, when she and Samson couldn't reach Uncle Ted, she called the Coast Guard.

Carole wrote that Anthony woke up amid the flurry of activity, and when he saw all of Carole's notes and phone numbers, he put his face in his hands and cried.

Eventually, Ted Kennedy called. He remained calm and reassuring. But everyone at the party, at what was supposed to be a celebration, began the slide into despair that Carole had been fighting since her phone rang.

Carole's insistent call to the Woods Hole Coast Guard set the full force of emergency services into action. Woods Hole called the First Coast Guard District in Boston, which then called the FAA, which finally checked to see if John's plane had rerouted and landed somewhere other than Hyannis Port or Martha's Vineyard.

Unable to locate the plane, the FAA called the Coast Guard back, as well as the Air Force Rescue Coordination Center at Langley Air Force Base in Virginia. Coast Guard cutters began an official search for the plane. Soon John Podesta, then White House chief of staff, called President Clinton at Camp David, who in turn authorized whatever measures necessary to find the plane, and asked to receive updates throughout the search.

This left Carole and Anthony with two more calls to make. Caroline was with Ed and their children on a rafting trip in Idaho, in an area known as the River of No Return. Unable to reach the lodge, Anthony tracked down police chief Philip Enright, who drove to the lodge at 4:30 a.m. and told Caroline that her cousin from Massachusetts was on the phone and it was urgent.

Carole then called the Freeman home in Connecticut. Dr. Freeman answered, and Carole quickly explained that Carolyn and John hadn't arrived and there was a search underway. Carole later wrote that she told him, "I'm sure it's fine, but I didn't want you to hear it on the news." Ann Freeman immediately called her back. She listened to Carole explain the airports and calls and missed connections.

"Well, everything's okay, right? Was anyone else on the plane with them?"

Carole was silent. Long enough for Ann to scream.

No one slept that night. And by the daylight on the seventeenth, word was out. News cameras were everywhere, including gathered on North Moore Street, which was already lined with hundreds of flowers and tributes; surrounding the Kennedy compound in Hyannis Port; and in studios, focused on reporters solemnly reviewing the lives of John and Carolyn between updates announcing that they had no updates. No one wanted to say it: Though not entirely gone, hope quickly and quietly became implausible.

Every television channel preempted its scheduled programming, instead showing various angles of the churning sea off Gay Head. Search and rescue began at 7:45 a.m. on Saturday, July 17, with fifteen Civil Air Patrol planes, two Coast Guard HH-60 Jayhawk choppers, an Air National Guard helicopter, and a Hercules cargo plane above the waters south of Martha's Vineyard. An armada of boats, including Coast Guard cutters and search-and-rescue patrol boats, were on the water.

Rory Kennedy and Mark Bailey delayed their nuptials, and instead of a wedding under the tent, the Kennedys' mass on Saturday morning was a prayer and vigil. The *Washington Post* reported, "[Rory] is on the beach with her fiancé, Mark Bailey, walking along the beach outside the Kennedy compound. Bailey's right arm is wrapped around her shoulders, her left hand clutching his fingers to her chest."

AROUND NOON, BRUCE MORTON of CNN began his broadcast with, "John Kennedy was thirty-eight years old . . ." when anchor Frank Sesno interrupted him. "Bruce, let's not put it in the past tense. The Coast Guard calls this a search-and-rescue operation. Hope is still alive."

Tim Shriver called Billy Noonan at John's Hyannis Port home and asked him to "put up a perimeter around the house. No one was allowed access—no one. It was Caroline's request." If there were any questions, they were to call Timmy. Caroline and her family prepared to fly back east, but they would seclude themselves at their home in Bridgehampton. Ann and Richard Freeman secluded themselves at their home in Greenwich, which was surrounded by police barriers. Barbara Walters had somehow gotten Carolyn and John's home number and called RoseMarie asking for a comment.

All Rose gave her was, "Anyone who is going to come on that air tonight doesn't know anything and is not a close friend of John's. Trust me."

"Streams of Strangers Keep Vigils, Waiting, but Expecting the Worst," read the headlines. "Visitors poured up the hill to the Kennedy graves here at Arlington National Cemetery," wrote the *New York Times*, "the sweltering summer heat compounding the day's dirgeful tinge as they left flowers and notes for the missing Kennedy."

One note read: "The world stands motionless and hearts are heavy with sadness."

The accident, and upcoming loss, were front-page news from Washington to New York, Boston to Dublin, and London to Paris.

The Kennedys, who had planned on a wedding, were trapped in their compound, surrounded by vans with camera crews. They coped with their anguish as best as they knew how—namely, physical activity. Biographer Christopher Andersen later wrote that Ethel Kennedy said, "We need to take a sail," and was seen with her son Max Kennedy and his wife, Victoria, walking barefoot down to the dock. Ted Jr., Bobby Jr., and several cousins swam and ran on the beach, staving off the grief for a short time.

Photographers pestered William Bessette around his home in White Plains so much that his brother, a former police officer, had to teach him defensive and avoidance maneuvers just so that he could go about his daily life.

Dan Rather hosted a CBS News special report at midday, covering a US Coast Guard press conference. Rear Admiral Richard M. Larrabee, First Coast Guard district commander, gave updates on the search: "I can tell you miraculous stories of people surviving. I can tell you that in previous cases like this we've searched as many as three or four days. We're not ready to give up on this yet." Despite the feeling that survival was unlikely, watching and waiting was the only thing to do.

But on July 18, by two p.m., all remaining hope began to fade as small pieces of foam insulation were found washed up over a mile along Philbin Beach. One of the captains on the search told the *New York Times* "the insulation was 'consistent' with insulation that would surround an airplane cockpit." Massachusetts State Police captain Robert Bird, who had announced the finding, conceded to a reporter: "It likely would take an impact of great force to produce such debris."

"I have spent some very painful moments with the families tonight," Admiral Larrabee announced later that day from Otis Air National Guard Base. "We are going to shift—and I say 'shift' very purposely—from our focus on search and rescue to search and recovery," he said.

By Monday, the headlines announced that Carolyn, John, and Lauren were presumed dead. The *New York Times* ran its obituary, "John F. Kennedy Jr., Heir To a Formidable Dynasty."

The public mourning was extreme. The flowers on North Moore Street were now accompanied by citizens sobbing and lighting candles. They left notes, American flags, and even sketches of the couple at a makeshift shrine on the steps of the Tribeca apartment. Once the area cleared, after midnight, a lone man stood playing a dirge on the bagpipes in the middle of the street.

Ted Kennedy went to Caroline's house in Bridgehampton to help comfort her. He was seen playing basketball with her children in the driveway. Soon after, he released a statement from the family: "We are filled with unspeakable grief and sadness by the loss of John and Carolyn, and of Lauren Bessette."

While Uncle Ted was there to grieve with Caroline, it turned out they had different ideas for the funeral. He was very aware that the world would be mourning with them. Even Pope John Paul II made a statement about the deaths from his vacation in the Italian Alps. Ted wanted a large public service at St. Patrick's Cathedral in New York City. He had a point.

Yet Caroline also had a point—namely that she favored St. Thomas More, a small venue that would lend the moment privacy and calm, and perhaps honor their mother, who had been a parishioner there until her death. The large service for her uncle Robert after his assassination in June 1968 had been held at St. Patrick's. The enormousness of the space and the number of mourners had left her, then a ten-year-old, traumatized. Rose-Marie, who helped with the planning, later wrote that she and Caroline bonded over the fact that John would've "hated the hoopla over his death," but put her foot down about which *George* staffers were invited. It was all or no one.

The kind of fame the Kennedys have makes it hard for a family to mourn in private. The commemorations of his father had always been hard on John, and he usually made sure he was out of the country on November 22, the date of the assassination. His own birthday was November 25. How could the Kennedys, Bessettes, and Freemans privately mourn in public? The moment the plane went down, everyone involved in their lives was in an impossible position.

There was a meeting of the families called that evening in New York City. Caroline was too distraught to attend, and Carole, who had planned to accompany Ann Freeman despite being told "family only," got fogged in at the Vineyard. At first, the idea was presented that John would be buried in Arlington, next to his mother and father. Then it was suggested that John and Carolyn be buried together at Holyhood, the Kennedy family cemetery in Brookline, Massachusetts, until it was pointed out that the Bessettes and Freemans, including Lauren, did not have a connection to Massachusetts. The families wanted to ensure that the place of burial did not become a tourist destination, so after much discussion, they collectively decided on a burial at sea for all three.

On July 22, of the Bessette-Freeman family, only Ann, Richard, Lisa, and William attended the scattering of the ashes held aboard the Navy guided-missile destroyer the USS *Briscoe*. A thirty-minute civilian ceremony on the ship's fantail was conducted by Catholic priests. Family members committed their ashes to the sea from a steep ladder at the ship's rear, aided by crew-members for safety. A brass quartet played "Eternal Father" while the flowers meant for Rory Kennedy's wedding were scattered after the ashes.

Orders were given that kept aircraft and chartered boats at a distance. Yet despite the request for privacy, some telephoto lenses found their way across ten miles of ocean to capture the mourners onboard, including Anthony Radziwill, whose sadness was etched on his face as he rested his hands and chin on top of a cane he was using as his body broke down.

The memorial service for John and Carolyn was held on Friday, July 23, at St. Thomas More Church on East 89th Street, just off Madison Avenue. The small size and side-street location allowed the police to keep the area under control. For the private, by-invitation-only ceremony, the cameras were, for once, banished. It was a sweltering 90 degrees as around 315 friends and relatives fought past barricades erected as far away as 72nd Street. Mourners had to brandish their invites to be allowed through and then walk seventeen blocks in the suffocating heat, past hundreds of onlookers lining the blocks. By contrast, the small church where Jackie's service had been held, was dark and cool. Despite the number of Carolyn's friends devastated by their loss, only a small number were invited, and there still wasn't enough room for them all. Yet the intimate space was an understandably deliberate choice to avoid spectacle.

Also in attendance were dignitaries such as John Kenneth Galbraith, John F. Kerry, and the Clintons. Reverend Charles O'Byrne, who had married them less than three years earlier on Cumberland Island, conducted the mass.

Intercessional prayers were read by family members—including Lee Radziwill, Eunice Kennedy Shriver, Mary Richardson Kennedy, Victoria Kennedy, Sydney Lawford McKelvy, and Tim Shriver—and friends such as RoseMarie Terenzio, Santina Goodman, and Sasha Chermayeff. Tim Shriver said, "For all those we love, united now with John and Carolyn and Lauren, for Jack and Jackie, for Carl Messina, that the many mansions of the Lord might be filled with their joy, their laughter, and their spirits, united now in heaven, we pray."

Anthony Radziwill, whose eulogy John had been writing the week before, read Psalm 23, "The Lord is my shepherd . . ." Mike Nichols read from Revelation, Caroline from Shakespeare's *The Tempest*, and Carole Radziwill from the book of Ruth: "Do not press me to leave you and to stop going with you. For wherever you go, I shall go."

Ann Freeman, in a feat of Herculean emotional strength, read from Henry Scott Holland's "Facts of Faith": "Death is nothing at all. It does not count. I've only slipped away into the next room . . . Why should I be out of mind because I am out of sight? I am waiting for you, for an interval, somewhere, very near, just around the corner. All is well. Nothing is hurt. Nothing is lost. One brief moment, and all will be as it was before. How we shall laugh at the trouble of parting when we meet again."

In his eulogy for John, Ted also quoted William Butler Yeats's "In Memory of Major Robert Gregory." "We dared to think, in that other Irish phrase, that this John Kennedy would live to comb gray hair, with his beloved Carolyn by his side. But like his father, he had every gift but length of years," Ted added. Referencing the Daniel Kelleher poem he had read on Carolyn and John's wedding day, he said, "He and his bride have gone to be with his

mother and father, where there will never be an end to love. He was lost on
that troubled night, but we will always wake for him, so that his time, which
was not doubled, but cut in half, will live forever in our memory and in our
beguiled and broken hearts."

Hamilton South gave a heartrending eulogy for Carolyn: "The void her
death leaves is unimaginable." He also recalled the intensity of her friendship.
"When she was your friend, it was like having a lion in your life. She was protective of her cubs, and woe to anyone or thing that would do them harm."
He remembered that she would call her friends on the phone and, after a
prolonged conversation, apologize for talking only about herself when, in
fact, it was all about them. Hamilton praised her caring ways and the simple
aspects of her style and approach to life; he spoke lovingly of "her graceful
bearing, her special allure" as "a physical expression of an inner fact," bringing
many of those present to tears.

On the way out of the church, Caroline's daughter Rose, then eleven,
paid homage to both Carolyn and John by sticking her tongue out at the
swarms of photographers. A reception was held at Convent of the Sacred
Heart, and then many friends went to McSorley's Old Ale House, which
housed a bronze bust of JFK behind the bar. From there, mourners went on
to yet another friend's apartment; they were not ready to say goodbye.

Dana Gallo Strayton, whom Carolyn nurtured through mourning both
her mother and father, spent the day crying on her couch, unable to put the
idea of her friend's suffering out of her mind. Dana was one of many who
did not get the invite for the private service due to the space constraints of
the small church. She did attend the service in Greenwich scheduled for the
next day.

Days earlier, when reporters were in wait outside the Freeman home,
both Ann and William, in a note read to reporters by family friend Grant
Stinchfield, described their daughters as "the embodiment of love, accomplishment, and passion for life."

The statement noted that "John and Carolyn were true soul mates, and
we hope to honor them in death in the simple manner in which they chose to
live their lives. We take solace in the thought that together they will comfort
Lauren for eternity."

A few days before the local service, Ann went to the church herself to
arrange for the candlelight memorial for her daughters, her cheeks stained

with tears. Mary Marks, parish secretary, was walking with Ann through the church when they overheard a woman say she had recently given birth to twins. Ann paused, turned to her, and said, "I used to have twins."

On Saturday, July 24, the Greenwich Christ Church service commemorated Lauren, Carolyn, and John. The day was sweltering, even outside the city, reaching 87 degrees as family and friends entered the church. Many who remembered the Bessette sisters came to pay their respects and knelt to pray outside the church, despite the heat. "Amazing Grace" was played, as it had been when Carolyn walked down the aisle in the one-room First African Baptist Church nearly three years earlier.

RoseMarie Terenzio, Mary Richardson Kennedy, and Marci Klein were among fourteen ushers. Among the eighteen honorary pallbearers, as there were no caskets, were Gordon Henderson, Bobby Kennedy Jr., Rob Littell, Chris Oberbeck, Anthony and Carole Radziwill, Narciso Rodriguez, Hamilton South, Jessica Weinstein, and Bobby, Tim, and Maria Shriver.

Teddy and Caroline attended the service, which Ann Freeman wanted "to be dignified and quiet, and to reflect the two daughters in a spiritual way." All of the Bessettes, Messinas, and Freemans were in attendance. Carolyn and Lauren's uncle Jack spoke, reminiscing fondly about Lauren playing putt-putt in the backyard in high heels and pajamas.

Ann asked Carole Radziwill to speak. Carole had just lost two family members and knew she was about to lose her husband. She later wrote, "It will take me years to forgive anyone that they have died." Yet somehow, she stood up to eulogize her friend:

When I was asked to read for Carolyn at this service I worried that nothing I would find could adequately describe what she meant to those of us who knew her. She was wild and vivid in a cautious and pale world. Always burning a little more brightly than any of us around her. She believed in me at times when I didn't believe in myself. And John was so beguiled and admiring of the alchemy she worked on her friends, transforming them into happier and bolder versions of themselves. Then I remembered a story written by Henry James. It was the story of a young girl named Isabel. A girl who was as brave as she was beautiful, who was pure of heart and as unafraid to love. His description of Isabel mirrored that of Carolyn and I wondered out loud how it was possible for him to have known her when he wrote that story over a century ago. But, I suppose, it was because he was writing about his dream of a pure and brave American girl, one who comes along maybe once every hundred years, if we are lucky. This is for the one who came along this century and for those who were lucky enough to have known her and been touched by the light of her sun. Henry James writes of her in *The Portrait of a Lady*:

"It had been her fortune to possess a finer mind than most of the persons among whom her lot was cast; to have a larger perception of surrounding facts and to care for knowledge that was tinged with the unfamiliar. It is true that among her contemporaries she passed for a young women of extraordinary profundity. She had a theory that one should be one of the best, should move in a realm of light, of natural wisdom, of happy impulse, of inspiration gracefully chronic. She had a fixed determination to regard the world as a place of brightness, of free expansion, of irresistible action. She had an infinite hope that she should never do anything wrong. The chance of inflicting a sensible injury upon another person always struck her as the worst thing that could happen to her. She was stoutly determined not to be hollow. Her way of taking compliments was to get rid of them as rapidly as possible. She was thought insensible to them whereas, in fact, she was simply unwilling to show how infinitely they pleased her.

"A very brilliant girl who would take a great deal of knowing, it was because she was fresh and natural and quick to understand, to speak . . . that he had fallen in love with her. A character like that is the finest thing in nature. It's finer than the finest work of art—than a Greek bas-relief, than a great Titain, or a Gothic cathedral." That is the Carolyn I loved. I will miss her for eternity.

The Rolling Stones' "She's a Rainbow" was played to emulate the brightness and vivacity of both Carolyn and Lauren: "She comes in colors everywhere."

EPILOGUE

I t was a shock to accept that Carolyn, Lauren, and John, three young people of promise, were lost without warning. Their life force was so strong that it was difficult to grasp that it no longer inhabited their physical forms. Suddenly, the media was kinder to Carolyn, lamenting the "loss of a princess" and recalling her "cool, regal demeanor" and "demure sparkle." But it would not last. And once again, the press relayed the story as the loss of Camelot, and much about how losing John and Carolyn was the loss of American royalty. As is often the case, they portrayed the humans involved as almost secondary to the dynasty.

Hilary Mantel, who wrote prolifically about the Tudors, nonetheless questioned whether we should have dynasties and monarchies. Yet we do indeed have them, but at what cost to ourselves and the members of said dynasties? "We are happy to allow monarchy to be an entertainment, in the same way that we license strip joints and lap-dancing clubs. Adulation can swing to persecution, within hours, within the same press report."

The swing is yet more extreme for women who marry into dynasties. They are always seen as interlopers, undeserving winners of a lottery and curtly assigned the task of breeding. Carolyn endured endless "pregnancy watches." That she wanted their lives to become less frantic before having a child, a precaution most people advise regardless of a couple's circumstances, was seen as unfair to John. Articles implied she was frigid, and ridiculed her when she showed anything but gratitude to be married to the dauphin. *Newsday's* "Mrs. JFK's Blues" needled Carolyn for being "depressed and even a bit weepy, bemoaning her fate as the wife of America's Most Famous Man."

Mantel also noted the short shrift for the females of the clan: "It may be that the whole phenomenon of monarchy is irrational, but that doesn't mean that when we look at it we should behave like spectators at Bedlam. Cheerful curiosity can easily become cruelty. It can easily become fatal. We don't cut off the heads of royal ladies these days, but we do sacrifice them, and we did memorably drive one to destruction a scant generation ago." Mantel was writing about Princess Diana, but similar circumstances apply when we look at Carolyn's plight.

Would just about anyone who married JFK Jr. have elicited this much enduring fascination during their life and in the decades since they died? I think the answer is no. There is something about Carolyn that is a cocktail of fascinating, intriguing, and exasperating. The clothes are impeccable, but that is not what draws us to her. When you combine her beauty and her style with the authenticity that came through in photos—whether posing happily at an event or scowling at the paparazzi—one can always see the emotion on her face: She is a revelation.

THE FACT THAT SO much of what was written was fabrication tormented Carolyn. "At any given moment," remembered Michelle Kessler, "in her own life, Carolyn could spot anything or anyone spurious, and she had no tolerance for it." Writing about truth in journalism while reviewing the book *How Democracies Die* for the *Washington Post*, Danielle Allen succinctly explains the damage done when one is continuously publicly accused of nefarious behavior: "When the allegation is false, it is equivalent to the brazen theft of the victim's reputation and standing in the community, and the fight to repair the damage can eviscerate that person's life force."

There is a very long history of male journalists fetishizing their famous female subjects, and Carolyn was described by her physical attributes again and again. Assumptions were made based on whether she smiled or frowned and narratives were spun, and none put her in a positive light.

To look at Carolyn in 1994 and then again in the summer of 1999 is to see stark change. The ongoing battle with the paparazzi was eviscerating her life force. She would have to grow thick skin. But, as Rob Littell put it, "Carolyn didn't want to have thick skin."

WHILE WRITING ABOUT A person like Carolyn—who was so private, particularly during the last months of her life spent in retreat from a menacing public glare and even more menacing photographers at her front door—I was often confronted with questions to which there were no answers. I sometimes questioned my own judgment in writing this biography, given the code of silence to which many of Carolyn's and John's friends adhered. Was it best to leave her legacy untouched, allowing time and the public to have their way? To let slander I knew to be untrue stand? But as I kept researching and discovering more information—and misinformation—I also eventually found friends, family members, and former colleagues who felt that setting the record straight took precedence over stoic silence. And then more friends emerged, and still more. As the work continued, I realized that my original hunches—such as that Carolyn was deeply empathetic, that she was a natural caretaker, that she valued moments of joy and saw fame as their thief, and even that sometimes her fear could turn to anger, which could come between her ideals and her reality—were closer to the mark than I ever could have imagined. As I peeled the layers back to reveal the true flavor of her life, I came to feel she was a vibrant soul who ran into many of the roadblocks that women face if they step outside the lines of feminine expectation.

In a sense, Carolyn's experience was a larger-than-life version of many of the impossible standards that women face. You must be chaste, but you cannot be frigid or prudish. You must be beautiful, but you cannot care about being such. You must never be angry, even if people (or in Carolyn's case, the tabloids) spread lies about you.

It's human nature to tell stories. They are how we understand life: our impulses, our foibles, and our path to becoming the better version of ourselves. Stories are our history. Yet many of the current incarnations of stories, news, and media seem to have taken an evolutional leap backward, and we use them as if we are, again, cave people relaying how best to entrap our prey. Rather than being about killing (outright, anyway), it has become about shame and ridicule, or, rather, technology has given the shame and ridicule that have always been present a velocity and reach they never had before. It feels as if Carolyn was one of the first quarries of the internet's worst traits: parasocial, herd-mentality-driven, toxic chaos.

Paparazzi photos of Carolyn staring glumly straight ahead, trying to avoid facing the cameras, sold like gangbusters to newspapers and magazines that gleefully printed them day after day. But it was the readers who drove this craze—readers who religiously devoured these images, barely masking their jealousy by consuming peddled narratives of Carolyn and John's marital woes, their professional stress as *George* struggled, and other tales of their private lives, all of which remain speculation to this day. Things accorded most of us were withheld from Carolyn on the assumption that, by simply marrying John, she had been given so much. It's hard to name what was withheld. Maybe it is as simple as: the benefit of the doubt. As Dana Gallo put it: "When I think of how the world treated her, it's mortifying."

THIS CRUELTY TOWARD CAROLYN may also partially explain her enduring status as a fashion icon. Those who contributed to the frenzy and obsession surrounding John and Carolyn—and I speculate that most of the American public alive at the time were guilty of playing a role; myself included, because even if I didn't read tabloids, I made assumptions about her privilege via pictures on newsstands—perhaps feel a deep sense of remorse for pinning Carolyn beneath a microscope, especially considering the way it all ended. So instead, we have collectively enshrined her in the halls of American fashion icons because perhaps doing so has allowed us to rewrite her story as one of quiet luxury and stealth-wealth style, of capsule wardrobes and intentional sustainability, not one of relentless paparazzi stalking and public scrutiny.

Vanessa Friedman, the fashion director and chief fashion critic for the *New York Times*, proposed a different theory to explain Carolyn's fashion resurgence, speculating in an October 2023 column that Carolyn "offered an example of a different way to be in the world, one that valorized what wasn't shown. And because she never gave a single interview after her marriage, what she wore has become a stand-in for who she was." Carolyn's style was intentionally unostentatious—no detail was overlooked, but nothing she wore meant to scream for attention. She had an interest in sustainability before it was in vogue—she was drawn to lasting timelessness and craftsmanship, the opposite of the fast fashion trend. Her commitment to these tenets has contributed to her securing fashion-icon status in recent years, with the likes of designer Sandy Liang, the downtown New York "It girl" designer known for her ubiquitous ballet flats and ribbon-adorned designs, viewing Carolyn as a muse and then explicit inspiration on her spring 2023 mood board.

Though she is now celebrated for her simple designs, sleek silhouettes, and no-frills outfits, Carolyn created her uniform in the hope of staving off the paparazzi pictures—she primarily wore neutrals, beige, and black, hoping that photographers would lose interest and stop chasing her, documenting her every move. There is a certain irony in the current obsession over her style: The very photos now posted and re-posted lauding Carolyn's choice of boots, coats, and even headbands were taken on the street, without permission and with a relentless intrusion that made her miserable. Their subtext is bleakness.

Yet in life, Carolyn was color: Blue jeans, a blue and white cloud T-shirt, a floral Chanel dress. A royal blue leather coat in Italy. Her red Prada coat, perhaps a Christmas gift. The colorful sarongs she wore in the Vineyard. The beautiful blue turtleneck John gave her to "match those matchless eyes." The white shirts, beige coats, and black Yohji Yamamoto pieces, his self-described armor and protection, were perhaps to preserve that color for her loved ones.

"She would have laughed at being called a fashion icon," Michelle Kessler remarked recently. "She was trying to be nothing of the sort. Carolyn was trying to have an interesting life and go about her day without interruption. After she left Calvin, she was not going to fashion shows or working her way back into the fashion business. She was running errands, traveling with John for *George*, and attending to friends and family in need while very carefully thinking about her next steps." That she had a great eye and chose exquisite fabrics and textures was secondary to her aspirations, and it was especially secondary to her energy. "She shifted a room when she walked in," added Kessler.

Therefore, it is not enough to say she is a style icon—it is the *spirit* in which she is an icon. And, as her friend Colleen Curtis said, it is a shame she is remembered as a fashion icon because there was so much more that was important about her. What she wore may have been beautiful, but it was not even close to what was most beautiful about her: her energy, the charisma that heightened and lit up everything, and everyone, around her.

Really, what Carolyn should be remembered for was her kindness. From her childhood days, all the way to how she treated the children of friends, she was very kind. She was, contrary to the image fabricated in certain quarters, especially kind to John. From being a sounding board after he lost his mother and a fellow soldier in the foxhole to create and sustain *George*, to explaining to Ralph Howard why he was so upset about a lost hat (a last gift from Jackie) and asking Jack Merrill to flatter his choice of home decor, to reassuring him when he fumbled with the rings at their wedding ceremony, Carolyn was kind to John.

JUST THREE DAYS AFTER John, Carolyn, and Lauren disappeared in the night, the *New York Times*'s Opinion team published a column mourning the loss, describing the tragedy as part of the Kennedy pattern of "magnetic personalities cut down far too early." John, Carolyn, and Lauren were lost during the years they were finding their footing in their lives. Any death of a young person leaves a whole set of opportunities unexplored, and these three people seem to have been on their way: Lauren in her climb up the ranks at Morgan Stanley; John in his role at *George* and his likely run for and holding of an office that could have meant, at the very least, a democracy less addled by partisan rancor and stalemates; and Carolyn, for . . . well, anything she set her mind to.

Her talents were many—an eagle eye for organization, natural empathy, ability to connect with children, and an intuition that her friend Hamilton South described as "being built to look around corners." It is easy to imagine she could have thrived running nonprofits, making documentaries to highlight the struggles of the forgotten and underprivileged, or captivating young minds in a classroom. In 1999, Carolyn ran into a friend and explained that she was hoping to work with kids in a school in East Harlem. It seemed like she was in a grounding process, a return to her first love: children. She had her degree in education and the talent to meet them where they were without coming on too strong. What is sad is that she never had the opportunity to be one of a thousand different women she could have been—a young and free professional with energy to spare for nights on the town without being watched, then moving on to elevated career accomplishment before possibly becoming a mother, and then, who knows, maybe a second career or giving it all up to live quietly in the country with lots of dogs—partly because the tabloids hemmed her into the roles of a druggie, a vapid gold digger, or vain arm candy, and then, of course, because her life was cut short. She missed out on the personal freedom to be all these things, both in her heart and in the eyes of the public.

The many "could have beens" are impossible to quantify, and one could spend hours speculating. Would John have run for president one day? Would he and Carolyn have started a family? Would Carolyn and John have remained married?

Of course, we will never know if they would have stayed together. Yet many of those close to the couple find it hard to imagine otherwise. "I don't know who they would find to replace each other," John Perry Barlow said. "That terrible experience, John's mother dying and all that press attention after they got married, was a kind of annealing process for them both. I can't see any circumstances so severe that they would give it all up at this stage."

WHAT MAKES THE LOSS of Carolyn, Lauren, and John that much harder is the feeling that tabloid attention, *our* attention, ultimately hurt them. They were not chased through the Pont de l'Alma tunnel in Paris by paparazzi like Princess Diana. But Carolyn was chased by the worry of what the press would say if she didn't go to Rory Kennedy's wedding. She was exhausted. The worry over John's magazine, Anthony Radziwill's health, and the public interest in her marriage had become too much. She wanted a break from travel and keeping up appearances. She called John's aunt Ethel to explain and apologize, and Ethel understood and told her to stay home and rest. But the thought of the rapacious headlines if John went stag was just too overwhelming. It would cause further complications for them both. So Carolyn agreed to go, directly as a consequence of the unwanted attention.

Though she felt pressure to attend the wedding festivities on that fateful July 1999 day, Carolyn had, despite the incessant attention, been growing more and more resilient. Just a couple of months before the crash, Carolyn told the *Daily News* that she no longer read stories about herself, because the gossip "has nothing to do with how I live my life. I have problems and issues just like anybody. I'm a happy person and maybe a better person for not knowing."

We are left to wonder what form the life of beautiful, captivating Carolyn would have taken, had it not been cut so short. But I'm willing to bet it would have been executed with sprezzatura and a wink.

ACKNOWLEDGMENTS

When people loved as dearly as Carolyn and John are lost, it is imperative to honor their legacy, and impossible to do perfectly. The last few years of research and interviews have been a practice in holding these two ideas at the same time, and the balance often felt tricky. I could not have made this attempt without the following people, to whom I will forever be grateful.

For Carole Radziwill and Hamilton South, thank you for sharing your memories, wisdom, and sense of humor that illuminated the same qualities in Carolyn.

Thank you to Michelle Kessler and MJ Bettenhausen for your insight, for sharing Carolyn's wit, and for your friendship.

Thank you to so many who were also willing to share their time and memories: Sasha Chermayeff, Ariel Paredes, Gustavo Paredes, Kimberly Wolf, Robert Curran, Gary Ginsberg, Betsy Reisinger Siegel, Nick Magliato, Peter Alson, Pam Thur, Sue Sartor, Jennifer Dermer, Lorain Kirk, Ann Mashburn, Molly McMahon, Jonathan Becker, Xanthipi Joannides, Jane Elezi, Jodi Savitch, Yuma Euell, Howard Brodsky, Brenda Spezialy, Victoria Giorgi, Frances Bazinet Puletz, Sherry Mansing, George Conlon, Irene Savage, Ann T. Edwards, Roseann Flood, Mimi Stein, Dr. Deena Manion, Timothy Dumas, Peter Wilson, Patricia Pulitano, Dana

Gallo Stratton, Jonathan Soroff, Blaine Applegate, Will Regan, Jack Merrill, Kim Vernon, Heather Ashton, Noona Smith Peterson, Diane von Furstenberg, Bruce Weber, Bruce Hanks, Russell Turiak, Lauren Fornes, Stephen Lyle, Steven M. Gillon, Richard Bradley, Hugo Lindgren, André Vivieros, Chris Simonetti, Chip Arndt, Christiane Amanpour, Lucy Clayton, Claire Sisco King, James Reginato, Dan Samson, George Carr, Hava Beller, Jack Kliger, William Ivey Long, Erin Lippmann, Geoffrey Freeman, Jefferson Arrington, Richard Wiese, Robert Becker, Adrian Dannat, Inigo Thomas, William D. Cohan, David Golden, Clifford Streit, Keith Stein, Jeff Bark, Matt Berman, Stormy Stokes, and all those who prefer to remain anonymous.

Thank you to Elena Gonzalvo, whose research on her Instagram page @bessetteandkennedy has been invaluable in connecting me with people who might not have otherwise come forward, nor would I have found.

Many thanks to Forbes Dudley for your help, and to Tatiana Jackson-Saitz, whom I was lucky to find through the University of Chicago's Research Program, and whose work was invaluable to this book.

Very special thanks to the Bessette family, Thomas, Kelly, and Mat, for sharing the warmth, love, and joy you experienced together.

Thank you to Andra Miller, Liana Blum, and Tara Johnson for your insightful editorial skills, my fact-checker Ben Kalin for working and worrying with me, and Geoff Shandler.

Special thanks to David Kuhn, Nate Muscato, Helen Hicks, Allison Warren, and everyone at Aevitas Creative Management for taking me on and championing this project. All of you are heroes.

I could not, and would not, have written this book without the extraordinary guidance, patience, and talent of Aimée Bell and the entire team at Gallery/Simon & Schuster, who guided and encouraged me throughout this odyssey, including but not limited to Jennifer Bergstrom, Pam Cannon, Jennifer Long, Sally Marvin, Jennifer Robinson, Kell Wilson, Caroline Pallotta, Emily Arzeno, Jamie Selzer, Jaime Putorti, Max Meltzer, and Sierra Fang-Horvath.

To my family: my late father, Frank, and my loving mother, Evelyn Pettinelli, thank you for this life. What a ride! Thank you also to Susan Hill, Tony and Emily Frazier, and Ken and Joan Schmidt.

Thank you to my New Orleans family, who tolerated me incessantly talking about this project, especially Melissa Phipps Gray and John Gray, Dawn Dedeaux, Vesta Fort, and Minor and Jill Pipes, and to Sara Ruffin and Paul Costello, our fellow co-parents, who helped set the ship to sail.

To my dear New York friends, who tolerated more talking and speculating: Natalie Valenzuela, Carolyn Sterling, Eliza Osborne, Sully Amos Hurley, Jamie Niven, Dorothy Spears and Alexis Rockman, Andy Meyers and Tanya Gallo, Elaina Richardson, Henry Davis, John and Vanessa Lilly, and Melissa Grace.

I am deeply grateful to my beautiful children, Evangeline and Alexander, for sharing time with this project and lending it inspiration, beauty, and joy. I love you beyond measure.

Most significantly, and eternally, thank you to my husband, Tom, who has been my partner and guide in everything—editorial, intellectual, emotional, and spiritual. I love you forever, and to quote Larry David, "till death do us part" isn't long enough. You are stuck with me.

NOTES

AUTHOR'S NOTE

Interview subjects include Sasha Chermayeff. Published sources include Mike Allen and Carey Goldberg, "Rescue Search in Kennedy Crash Ends; Coast Guard Tells Family There Is Little Hope," *New York Times*, July 19, 1999; Noonan and Huber, *Forever Young*, page 207.

CHAPTER 1: LAST NIGHT

Interview subjects include Steven M. Gillon, Carole Radziwill. Published sources include Bruce Landsberg, "Landmark Accidents: Vineyard Spiral: Low Visibility Contributes to JFK Jr.'s Accident," news release, AOPA.org, September 5, 2000, https://www.aopa.org/news-and-media/all-news/2000/september/pilot/land mark-accidents-vineyard-spiral#:~:text=The%20probable%20cause%20of%20the, haze%20and%20the%20dark%20night; William D. Cohan, " 'You Just Don't Wallow in Death. You Move On. You Hold It Inside.': The Struggle of John F. Kennedy Jr., American Prince," *Vanity Fair*, July 2019; Andersen, *The Day John Died*, pages 45, 50; National Transportation Safety Board, "History of Flight," NTSB Identification NYC99MA178, report of investigation, NTSB.gov, July 6, 2000; Noonan and Huber, *Forever Young*, page 15; Gillon, *America's Reluctant Prince*, page 389; Dale Russakoff and Lynne Duke, "JFK Jr. Gave Up Copilot as Ankle Healed," *Washington Post*, July 21, 1999; Elizabeth Wolff, "Inside JFK Jr.'s Daze of Doom," *New York Post*, June 17, 2007; Cohan, *Four Friends*, page 354; Adrienne Gaffney, "The Other Passenger: Who Was Lauren Bessette?," *Town & Country*, July 2019; Martin Kettle, "Doomed Flight into Darkness," *Guardian*, July 19, 1999.

CHAPTER 2: WESTCHESTER

Interview subjects include Thomas Bessette, Jane Elezi, Yuma Euell, Jodi Savitch, Howard Brodsky, Victoria Giorgi, Frances Bazinet Puletz, Sherry Mansing, George Conlon, Irene Savage, Roseann Flood, Mimi Stein. Published sources include Edward Lewine, Lisa Colangelo, and Bill Hutchinson, "The Bessette Sisters," *Daily News*, July 19, 1999; Land deed, 16 Fieldstone Drive, Hartsdale, New York, July 1, 1969; Land deed, 12 Old Knollwood Road, White Plains, New York, January 27, 1977; Mary McAleer Vizard, "If You're Thinking of Living in: Hartsdale," *New York Times*, April 28, 1991; Mary Ann Lachat, "The Dimensions of Integration in Greenburgh Central No. Seven, Greenburgh, New York," report, Office of Education, Columbia University Teachers College, November 1973; Library of Congress, "Immigration and Relocation in U.S. History: Under Attack," https://www.loc.gov/classroom-materials/immigration/; Ben Lariccia, "The U.S. Italian Community and the Immigration Act of 1924," *la Gazetta Italiana*, March 2017; David A. Taylor, "During World War II, the U.S. Saw Italian-Americans as a Threat to Homeland Security," *Smithsonian Magazine*, February 2017; "Foreman Burned by Power Line," *Hartford Courant*, October 12, 1962; Ann Gerhart, "Who's That Girl? Quite Possibly the Perfect Match," *Los Angeles Times*, October 18, 1996; Marriage Index, William J. Bessette Married Ann Marie Messina, New York State Vital Records, June 29, 1963; Berman, *JFK Jr., George, and Me*, page 125; Jane Meredith Adams, "Doctor Divorce," *Baltimore Sun*, July 14, 1997; George Judson, "Greenwich Feels Pain of Change," *New York Times*, April 12, 1993; Lisa Chamoff, "Greenwich's Departed Mom-and-Pops," *Greenwich* (CT) *Time*, April 19, 2010; Colleen Curtis, "She Was a Magnet," *Daily News*, July 25, 1999; Stephen S. Hall, "Italian Americans Coming into Their Own," *New York Times*, May 15, 1983; Heymann, *American Legacy*, pages 205, 207.

CHAPTER 3: GREENWICH TIME

Interview subjects include Thomas Bessette, Victoria Giorgi, Frances Bazinet Puletz, Irene Savage, Roseann Flood, Mimi Stein, Dana Gallo Strayton, Lucy Milby, Sherry Mansing, Gregory Conlon, Ann T. Edwards, Patricia Pulitano, Rob Pedicano, Deena Manion. Published sources include Lisa Chamoff, "Greenwich's Departed Mom-and-Pops," *Greenwich* (CT) *Time*, April 19, 2010; Richardson, *Greenwich Before 2000*, page 176; Ann Gerhart, "Who's That Girl? Quite Possibly the Perfect Match," *Los Angeles Times*, October 18, 1996; Denise Lavoie, "Bessette Family Deals with Tragedy," *South Coast Today*, July 19, 1999; George Judson, "Greenwich Feels Pain of Change," *New York Times*, April 12, 1993; Maxine King, "A Look Back—GHS in the 70's: A Transition Under Headmaster John Bird," *Greenwich* (CT) *Free Press*, August 4, 2017; Thomas P. Ronan, "8 Striking Westchester Teachers Jailed for Contempt," *New York Times*, October 29, 1977; Colleen Curtis, "She Was a Magnet," *Daily News*, July 25, 1999; Rick Marin and Tessa Namuth, "Crazy for Carolyn," *Newsweek*, October 21, 1996; Jeannine Stein, "John-John Is Gone-Gone," *Los Angeles Times*, September 24, 1996; Ann Caron, "Passion for Retail Business Runs in the Family," *Greenwich* (CT) *Time*, January 11, 2012.

CHAPTER 4: BOSTON UNCOMMON

Interview subjects include Thomas Bessette, Jen Curran, Deena Manion, Timothy Dumas, Roseann Flood, Peter Wilson, Dana Gallo Strayton, Blaine Applegate, Jonathan Soroff, Chris Matchett. Published sources include Bob Monahan, "Cullen Has Been Scoring His Points for the Family," *Boston Globe*, January 6, 1984; Wallerstein, Lewis, and Blakeslee, *The Unexpected Legacy of Divorce*, page 55; Patrick Kennedy, "The Little Dive with a Long History," *BU* (Boston University) *Today*, September 30, 2014; "Carolyn of Camelot," *Sun Sentinel* (Fort Lauderdale, FL), September 26, 1996; Alessandro Benetton, "My Father, My Children and Carolyn Bessette," *Vanity Fair Italia*, May 2022; Heymann, *American Legacy*, page 407; Benetton, *La Traiettoria*, pages 157–158, 185–188.

CHAPTER 5: CHAMPAGNE SUPERNOVAS

Interview subjects include Will Regan, Michelle Kessler, Jennifer Dermer, George Carr, MJ Bettenhausen, Sue Sartor, Ann Mashburn, Xanthipi Joannides, Deena Manion, Madonna Badger, Heather Ashton, Richard Wiese, Steven M. Gillon, Betsy Reisinger Siegel, Molly McMahon, Bruce Weber, Stormy Stokes. Published sources include Marisa Meltzer, "Remembering Grace Mirabella and Her Inventive Magazine," *New York Times*, February 9, 2022; Rosemary Feitelberg, "The House That Calvin Klein Built," *Women's Wear Daily*, October 19, 2011; Ginia Bellafante, "Zack Carr, 55, Fashion Designer at Calvin Klein," *New York Times*, December 25, 2000; Heymann, *American Legacy*, page 358; Ann Gerhart, "Who's That Girl? Quite Possibly the Perfect Match," *Los Angeles Times*, October 18, 1996; Ann Gerhart, "Myth America," *Washington Post*, October 9, 1996.

CHAPTER 6: ANN'S GIRL, JACKIE'S BOY

Interview subjects include Carole Radziwill, Michelle Kessler, Jennifer Dermer, MJ Bettenhausen, Deena Manion, Madonna Badger, Heather Ashton, Richard Wiese, Steven M. Gillon, Betsy Reisinger Siegel, Molly McMahon, Sasha Chermayeff, Kim Vernon. Published sources include Jane Delynn, "Don't Bungle the Benefit," *New York Times*, May 24, 1992; "Finally, They Both Found True Love," *New York Post*, July 19, 1999; Charles Strum, "For the People, Kennedy. For Jurors, Kennedy!," *New York Times*, July 10, 1992; "Murf's Backstreet Tavern," Sag Harbor, *Foursquare City Guide* (app), https://foursquare.com/v/murfs-backstreet-tavern/4c2a0b5ed26eb713908e14d1; Radziwill, *What Remains*, page 95; Richard Corkery, "Carolyn: A Woman of Intrigue," *Daily News*, July 22, 1999; Lois Romano, "The Reliable Source," *Washington Post*, July 21, 1992; Michael Powell, "JFK Jr.: As Child and Man, America's Crown Prince," *Washington Post*, July 18, 1999; Maureen Downey and Bette Harrison, "Neiman Marcus in Atlanta for the Atlanta Ballet Ball," *Atlanta Constitution*, March 1, 1993; Cathy Horyn, "Calvin Klein Is Seeking Treatment for Substance Abuse," *New York Times*, April 5, 2003; Gillon, *America's Reluctant Prince*, page 208; Andersen, *The Day John Died*, page 270; John F. Kennedy Jr. and Caroline Kennedy, interview with Jay

Schadler, *Prime Time Live*; Associated Press, "Ted Kennedy Jr.'s October Wedding," *Standard-Star* (New Rochelle, NY), October 11, 1993; Linda Grant, "Can Calvin Klein Escape?: He Built an Empire on Raunch and Elegance. Then, Overpriced Jeans and Junk-Bond Debt Pushed It to the Edge. But Look Out, Here Comes His Spring Collection," *Los Angeles Times*, February 23, 1992; Charlotte Cowles, "Her Mossness: Kate Moss on Heroin, Johnny Depp, Galliano, and 'Facial Tourette's,'" *The Cut*, October 31, 2012; James Kaplan, "What Makes Calvin Run," *New York* magazine, September 18, 1995; Heymann, *American Legacy*, page 419; Littell, *The Men We Became*, page 170; Rose Minutaglio, "Inside John F. Kennedy Jr.'s 'Adventurous' Relationship with Model Julie Baker," *Town & Country*, January 2019; Associated Press, "Kennedy Kept Waiting at the Altar," *Standard-Star* (New Rochelle, NY), October 11, 1993; "Marriage or Nothing Daryl Tells JFK," News in Brief, *Evening Standard* (London), August 18, 1994; Pat Weschsler, "Hunk and Daryl in the Dumper," *Newsday* (Long Island, NY), November 24, 1993; Liz Smith, "Daryl, John, Not Kaput?," *Newsday* (Long Island, NY), December 3, 1993; Bergin, *The Other Man*, page 132; Lauren Hubbard, "The Last Love of Jackie Kennedy Onassis," *Town & Country*, May 2019; Terenzio, *Fairy Tale Interrupted*, page 14; Cohan, *Four Friends*, page 295; Colleen Curtis, "She Was a Magnet," *Daily News*, July 25, 1999; Jon Levine, "The Secret Life of Carolyn Bessette's Sister 20 Years After Doomed JFK Jr. Flight," *New York Post*, July 13, 2019; "Kate Moss on Her 'Years of Crying' over Johnny Depp—and How She's Still a Total 'Hell-Raiser' Behind Closed Doors," *Vanity Fair*, October 2021; Martha Brant, "Coming of Age," *Newsweek*, August 13, 1995; Nina J. Easton, "Is John Kennedy Jr.'s 'George' Making American Politics Sexy?," *Los Angeles Times*, August 11, 1996.

CHAPTER 7: MUCH ADO

Interview subjects include Bruce Hanks, MJ Bettenhausen, Michelle Kessler, Deena Manion, Sara Ruffin Costello, Heather Ashton, Betsy Reisinger Siegel, Jen Dermer. Published sources include Bergin, *The Other Man*, page 98; Betty Goodwin, "Benefit by Calvin Klein an Event to Remember," *Los Angeles Times*, June 7, 1993; Bernadine Morris, "Enough Calvin Klein Minimalism to Fill Hollywood Bowl," *New York Times*, June 8, 1993; William Norwich, "Prize Partnership," *Vogue*, June 1993; John F. Kennedy Jr., "A Kayaking Expedition in the Baltic," *New York Times*, July 26, 1992; Linda Stasi, A. J. Benza, and Michael Lewittes, "JFK Indoscene," *Daily News*, July 1, 1993; George Rush Jr. and Joanna Molloy, "RFK's Son Ready to Marry Again, Will JFK Be Next to Wed?," *Star-Gazette* (Elmira, NY), July 19, 1993; Andersen, *The Day John Died*, page 137; Heymann, *American Legacy*, page 419; Don Singleton, "Photog Preys on JFK After DeNiro Fiasco," *Daily News*, October 15, 1995; Maer Roshan, "Prince of the City," *New York* magazine, August 2, 1999; Francesca Stanfill, "The Private Jackie," *Vanity Fair*, November 1995; Littell, *The Men We Became*, pages 177, 301; Gillon, *America's Reluctant Prince*, pages 103, 209, 214; Cohan, *Four Friends*, page 295; Pat Wechsler, "Hunk and Daryl in the Dumper," *Newsday* (Long Island, NY), November 24, 1993; Laura Fleischmann, "If the Washington Square Hotel Could Talk (or Write, or Sing)," *Off the Grid* (blog), Village Preservation,

July 12, 2019, https://www.villagepreservation.org/2019/07/12/washington-square-ho
tel-earle/; Fergal Keane, "After All the Eulogies for the Kennedys, Here's One for Lauren," *The Independent* (UK), July 23, 1999; Isabel Jones and Krista Carter, "JFK Jr. and
Daryl Hannah's Relationship Timeline: A Look Back," *InStyle*, updated August 24,
2023; Terenzio, *Fairy Tale Interrupted*, page 14; Erin Blakemore, "How JFK's Brief Stint
as a WWII Journalist Influenced His Presidency," *History Classics*, A&E Television Networks, November 27, 2018, https://www.history.com/news/jfk-journalist-wwii-pots
dam-conference-hearst; Kennedy, *Profiles in Courage*; Andersen, *The Good Son*, page
283; *I Am JFK Jr.*, documentary film.

CHAPTER 8: WORKING GIRL

Interview subjects include Gary Ginsberg, Richard Wiese, Hugo Lindgren, Sasha
Chermayeff, Erin Lippmann, Gustavo Paredes, Libra Max, Jack Merrill, Betsy
Reisinger Siegel, Stephen Lyle, Jen Dermer. Published sources include *A Current
Affair*, Fox television, August 29, 1994; "Hyannis Port Kennedy Compound," *Scene
Therapy*, January 14, 2023, https://scenetherapy.com/hyannis-port-kennedy-com
pound/; Taraborrelli, *Jackie*, page 404; Taraborrelli, *After Camelot*, page 34; Tarabor-
relli, *The Kennedy Heirs*, page 52; Flaherty, *What Jackie Taught Us*, page 38; Lois
Smith Brady, "In the Shadow of the Very Rich," *Harper's Bazaar*, September 1993; *I
Am JFK Jr.*, documentary film.

CHAPTER 9: MEET THE FAMILY

Interview subjects include Gary Ginsberg, Carole Radziwill, Erin Lippmann, MJ
Bettenhausen, Richard Wiese, Betsy Reisinger Siegel, Peter Alson, Pam Thur, Chris-
topher Simonetti, Jack Merrill, Richard Bradley, Chris Oberbeck, Hugo Lindgren,
Hamilton South, Michelle Kessler, Dana Gallo Strayton, David Golden, Noona
Smith-Petersen. Published sources include Isabel Vincent and Melissa Klein, "Ken-
nedys Feuded Before Bodies Were Recovered," *New York Post*, November 3, 2013;
Andersen, *The Day John Died*, pages 172–173; Littell, *The Men We Became*, pages 170,
177; "JFK Jr.'s Collared for Leash," *Herald-News* (Passaic, NJ), December 24, 1994;
New York Times Syndicate, "The New Ms. Kennedy 'There's Something Sexy—
Even Raunchy—About Her,' Says One Ex-Colleague," *Spokesman-Review* (Spokane,
WA), September 29, 1996; Rod Stafford Hagwood, "Seen on the Scene," *Sun Sentinel* (Fort Lauderdale, FL), April 16, 1995; Radziwill, *What Remains*, page 129;
@carolyn_iconic, "May 19, 1996. At the memorial for Jackie, John's mother. I am loving her pants suit, with no shirt underneath," Instagram, July 22, 2020, https://www
.instagram.com/p/CC828ZqnJmF/?img_index=1; Terenzio, *Fairy Tale Interrupted*,
pages 94, 97; Bradley, *American Son*, pages 60, 85; Nina J. Easton, "Is John Kennedy Jr.'s 'George' Making American Politics Sexy?," *Los Angeles Times*, August 11,
1996; Cohan, *Four Friends*, page 342; Frederick M. Winship, "JFK Jr. Unveils
His Political Magazine," UPI.com, September 7, 1995, https://www.upi.com
/Archives/1995/09/07/JFK-Jr-unveils-his-political-magazine/7032810446400/;

George Rush Jr. and Joanna Molloy, "Three of Good Cheer: B'days for Woody, Bette and JFK Jr.," *Daily News*, December 5, 1995; Colleen Curtis, "She Was a Magnet," *Daily News*, July 25, 1999; Kate Storey, "The Inside Story of John F. Kennedy Jr.'s *George* Magazine," *Esquire*, April 22, 2019, https://www.esquire.com/news-pol itics/a27031243/john-kennedy-jr-george-magazine-true-story/; Rob Littell, in *Final 24, "JFK Junior"*; Karen Schneider, "Nobody Seemed to Care About Who He Really Is," *People*, January 16, 1995; Karen Schneider, "And Now, the Rest of His Life," *People*, January 16, 1995; Linda Stasi, A. J. Benza, and Michael Lewittes, "Sound Bites," *Daily News*, October 5, 1994; Susan Bickelhaupt, Names & Faces, *Boston Globe*, September 29, 1994; Taraborrelli, *The Kennedy Heirs*, page 22; Hey- mann, *American Legacy*, page 419; Flaherty, *What Jackie Taught Us*, page 38; Karen Duffy, "John and Carolyn, the Spell They Cast," *Glamour*, October 1999; Laurent Guyénot, "The Broken Presidential Destiny of JFK, Jr.: Israel's 'Kennedy Curse'?," *Unz Review*, February 11, 2019; "JFK Jr. on His Own," *People*, January 16, 1995; Gil- lon, *America's Reluctant Prince*, page 296; George Rush Jr. and Joanna Molloy, "JFK's New Squeeze Denies She's Torn Between 2 Lovers," *Daily News*, March 2, 1995; Berman, *JFK Jr., George, and Me*, page 51; Mark Ganem, "Paradise Lost," *Wom- en's Wear Daily*, July 19, 1999; Jane Martinson, "The Bessette Sisters," *Guardian*, July 19, 1999; Hilary Mantel, "Royal Bodies," *London Review of Books*, February 21, 2013; Frederick M. Winship, "JFK Jr. Unveils His Political Magazine," UPI.com, September 7, 1995, https://www.upi.com/Archives/1995/09/07/JFK-Jr-unveils -his-political-magazine/7032810446400/; Larry Sutton, "JFK Jr. Ready to Let George Do It," *Daily News*, September 8, 1995; Robert Dominguez, "They Angle for Tabloid Hit Parade," *Daily News*, October 15, 1995; A. J. Benza and Michael Lewittes, "In the 'Zona,'" *Daily News*, January 3, 1996.

CHAPTER 10: SUNDAY IN THE PARK WITH *GEORGE*

Interview subjects include Carole Radziwill, Erin Lippmann, MJ Bettenhausen, Rich- ard Wiese, Betsy Reisinger Siegel, Christopher Simonetti, Jack Merrill, Richard Brad- ley, Chris Oberbeck, Hugo Lindgren, Hamilton South, Michelle Kessler, Dana Gallo Strayton. Published sources include Gillon, *America's Reluctant Prince*, page 287; Madonna, "If I Were President," *George* magazine, October 1995; Associated Press, "Kennedy, Girlfriend Caught in Dramatic Lovers' Quarrel," *Chicago Tribune*, March 1, 1996; George Rush Jr. and Joanna Molloy, "Fights, Camera, Action," *Daily News*, March 9, 1996; Associated Press, "Enquirer Takes Offers on Video of Fight Between JFK, Girlfriend," *Star-Gazette* (Elmira, NY), March 2, 1996; Geri Anne Kaikowski, "Return to Your Roots for Best Hair Color," *Citizens' Voice* (Wilkes-Barre, PA), May 20, 1997; "JFK Jr., Girlfriend Scuffle in Central Park," Inside Color, *San Fran- cisco Examiner*, March 1, 1996; Richard Corkery, "Seems like This Must Be the Real Thing for John-John," *Daily News*, February 28, 1996; "JFK Jr. Rips Ring Off in Lover's Spat," Names, Faces, *Cincinnati Post*, March 1, 1996; Francesca Chapman, "JFK Jr. and Squeeze Had Swinging Time in Park," *Philadelphia Daily News*, March 5, 1996; Jean Seligmann, "Sunday in the Park with George," *Newsweek*, March 10, 1996; George

Rush Jr., "Hunk and Lover's Quarrel," *Daily News*, March 1, 1996; Tom Kelly, "The Week," *Daily News*, March 2, 1996; "Pretending to Run a Magazine," Spade in America, *Saturday Night Live*, season 21, episode 16, NBC, March 23, 1996; Corky Siemaszko, "Kennedy Walks," *Daily News*, September 23, 1996; Isabel Jones, "John F. Kennedy Jr. Used to Avoid the Paparazzi by Dressing Up like a Woman," *InStyle*, June 2019; Kate Storey, "The Inside Story of John F. Kennedy Jr.'s *George* Magazine," *Esquire*, April 22, 2019; George Rush Jr. and Joanna Molloy, "A Leg of Stars at Bash for 'Birdcage,'" *Daily News*, March 5, 1996; McKeon, *Jackie's Girl*, page 295; Holly Lambery, "Carolyn Bessette and John F. Kennedy Jr. in 24 Images," *Vogue France*, November 2018; George Rush Jr. and Joanna Molloy, "Is Girlfriend Bessette in the Kennedy Way?," *Daily News*, March 4, 1996; Liz Smith, "Now Take It from Me," *Newsday* (Long Island, NY), March 18, 1996; Noonan and Huber, *Forever Young*, page 153; Heymann, *American Legacy*, page 419.

CHAPTER 11: SPREZZATURA

Interview subjects include Hamilton South, Carole Radziwill, Sue Sartor, Michelle Kessler, Alexandra Kotur, Nancy Haas, MJ Bettenhausen, Bryan Huffman, Heather Ashton, Chris Oberbeck, Kim Vernon, Jonathan Soroff, Sasha Chermayeff, Claire Sisco King, Chris Simonetti. Published sources include Jane Martinson, "The Bessette Sisters," *Guardian*, July 19, 1999; Ann Gerhart, "Myth America," *Washington Post*, October 9, 1996; Bradley, *American Son*, page 117; Lisa Bessette, "The Visualization of the Contents of the Psalms in the Early Middle Ages," dissertation, University of Michigan, 2005; N. R. Kleinfield, with Carol Vogel, "Fans Throng to See Mrs. Onassis' Items Shown at Sotheby's," *New York Times*, April 20, 1996; David Colman, "Did Thoughts of April 15 Influence Auction Bids?," *New York Times*, April 28, 1996; Paula Span and Judd Tully, "Auction of an Aura in History," *Washington Post*, April 27, 1996; Radziwill, *What Remains*, page 146; Gillon, *America's Reluctant Prince*, page 375; Heymann, *American Legacy*, page 448; Associated Press, "Italy: John F. Kennedy Jr. Visits Famous Design House Valentino," video, Associated Press Archive, April 20, 1996, https://www.youtube.com/watch?v=dXb4cRBZCJ8&list=PPSV; Donatella Chiappini, "Divise d'Autore per Kennedy Jr.," *la Repubblica* (Italy), April 21, 1996; Castiglione, *The Book of the Courtier*, page 209.

CHAPTER 12: BACK TO WORK

Interview subjects include Michelle Kessler, Alexandra Kotur, Nancy Haas, MJ Bettenhausen, Carole Radziwill, Bryan Huffman, Heather Ashton, Chris Oberbeck, Kim Vernon, Jonathan Sarnoff, Sasha Chermayeff, Hamilton South, Bryan Huffman, Chris Zimonetti, Claire Sisco King. Published sources include Knight-Ridder, "Playing the Political Name Game," *Buffalo News*, May 10, 1996; Paul D. Colford, "Some Press Hounds Heel for Kennedy," *Los Angeles Times*, November 5, 1996; Terenzio, *Fairy Tale Interrupted*, page 139; Littell, *The Men We Became*, page 178; Haag, *Come to the Edge*, page 160; Brooke Bobb, "The Kennedy Family Wedding Photographer Shares His

Most Iconic Images and the Stories Behind Them," *Vogue*, April 2016; Aaron Pars-
ley, "JFK Jr. Married Carolyn Bessette in Secret 25 Years Ago: Remembering All the
Wedding Details," *People*, September 23, 2021; Christopher Mason, "He Said It with
Flowers," *New York Times*, July 17, 2009; Berman, *JFK Jr., George, and Me*, page 50;
W. Speers, "Talk Is Percolating That JFK Jr. Is on the Brink of Announcing His Engage-
ment to Carolyn Bessette," *Philadelphia Inquirer*, June 18, 1996; "News Lite: Spielberg
Ride-Along a Glitzy 'Incident,'" *Los Angeles Times*, July 26, 1996; Cohan, *Four Friends*,
page 332; Julie Miller, "Inside John F. Kennedy Jr. and Carolyn Bessette's Fraught Final
Summer," *Vanity Fair*, July 2019; Laird Borrelli-Persson, "Karl Lagerfeld Took Us
Around the World in 200 Looks at His Spring 1996 Chanel Show," Vogue Runway
(app), December 30, 2019; George Rush Jr. and Joanna Molloy, "Wild Nights Appear
Over for Morrison and Fiancé," *Daily News*, June 14, 1996; Jim Davis, "Encore," *Fort
Worth Star-Telegram*, September 15, 1996; Rick Bonino, "But We Still Kinda Doubt
She's His First Lady," *Spokesman-Review* (Spokane, WA), July 28, 1996; "Who's That
Girl?," Accent, *Palm Beach Post*, September 25, 1996; "You've Picked the Wrong Place,
Diana," Features, *Evening Standard* (London), July 23, 1996; John F. Kennedy Jr.,
"National Enquirer Publisher Iain Calder," *George* magazine, August 1996; Nina J.
Easton, "Is John Kennedy Jr.'s 'George' Making American Politics Sexy?," *Los Angeles
Times*, August 11, 1996; Jim Davis, "Couples," *Fort Worth Star-Telegram*, September
15, 1996; George Rush Jr. and Joanna Molloy, "Kennedy Marriage Watch: Opinions
Are Split," *Daily News*, September 19, 1996; Jon Anderson, "JFK Jr. Party at Art Insti-
tute Stars Good Mix of Names," *Chicago Tribune*, August 28, 1996.

CHAPTER 13: THE WEDDING

Interview subjects include Hamilton South, Jonathan Soroff, Chris Simonetti,
Christiane Amanpour, Claire Sisco King, Sasha Chermayeff, Betsy Reisinger Siegel,
William D. Cohan, Richard Bradley, MJ Bettenhausen, Dan Samson. Published
sources include Rob Littell, in *Final 24*, "*JFK Junior*"; George Rush Jr. and Joanna
Molloy, "Kennedy Marriage Watch: Opinions Are Split," *Daily News*, September 19,
1996; billmad2509, "The '90s," r/popculturechat, Reddit, January 29, 2022; Morris,
Cumberland Island, page 26; Greyfield Inn, Cumberland Island, Georgia, website,
https://greyfieldinn.com; Alainna Lexie Beddie, "I Traveled to a Magical Island—
Alone," *New York Times*, January 25, 2017; Rachel Burchfield, "25 Years Later, Car-
olyn Bessette-Kennedy's Wedding Dress Still Stuns," *Vanity Fair*, September 2021;
Rob Littell, in *Final 24*, "*JFK Junior*"; Bradley, *American Son*, pages 109–110;
Littell, *The Men We Became*, pages 181, 183–184, 187–188; Heymann, *American
Legacy*, pages 455, 457; Terenzio, *Fairy Tale Interrupted*, pages 138, 144; Radziwill,
What Remains, pages 155–156; *JFK Jr. and Carolyn's Wedding*, documentary film;
Taraborrelli, *The Kennedy Heirs*, page 113; Taraborrelli, *After Camelot*, page 419;
Andersen, *The Day John Died*, page 288; Andersen, *The Good Son*, page 309; Kevin
Sack, "The Island That Kept a Wedding a Secret," *New York Times*, September 26,
1996; Noonan and Huber, *Forever Young*, page 186; Ann Gerhart, "Myth America,"
Washington Post, October 9, 1996; Robert D. McFadden, "John F. Kennedy Jr. Is

Married, Quietly, Reports Say," *New York Times*, September 23, 1996; Daniel Kelleher, "On the Birth of a Child in Ireland," in Noonan and Huber, page 185.

CHAPTER 14: DAYS OF WINE AND ROSES

Interview subjects include Hamilton South, Christiane Amanpour, Richard Bradley, MJ Bettenhausen, Dan Samson, Russell Turiak. Published sources include "Remembering John," *People*, August 1, 1999; David Freed, "Pilots and Fans Dedicated to Prolonging the Stardom of the Beech 18," *Smithsonian Magazine*, January 2013; Ann Gerhart, "John F. Kennedy Jr., a Bachelor No More," *Washington Post*, September 23, 1996; Celaleddin Celeb, "Sema: Human Being in the Universal Movement," Umass Rumi Club website, September 2005, https://www.umass.edu/gso/rumi/sema3.htm; Russell Turiak, "JFK Jr.'s Exotic Honeymoon," *Globe* (Canada), October 8, 1996; George Rush Jr. and Joanna Molloy, "For the Newlyweds, No Turkish Delight," *Daily News*, October 8, 1996; Liz Smith, "JFK Jr.'s Last Laugh," *Newsday* (Long Island, NY), September 24, 1996; Corky Siemaszko, "Kennedy Walks," *Daily News*, September 23, 1996; Joanna Molloy, "The Aisle on the Isle," *Daily News*, September 23, 1996; Associated Press, "New Kennedy Tailor-Made to Suit Camelot," *Democrat and Chronicle* (Rochester, NY), September 30, 1996; Nathan Cobb, "OK, She Hooked JFK Jr.— But Just Who the Heck Is She?," *Des Moines Register*, September 27, 1996; John F. Kennedy Jr., Editor's Letter, *George* magazine, October 1996; George Rush Jr. and Joanna Molloy, "Psssst, They're Baaaack!," *Daily News*, October 6, 1996; Paul D. Colford, "Some Press Hounds Heel for Kennedy," *Los Angeles Times*, November 5, 1996; Lisa Sandberg, "JFK Jr. Asks Media for Honeymoon," *Daily News*, October 7, 1996; "Paradise Lost," *Women's Wear Daily*, July 19, 1999; Gillon, *America's Reluctant Prince*, page 299; Alderman and Kennedy, *The Right to Privacy*, page xvi; Yonette Joseph, "Down Boy! Good Dog," *Miami Herald*, January 31, 1997; Marie Cocco, Asides, *Newsday* (Long Island, NY), September 29, 1996; Corky Siemaszko, "Connecticut Beauty Won Jackie's Approval," *Daily News*, September 23, 1996; Elisabeth Bumiller, "Enter Smiling, the Stylish Carolyn Bessette," *New York Times*, September 29, 1996; Cindy Adams and George Wayne, "Gossip Queens," *New York* magazine, November 4, 1996; Anne Kornblutt, William Goldschlag, Virginia Breen, and Helen Kennedy, "Royal Wedding," *Daily News*, September 24, 1996; Judy Klemesrud, "The Reaction Here Is Anger, Shock and Dismay," *New York Times*, October 19, 1968; Theodore H. White, "For President Kennedy an Epilogue," *Life*, December 6, 1963; "Jackie," *Newsweek*, May 29, 1994; George Rush Jr. and Joanna Molloy, "Lotsa Q, Little A as Kennedys Meet the Press," *Daily News*, November 6, 1996; Virginia Breen, James Rutenberg, and Stephen McFarland, "Papa John-John?," *Daily News*, October 24, 1996; William Norwich, "No Assistants. No Entourage. Just John," *New York Observer*, July 26, 1999.

CHAPTER 15: FRIENDS AND FOES

Interview subjects include Sasha Chermayeff, Hamilton South, Jack Merrill, Hugo Lindgren, Steven M. Gillon, Heather Ashton, Betsy Reisinger Siegel, MJ Bettenhausen, Biz Mitchell, Gary Ginsberg, William D. Cohan. Published sources include Heymann, *American Legacy*, page 448; Noonan, and Huber, *Forever Young*, page 189; Littell, *The Men We Became*, page 179; "Money Magazine Profitable for Time Inc.," *New York Times*, October 25, 1982; Carl Swanson, "Pecker Dumps Hachette, Begins Tabloid Reign," *New York Observer*, February 22, 1999; @carolyn_iconic, "The Green Valentino Coat Clip," Instagram, July 28, 2020, https://www.instagram.com/p /CDNPIvYH00j/; Bradley, *American Son*, page 115; Berman, *JFK Jr., George, and Me*, pages 29, 77–88; "Sipple Suit Dismissed," *Mother Jones*, January/February 1998; Maureen Dowd, "The No Frontier," *New York Times*, October 3, 1996; Ann Gerhart, "Myth America," *Washington Post*, October 9, 1996; Elisabeth Bumiller, "Enter Smiling, the Stylish Carolyn Bessette," *New York Times*, September 29, 1996; "Paradise Lost," *Women's Wear Daily*, July 19, 1999; Alona Wartofsky, "The List: 1997," *Washington Post*, December 31, 1996; Associated Press, "Jacqueline Kennedy Onassis, JFK Items Being Auctioned," Boston.com, May 11, 2017, https://www.boston.com /news/history/2017/05/11/jacqueline-kennedy-onassiss-painting-watch-head -to-auction/; Gillon, *America's Reluctant Prince*, page 294; Kate Storey, "The Inside Story of John F. Kennedy Jr.'s *George* Magazine," *Esquire*, April 22, 2019; Punch Lines, *Los Angeles Times*, October 25, 1996; Corky Siemaszko, "He's 'Shutter Buggin'," *Daily News*, December 16, 1996; Andersen, *The Day John Died*, page 298; Anna Mundow, "Bessette by Difficulties?," *Irish Times*, January 18, 1997; Radziwill, *What Remains*, pages 95, 171.

CHAPTER 16: HELP WANTED

Interview subjects include Russell Turiak, Hugo Lindgren, Gary Ginsberg, MJ Bettenhausen, Kim Vernon, Hamilton South, Donatella Versace, Christopher Simonetti, Gustavo Paredes, Lucy Clayton, Jonathan Soroff, Carole Radziwill, Michelle Kessler, Christiane Amanpour. Published sources include Kate Storey, "The Inside Story of John F. Kennedy Jr.'s *George* Magazine," *Esquire*, April 22, 2019, https://www.esquire .com/news-politics/a27031243/john-kennedy-jr-george-magazine-true-story/; "Show," *Star-Gazette* (Elmira, NY), October 24, 1996; Andersen, *The Day John Died*, page 300; "Turning Point: Paparazzi: Shooting Stars," *ABC News*, TV broadcast, March 27, 1997; Corky Siemaszko, "He's 'Shutter-Buggin'," *Daily News*, December 16, 1996; David Carr, "The Tell-All Steven Florio Won't Sell," *New York Times*, June 27, 2005; Melissa Orlov, "The ADHD Effect on Marriage," A.D.D. Resource Center website, September 20, 2012, https://www.addrc.org/the-adhd-effect-on -marriage/; Mark Tran, "Kennedy Allies Slate Marriage-Rift Claims," *Guardian*, January 14, 1997; Ann Gerhart, "Who's That Girl? Quite Possibly the Perfect Match," *Los Angeles Times*, October 18, 1996; Heymann, *American Legacy*, pages 448, 472; Andersen, *The Good Son*, page 294; Eileen Reslen, "JFK Jr.'s College Application and Jackie

Kennedy's Letters to His Professors Are for Sale," *Harper's Bazaar*, October 2017; Radziwill, *What Remains*, page 162; A. J. Benza and Michael Lewittes, "The Kennedy Case," *Daily News*, February 11, 1997; Lloyd Grove, "'Retired' National Enquirer Chief David Pecker Is Still in Charge and 'Still Protecting Trump,' Insiders Say," *Daily Beast*, January 25, 2021; George Rush Jr. and Joanna Molloy, "A Jolly Good Fella, Not a Raging Bull Artist," *Daily News*, March 6, 1997; Kimberly Ryan, "The Cult of Carolyn," *Vogue*, February 1997; Orla Healey, "Beaded Belles," *Daily News*, April 8, 1997; Liz Smith, "Night of a Thousand Blondes," *Newsday* (Long Island, NY), April 7, 1997; Gillon, *America's Reluctant Prince*, pages 301–304; Noonan and Huber, *Forever Young*, pages 191–192; Littell, *The Men We Became*, pages 178, 211–212.

CHAPTER 17: CRUEL SUMMER

Interview subjects include Carole Radziwill, Betsy Riesinger Siegel, Billy Strauss, Ariel Paredes, Hamilton South, Richard Bradley, MJ Bettenhausen, Jack Merrill, Dan Samson, Ralph Howard, Chelsea Howard. Published sources include Matthew Fenton, "Splitting the Difference," *Broadsheet* (blog), April 9, 2018, https://www.ebroadsheet.com/splitting-the-difference/; "Carolyn 'Bassinet' Kennedy? She Glows!" *Daily News*, November 7, 1997; George Rush Jr. and Joanna Molloy, Surveillance, *Daily News*, May 18, 1997; Mark Ganem, "Paradise Lost," *Women's Wear Daily*, July 19, 1999; George Rush Jr. and Joanna Molloy, "John-John to Be Dada?" *Daily News*, June 12, 1997; @ttigerlily, "Carolyn Bessette Kennedy and JFK Jr. at a memorial Mass for Jackie," Pinterest, August 8, 2021, https://www.pinterest.com/pin/1117234396542087308/; Radziwill, *What Remains*, pages 165–166; Terenzio, *Fairy Tale Interrupted*, page 232; Lisa Lockwood and Susan Watters, "Kennedys Out in 'Force,'" *Women's Wear Daily*, July 25, 1997; "'Lapsed Pilot' JFK Jr. Visits Oshkosh Air Show," *Chicago Tribune*, August 2, 1997; Associated Press, "Kennedy at Fly-In," *Dispatch* (Moline, IL), August 2, 1997; William K. Rashbaum and Jere Hester, "Celebrities Cry for Gianni," *Daily News*, July 23, 1997; John F. Kennedy Jr., "Don't Sit Under the Apple Tree," Editor's Letter, *George* magazine, September 1997; Littell, *The Men We Became*, page 204; Noonan and Huber, *Forever Young*, pages 202–203, 233; "Kiss My Shamrock," The People, *Miami Herald*, January 5, 1997; Scott Malone, "Ex-Kennedy Wife Says Vatican Overturns Annulment," *U.S. News & World Report*, June 21, 2007; "By George, JFK Jr. Bares a Lot," CNN, TV broadcast, August 11, 1997; Taraborrelli, *The Kennedy Heirs*, pages 126–127; Reuters, "By George, JFK Jr. Breaks the Code of Silence," *Los Angeles Times*, August 12, 1997; Maureen Dowd, "Kennedy Family Values," *New York Times*, May 3, 1997; Richard Cohen, "Suffering from the Sins of the Fathers," *Washington Post*, September 2, 1997; James Pinkerton, "It's a Real Hate-Hate Family Relationship," *Newsday* (Long Island, NY), August 14, 1997; Tina Brown, "A Woman in Earnest," *New Yorker*, September 7, 1997; Andersen, *The Day John Died*, page 300; Lisa DePaulo, "John F. Kennedy Jr. and George Magazine: A Story of Politics, Love and Loss, 20 Years Later," *Hollywood Reporter*, April 9, 2019; McKeon, *Jackie's Girl*, pages 291–294; Heymann, *American Legacy*, page 478.

CHAPTER 18: BURNING AT BOTH ENDS

Interview subjects include Carole Radziwill, Betsy Riesinger Siegel, Ariel Paredes, Hamilton South, MJ Bettenhausen, Jack Merrill, Dan Samson, Ralph Howard, Chelsea Howard. Published sources include Julie Hinds, "JFK Jr. Wining, Dining," *San Francisco Examiner*, September 20, 1997; George Rush Jr. and Joanna Molloy, "In-Flight Turbulence for John and Carolyn," *Daily News*, October 10, 1997; George Rush Jr. and Joanna Molloy, "Carolyn 'Bassinet' Kennedy? She Glows!," *Daily News*, November 7, 1997; Ronald Sklar, "Robert Littell Watching Kennedy Grow," PopEntertainment.com, July 21, 2004, https://www.popentertainmentarchives.com/post/robert-t-littell-watching-kennedy-grow; Noonan and Huber, *Forever Young*, page 224; Andersen, *The Day John Died*, pages 306, 308; Gillon, *America's Reluctant Prince*, pages 299–300, 344–346; Heymann, *American Legacy*, pages 443, 466, 471, 474–475; "Georgian Manner," *Women's Wear Daily*, November 10, 1997; Radziwill, *What Remains*, pages 169–171; Nicole Bietette, "JFK Jr.'s Wife Carolyn Bessette-Kennedy Was 'Terrified' of Paparazzi," *Daily News*, April 28, 2017.

CHAPTER 19: MRS. KENNEDY AND THE VICIOUS CIRCLE

Interview subjects include Carole Radziwill, Dan Samson, Hamilton South, Jack Merrill, Chip Arndt, Deena Manion, Bruce Weber, Jefferson Arrington, Gary Ginsberg, MJ Bettenhausen, Betsy Reisinger Siegel, Michelle Kessler, Sasha Chermayeff, William D. Cohan, Geoffrey Freeman, André Vivieros, Ariel Paredes, Matt Berman. Published sources include Andersen, *The Day John Died*, pages 308–309; Andersen, *The Good Son*, page 319; Knight-Ridder, "Spitting Images," *Province* (British Columbia), January 11, 1998; Michael Daly, "Matriarch Embodies the Clan's Resilience," *Daily News*, January 4, 1998; Gillon, *America's Reluctant Prince*, page 103; Bradley, *American Son*, page 144; Sandra Sobieraj, "British Welcomed with D.C. Star-Studded Affair," *Daily Journal* (Vineland, NJ), February 6, 1998; Noonan and Huber, *Forever Young*, page 194; Alderman and Kennedy, *The Right to Privacy*, page xvi; Liz Smith, "Watch Bill Dance," *Newsday* (Long Island, NY), February 8, 1998; Loretta Grantham, "Diamonds Still a Girl's Best Friend," *Palm Beach Post*, February 22, 1996; Anna Wintour, "Letter from the Editor: Fantasy and Reality," *Vogue*, April 1998; Julia Reed, "How Sexy Is Too Sexy," *Vogue*, April 1998; "JFK Jr. on Monicagate," *AdAge*, February 13, 1998; Hersh, *The Dark Side of Camelot*; Steve Pionki, "JFK Jr. Buys into Clinton's Denial," *Indianapolis Star*, February 18, 1998; Adrienne Gaffney, "The Other Passenger: Who Was Lauren Bessette?," *Town & Country*, July 2019; Christopher Gray, "A Glimpse of What SoHo Used to Be," *New York Times*, March 18, 2007; Littell, *The Men We Became*, page 193; "JFK Jr. at 'From Earth to Moon,'" *Lancaster* (PA) *New Era*, March 26, 1998; "JFK Jr. Has Praise for 'Earth to Moon' Series," *Charlotte* (NC) *Observer*, March 27, 1998; Radziwill, *What Remains*, pages 176–177; Andrea Shea King, "JFK Jr., Wife, Take in HBO's 'From Earth to Moon' Preview," *Florida Today*, March 31, 1998; Mark Ganem, "Paradise Lost," *Women's Wear Daily*, July 19, 1999.

CHAPTER 20: THE RUMOR MILL

Interview subjects include Carole Radziwill, MJ Bettenhausen, Hamilton South, Betsy Reisinger Siegel, Michelle Kessler, Sasha Chermayeff, William D. Cohan, Bruce Weber, Geoffrey Freeman, Joan Ford, André Vivieros, Ariel Paredes. Published sources include Sherryl Connelly, "More Than a Wife," *Daily News*, July 22, 1999; Ann Gerhart, "Myth America," *Washington Post*, October 9, 1996; George Rush Jr., "PR Exec's Linked to Kennedy and Calvin Klein Supermodel," *Daily News*, March 1, 1995; "Sex in High Places," *George* magazine, April 1998; *The Tonight Show with Jay Leno*, season 6, episode 7, NBC, September 24, 1997; Corky Siemaszko, "JFK Jr. and Wife Just Wingin' It," *Daily News*, May 19, 1998; Michael Grunwald, "JFK Jr. Feared Dead in Plane Crash," *Washington Post*, July 18, 1999; Claire Johnson, "With the Award Comes the Media, Social Whirl," *Billings* (MT) *Gazette*, May 30, 1998; George Rush Jr. and Joanna Molloy, "Dance Partners," *Daily News*, May 7, 1998; @allforcarolyn, "On July 4, 1998, John and Carolyn joined the Kennedys for a major family celebration of the Independence Day holiday at the Kennedy compound," Instagram, July 3, 2023, https://www.instagram.com/reel/CuPin5hOh3b/; "Party of the Summer," *Wichita Eagle*, July 20, 1998; Alex Kuczynski, "Washington Memo: A Melding of Extremes at Correspondents Dinner," *New York Times*, May 3, 1999; "Jamie Rubin, Christiane Amanpour," Weddings, *New York Times*, August 9, 1998; "Rubin Amanpour Wedding in Italy, 1998," *CBK Wardrobe* (blog), July 29, 2011, https://cbkwardrobe.blogspot.com/2011/07/rubin-amanpour-wedding-in-italy-1998.html; Valerie Fortney Schneider, "Lake Bracciano—Central Italy's Appealing Lake District," *International Living*, April 28, 2019; Mark Ganem, "Paradise Lost," *Women's Wear Daily*, July 19, 1999; Noonan and Huber, *Forever Young*, pages 206, 209, 212; Littell, *The Men We Became*, pages 199–200; Andersen, *The Day John Died*, pages 28–31, 313; McKeon, *Jackie's Girl*, page 294.

CHAPTER 21: ALL THE WORLD'S A STAGE

Interview subjects include RoseMarie Terenzio, Sasha Chermayeff, Chris Oberbeck, Jack Merrill, MJ Bettenhausen, Hamilton South, Dan Samson, Carole Radziwill, Richard Wiese, Ariel Paredes, Pam Thur, Clifford Streit, Steven M. Gillon. Published sources include Wallerstein, Lewis, and Blakeslee, *The Unexpected Legacy of Divorce*, page 55; Cohan, *Four Friends*, page 338; Andersen, *The Good Son*, page 318; "First Class," Tattle, *Philadelphia Daily News*, September 8, 1998; Heymann, *American Legacy*, pages 258, 479, 481, 484; George Rush Jr. and Joanna Molloy, Surveillance, *Daily News*, September 21, 1998; Terenzio, *Fairy Tale Interrupted*, pages 90–91, 178–179; Matt Berman, cover, *George* magazine, September 1998; @carolynjean nebessette, "Summer," Instagram, July 24, 2021, https://www.instagram.com/p/CRuEG9zF3dk/; "John Kennedy Jr. Claims Many Talents," Living, *Times Herald* (Port Huron, MI), October 12, 1998; George Rush Jr. and Joanna Molloy, "Bessette to the Barricades," *Daily News*, October 29, 1998; David W. Dunlap, "For Once-Gritty TriBeCa, a Golden Glow," *New York Times*, July 30, 2000; Littell, *The Men We Became*, page 235; Gillon, *America's Reluctant Prince*, pages 332, 376–377; Candace Bushnell, "Spoiled in the City," *Manhattan File*, November 1998; Andersen, *The Day John Died*, page 317; John Smyntek, Names and Faces, *Detroit Free Press*, December 3, 1998; Liz Smith, "My Item," *Newsday* (Long Island, NY), January 7, 1999; Trish Hall, "American Cities: New York, Renewed and Restored," *New York Times*, May 16, 1999; Mitchell Fink, "John-John and Carolyn Are a Hands-On Couple," *Daily News*, December 3, 1998; Associated Press, "FBI Tells of 3 JFK Jr. Kidnapping Threats," *Los Angeles Times*, June 20, 2000; Mark Ganem, "Paradise Lost," *Women's Wear Daily*, July 19, 1999; George Rush Jr. and Joanna Molloy, "Gem Dandy Party," *Daily News*, December 21, 1998; Radziwill, *What Remains*, page 206.

CHAPTER 22: GREY GARDENS IN MANHATTAN

Interview subjects include Carole Radziwill, Chris Oberbeck, Richard Wiese, Hamilton South, Sasha Chermayeff, Ariel Paredes, Dan Samson, Erin Lippmann, Steven M. Gillon. Published sources include Littell, *The Men We Became*, pages 197, 213–214, 220; Gillon, *America's Reluctant Prince*, pages 356–358; Terenzio, *Fairy Tale Interrupted*, pages 193, 196; Noonan and Huber, *Forever Young*, page 208; Klein, *The Kennedy Curse*, page 204; Andersen, *The Day John Died*, page 41; *Biography: JFK Jr.: The Final Year*, documentary film; George Rush Jr. and Joanna Molloy, "Gala Rocks with JFK Jr. and Rap Royalty," *Daily News*, March 11, 1999; George Rush Jr. and Joanna Molloy, Surveillance, *Daily News*, May 18, 1997; Keith J. Kelly, "John Jr. Searching for New No. 2," *New York Post*, January 6, 1999. See also @carolynbessettehd, "January 27, 1999. Opening night of 'The Blue Room,' Broadway," Instagram, November 7, 2022, https://www.instagram.com/p/CkrRFF1LN5_/; Radziwill, *What Remains*, pages 203–204, 208; Walter Scott, "Personality Parade," *Washington Post*, September 6, 1998; Heymann, *American Legacy*, pages 19, 466; Bradley, *American Son*, page 144; Laura Castaneda, "Inside Story About Prenuptial Agreements/Even If You're Not Rich, or Famous, It Can Pay to Have One," *San Francisco Chronicle*, November 4, 1996; Sasha Chermayeff, letter to Andover Alumni page, October 2019; John F. Kennedy Presidential Library and Museum, *Eunice Kennedy Shriver*; *Final 24, "JFK Junior"*; George Rush Jr. and Joanna Molloy, "'Psycho' Drama Disrupts Toronto Movie Set," *Daily News*, March 11, 1999; Alexandra Kotur, "Talking Back: Museum Mix," *Vogue*, June 1999.

CHAPTER 23: PRESENT TENSE

Interview subjects include Chip Arndt, Jonathan Becker, Diane von Furstenberg, André Vivieros, Sasha Chermayeff, Jack Kliger, David Kuhn, Carole Radziwill, Hamilton South, Michelle Kessler, Erin Lippmann, Richard Bradley, Gary Ginsberg, Ariel Paredes, Keith Stein. Published sources include George Rush Jr. and Joanna Molloy, "Ciao, Bella," *Daily News*, April 16, 1999; Andersen, *The Day John Died*, page 321; Radziwill, *What Remains*, pages 199, 217, 221–223; George Rush Jr. and Joanna Molloy, Surveillance, *Daily News*, May 4, 1999; Taraborrelli, *The Kennedy Heirs*, page 300;

Richard Bradley, "Camelot's Son," *Vanity Fair*, May 2002; Mitchell Fink, "A Couple at Peace with Themselves," *Daily News*, July 19, 1999; Heymann, *American Legacy*, pages 466, 491; Mitchell Fink, "JFK Jr.'s Humanity Reduces Al to Tears," *Daily News*, July 20, 1999; Noonan and Huber, *Forever Young*, page 213; Littell, *The Men We Became*, pages 179, 219–220; Kirsten Danis, "JFK Jr. Puts His Best Foot Forward," *New York Post*, June 6, 1999; Caroline Framke, "A History of Male Journalists Fetishizing Their Famous Female Subjects, in 8 Profiles," *Vox*, July 25, 2016, https://www.vox.com/2016/7/12/12110190/sexist-celebrity-profiles-margot-robbie-renee-zellweger; Mark Ganem, "Paradise Lost," *Women's Wear Daily*, July 19, 1999; Liz Smith, "Surprise, Hillary!" *Newsday* (Long Island, NY), October 29, 1997.

CHAPTER 24: REFERENCE POINTS

Interview subjects include Jack Kliger, Sasha Chermayeff, David Kuhn, Carole Radziwill, Hamilton South, Michelle Kessler, Erin Lippmann, Richard Bradley, Gary Ginsberg, Ariel Paredes, Keith Stein. Published sources include Radziwill, *What Remains*, pages 222–223, 231; Gillon, *America's Reluctant Prince*, page 366; Andersen, *The Day John Died*, page 26; Heymann, *American Legacy*, pages 19, 23–24; Terenzio, *Fairy Tale Interrupted*, page 197; Littell, *The Men We Became*, page 175; Mike Allen and Carey Goldberg, "Kennedy Flight Ended in a Plunge, Possibly Complicating Recovery," *New York Times*, July 20, 1999; Bradley, *American Son*, pages 254, 257–258; Edward Klein, "Secrets and Lies," *Vanity Fair*, April 18, 2014; Leamer, *Sons of Camelot*, pages 527–528; Ruth Reichl, Restaurants, *New York Times*, March 7, 1997; Rene Chun, "How David Pecker Built His Tabloid Empire AMI on Fear," *Daily Beast*, March 11, 2019; "Carole Radziwill Reflects on Losing John Kennedy Jr. and His Wife Carolyn on 20th Anniversary of Fatal Plane Crash . . . ," *Daily Mail*, July 17, 2019; Sarah Hampson, "History Is, of Course, About Dead People," *Globe and Mail*, July 19, 2003; Libby Calaway, "Carolyn's Terrible Premonition—She Told Saks Girl She Dreaded Flying That Night," *New York Post*, July 22, 1999; William Sherman and Kevin McCoy, "Retracing Hours Before Sad Fate, Delays Plagued Kennedy and Bessettes," *Daily News*, July 22, 1999.

CHAPTER 25: THE OTHER SIDE

Interview subjects include Dana Gallo. Published sources include "While the World Watched and Waited," *Cape Cod Times*, July 25, 1999; Mike Allen and Carey Goldberg, "Coast Guard Sees Little Hope for Kennedy," *New York Times*, July 19, 1999; Francis X. Clines, "Streams of Strangers Keep Vigils, Waiting, but Expecting the Worst," *New York Times*, July 19, 1999; "Comparisons Follow Bessette Kennedy," *Tampa Bay Times*, July 18, 1999; Andersen, *The Day John Died*, pages 338, 345; K. C. Baker and Bill Hutchinson, "Grieving Bessette Family Sets Service," *Daily News*, July 22, 1999; Peter Grant, Dave Saltonstall, and Dave Goldiner, "Time Runs Out for a Miracle," *Daily News*, July 19, 1999; Sherryl Connelly, "More Than A Wife," *Daily News*, July 22, 1999; Radziwill, *What Remains*, pages 234–237, 239–242, 244; Taraborrelli, *After Camelot*, pages 465, 468; Terenzio, *Fairy Tale Interrupted*, pages 200, 205, 207–209;

Noonan and Huber, *Forever Young*, pages 14, 216, 218–219, 224–226; Andersen, *The Day John Died*, pages 327, 330–332, 334–336, 338, 340–341, 343, 345; Lynne Duke, "Family Memorializes Another JFK," *Washington Post*, July 24, 1999.

EPILOGUE

Interview subjects include Carole Radziwill, Dan Samson, Hamilton South, Michelle Kessler. Published sources include Hilary Mantel, "Royal Bodies," *London Review of Books*, February 21, 2013; Vanessa Friedman, "Carolyn Bessette Kennedy, Ghost Influencer," *New York Times*, October 24, 2023; "Tragedy Revisits the Kennedys," Opinion, *New York Times*, July 19, 1999; Erica Noonan, "Search Continues; Debris, Luggage from Craft Found," *Ledger* (Lakeland, FL), July 18, 1999; "Crash and Search Timeline," *Washington Post*, 1999; Francis X. Clines, "Streams of Strangers Keep Vigils, Waiting, but Expecting the Worst," *New York Times*, July 19, 1999; Radziwill, *What Remains*, page 246; Andersen, *The Day John Died*, pages 345–349; *JFK Jr. and Carolyn's Wedding*, documentary film; Mike Allen and Carey Goldberg, "Rescue Search in Kennedy Crash Ends; Coast Guard Tells Family There Is Little Hope," *New York Times*, July 19, 1999; *I Am JFK Jr.*, documentary film; Ann Gerhart, "Bessette Tried to Avoid Kennedy Spotlight," *Washington Post*, July 18, 1999; Lynne Duke, "Family Memorializes Another JFK," *Washington Post*, July 24, 1999; Al Baker, "Ashes to the Sea," *Newsday* (Long Island, NY), July 23, 1999; Ellis Henican, "Ashes, Saltwater and Wind," *Newsday* (Long Island, NY), July 23, 1999; Casey Baker and Bill Hutchinson, "Bessette Clan Talk of Sorrow," *Daily News*, July 20, 1999.

BIBLIOGRAPHY

Alderman, Ellen, and Caroline Kennedy. *The Right to Privacy*. New York: Knopf, 1995. Citations refer to the 2010 ebook edition.

Andersen, Christopher. *The Day John Died*. New York: HarperCollins, 2000. Citations refer to the 2001 Avon paperback edition.

———. *The Good Son: JFK Jr. and the Mother He Loved*. New York: Gallery, 2014. Citations refer to the 2015 paperback edition.

———. *Jackie After Jack: Portrait of the Lady*. The Jackie (Kennedy) Chronicles. New York: William Morrow, 1998.

Anthony, Carl Sferrazza. *Camera Girl: The Coming of Age of Jackie Bouvier Kennedy*. New York: Gallery, 2023.

Benetton, Alessandro. *La Traiettoria*. Milan: Mondadori, 2022.

Bennett, Jessica. *Feminist Fight Club: An Office Survival Manual for a Sexist Workplace*. New York: Harper Wave, 2016.

Bergin, Michael. *The Other Man: John F. Kennedy Jr., Carolyn Bessette, and Me*. New York: William Morrow, 2004. Citations refer to the 2005 Regan paperback edition.

Berman, Matt. *JFK Jr., George, and Me: A Memoir*. New York: Gallery, 2014.

Bradley, Richard. *American Son: A Portrait of John F. Kennedy Jr*. New York: Henry Holt, 2002.

Callahan, Maureen. *Champagne Supernovas: Kate Moss, Marc Jacobs, Alexander McQueen, and the '90s Renegades Who Remade Fashion*. New York: Touchstone, 2014.

Castiglione, Baldassare. *The Book of the Courtier*, 1522. English translation by George Bull. Glasgow: Good Press, 2022.

Cohan, William D. *Four Friends: Promising Lives Cut Short*. New York: Flatiron Books, 2019.

Eskin, Blake, and *George* Magazine. *The Book of Political Lists.* New York: Villard, 1998.

Flaherty, Tina Santi. *What Jackie Taught Us: Lessons from the Remarkable Life of Jacqueline Kennedy Onassis.* Revised and expanded, with introduction by Liz Smith. New York: TarcherPerigee, 2014.

Gillon, Steven M. *America's Reluctant Prince: The Life of John F. Kennedy Jr.* New York: Dutton, 2019.

Ginsberg, Gary. *First Friends: The Powerful, Unsung (And Unelected) People Who Shaped Our Presidents.* New York: Twelve, 2021.

Haag, Christina. *Come to the Edge: A Love Story.* Paperback reissue. New York: Random House, 2012.

Hagan, Joe. *Sticky Fingers: The Life and Times of Jann Wenner and Rolling Stone Magazine.* New York: Knopf, 2017.

Hersh, Seymour M. *The Dark Side of Camelot.* Boston: Little Brown, 1997. Citation refers to the 1998 Back Bay paperback edition.

Heymann, C. David. *American Legacy: The Story of John and Caroline Kennedy.* New York: Atria, 2007. Citations refer to the 2008 paperback edition.

Hill, Clint, and Lisa McCubbin. *My Travels with Mrs. Kennedy.* New York: Gallery, 2022.

Jewell, Karen. *A History of the Greenwich Waterfront: Tod's Point, Great Captain Island and the Greenwich Shoreline.* Charleston, SC: History Press Library, 2011.

Kennedy, John Fitzgerald. *Profiles in Courage.* New York: Harper & Brothers, 1956.

Klein, Edward. *Just Jackie: Her Private Years.* New York: Ballantine Books, 1998.

———. *The Kennedy Curse: Why Tragedy Has Haunted America's First Family for 150 Years.* New York: St. Martin's, 2003. Citations refer to the 2004 paperback edition.

Leamer, Laurence. *Sons of Camelot: The Fate of an American Dynasty.* New York: William Morrow, 2004.

Littell, Robert T. *The Men We Became: My Friendship with John F. Kennedy, Jr.* New York: St. Martin's, 2004. Citations refer to the 2005 paperback edition.

Littlefield, Nick, and David Nexon. *Lion of the Senate: When Ted Kennedy Rallied the Democrats in a GOP Congress.* New York: Simon & Schuster, 2015.

Malcolm, Janet. *The Silent Woman: Sylvia Plath and Ted Hughes.* New York: Knopf, 1994.

Mantel, Hilary. *Bring Up the Bodies: A Novel.* Wolf Hall Series Book 2. New York: Henry Holt, 2012.

———. *Mantel Pieces: Royal Bodies and Other Writing from the* London Review of Books. London: Fourth Estate, 2020.

McKeon, Kathy. *Jackie's Girl: My Life with the Kennedy Family.* New York: Gallery, 2017.

Morris, Thornton. *Cumberland Island: A Place Apart.* Cumberland Island, GA: Cumberland Island Conservancy, 2008.

Noonan, William Sylvester, and Robert Huber. *Forever Young: My Friendship with John F. Kennedy, Jr.* New York: Viking, 2006.

Radziwill, Carole. *What Remains: A Memoir of Fate, Friendship, and Love.* New York: Scribner, 2005. Citations refer to the 2007 illustrated paperback edition.

Reeves, Richard. *President Kennedy: Profile of Power.* New York: Simon & Schuster, 1993. Citation refers to the 2000 leatherbound Easton Press reprint.

Richardson, Susan. *Greenwich Before 2000: A Chronology of the Town of Greenwich, 1640–1999.* Greenwich, CT: Historical Society of the Town of Greenwich, 2000.

Simon, Carly. *Touched by the Sun: My Friendship with Jackie.* New York: Farrar, Straus and Giroux, 2019.

Taraborrelli, J. Randy. *After Camelot: A Personal History of the Kennedy Family—1968 to the Present.* New York: Grand Central, 2012.

———. *Jackie: Public, Private, Secret.* New York: St. Martin's, 2023.

———. *The Kennedy Heirs: John, Caroline, and the New Generation—A Legacy of Tragedy and Triumph.* New York: St. Martin's, 2019.

Terenzio, RoseMarie. *Fairy Tale Interrupted: A Memoir of Life, Love, and Loss.* New York: Gallery, 2012.

Wallerstein, Judith, Julia M. Lewis, and Sandra Blakeslee. *The Unexpected Legacy of Divorce: A 25 Year Landmark Study.* Second edition. New York: Hyperion, 2000.

Wenner, Jann S. *Like a Rolling Stone: A Memoir.* New York: Little, Brown, 2022.

Yarrow, Allison. *90s Bitch: Media, Culture, and the Failed Promise of Gender Equality.* New York: Harper Perennial, 2018.

BROADCASTS

Associated Press. "Italy: John F. Kennedy Jr Visits Famous Design House Valentino." Video, Associated Press Archive, April 20, 1996. https://www.youtube.com/watch?v=dXb4cRBZCJ8/.

Biography: JFK Jr.: The Final Year. Documentary, A&E network. Aired July 16, 2019. https://www.aetv.com/specials/biography-jfk-jr-the-final-year.

Final 24, "JFK Junior." Season 1, episode 5. TV series directed by Karl Jason and William Hicklin, aired 2006.

I Am JFK Jr. Documentary directed by Derik Murray and Steve Burgess, August 1, 2016.

JFK Jr. and Carolyn's Wedding: The Lost Tapes. Documentary directed by David Metzler, produced by Meredith Wright. Released July 13, 2019.

John F. Kennedy Jr. and Caroline Kennedy. Interview with Jay Schadler. *Prime Time Live*, ABC Television, May 1992.

INDEX

ABOUT THE AUTHOR

Elizabeth Beller is a writer and journalist specializing in culture, art, and travel, with more than fifteen years of experience as a book and story editor. Her work has appeared in the *Guardian*, *Vogue*, and *Travel + Leisure*, among other outlets. Before turning to writing and editing, she spent two years as a script reader for Miramax, followed by twelve years in the art world at Sotheby's auction house. She splits her time between New York and New Orleans with her husband, writer Thomas Beller, and their two children.